The Role of Government in the History of Economic Thought

The Role of Government in the History of Economic Thought

Annual Supplement to Volume 37
History of Political Economy

Edited by Steven G. Medema
and Peter Boettke

Duke University Press
Durham and London 2005

Printed in the United States of America
on acid-free paper. ISBN 0-8223-6652-5
This is the 2005 supplement to
History of Political Economy, ISSN 0018-2702.

Contents

Setting the Table

Steven G. Medema

The analysis of the appropriate role for government within the economic system has been a centerpiece of economic thinking from its inception. No area of economic analysis has been untouched by this issue: public finance, money, labor, development and growth, industrial organization, international economics . . . all have wrapped up within them, throughout the history of economic thought, issues regarding the role that government plays or ought to play, the analysis of the impacts of policy or potential policies, and other, related, concerns. It is also, of course, the most controversial area of economic analysis. Yes, economists debate things like models of price determination, the appropriate role for dynamics in economic modeling, the potential limitations of certain forms of econometric analysis. But nothing charges the debates like issues that reach into the policy arena. Positive theories and descriptions, and normative prescriptions alike, all take on a strong normative cast—as

We would like to thank Duke University Press and the Mercatus Center at George Mason University for their generous financial support of the conference, the papers from which are published in the present volume. Craufurd Goodwin, *HOPE*'s editor, and Paul Dudenhefer, *HOPE*'s managing editor, were incredibly helpful to us in putting together the conference, particularly when the original conference hotel informed us just weeks before the conference that they had accidentally overbooked the hotel and could not host us for the weekend. We would also like to thank the scholars whose work is published here for contributing to what was both an excellent and spirited conference and what we believe is a volume that makes an important contribution to the literature in the history of economic thought. We are particularly grateful to Warren Samuels for his willingness to serve as a general discussant and to present the assessment that concludes this volume.

Warren Samuels both points out and illustrates in the essay that concludes this volume. Indeed, it is often difficult, if not impossible, to discern among them.

It would not be exaggerating the case to say that the theory and analysis of the economic role of government is the most broad-based, nuanced, and heterogeneous stream of economic thinking. In part because of this, there are countless entrées into the study of this subject: the view of the appropriate role for government espoused by individuals or schools and comparative studies of the same; the evolution of views over time and the underlying reasons for it; varieties of approaches to the subject within particular schools of thought; the evolution of particular aspects of the theory (e.g., regulation, taxation); the role of internal (e.g., tools) and external (e.g., contemporary events) factors in the development of ideas; the role of ideology; positive versus normative analysis; the determination of the role ascribed to government within the economic system (e.g., apriorist versus "theoretically derived"); the impact of service in government on attitudes toward this question; the effect of the general gestalt in which economists live; the modeling of governmental behavior; the efficacy of markets versus government; policy instruments (e.g., law, direct regulation, taxation); the role of implicit assumptions in models of the economic role of government; sophisticated versus naive formulations of particular approaches. A number of these themes are evidenced in the present volume, and the reader can doubtless think of many more.

As such, it comes as no surprise that the evolution of economists' views of the policy process, the economic role of government, and related ideas has been the focus of a not insignificant body of scholarship by those working in the history of economics. Yet there has been no broad-based integrated study, no magisterial treatment (to use Mark Perlman's term) of this subject. We have the treatises on the classical theory of economic policy by Lionel Robbins (1952) and by Warren Samuels (1966), articles and bits in textbooks examining the stances of individual authors or perhaps juxtaposing the views of two or three authors or attempting to make sense of a particular "school," but practically nothing has been done by way of pulling out and juxtaposing larger themes in the evolution of thought and attempting to trace the forces that account for the development of ideas across schools and epochs.[1]

1. Medema forthcoming examines certain facets of the evolution of the theory of the economic role of government from the mid-nineteenth century through the end of the twentieth.

Nor does the present volume fill this gap. The goal that Peter Boettke and I had in putting together this conference was more simple: to bring together a group of scholars with substantial interest and expertise in this subject who would take on the subject from a variety of perspectives—bringing to the table new ideas, perspectives, and topics in a way that would add both breadth and depth to this literature. Of course, the challenge here was to do so in a way that resulted in a conference that would be useful for the participants and a conference volume that was sufficiently thematic. These concerns led us to emphasize the period from the mid-nineteenth century onward—not because we had a particular interest in that period over others but because that is the period dealt with by the bulk of the best proposals we received. But then, given that the post-classical period is relatively underanalyzed in the literature as compared with the classical one, and as much of the most innovative work in our subject at present is being done on this period, perhaps this should not come as a surprise.

Political Economy, Old and New

The volume leads off with an article by Peter Boettke and Steven Horwitz that offers an overarching framework for thinking about the evolution of economists' views on the economic role of government. In Boettke and Horwitz's schema, economists can be thought of as students or saviors of society, while economics as a discipline can be characterized as evidencing epistemic modesty or hubris in its scientific knowledge claims. Boettke and Horwitz then apply this framework to the analysis of the history of development economics from the eighteenth century onward. This framework, while only one of several possible means for naming and framing issues related to the economic role of government, offers an interesting lens through which to view the essays in this volume.

The detailed analysis of the economic role of government really begins with the classical period. And, while much has been written on this subject, contemporary scholarship is causing us to view both the classical literature and its relationship to modern economic analysis in new and interesting ways. The essays by Alain Marciano, Andrew Farrant and Maria Pia Paganelli, Jeffrey Young, and David Levy and Sandra Peart are emblematic of this new scholarship. Marciano and Farrant and Paganelli take on the question of modeling government behavior by taking us back to the work of David Hume. Both essays treat Hume's theory of human nature, its relationship to the modern economic theory of human behavior, and the implications of this for modeling government behavior in modern political economy. One of the interesting things that emerge from these two articles is a good sense for the contingency of the view of government on the underlying assumptions about agent behavior.

The problem of multiple interpretations is evidenced in Jeff Young's examination of the tension in Smith's theory of the state, a tension reflected in his "only three duties" assertions about the role of the sovereign when juxtaposed against the lengthy list of action functions that Smith thought the government should perform. This has led some to characterize Smith as a die-hard advocate of laissez-faire, others to see him as promoting wide-ranging government "interference," and no less a scholar than Lionel Robbins to suggest that Smith's "invisible hand" is actually the state. Young offers a reconciliation of these seemingly inconsistent aspects of Smith's theory of the state, drawing on Smith's discussion in *The Theory of Moral Sentiments* to suggest an overarching framework grounded in commutative justice, distributive equity, and public utility.

While Marciano and Farrant and Paganelli look forward from the classical tradition to modern political economy, Levy and Peart reverse the lens, applying the notion of "politics as exchange"—the catallactic process at the heart of important strands of modern public choice theory[2]—to the nineteenth-century classical period. Here, though, the political exchange process is grounded in then current notions of sympathy, which have a tempering effect on self-interest and play a prominent role in its translation to the general interest.

New World Economics

The analysis of the American view is almost altogether absent from the extant literature on the economic role of government. Apart from some work on the institutionalists and the more contemporary happenings at Chicago and Virginia, the underanalyzed history of American economics has perhaps its greatest deficit in this area.[3] Yet, as the articles by Stephen

2. This notion actually dates to Richard Whately, despite its really only coming to the fore within economics in the last half century.

3. On aspects of the history of American economics in the twentieth century, see the volume from the 1998 *HOPE* conference on this topic, *From Interwar Pluralism to Postwar Neoclassicism* (Morgan and Rutherford 1998). On institutional economics, see both Rutherford 1994 and

Meardon, Bradley Bateman, Thomas Leonard, and Malcolm Rutherford demonstrate, there is a rich and underappreciated literature that tells a story very distinct from the British and Continental experiences during this period.

A great deal of the American literature in the eighteenth and nineteenth centuries focused on trade-related issues, and Steve Meardon's essay hones in on one particular facet of that discussion—the protection of intellectual property and its relation to international trading practices. Meardon looks at the relationship between William Cullen Bryant's and Henry C. Carey's respective positions on international copyright and their views of trade policy generally, and their larger perspectives on the role of government in the economy. In the process, Meardon is also able to show that intellectual history sheds a somewhat different light than does economic history on the relationship between intellectual copyright, trade policy, and economic welfare.

Brad Bateman's essay examines the evolution of the doctrine of laissez-faire as the dominant credo in nineteenth-century American popular and economic discourse. Bateman traces the discussion through views of trade, slavery, and labor issues in the first part of the century, to the rise of industrialization and the challenges it posed in the latter part of the century. With this came the beginnings of a challenge to laissez-faire. Specifically, arguments for an increasingly activist role for government developed through what we now call the Social Gospel movement within American Protestantism, informed by the German historical tradition of economic thinking—a process that set the stage for, among other things, the reformist aspects of the Progressive and institutionalist movements on the popular and academic fronts in the late nineteenth and early twentieth centuries.

Tim Leonard picks up the story at the point of the Progressive ascendancy to examine the influence of eugenic ideas on the theory of economic policy during this period. The role of race, eugenics, and related issues in the development of economic ideas has been almost totally unexplored until recently. The work of David Levy and Sandra Peart has confronted this head-on in its British classical and postclassical manifestations,[4] and Leonard's essay here shows how many of these same issues played a role in the American experience as well by informing

Rutherford's numerous recent articles on interwar institutionalism in *HOPE* and the *Journal of the History of Economic Thought*.

4. See Levy 2001 and Levy and Peart 2005.

thought and policy on social reform, particularly issues related to wages and employment that were at the heart of the Progressive agenda.

Malcolm Rutherford's piece on Walton Hamilton is very much a case study in the analysis of the economic role of government during the interwar institutionalist ascendancy. Hamilton was an early proponent of the study of law and economics—defined as the interrelations between legal and economic processes—and a pragmatist with a reformist bent. He was neither an unabashed supporter of business nor a proponent of heavy-handed control of business operations. Nor was he of the mind that the answers to the questions of economic policy are likely to be revealed through a priori reasoning. Rather, Hamilton took a case-by-case approach to these issues and, with this, promoted legal-political decision making with the broadest possible range of interests directly represented at the table. Rutherford's discussion also illustrates how Hamilton's analysis both informed and was informed by his extensive participation in governmental affairs, including the New Deal—an activism that was not unique among American economists of that period but which, in degree at least, does distinguish the American economists from their British counterparts.

Applying Doctrine to the Policy Arena

The discussion of the theory of economic policy has for several decades now included references to the virtues and vices of "blackboard economics," a term that Ronald Coase applied to theories that he considered glorious in the world of the blackboard but wholly inapplicable to the world in which we live, and which has subsequently been popularized by Deirdre McCloskey. David Colander puts this debate in historical context by analyzing the views on the theory-policy linkage reflected in John Neville Keynes's distinction between the science and the art of economics, Alfred Marshall and A. C. Pigou's quest for a realistic economic theory, and Abba Lerner's pure theory of economic policy. Colander probes the implications of this for the extent to which one can draw policy conclusions from theory and examines how our teaching of economics reflects these ideas.

Certain of the issues touched on in Colander's discussion bear on the question asked by Yakir Plessner and Warren Young—that of the link between academic economics and economists, and the role of economist as policy adviser and the willingness and ability of economists to translate the theories they teach into the policy arena. The theoretical difficulties pointed to by Colander are amply evidenced by Plessner and Young's examination of the role of economists as policy advisers in Israel from the early 1970s through the mid-1980s and their attempts to deal with the substantial inflationary pressures of the day. The story is not one of success for the market, government, or economists.

Another issue foreshadowed by the theory-policy linkage discussed by Colander and the policy failures analyzed by Plessner and Young is that of coming to grips with what governments and government agents actually do when they make economic policy and the implications of this for understanding and modeling the political element of the policy-making process. The Anglo-Saxon tradition, in both its classical and its marginalist-neoclassical variants, lacked a theory of government behavior. The classical pessimism about "interference" with the market and the neoclassical analysis of efficiency-enhancing government policies were all predicated on a priori views of the state. As Jürgen Backhaus and Richard Wagner point out, the Continental tradition of the late nineteenth and early twentieth centuries was rather different, with distinct German, Italian, and Swedish approaches to the analysis of public economics and the political factors that attend it. Backhaus and Wagner bring out both the foundational elements of these Continental approaches and certain of their relations to modern public choice theory.

Both theoretical economics and real-world economies evolved away from laissez-faire ideology over the first half of the twentieth century. Socialism held certain attractions both in theory and in reality, the Cambridge tradition espoused a strongly reformist view of the market process, and, as I have already noted, the American Progressive and institutionalist movements evidenced a strong belief in the ability of government to modify market performance in socially desirable directions. The corporatist movement on the Continent during the interwar period paralleled the increasing calls for a larger role for government management in the British and American capitalist systems during that same period. António Almodovar and José Luís Cardoso look at the rise of corporatist ideas as a third way between the classical–free market and socialist alternatives that had dominated the debates, one that would attempt to overcome some of the limitations of the laissez-faire approach while availing itself of the advantages offered by the market system. They also show how certain aspects of corporatism were enfolded into the Keynesian ideas that emerged in the postwar period.

If the first two-thirds of the twentieth century were dominated by the economist as savior-cum-engineer with increasingly sophisticated models of efficient government policymaking, as Boettke and Horwitz suggest, the last several decades have witnessed something of a reversion to classicism in the reawakening of what Backhouse calls "free market economics." Here, though, we see a more sophisticated modeling of the market process than evidenced in the classical tradition and a more detailed depiction of government behavior than can be found in either the pessimism of the classicals or the optimism of the neoclassicals. Backhouse's essay attempts to address the "why" behind this transformation by examining forces within the profession and without, and how they came together to revolutionize the theory of economic policy and its application on both the macro and micro sides—first in the United States and then throughout much of the West.

Conclusion

Given the enduring importance of the analysis of the economic role of government within the history of economic thought, as well as the still relatively unsettled, or controversial, nature of this issue within contemporary thinking, we believe that this volume is highly topical. In the end, our hope is that it will contribute to an enhanced understanding of the evolution of economists' views about the economic role of government and stimulate new lines of research that build on the ideas suggested in the present essays.

References

Levy, David M. 2001. *How the Dismal Science Got Its Name: Classical Economics and the Ur-Text of Racial Politics*. Ann Arbor: University of Michigan Press.

Levy, David M., and Sandra J. Peart. 2005. *The "Vanity of the Philosopher": From Equality to Hierarchy in Post-Classical Economics*. Ann Arbor: University of Michigan Press.

Medema, Steven G. Forthcoming. *The Hesitant Hand: Market and State in the History of Modern Economic Thought*. Princeton, N.J.: Princeton University Press.

Morgan, Mary, and Malcolm Rutherford, eds. 1998. *From Interwar Pluralism to Postwar Neoclassicism*. *HOPE* 30 (supplement).

Robbins, Lionel. 1952. *The Theory of Economic Policy in English Classical Political Economy*. London: Macmillan.

Rutherford, Malcolm. 1994. *Institutions in Economics: The Old and the New Institutionalism*. Cambridge: Cambridge University Press.
Samuels, Warren J. 1966. *The Classical Theory of Economic Policy*. Cleveland: World.

The Limits of Economic Expertise: Prophets, Engineers, and the State in the History of Development Economics

Peter Boettke and Steven Horwitz

What role is there for government in promoting the economic well-being of citizens within its national boundaries? This question has vexed social philosophers for centuries. If we assume that political authority derives its legitimacy in part from the satisfaction it affords its subjects, then it follows that a "good" government will adopt policies that will enhance the economic well-being of its citizens. What exactly those policies are has been one of the main subjects of controversy in economics since its founding. Some have contended that the role of government is to be at best a referee, whereas other economists have argued the government must actively participate in the economic game.

We identify two theoretical tensions that exist in this debate. First, from Adam Smith onward a large part of the teachings of economics has stressed the mutually beneficial aspects of trade. But for the gains from exchange to be had, some level of coercion is postulated by the economist to ensure the provision of the basic framework of property and contract. Without the government providing the legal infrastructure, mutual gains from exchange will go unrealized. To fund government provision of this framework and to empower government to enforce this framework, the presumption toward voluntarism must be suspended. How precisely to negotiate this divide is something that economics and political economy wrestles with to this day.

We thank the conference participants and an anonymous referee for challenging and helpful comments on earlier drafts.

Table 1 The Status of Economics and the Role of the Economist

	Economist as Student	Economist as Savior
Economics has epistemic modesty	Happy cautionary prophet	Frustrated engineer
Economics has epistemic hubris	Frustrated cautionary prophet	Practicing engineer

Second, there is an interesting relationship between the epistemic outlook of economics and the disposition of the economist that plays itself out in the history of development economics. To simplify two continuums down to their poles, we can see the discipline of economics as moving between "epistemic modesty" and "epistemic hubris" in the way it understands its own claims to scientific knowledge (particularly in the sense of prediction and control), and we can envision economists as approaching their work as either "students of society" or "saviors of society." The interaction between the dominant culture of the discipline and the disposition of the economist is portrayed in table 1.

We broadly categorize the results in terms of "cautionary prophets" or "engineers." We use "prophet" in the sense of a person who offers predictive warnings ("if you do x, y will happen") rather than someone who is divinely inspired or the like. By using the adjective "cautionary," we are suggesting that the economist as prophet is largely in the business of cautioning us about the limits of what we can and cannot do. The economist as prophet is more likely to utter "Thou Can Not" than "Thou Shalt Not." This sort of economist has a default, though not inviolable, respect for the workings and value of institutions that have survived the process of social evolution. This puts him or her in the position of cautioning those who would remake or ignore the lasting results of those historical processes.

Over the last 150 years, the economist as engineer, by contrast, has moved through two distinct though related worldviews with respect to historically emergent institutions. During the late nineteenth century, a period characterized by "frustration," the engineering-oriented economist was interested in the role of institutions but concerned with designing new social institutions to replace those seen as responsible for the problems of the day. The spirit of science and engineering, which had been apparently so successful in taming nature, would be used to rein in the forces of the social world so that they would serve the cause of human betterment by being the results of human reason rather than blind evolution. By the middle of the twentieth century, with the failures of wholesale institutional redesign more obvious, the economist as engineer was more likely to ignore historically emergent institutions, focusing instead on the problems of optimal resource and income allocation as explored in what amounted to an institutional vacuum. What unites the engineers of the two centuries, and makes grouping them together intellectually coherent, is their rejection of the cautionary prophet's default respect for historically successful social institutions. The older ones rejected it because they thought they could do better; the more recent ones simply ignore the issue.

In this essay, we explore how these interrelationships between economists as prophets or engineers and economics as epistemically modest or hubristic play out in the debates over the state's role in promoting economic development. Clearly the state plays a role, but does it do so by establishing the framework within which economic transactions occur or by serving as a corrective to the failure of voluntary actions to promote development? That is, how modest or self-confident is economics about what economists can directly contribute to economic development? Douglass North (1981, 24) has written that it is important in these discussions to remember that no matter how predatory and exploitive the state may in fact be, the state is necessary for economic development. Adam Smith ([1776] 1976, xliii) provided a classic statement of this when he argued in the notebooks that eventually led to the *Wealth of Nations* that "little else is requisite to carry a state to the highest degree of opulence from the lowest barbarism, but peace, easy taxes and a tolerable administration of justice; all the rest being brought about by the natural course of things." This is a call for limited government, but still an effectively organized government capable of defining property rights and enforcing contracts. On the other hand, the mercantilist writers before Smith and the German protectionist economists as well as the Keynesian economists after Smith argued vigorously that the state cannot remain on the sidelines and referee the economic game. The state is in a unique position to serve as a corrective to social ills and thus plays a definite and active role in promoting the wealth of a nation. Intertwined in the history of these debates over the state's role in political economy are questions of the nature of economic expertise, the epistemic assumptions of economics, and the disposition of the economist.

From Moral Philosophy to Science and Back Again?

Before we focus more precisely on the history of development economics, we need a broad, if brief, overview of economics' self-understanding of its own epistemic standpoint. Restricting ourselves to the last 350 years or so, we can see an oscillation between epistemic modesty and epistemic hubris about the scientific status of economics and its implications for economic policy. In Smith we find repeated cautions about the limits of the expertise of the moral philosopher, particularly in light of what the state can do with respect to economic policy and the differences between the knowledge of the economist and the knowledge of the economic actor. Jeffrey Young (this volume) distinguishes between two forms of knowledge present in Smith—"contextual" and "system." The former refers to the knowledge actors use, based on their experiences, to make their day-to-day decisions of "ordinary life." The latter, by contrast, is what the philosopher produces and, in so doing, "reveals what is hidden to agents in ordinary life." Young's distinction is also seen in Smith's famous "chessboard" passage from *The Theory of Moral Sentiments* ([1759] 1982, 234), where he distinguishes between the "principle of motion" of individual actors and the systemic rules laid down by the legislature. Of particular importance in that passage is Smith's discussion of the "arrogance" of those who would seek to arrange actors as if they were pieces on a chessboard. The whole notion of the invisible hand, particularly as Smith understood it to be linked with the divine, is yet another example of his call for philosophical humility before greater social forces.

During the early nineteenth century, economics remained largely under the sway of relatively modest views of its own position among the sciences. In the decades to follow, two developments began to push at the prevailing methodological self-conception. The first, to be explored in more detail below, was an emphasis on the importance of the "folk" knowledge of the actor and an increased skepticism about the knowledge of the expert. This argument was linked with the historical school and some of the protectionist thinkers in Germany and the United States. They attacked the then current orthodoxy from one side, arguing that it was, in some sense of the term, "too" scientific because it paid insufficient attention to how actors saw the world. At the same time, some of these thinkers also argued that economics was *unscientific* for not paying enough attention to how natural laws of human development functioned and how best to facilitate those processes.

The second development was the rise of socialist thought, particularly Marxism, which began to criticize classical orthodoxy for, in some sense of the term, not being scientific enough. Marx's laws of history represented, in his view, a more scientific approach to understanding the developmental path of industrial economies than did the classical worldview. Although Marxism suggested humility in the face of these larger historical laws, the culmination of that historical process would be a world where humans used their knowledge of social forces to make history rather than be subject to it. The Marxian future where production would be directed "in accordance with a settled plan" would be a social order rationally constructed according to our knowledge of the laws of production (Marx 1906, 92). Engels ([1892] 1972, 68–70) captured this nicely by analogizing capitalism to lightning and socialism to electricity under human control. Just as a scientific understanding of nature had enabled us to take powerful natural forces and subject them to human control, so could a scientific understanding of the social world, led perhaps by economics, enable us to use rationality to control the forces of production.

Despite their attempts to change the basic outlook of the discipline, both the historicists and the Marxists remained part of heterodoxy. Nonetheless, they, especially the Marxists, did have their effects. At the same time, the disposition of many coming to study economics was changing as well. Given the events surrounding the Industrial Revolution, including factory conditions and changes in the distribution of wealth and income, more people came to economics predisposed to be saviors rather than students.[1] Combined with the Progressive movement in the United States and similar movements elsewhere in the world, this move toward the savior approach put increasing pressure on the discipline of economics to shift its self-understanding.

Into the late nineteenth and early twentieth century, economics continued to borrow from the natural sciences with increasing frequency. As Philip Mirowski's (1989) work demonstrates, the importation of natural science concepts profoundly affected the development of neoclassical economics. The marriage of the language of equilibrium, energy, and

1. The Social Gospel movement of the nineteenth century, discussed by Bradley Bateman in this volume, is a good example of the rise of the savior disposition among those with an interest in economic issues.

"forces" to the rise of positivist philosophy in the early twentieth century began to increase the level of intellectual self-confidence among economists. With a philosophical outlook that emphasized prediction and control, and a set of theoretical tools that emphasized modeling and empirical testing, neoclassical economics looked increasingly like an extension of engineering. The belief in the real-world applicability of general equilibrium models reached its peak in the 1930s and 1940s in the literature on planning and market socialism. The growing interaction between economists, game theorists, and the military-industrial complex further cemented the view of economic problems as static, allocative, quasi-engineering problems. Books like Abba Lerner's *The Economics of Control* (1944) were examples of this vision of economics at work.

For the young person approaching economics with the savior disposition, the newfound scientific self-confidence of economics presented a perfect match. Economics became an opportunity to put one's desire to save the world to work by becoming a practicing social engineer. For those less inclined to be the savior, the state of the discipline became a source of frustration. Although the "student" is always inclined to play the role of cautionary prophet, that role is largely reduced to irrelevance when the dominant discourse of the discipline is closer to that of the engineer. During the middle of the twentieth century, economics was too busy imagining what it could do and had little time for those who kept warning that it could not be done. Many heterodox economists of the period, mostly those skeptical of significant state intervention, but even some Marxists as well, found themselves in the role of frustrated cautionary prophet, believing that the scientific self-confidence was really intellectual hubris. In the face of the triumph of science, views akin to those of the moral philosophers of 150 years earlier were seen as mere metaphysics.

In the last thirty years, however, the discipline has shifted somewhat. For various reasons, including the real-world failures of policies based on the engineering approach, economics has swung away from the most extreme sorts of hubris found earlier in the twentieth century. Advances in philosophy and our understanding of the human mind have challenged the stronger claims of positivism and rationalism, and led to renewed appreciation for the role of social institutions in guiding fallible humans of bounded or limited rationality through a world of complexity and uncertainty. The increased emphasis on the rhetoric of economics and the history of the discipline, and not just the history of ideas, have all helped rein in the unrealistic ambitions of the early twentieth century. One interesting twist is that the engineering mentality remains in form but not function in the increasing complexity of mathematical economics. The result is that those who come to the discipline as saviors find themselves frustrated by the arid policyless world of supposedly "pure" economics yet also perhaps frustrated by the swing back toward epistemic modesty. In addition, the student is heartened, perhaps, by the newfound modesty, as he or she sees the role of cautionary prophet as somewhat more available. However, the institutional structures of the discipline continue to reward disproportionately those with the engineering skills, even if they do not perform the engineering functions. The result is frustration of one sort or another for all but those who see beauty inherent in the tools.

In the rest of the essay, we overlay this story on the history of the state's role in development economics to explain the twists and turns it has taken in trying to account for why some nations are rich and others are not.

The Modest Economist and the Limited State

The history of the state's role in economic thought begins with the earliest contributors to modern economic thought. The liberal moral philosophers of the eighteenth century, particularly those associated with the Scottish Enlightenment, saw a clear connection between the development of trade and commerce and the development of the various measures of "civilization." In their view, the extension of trade was the result of limiting the state's role in attempting to be the direct source of economic development and of restricting that role to providing the institutional infrastructure that facilitates trade. In turn, this view of the state implied a much more modest role for the economist/moral philosopher in contributing to the wealth of nations.

The civilizing effect of trade could be seen at three levels. First, the spread of trade created incentives for individuals to interact through persuasion via mutual benefit, rather than through zero- or negative-sum games of force or deception. In doing so, trade engendered peaceful relations among individuals by creating interdependencies through the division of labor and exchange. Second, trade promoted orderly and prosperous societies through the invisible hand/spontaneous ordering processes of the market. Not only did it create more civilized relationships among individuals, it created more civilized social orders. Finally, trade promoted more civilized relationships among nations through the extension of the Ricardian law to international trade: nations that kept barriers to international trade low developed cooperative and interdependent relationships with other nations, reducing the net benefits, and thus the frequency, of armed conflict. This section explores each of these arguments in turn.

Adam Smith recognized early in the *Wealth of Nations* that market economies had civilizing effects on individuals in several ways. The transition from older forms of economic organization to markets entailed a movement from societies that were frequently coordinated by face-to-face interaction to ones that required new processes of social coordination that could work among anonymous actors. As Smith ([1776] 1976, 18) put it in the well-known passage near the start of the *Wealth of Nations*,

> In civilized society [man] stands at all times in need of the co-operation and assistance of great multitudes, while his whole life is scarce sufficient to gain the friendship of a few persons.

Smith argues that we could try to gain this cooperation by appealing to the benevolence of others with beneficent acts, but that is unlikely to work where their motive for cooperation is not some personal connection but only self-love. Our beneficence leads to the reward of self-approbation from the impartial spectator but not to the concrete sorts of cooperation and pecuniary benefits that economic processes depend on.[2] Thus, says Smith, we must find a way to appeal to others' self-love, and the famous passage about the butcher, baker, and brewer follows in turn.

In addition to the ways in which Smith et al. argued that commerce demonstrated that direct action by the state was not necessary for encouraging cooperative behavior among individuals, it was also clear that such action was not necessary for the generation of broader notions of social order. The invisible hand of the Scottish Enlightenment helps explain how a nation's internal trade could generate orderly, but unplanned, institutions and outcomes. The thrust of the Smithian system was that the "system of natural liberty" would generate the wealth of nations, and not the state's intentional attempts to create national wealth. However one reads the metaphor of the invisible hand, its very invisibility invokes

2. We thank an anonymous referee for a particularly useful suggestion for clarifying this argument.

processes other than the very visible activities of the state in generating economic development.

This increase in commerce, which was mainly focused on the towns, had other salutary effects on the broader social order. As Smith argues in the chapter "How the Commerce of the Towns Contributed to the Improvement of the Country," there were three ways that town-based commerce generated beneficial unintended consequences for the country areas. The first two were more narrowly economic, but the third, which he attributes to Hume, was the one he thought was most important:

> Commerce and manufactures gradually introduced order and good government, and with them, the liberty and security of individuals, among the inhabitants of the country, who had before lived almost in a continual state of war with their neighbors, and of servile dependency upon their superiors. (433)

This argument is a nice condensation of the views of the Scots with respect to the necessary and unnecessary roles of the state. Smith argues here that it is commerce, which clearly in some sense precedes the state, that generates the "demand" for political reform and good government, and the spread of civilization to the countryside. Trade is, for Smith, a natural human proclivity, but one that will generate the best consequences when property and liberty are secure. An increased volume of trade leads to greater benefits from the state being both limited and well respected.

The third way in which the state's forbearance was believed to generate civilizing effects was through international trade. The idea that specialization and the division of labor led to salutary effects within the nation was clear in Smith's mind. His linking that division of labor to the "extent of the market" provided a principle by which the ongoing evolution and growth of economies could be rendered intelligible. Both Jean-Baptiste Say and David Ricardo extended that insight in important ways, with Say's law explaining how production was the source of demand and Ricardo using the concept of comparative advantage to extend the Smithian insight to trade among nations. Commerce could generate the very same interdependencies among nations as it did among individuals. In the case of nations, these interdependencies would lead to a reduction in the level of conflict among them.

For the early political economists, the state's role was largely limited to the protection of person and property, as they argued that unhampered trade would generate the beneficial effects that some believed required an activist state. The state's job was to provide the legal-political infrastructure that made commerce possible. Like the gardener who cultivates an environment in which plants can thrive, the state was seen, largely, as providing the institutions that individuals required to benefit from the gains from trade. Smith, it could be argued, saw himself as explaining the economic and social forces that were actually at work in the social world of his time, and, in identifying them, he offered a vision of humility for the ability of humans to consciously manipulate those economic processes. The institutional infrastructure was the key to the wealth of nations, as it would direct our passions into channels that generated public benefits, if only unintentionally.

For Smith and his contemporaries, the claims of economics were modest ones. It made no claim to being able to remake the world; it could only offer some general advice about what needed to be done, but it could say a great deal about what not to do. The student would find this a congenial atmosphere and would happily play the role of cautionary prophet. It is worth noting that from the early years of the Enlightenment and well into the nineteenth century, the role of cautionary prophet was more radical than conservative, given that Smith's work was an attempt to bring reason to the study of society.[3] The cutting edge of knowledge was, in fact, the ability to talk about how reason demonstrated, in Hume's words, the limits to reason. We are often accustomed to seeing the cautionary prophet as a "conservative" voice, but in the context of Smith's time it was quite the opposite. Not surprisingly, this modest role for economics and the economist did not sit well with those who approached economics as saviors. They would have their turn in the next stage of development economics.

Protectionism and National Identity: The Savior as Frustrated Engineer

The argument for unhampered trade, particularly among nations, put forward by Smith et al. was in response to earlier arguments that we now

3. A good example of just such a radical cautionary prophet was Richard Cobden in nineteenth-century England. Largely in agreement with Smithian arguments, Cobden was particularly effective in advocating the epistemically modest vision of economics and in actually affecting policy concerning free trade as a result. He was both committed to free trade and clearly radical. We thank an anonymous referee for suggesting Cobden as a good example of the point in the text.

broadly categorize under the name "mercantilism." There remains much debate as to whether the mercantilism of the pre-Smithian period can be understood as a coherent theoretical system. In his overview of mercantilist thought, Lars Magnusson (2003, 56) argues that although there was no cohesive doctrine or set of policy proposals, what the various pre-Smithian British mercantilist thinkers "mainly shared was a preoccupation with the question of how a nation could become rich and thus also achieve greater national power and glory." For most mercantilists, doing so required that the state manage trade, especially with the goal of generating a favorable balance of trade. The response from the classical economists, as we have shown, was to argue that national wealth was better understood in terms of how goods and services were best delivered to the population, and that markets and trade were the best means to that end.

At much the same time as these promarket arguments were being developed in Great Britain and in areas of the Continent, another school of mercantilist thought was emerging in the United States and in Germany.[4] Like the earlier mercantilists, these thinkers did not always form a coherent school of thought. However, the most full-fledged statement of the general thrust of their ideas came from the German Friedrich List in his *Nationale System der Politischen Ökonomie* in 1841. List's ideas, and those of similar thinkers in the United States (e.g., Alexander Hamilton and Henry Carey), are often categorized as "national economics," as they, like their British predecessors, were focused on the development of the nation's wealth and power. List's work is also sometimes linked to the German historical school, as his central idea was that the economic theory and policy that was appropriate to a particular country depended on that country's stage of development. By making economic theory historically dependent, List fits with the German historicists, and by arguing that free trade was sometimes not the best policy option, List followed in the tradition of the pre-Smithian mercantilists.

At the time List was writing, the highly decentralized nature of the multiple political entities that comprised Germany led to a number of tariffs among them that limited intranational trading. Combined with very low to nonexistent import tariffs, the various German states were lucrative markets for foreign sellers, especially the British. With foreign goods making up a relatively large part of the economy, the various

4. See Stephen Meardon's essay in this volume for more on the U.S. economists William Cullen Bryant and Henry C. Carey.

German states wanted some way to rebuild their national industries and national identities. List's work landed nicely into this historical environment. As we argue later, much of List's work, and the circumstances that produced its reception, foreshadows similar ideas and historical contexts in the emergence of approaches to economic development in the twentieth century, as Magnusson (2003, 58–59) notes as well.

List argued that economic development was best understood as a series of stages of maturation, from "barbaric" to "pastoral" to "agricultural" to "agricultural-manufacturing" to "agricultural-manufacturing-commercial." Specifically, List claimed nations could pass from the first to third stage making use of free trade, but that some form of protectionism was necessary to reach the final stage when, once again, free trade was most desirable. The central theoretical premise was that the very unevenness of world economic development precluded free trade from being desirable in all circumstances. When one country moved to the later developmental stages, its ability to export cheaper manufactured goods to countries in earlier stages would preclude the development of their own manufacturing industries, preventing the less-developed country from moving to the higher stages of development. The implication is that nations should adopt protectionist strategies, in particular what today would be called "infant industry" protections, to make sure that internal industries have sufficient time to develop without the competition from cheaper imports.

The nationalist aspect of List's approach demands some further attention. Like others in the early nineteenth century (e.g., Thomas Carlyle, as David Levy [2002] demonstrates), List objected to the "cosmopolitanism" of the classical economists. Where the focus for some critics was on the implication that free trade would overthrow long-standing hierarchies of race or gender, for List the concern was with the cross-national application of economic theory and its focus on the individual rather than the nation. As his stages-of-development approach indicates, one at the very least had to recognize that different theories might apply to different countries. In addition, List was concerned with the effects of free trade on the nation as a whole. For example, if such trade meant that industries or people were displaced, it should be seen as harmful. He also claimed that nations should attempt to husband "productive power" rather than wealth itself. In an interesting turn on the older mercantilist tradition, he saw the real national goal as not the collection of money but the increase of the productive powers of industry. And unlike the charge sometimes leveled at the older mercantilists, he understood that productive power was not the same as wealth and explicitly preferred the power to the wealth.

One element that List brought to his version of the mercantilist view is that nationalism and national identity were part of what was at stake in economic development. Writing in Germany of the early to mid-nineteenth century, List naturally would see nation building as central to his theoretical stance. Much of the concern with the infant-industry argument is that free trade makes the development of a nation's economy dependent on forces that it cannot control. When world prices and free trade guide the direction of economic development, nations cannot control whether and how their own productive powers evolve, thus they cannot determine their own national identity and destiny. In some ways, this is a precursor of Marxian arguments about the hidden nature of capitalist laws and the need to take control over what has previously controlled us. In the twentieth century, the building of national identity and these elements of Marxism would come together in the economic development policies of the postcolonial world.

Three aspects of List's framework are noteworthy for the broader story we are telling. The first is that this view assumes that industrialization is central to economic development. List was explicit in believing that rapid and early industrialization was desirable even if it meant that the nation was worse off temporarily. As we show later, this claim was at the center of debates in the emergence of both the Soviet model in the 1920s and postwar development economics. The second aspect is that it focuses on the nation as the unit of analysis. By starting with the stage of development that the nation is in and asking what is necessary for enhancing the nation's industrial strength, List's approach can avoid asking whether the policies it recommends actually work to the benefit of most or many individuals. Where it does ask that question, it answers it by putting the interests of the "nation" over those of the individual. Finally, List's approach is a clear precursor of the "import substitution" policies that dominated much of development economics in the mid-twentieth century.

The views associated with List and the historical school redefined the role that economists, or those knowledgeable about economics, might play with respect to the broader society. Economists disposed to be saviors could make a claim to understanding the "real" processes at work and staking a further claim to having sufficient knowledge to design policies that would produce both better economic outcomes and other goals, such as enhanced national identity. Though not as comprehensively as would be seen in the twentieth century, List and the historicists gave the savior some scope to become an engineer. Rather than humility in the face of social processes that could be understood but not controlled, this critique of the Smithian paradigm suggested that economists should have confidence that they could be key contributors to the activist work of the state. Later in the nineteenth century, this confidence would reach a higher plateau in the role played by members of the later German historical school, as the so-called Socialists of the Chair. Seeing themselves as the intellectual defenders of those in power, they came even closer to the engineer than the cautionary prophet.

We also wish to suggest that the relationship between policy and the economist's role can be cumulative. That is, changes in the dominant perception of policy can alter economists' perceptions of their own roles in society. We do not mean to suggest that narrow self-interest in access to power explains the changes in ideas; rather, it is more likely the other way around: changes in beliefs about "how the world works" will change economists' self-perceptions. In addition, once that self-perception begins to change, and economists both see themselves and are treated as saviors, it can in turn affect how they attempt to understand the world. If the savior can become an engineer and appear to have success in doing so, more potential saviors will be attracted to economics. As the saviors become engineers, they will look for ways of understanding the world that play to the strengths of the savior-cum-engineer. They will see the world in engineering terms. There is, perhaps, a kind of lock-in here where self-perceptions, actual access to power, and the human capital of economists are mutually reinforcing in ways that make alternative visions appear to have very high transition costs.

Nonetheless, by the mid-nineteenth century, the saviors of the List/historical school remained frustrated engineers, as the dominant self-understanding of the discipline stayed largely in the same camp as Smith's time. Put somewhat differently, being the savior at this time required that one be heterodox, and thus it largely meant frustration in terms of influencing both the discipline and policy. Only when the discipline changed in ways that enabled the savior-cum-engineer to be part of orthodoxy would that frustration end.

The Rise of the Engineers in the Twentieth Century

Despite the potential for such an intellectual lock-in, the late nineteenth century and early twentieth century saw both the rise of the savior and the continued strength of the student. With respect to the latter, Max Weber emerged as one of the leading social scientists in the world. Of his many scholarly contributions, the one his name is most identified with is his claim about the protestant work ethic and capitalist development. In *The Protestant Ethic and the Spirit of Capitalism*, Weber sought to explain how religious beliefs affect economic organization and performance. Whether one agrees with him or not, one must agree with the importance of the way Weber addressed the question of the wealth and poverty of nations. Too often in the history of political economy, thinkers sought to explain the differences between nations by reference to natural resource endowment. But Weber sought to blend an analysis of material resources with noneconomic factors to address why industrial capitalism appeared in the West, specifically northwestern Europe, and not in China, even though, only a few centuries earlier, China was by far richer and more technologically advanced than Europe. Weber ([1904–5] 1958) did not provide the monocausal answer to that question that his critics often accuse him of. Protestantism is only one of the differentiating characteristics in his explanation. Protestantism provided the ethical or moral justification for practices conducive to economic development, but it was not the source of development.[5] In his *General Economic History* (1927), Weber contrasted the legal structure of Chinese society, which was not conducive to the development of capitalism, with the Western legal structure, which was conducive to capitalist development. Chinese law, according to Weber, was based on spiritual and magical practices, whereas the Western legal tradition was inherited and evolved out of the formal legal rules of Judaism and Roman law. The Western legal tradition relied on a logical mode of juristic reasoning, instead of discretionary, ritualistic, religious, or magical considerations found in the Chinese legal system.

The main reason that the legal system mattered for economic development is that it enabled the calculative capabilities of individuals to be used in making decisions about enterprise activities. Because the legal system possessed some certainty in its rules, individuals could engage

5. See Swedberg 1998 for an overview of Weber's project for the social sciences.

in rational calculation about the consequences of decisions. Another major factor in Weber's analysis is a fixed tax system, rather than an arbitrary one, and the reason that this fiscal arrangement is vital to economic growth is the same as that for legal certainty; it encourages a longer-term horizon among decision makers, and it provides an incentive for responsible decision makers. We return to this explanation in the section on the institutional revolution in development economics. But first we explore the consequences for economic theory and policy from not following in the Weberian path of focusing on the comparative historical political economy of development. From the time of Adam Smith to Max Weber it was common practice to distinguish between the capitalist civilized world and the noncapitalist barbaric world. The idea of an advanced civilized world that was not capitalistic in orientation was simply a contradiction. Weber's focus on institutions harkened back to the Smithian vision, and Weber's recognition of the power of economic calculation under decentralized decision making suggested a Smithian humility in the economist's own role in second-guessing the products of undesigned social processes.

The Smith-Weber distinctions among countries would fade for a variety of reasons with the rise of the engineering mentality in the twentieth century. Questions about how the institutional infrastructure of a society was or was not conducive to growth were replaced with those about the appropriate policy mix to be implemented by government to achieve economic development. As we show, this, not surprisingly, changed the role played by economists in the process. Poor countries had to catch up to the rich countries, and the process of capital accumulation and capitalist development that occurred in the West was simply too slow. The advantage of backwardness was that concerted effort by the state could speed economic development (see Gerschenkron 1962). Three developments in twentieth-century thought and history undermined the earlier emphasis on the institutional infrastructure of society and how that affected economic performance:

1. Formalism and positivism in economics
2. The Bolshevik revolution and the rise of socialism
3. The Keynesian revolution in macroeconomics and the rise of international public policy institutions grounded in that revolution

Each of these three shifted attention away from the appropriate *institutional* structure of good governance to the necessary *activities* that government must undertake—a move from designing rules to direct action. This in turn facilitated the emerging shift from cautionary prophet to engineer and the corresponding attraction of the savior to economics.

Formalism directed economists' attention away from how the institutional structure of society directed actors to behave in directions more or less conducive to economic development. Instead, optimization against given constraints, the classic technique of the engineer, became the focus of intellectual attention. Positivism also contributed in the shift away from institutions by delegitimizing the study of ideology as an important component in social theory. Political, legal, and economic institutions are sustained through ideological systems of thought. Out of fear of ideological campaigns such as fascism, positivism sought to eliminate all nontestable propositions from economic science.

The combination of the formalistic preoccupation with equilibrium properties and the positivistic disregard for ideas meant that the sorts of questions that dominated the discussion of the wealth and poverty of nations from Smith to Weber were pushed aside in the field of political economy. In fact, political economy was pushed aside in favor of the idea of scientific economics. The natural tendency of neoclassical development economics was to ignore political, legal, and economic institutions and instead search for empirical measures of development. The question of the institutional infrastructure of development was considered to be unscientific. Measurement equaled science, whereas discussions of property rights, rule of law, constitutional constraints, and legitimating belief systems were dismissed as prescientific musings by worldly philosophers. The triumph of the engineer was at hand.

The Keynesian mind-set and analytical tool kit were suited to fill the void once the classical and Weberian treatment of the wealth and poverty of nations was pushed aside. First, Keynesian theory reinforced the general post–Great Depression intellectual climate of opinion that capitalism was inherently unstable. Aggregate demand failure periodically results from the chaotic and irrational decisions of investors. Free market competition could not be relied on to self-correct for the systemic consequences of the errors committed by private actors. Laissez-faire was dead as a legitimating ideology. Second, the aggregate techniques developed in the Keynesian revolution provided economists with a way to measure economic development. Economic development became synonymous with measured growth in per capita income. Obviously the equating of economic development with the emerging neoclassical theory of economic growth had profound consequences for the theoretical foundations of economic development. Third, as the Keynesian hegemony emerged after World War II, various international institutions were formed to carry out public policy grounded in the Keynesian vision and analysis of the government's role in economic development.

The effect of these philosophical and methodological changes on the economist's role was profound with respect to the practice of economics. With the claim to scientific status at their fingertips, economists could move from cautionary prophet to engineer because they now had the tools of objective science to guide policy in ways that did not appear to invoke ideology. Moreover, with the philosophical shifts reflected by positivism and formalism, the engineer not only had the tools but the philosophical blessing to pursue his craft. The shift in focus from the institutional framework to the levers of policy, combined with the rise of formalist and scientistic modes of thought, fed powerfully into the state's own interest in having such policy tools at *its* fingertips. For obvious reasons, the state's interests are conservative here, in that it does not wish to challenge the prevailing set of institutions and would prefer to work within that set to affect policy. This coincidence of interests made for another powerful form of intellectual lock-in that reinforced the role of economist as savior, though this time disguised, through the language of science and objectivity, as a "mere" student.

Although we turn to the Soviet case in the next section, it is important to mention here how that experience influenced thought precisely at the moment of positivist and Keynesian ascendancy. The perceived success of Soviet planning in modernizing a peasant society into an industrial and military power demonstrated that an alternative to the capitalist path to modernity was indeed viable and that the savior as engineer was a model to emulate. Even if the Soviet case was marred by political tyranny in the 1920s and 1930s, surely a more democratic society could accomplish the same societal transformation without the abuse of human rights.

It is important to acknowledge that the promise of Soviet planning in terms of economic development was first accepted in the 1920s and 1930s prior to full knowledge of the political repression of the purges and collectivization. At the time the Western democracies were trapped in the crisis of the Great Depression, and the Soviet system seemed to avoid that problem through rational central planning of the economy. The Soviet system promised to be more economically efficient and more socially just. After knowledge of the political purges and the death toll of collectivization became common, the argument switched from one of Soviet promise to one of merging socialist planning with the democratic institutions of the West. Soviet political institutions lost intellectual legitimacy, but Soviet economic policies continued to hold sway over the hearts and minds of economic reformers. These reformers would occupy the key policy positions throughout the Western democracies and international agencies entrusted with world economic development after World War II.

By the war's end, the distinction between the capitalist and noncapitalist world had given way to a distinction between first world (capitalist-developed), second world (socialist-developed), and third world (underdeveloped) countries. An intellectual and geopolitical battle began between the first world and second world countries to export policy advice to third world countries on how to pursue the path to modernity. It is our contention that the intellectual and historical evidence demonstrates that policy advice provided to the underdeveloped world by the capitalist nations as well as the socialist ones was almost identical and reflected the intellectual transformation of the political economy of development economics that we have just outlined, in addition to giving economists a starring role as saviors of the third world as "practicing engineers." Both first world and second world economists jettisoned the older focus on the institutional infrastructure in society and emphasized a proactive role of government (and its economists) in engineering the path of economic development.

The Soviet Model and the Collapse of Development Planning

When the Bolsheviks rose to power in 1917, Lenin and his colleagues sought to construct a communist economy. Paul Roberts (1971) and Peter Boettke (1990) provide evidence of the ideological motivation of the policies of comprehensive centralized planning that were followed between 1917 and 1921. However, those policies met with a refractory reality that forced the Bolshevik regime to change course with the New Economic Policy (1921–28). The ideological tension that existed over the NEP led to a major intellectual debate among the Bolshevik ruling elite on the nature of socialism and the path of development. The quality of the economic debate was sophisticated as far as politicized discussions of economic policy permit. Nikolai Bukharin argued for a market-based policy that served socialist goals by permitting accumulation and retaining planning control over the "commanding heights" so that peasant Russia would be transformed under a balanced growth policy into an industrialized society, at which time full-blown socialism would once again be pursued to its logical end of the eradication of the market mechanism. Lev Shanin argued that Soviet Russia had a comparative advantage in agricultural production and thus Russia should pursue a policy of agricultural exportation and capital importation (unbalanced growth policy) to industrialize the economy to prepare for full-blown socialism. Evgeny Preobrazhensky, in contrast to both Bukharin and Shanin, never retreated from the communist policies adopted during 1917–21. The first act of any socialist state, Preobrazhensky argued, was to nationalize industry, and the path from capitalism to socialism will be planned and follow a rational strategy.

On an academic level these alternative positions were developed in the Soviet journal, the *Planned Economy*.[6] Alec Nove (1969, 129) suggests that it was in these pages that "development economics could be said to have been born." Nove makes an interesting point in intellectual history. The emphasis in postwar development economics on "growth" and "long-range" planning of an economy follows directly from Soviet discussions in the 1920s. Evsey Domar (1957, 10) has remarked that his study of the debates in the *Planned Economy* was "a valuable source of ideas" in the development of the Harrod-Domar model of economic growth. However, Domar's reconstruction of the Soviet debates minimizes the intellectual influence of Karl Marx and plays up the anticipation of Keynesian ideas. Although the Keynesian interpretation possesses some appeal because of the shared engineering mentality, it does not do justice to the Marxian background of the arguments in the Soviet industrialization debate. For the purposes of this essay, however, we are not concerned with getting the interpretation of the Soviet debate right. Instead, our focus is on simply pointing out the link between the debate and the subsequent development of postwar development economics.

The belief that emerged out of the Soviet experience and the rise of Keynesianism was that development economics was synonymous with

6. A comprehensive discussion of the Soviet industrialization debate can be found in Alexander Erlich's *Soviet Industrialization Debate, 1924–1928* (1960). Erlich, however, tends to reconstruct the arguments from the debate in terms that are understood in the neoclassical synthesis. Boettke (1990, 147–91) provides an interpretation of these debates that attempts to put them within the context of the ideological debates inside the Bolshevik leadership.

macroeconomic growth, and the public policy implications were that government could design, control, and engineer economic growth through various crucial interventions. Underdevelopment was a consequence of weak investment, lack of technology, and shortfalls in the stock of human capital. Government policies were to serve as correctives to the failures of market-driven development and as an engine of economic growth and development in their own right. A fixation on industrialization as the path and measure of development was central to the development planning process, and this was oftentimes complemented by the adoption of import-substitution policies that saw protectionism as a means to the end of statistically measured growth.

As we have shown earlier, this line of thought was hardly original in its broad contours, which recall the nationalism and protectionism of List and other nineteenth-century thinkers. The difference this time was the additional support garnered from the misinterpretation of the Soviet experience and the theoretical framework of Keynesianism that had begun to dominate economic thought, and economists' abilities to ground their roles as saviors in the language of science and the tools of engineering. One reason for the confidence of economists was that the arguments for development planning made during the twentieth century grew out of the then mainstream of economic thinking, in contrast to the heterodoxy of their predecessors a century before. As a result, these ideas had a practical influence on real-world economies that the economic nationalism of List et al. never really achieved. The changes in the methodological and philosophical winds in the early twentieth century made the later versions of economic nationalism into orthodoxy and turned frustrated engineers into practicing ones.

One of the more fascinating puzzles of the middle of the twentieth century is the disjunction between generally accepted beliefs about the success of the industrialization of the Soviet economy and the reality of its effects on the lives of the citizenry. After Stalin consolidated his power, he moved to rapidly industrialize the Soviet economy, believing that it was the path to both the growth needed to implement socialism and the power needed to counterbalance the West. The five-year planning model involved transfers of wealth from agriculture to industry via the forced collectivization of the former and state planning of the latter. By many of the accepted measures, this attempt was successful. Reported growth rates in per capita GDP and other macroeconomic variables, as well as the buildup of military resources, pushed the Soviet

Union into the ranks of a world power. The strategy of forced industrialization appeared to be the path to economic development and political influence.

In retrospect, many of the beliefs about the strength of the Soviet economy turned out to be illusory. This illusion came in three forms. First, the data produced by the Soviets themselves were systematically overstated, both intentionally for propaganda purposes and through mismeasurement and miscommunication. Second, the estimates made by CIA economists also systematically overstated the health of the Soviet economy: "In 1986, for example, the CIA estimated that Soviet per capita GNP was about 49 percent of that in the United States. The revised estimate now put that figure at about 25 percent" (Boettke 1994, 7).

The third source of illusion was perhaps the most important. Whatever the truth of the macroeconomic variables, day-to-day life for the Soviet citizenry did not match the picture they painted. The reality of breadlines, backward and dysfunctional technology, inadequate medical care, and dangerous employment conditions was more like that of a third world country than a developed world power. Various measures of well-being demonstrated the ways in which the Soviet citizenry lagged behind the West to a degree that far exceeded the differences in conventional measures of economic success. Comparative data on consumer items such as passenger cars and telephones show the Soviet economies, and Soviet-style economies of Eastern Europe, as lagging significantly behind those of the West. Per capita food consumption and a variety of health indicators, including infant mortality, show similar trends (Boettke 1993, 35–36). The measured industrial output did not translate into better opportunities and outcomes for most economic actors, and the investments in military equipment did not translate into effective military power, as the failure of Soviet technology in the first Gulf War demonstrated. The emergence of economic doctrines that saw *C*, *I*, and *G*, or their sum, as measures of economic development precluded analysts from asking important questions about the *composition* of those variables or whether they translated into meaningful gains in living standards for those affected by them. The doctrines also were both the cause and the effect of the savior-cum-engineer approach to economics.

The problem with the equation of statistical aggregates that measure "growth" with the more general notion of "development" is that, paraphrasing a remark of Friedrich Hayek's in a different but not unrelated context, the aggregates "conceal the most fundamental mechanisms of change" ([1931] 1995, 128). In the Smithian tradition, economic development was seen as the progressive extension of the division of labor (and the extent of the market), along with the emergence of institutional arrangements that would both facilitate that evolution and respond to the new practices and structures that it produced. For example, the focus on aggregates made it difficult to see how investment expenditures were or were not producing a structure of capital that was sustainable and that could actually produce consumer goods that added to well-being, not to mention whether the existing political and economic institutions were capable of generating a sustainable capital structure. The generation of such a structure was emphatically not an engineering problem of maximizing *K* against constraints, as Hayek attempted to argue in that same response to Keynes.

In addition, in many places in the developing world, the aggregates concealed the fact that many of the resources counted in official GDP figures were actually diverted to the more narrow well-being of the political class. The classic picture of the gleaming third world capital surrounded by extreme poverty is symbolic of that concern. The understanding of development that pervaded the twentieth century could easily be blind to those differentials and their underpinnings in the particular political and economic institutions in these countries. These concerns were especially noteworthy with respect to the role of aid from the West. Even where aid made up a very small portion of GDP, it was often a substantial portion of government revenues, which in turn frequently benefited government officials rather than those in need of assistance (Osterfeld 1992, 150–51). All of this emphasis on measurement and aggregates distracted attention from the institutional concerns of the Smithian vision.

The data on the effects of development planning in the non-Soviet world bear out these concerns. In India, over forty years of development planning leading up to the early 1990s had left India's per capita income at around $300, with approximately 40 percent of the population living below the poverty line. Because population grew significantly over that period, the lack of growth meant an increase in the absolute number of Indians below the poverty line during the peak decades of development planning (Kamath 1994, 91). The story in Africa was similar, with the continent's annual GNP growth rate from 1965 to 1986 averaging 0.9 percent. Put against rising population, this meant a decline in per capita GNP of about 14.6 percent for sub-Saharan Africa. In addition, food production per person "fell by 7 percent in the 1960s, 15 percent in the 1970s, and continued to deteriorate in the 1980s" (Ayittey 1994, 155). As George Ayittey also notes, the grandiose plans of African governments were expected to be paid for by "huge surpluses in the rural sector" (162). This is a good example of the borrowing of the failed Soviet model by postcolonial planners.

A story that remains untold in the evolution of theories of economic development is the role of Western universities as the intellectual conduit from the Soviet model and early Keynesian models to development planning in the third world. Many of the postcolonial leaders, as well as the civil servants who staffed the planning bureaucracy, were educated in Western universities during the 1950s and 1960s when Keynesianism and the related growth models were the mainstream of economic thinking. Some postcolonial leaders were also trained in the Marxist tradition, which was also reasonably alive and well in the universities, but even those who pursued advanced degrees in economics at topflight universities came away with a set of beliefs about what produced development that included doctrines that would later be shown to be, at the very least, inadequate and, more often, destructive. It was through these institutions that the economist as savior moved from the first world to the third world. Where Western doctrines were translated into guidance for development in the South and East, the economist, with the engineering tools of science at hand, was easily seen as the savior. The ways in which many students from the third world of that era, and still today, imagine themselves using their Western educations to return home and solve the problems of their native lands reflect this marriage of activist government and the economist as savior-cum-engineer. The intellectual environment and economics' self-understanding enabled these engineers to practice their trade on their home countries. The Western universities continue to be an intellectual conduit for policymaking in the third world, but as economic thought has evolved on these questions, Western-trained economists are now more critical of planning-based approaches and have turned more attention to the institutional environment.

A Return to Humility?

At the close of the twentieth century, a coincidence of three empirical facts of political economy worldwide forced economists and public policymakers to rethink the underlying engineering vision of economic policy. The three empirical facts were (1) the breakdown of the Keynesian consensus on macroeconomic policy (see Buchanan and Wagner [1977] 2000), (2) the collapse of state communism in Eastern and Central Europe (see Boettke 1993), and (3) the frustration with foreign-aid programs in less-developed countries (see Easterly 2001). At the same time that these facts came to be increasingly recognized by scholars, policymakers, and the public, economic scholarship had undergone a transformation. While new Keynesian economics, information economics, and game theory came to be part of the tool kit of modern economics, so did rational expectations theory and new classical macroeconomics, the Chicago school of law and economics, the Chicago new learning in industrial organization, the Washington and UCLA schools of property rights economics, Schumpeterian evolutionary economics, the market process of economics of the Austrians as well as neo-Marshallian industrial organization, and public choice theory of political economy. Many of these scholarly developments in economics eventually would go under the banner of new institutionalism in economics, political science, and sociology.

One could argue that the breakdown of Keynesianism led to a reemergence of laissez-faire policy in economic debates, and the transition experience in the wake of the collapse of communism led to the focus on the vital role of institutions. Unlike the nineteenth-century critics of laissez-faire, whose focus on institutions was an attempt to redesign them through the use of reason, the recent resurgence of interest in institutions reflects a return to the cautious respect of an earlier era. To some, a defense of laissez-faire and an emphasis on institutions would be at odds, given the belief that the institutionless approach of much of twentieth-century economics was also a defense of laissez-faire. But there is no conflict between laissez-faire policy prescriptions and an analytical emphasis on institutions, as demonstrated by the work of classical economists such as David Hume and Adam Smith as well as more modern economists such as F. A. Hayek and James Buchanan. It is not the laissez-faire tradition that ignored institutions, rather it was the engineering vision of economics that first thought it could transcend evolved institutions, then later saw institutions as irrelevant to a framework of optimization and equilibrium. Both engineering approaches effectively ruled out as "unscientific" serious discussion of the role of historically evolved institutions, and neither approach was one that unambiguously supported laissez-faire.[7]

7. Paul Krugman (1995) argued that the resistance of mainstream economists to discuss ideas that defy immediate formalization often leads them to ignore ideas which in the end prove

Only the very sterile engineering version of economics could ignore the crucial role of institutions, or could imagine that the transition problem or the economics of underdevelopment could be boiled down to a prescription for getting the prices right. Of course, allowing prices to float freely to clear markets and guide producers and consumers in orienting their behavior to one another is necessary but not sufficient for development, as the ability to get the prices right is a function of the effective operation of a complex array of institutions such as those associated with the definition and enforcement of private property rights.[8]

Overviews of the role of institutions in economic development can be found in Ostrom et al. 2001 and Ahrens 2002. Although this work stresses our need to overcome the market-government dichotomy that reflected the ideological battle from the classical to neoclassical period, there should be no mistaking that the government's role in economic development has been severely restricted in comparison with the postwar policy consensus of government as a corrective to the social ills that result from market failures.[9] The quality of the institutions of governance (both the private and public devices in operation in a society for warding off predation) determine the capacity of a society to realize the gains from specialization and exchange and stimulate the long-term

---

to be the most fundamental to solving the pressing problems of economic policy. Krugman uses the fields of both economic development and economic geography as examples to show how the obsession with formalization led to their decline as fields of research in the economics profession. The story of the rise and fall and rise again of development economics is a complicated one. But the fact, as Krugman points out, that the field defied formalization even by its top practitioners in a discipline where formalization was the sign of scientific advance played a significant role. It is important to note that in Krugman's analysis the reason for the difficulty in formalization was not related to the issues we have discussed, but instead technical—the difficulty of squaring economies of scale with models of perfect competition. In fact, what Krugman argues in these lectures is that a new class of models that have challenged the competitive market structure model is now able to absorb in a rigorous way the ideas of economies of scale and economic geography. Ideas that defied formalization can now be taken off the shelf, dusted off, and incorporated into contemporary thinking in economics and public policy.

8. See the interesting note by Raghuram Rajan (2004) in "Assume Anarchy? Why an Orthodox Economic Model Might Not Be the Best Guide for Policy." Rajan's argument is straightforward. The complete market model assumes that the institutional framework necessary for its operation is in place, whereas in the former socialist countries and in the less-developed world it is precisely the absence of this framework that must be addressed if a successful transition to a more peaceful and prosperous social order is to be achieved.

9. As we have stressed, the classical economists did not subscribe to this dichotomy either, so while people characterize their position as representative of this dichotomy, this is actually a false depiction. However, the neoclassical synthesis did speak in terms of this dichotomy and in particular by stressing market failure and government correctives to questions of insufficient aggregate demand, unemployment equilibrium, capital market instability, and underdevelopment.

investment behavior that leads to wealth creation. As Mancur Olson (1996, 22) summarizes the point,

> Though low-income societies obtain most of the gains from trade from self-enforcing trades, they do not realize many of the largest gains from specialization and trade. They do not have the institutions that enforce contracts impartially, and so they lose most of the gains from those transactions (like those in the capital market) that require impartial third-party enforcement. They do not have the institutions that make property rights secure over the long run, so they lose the gains from capital-intensive production. Production and trade in these societies is further handicapped by misguided economic policies and by private and public predation. The intricate social cooperation that emerges when there is a sophisticated array of markets requires far better institutions and economic policies than most countries have.

The most drastic change in modern economic thought is in fact the emphasis now placed on the study of the institutions (rules of the game and their enforcement) required to realize the intricate social cooperation of an advanced market economy. This requires not just economic and financial institutions but also political, legal, and social institutions that serve to align incentives, and utilize and communicate information effectively so that millions of individuals can coordinate their affairs with one another. Without the effective operation of these institutions that afford complex coordination, individuals will not generate the material standards of living that are prerequisites for human flourishing.

The dilemma of underdevelopment is that while there are many different ways for individuals to live their lives, there are few ways that they can live prosperously. For generalized societal prosperity to be realized, an alignment of cultural norms, formal legal rules, and economic organizations must occur. Absent this alignment of informal and formal rules and organizations, generalized prosperity will go unrealized.

Whether the state plays a positive role in this alignment is unimportant for our present purpose. What matters for the metadiscussion of the vision of the state in economic development is that under this configuration the state is not an active player entrusted to correct social ills, and economists are not engineers putting that vision into practice under the guise of science. That vision of the state is consistent with another era of economic thinking and policy. Rather than a focus on the state's role in correcting market failures, the focus is now on the governing capacity of an array of private and public institutions that are entrusted to ward off predation by either private opportunists or public exploiters. Overcoming poverty is not a consequence of the state closing an investment gap or fixing human capital shortfalls in a society, let alone population control through contraceptive education.

The state's role has indeed withered away and with it, perhaps, will wither the role of the economist. Vernon Smith (2003) has characterized the visionary implications of the new thinking in economics that emerges from both experimental research and the analytical focus on institutions as a transformation from "constructivist rationality" to "ecological rationality." In the field of development economics, this is a move from the government directly orchestrating economic activity to providing the fertile conditions for bottom-up development. This represents a swing back toward the more humble self-understanding of what economics can contribute, in that the role of the economic policymaker moves from engineering economic development to cultivating economic development. As a result, the savior moves back to the frustrated engineer, and more room opens up for the student to play the role of cautionary prophet and have that role respected. Furthermore, the fact that the move back toward humility can be defended on the basis of better scientific knowledge about the workings of the human brain (e.g., Hayek 1952) gives, ironically, the cautionary prophet newfound scientific legitimacy and makes the savior-cum-engineer seem somewhat unscientific.[10]

With the swing back toward humility in the discipline, the economist as student is perhaps in the ascendance, and the debate over the economic role of the state in economic development has come full circle. We are back again to Smith's admonition that "little else is requisite to carry a state to the highest degree of opulence from the lowest barbarism, but peace, easy taxes and a tolerable administration of justice; all the rest being brought about by the natural course of things." An emphasis on how actors make choices in alternative institutional contexts also pushes the economist away from being the savior-cum-engineer and back toward being the student-cum–cautionary prophet: humble in the face of processes that economists did not design and cannot control.

10. This view is consistent with the argument Bruce Caldwell (2003) makes about Hayek's contribution. Hayek's work on the philosophy of mind provided a scientifically based critique of scientism.

References

Ahrens, J. 2002. *Governance and Economic Development: A Comparative Institutional Approach*. Cheltenham, U.K.: Elgar.

Ayittey, George. 1994. The Failure of Development Planning in Africa. In *The Collapse of Development Planning*, edited by Peter J. Boettke. New York: New York University Press.

Boettke, Peter J. 1990. *The Political Economy of Soviet Socialism: The Formative Years, 1918–1928*. Boston: Kluwer Academic.

———. 1993. *Why Perestroika Failed*. New York: Routledge.

———, ed. 1994. Introduction to *The Collapse of Development Planning*. New York: New York University Press.

Buchanan, James, and Richard Wagner. [1977] 2000. *Democracy in Deficit: The Political Legacy of Lord Keynes*. Vol. 8 of *The Collected Works of James M. Buchanan*. Indianapolis, Ind.: Liberty Fund.

Caldwell, Bruce. 2003. *Hayek's Challenge*. Chicago: University of Chicago Press.

Domar, Evsey. 1957. *Essays in the Theory of Economic Growth*. New York: Oxford University Press.

Easterly, William. 2001. *The Elusive Quest for Growth: Economists' Adventures and Misadventures in the Tropics*. Cambridge, Mass.: MIT Press.

Ehrlich, Alexander. 1960. *The Soviet Industrialization Debate, 1924–1928*. Cambridge, Mass.: Harvard University Press.

Engels, Frederick. [1892] 1972. *Socialism: Utopian and Scientific*. New York: International Publishers.

Gerschenkron, A. 1962. *Economic Backwardness in Historical Perspective*. Cambridge, Mass.: Harvard University Press.

Hayek, F. A. 1952. *The Sensory Order*. Chicago: University of Chicago Press.

———. [1931] 1995. Reflections on the Pure Theory of Money of Mr. J. M. Keynes. Reprinted in *Contra Keynes and Cambridge*, vol. 9 of *The Collected Works of F. A. Hayek*, edited by Bruce Caldwell. Chicago: University of Chicago Press.

Kamath, Shyam. 1994. The Failure of Development Planning in India. In *The Collapse of Development Planning*, edited by Peter J. Boettke. New York: New York University Press.

Krugman, Paul. 1995. *Development, Geography, and Economic Theory*. Cambridge, Mass.: MIT Press.

Lerner, Abba. 1944. *The Economics of Control*. London: Macmillan.

Levy, David M. 2002. *How the Dismal Science Got Its Name: Classical Economics and the Ur-Text of Racial Politics*. Ann Arbor: University of Michigan Press.

Magnusson, Lars. 2003. Mercantilism. In *The Blackwell Companion to the History of Economic Thought*, edited by Warren J. Samuels, Jeff E. Biddle, and John B. Davis. Malden, Mass.: Blackwell.

Marx, Karl. 1906. *Capital*. New York: Modern Library Edition.

Mirowski, Philip. 1989. *More Heat Than Light: Economics as Social Physics, Physics as Nature's Economics*. Cambridge: Cambridge University Press.

North, Douglass. 1981. *Structure and Change in Economic History*. New York: Norton.

Nove, Alec. 1969. *An Economic History of the USSR*. Baltimore, Md.: Penguin.

Olson, Mancur. 1996. Big Bills Left on the Sidewalk: Why Some Nations Are Rich, and Others Poor. *Journal of Economic Perspectives* 10.2:3–24.

Osterfeld, David. 1992. *Prosperity versus Planning: How Government Stifles Economic Growth*. New York: Oxford University Press.

Ostrom, E., et al. 2001. *Aid, Incentives, and Sustainability: An Institutional Analysis of Development Cooperation*. Stockholm, Sweden: SIDA.

Rajan, Raghuram. 2004. Assume Anarchy? Why an Orthodox Economic Model Might Not Be the Best Guide for Policy. *Finance and Development* 41.3:56–57.

Roberts, Paul Craig. 1971. *Alienation and the Soviet Economy: The Collapse of the Socialist Era*. Albuquerque: University of New Mexico Press.

Smith, Adam. [1776] 1976. *An Inquiry into the Nature and Causes of the Wealth of Nations*. Edited by Edwin Cannan. Chicago: University of Chicago Press.

———. [1759] 1982. *The Theory of Moral Sentiments*. Indianapolis: Liberty Press.

Smith, Vernon. 2003. Constructivist and Ecological Rationality in Economics. *American Economic Review* 93.3:465–508.

Swedberg, Richard. 1998. *Max Weber and the Idea of Economic Sociology*. Princeton, N.J.: Princeton University Press.

Weber, Max. [1904–5] 1958. *The Protestant Ethic and the Spirit of Capitalism*. New York: Scribners.

———. [1927] 1995. *General Economic History*. New Brunswick, N.J.: Transaction.

Part 1

New Perspectives on the British Classical Tradition

Benevolence, Sympathy, and Hume's Model of Government: How Different Is New Political Economy from Classical Political Economy?

Alain Marciano

> What a malignant philosophy must it be, that will not allow, to humanity and friendship, the same privileges, which are undisputably granted to the darker passions of enmity and resentments? Such a philosophy is more like a satire than a true delineation or description of human nature; and may be a good foundation for paradoxical wit and raillery, but is a very bad one for any serious argument or reasoning.
>
> —David Hume, *An Enquiry concerning Human Understanding* (1748)

This essay is about the theory of human nature proposed by David Hume and how it relates to his model of government. This is of particular interest from the perspective of a historical discussion of the way economists have modeled institutions and governments. Indeed, the standard model of government proposed by *new* political economists—usually labeled the "worst case" model of government (see Farrant and Paganelli, this volume)—is based on the assumption that individuals are rational utility maximizers who act out of egoist motives. This postulate about human behavior is not only a core assumption in mainstream economics; it is also presented as having its roots in the writings of one of the founders of political economy, namely, Hume. This is shown by the quotation new political economists frequently borrow from the Scottish scholar: "In constraining any system of government, and fixing the several checks

I would like to thank all the participants at the 2004 *HOPE* conference and the anonymous referee for helpful comments. A preliminary version of this essay was presented at the University of Saint-Etienne (CREUSET). I would also like to thank Maud Pélissier and Philippe Solal for helpful comments.

and controls of the constitution, each ought to be supposed as a knave, and have no other end, in all his actions than his private interest" (Hume, *Essays*, I.IV; quoted, for instance, in Brennan and Buchanan 1985; Buchanan 1987, 1990).[1] This sentence, at the same time, shows, first, that any model of government has to be founded on the assumption of human knavery—the eighteenth-century equivalent of rationality and egoism—and, second, designates Hume as a precursor of the model of government that new political economists adopt. That is, new political economists revive "the spirit of the classical political economists" (Brennan and Buchanan 1985, 10): both new and classical political economists share the same conception of man (individuals are knaves) and, as a consequence, develop the same (worst case) model of government.[2]

Now, despite their claims, new political economists do not really assume the heritage of classical political economy. Indeed, and this is the argument that we develop in this essay: Hume's model government and theory of institutions differ from the conception proposed by new political economists *because* his conception of humanity differs from that of new political economy. In fact, it is sometimes admitted that Hume's model of humanity cannot be restricted to what is put forward in this famous sentence. Even authors who previously defended the standard "new political economy" vision of humanity now acknowledge that "the procedure that public choice orthodoxy routinely adopts . . . is *unduly* restrictive" (Brennan 2000, 6). However, Hume's theory is rarely (if ever) discussed, and his assumption regarding individual "knavery" remains undisputed. This is an obstacle to seeing that Hume's model of government differs from what is usually assumed.

Our demonstration develops as follows. We show that Hume's representation of human nature is not only different but also richer than the narrow conception of human nature proposed by neoclassical economics and accepted by new political economists. In effect, classical political

1. The following abbreviations are used hereafter: *THN* (*A Treatise of Human Nature*); *EHU* (*An Enquiry concerning Human Understanding*); *EPM* (*An Enquiry concerning the Principles of Morals*); *Essays* (*Essays, Moral, Political, and Literary*). They are cited by section and paragraph numbers.

2. This perspective contrasts with new law and economics where references to past authors were abandoned (see Medema 1998) and even criticized for making it impossible to renew law and economics. Past authors, in particular old political economists, are viewed as obstacles to a renewed approach in law and economics. For instance, Richard Posner, an advocate of Friedman's instrumentalism, opposes Coase's law and economics and criticizes his approach for being old, in the sense of being in the vein of Adam Smith's political economy.

economists depict humans as totally different from the rational egoist individual of new political economists. Indeed, in contrast to what is usually assumed, classical political economists, in particular Hume, propose a *sensualist* theory of human nature in which sensory perception is decisive. Thus, taking into consideration the philosophical and psychological foundations of human behavior, classical political economists insist on the subjectivist dimension of human cognition as well as the weakness, or the limitations, of human rationality and stress the role of benevolence and sympathy in interactions with others. Benevolence and sympathy are not only the most important, noticeable, and undisputable characteristics of human nature; they have to be taken into account in any analysis of social interactions. That is, using such a conception of individuals necessarily leads to a different conception of institutions and a different theory of the government's role. This clearly appears when one analyzes what Hume writes about the characteristics of the governments of civil societies and how these considerations were linked with limited rationality, benevolence, or sympathy.

In the first two sections of this essay, we discuss human cognition in a sensualist framework. We then show that reason is limited and dependent on experience. In the third and fourth sections, we analyze the role of sympathy and how it combines with benevolence, and discuss the limitations of generosity and sympathy. In the fifth section, we present important elements in Hume's model of government and show how it stems from his theory of human nature. The last section presents concluding comments.

Sensualism and the Limits of Human Reason

Individual rationality is undoubtedly the point of departure for a comparison between Hume's conception of human nature and the standard new political economy model of human behavior. From the perspective of a neoclassical theory in which individuals are "*resourceful* evaluating maximising men" (Brunner 1987; emphasis added), reason is not only a powerful capacity that allows us to choose optimal means to reach certain goals; it also preserves and nourishes individual identity (Davis 1995, 41). Thus, individual preferences and resources are indeed indispensable for the exercise of human rationality. In other words, rationality presupposes knowledge (under the form of initial endowments). Certainly, endowments do change, but these modifications can also be considered as the consequence of a rational calculus. Learning, therefore, which consists in accumulating information and adding more to the existing data, is a rational operation that originates within the human mind. In total contrast to this approach, sensualist theorists—among them Hume and Étienne Bonnot de Condillac—insist on ignorance, rather than knowledge, as the basic characteristic of the human condition. This line of reasoning is exemplified by the fact that sensualism, according to a conception that can be traced back to John Locke, assumes that the human mind is a tabula rasa. This is not to say, as G. A. J. Rogers (1993, 83) stresses, that sensualism denies the existence of a human nature, of typically human dispositions. However, the capacity or possibility to act in human ways does not depend on any initial endowments. On the contrary, our experience determines the content of the mind. To insist on the role of experience, Condillac imagines the fiction of a marble statue that, although having the same internal organization as a living person, has none of the five senses that characterize human beings. This perspective thus clearly contradicts other metaphoric representations of humanity, such as those envisaged by the social contract theorists or the nineteenth-century economists. While the latter depict rational and isolated individuals, Condillac argues that individuals insulated from their environments cannot be considered as human beings; they are not different from a marble statue. The first characteristic that makes individuals human are the senses, which allow them to perceive the world, and not their reason, which would permit them to "build" it beyond experience. These individuals, who thus resemble statues because they are deprived of sensory perceptions, are incapable of any form of knowledge, even self-knowledge. This clearly appears in Hume's argument based on the example of a sleeping man: "When my perceptions are remov'd for any time, as by sound sleep; so long am I insensible to myself, and may truly be said not to exist" (*THN*, 252). Here, in contrast to rationalism, the source of knowledge does not lie in the human mind but in the external world. Sensualism makes knowledge dependent on the capacity to perceive and to experience one's environment.

As to these perceptions, Hume considers that they take the form of impressions and ideas. In the very first sentence of his *Treatise of Human Nature*, he writes that "all the perceptions of the human mind resolve themselves into two distinct kinds, which I shall call IMPRESSIONS and IDEAS" (1). Interestingly, although Hume describes impressions and ideas as "distinct," he joins them as two forms of perception. That is, impressions and ideas are produced by the same cognitive operation, namely, the *perception* of the external world. Perception thus consists of two complementary operations, receiving impressions and forming ideas. This suggests that impressions are not qualitatively different from ideas; consequently, Hume writes that impressions and ideas "differ only in degree, not in nature" (3). The differences that Hume envisages between impressions and ideas are quantifiable and could be measured in terms of the "degrees of force and liveliness with which they strike upon the mind, and make their way into our thought or consciousness" (1) and impressions and ideas could be "distinguished by their different degrees of force and vivacity" (*EHU*, 18). In fact, these differences acknowledge the hierarchy Hume establishes between impressions and ideas: the former do not only always chronologically precede the latter, but they also make them possible.

Hume names impressions "those perceptions which enter with most force and violence . . . ; all our sensations, passions and emotions, as they make their *first* appearance in the soul" (*THN*, 3; emphasis added). Thus impressions precede ideas because they correspond to the immediate perception of an object or, rather, the perception of an object that is immediately present to our senses (cf. 73). On this very first moment of the perception, impressions are received through the senses and render an object present. The presence of the object in our mind does not involve the mediation of any intellectual faculty, which could give a particular meaning to the impression received and go beyond to the immediate appearance of the object. Objects are perceived *as they are* because this operation, which Hume names perception "properly speaking," consists in the "passive admission of the impressions throu' the organs of sensation" (73). Thus perception, a passive operation, is guided by the external object itself: "The external objects become known to us only by those perceptions *they occasion*" (67; emphasis added). Once an object, or any element from the external world, is presented to the mind through an impression, the latter is copied and transformed into the second form of perception, namely, an idea. Hume indeed names an idea a copy, image, or representation of an impression. Therefore, the perception of an object appears "both as impressions and ideas" (3). But, of course, the idea is weaker than an impression for two reasons: first, it is only an image that, second, corresponds to an object no longer or not immediately present to our senses. The object remains present to our mind only through the mediation of an image. Obviously, because something that does not exist cannot be copied, an idea is necessarily derived from and caused by an impression, while the reverse cannot be true.[3] For that reason, no idea can be present in the mind without a corresponding impression,[4] and, as a corollary, every impression or any idea that is present to the human mind can be traced back to an impression.

As a consequence, because an idea is "fainter" than the impression it depends on, the cognitive operation associated with the formation of ideas depends on what has been received and transmitted to the mind through the senses and is also weaker than the passive reception of impressions. This operation corresponds to what Hume names "thinking" or, more interestingly, "reasoning." Ideas are thus considered as "the faint images of [impressions] in thinking and reasoning" (7). To be more precise, reasoning consists in transforming—through copy and derivation—an impression, which is a form of perception, into an idea, another form of perception. This confirms that, as said above, to receive "impressions" from and to form "ideas" about the external world do not refer to two different cognitive operations but, more precisely, to the two different stages of the same cognitive operation, perceiving the external world. Thus reasoning, the use of this capacity named "reason," can indeed be assimilated to a form of perception. As a consequence, reasoning is not only impossible without an experience of the world, it cannot go beyond an experience of the world. Hume describes the same phenomenon presented by Condillac: "A blind man can form no notion of colours; a deaf man of sounds. Restore either of them that sense in which he is deficient; by opening this new inlet for his sensations, you also open an inlet for the ideas; and he finds no difficulty in conceiving these objects" (*EHU*, 20). Furthermore, reasoning is determined and strictly delineated by what has been experienced; Hume thus notes that "though our thought seems to possess this unbounded liberty, we shall find, upon a nearer examination, that it is really confined within very narrow limits, and that all this creative power of the mind amounts to no more than the faculty of compounding, transposing, augmenting, or diminishing the materials afforded us by the senses and experience" (19). Vary the experience,

3. Hume thus writes, "Our ideas upon appearance produce not their correspondent impressions" and adds that "our impressions are the causes of our ideas, not our ideas of our impressions" (*THN*, 5).

4. For Hume, "all our simple ideas proceed either mediately or immediately from their correspondent impressions" (*THN*, 7). Hume considers as "complex" those ideas that can exist independently from a corresponding impression. However, because ideas are separable, complex ideas are composed by simple ideas that can be traced back to a corresponding impression. Thus, complex ideas are, even if indirectly, connected to an impression.

Hume writes; it will change reasoning. Thus reason, in the sensualist meaning of the word, is different from the "rational reason" that characterizes human beings in the rationalist framework. "Humean" individuals are deprived of this specifically human capacity,[5] susceptible not only to organizing the impressions received from the environment but also to allowing human beings to identify the false information conveyed by the senses as well as speculate about facts and events that have not been experienced. As a consequence, reasoning cannot be considered as a capacity susceptible to organizing and structuring impressions received from the outside. Reasoning is nothing more than a stage, a step in the process of perceiving objects. This operation, the use of reason, thus does not imply any capacity to organize and structure the perception of the external world.

So far we have presented the basic units of knowledge (impressions and ideas) and described the related cognitive operations through which individuals perceive the external world. At this stage of cognition, individuals are only "a heap or collection of different perceptions" (*THN*, 207). No mechanism has been presented to explain how impressions are stored (memorized), which impressions are used to be transformed into ideas, and how this occurs. That is, how are perceptions transformed into meaningful, structured, and stable knowledge?

From Sensualism to Associationist Psychology

Having identified the basic units of knowledge transmitted to the mind by the senses and having also rejected reason as an organizing capacity, Hume then argues that this "heap" or "chaos" of impressions is transformed into knowledge thanks to a "gentle force," a "kind of ATTRACTION, which in the mental world will be found to have as extraordinary effects as in the natural, and to show itself in as many as various forms" (10, 13). To assume that there exists a "Newtonian" force within the human mind indicates how spontaneous is the process through which impressions and ideas associate with each other. The reference to association, particularly frequent in *A Treatise of Human Nature*, makes clear that Hume's theory—just like Condillac's—is rooted in associationist psychology (cf., for instance, Young 1985, 65). This is no surprise.

5. From this perspective, Hume considers that animals do not differ from human beings in the use of reason. He describes cognition in animals as following the same mechanisms as human cognition (see *THN*, 176–79).

Historically, the origins of associationism can be traced to the publication in 1749 of a book titled *Observations on Man, his Frame, his Duty and his Expectations*, written by David Hartley, a Scottish "psychologist" with whom Hume was acquainted. Furthermore, associationism, in psychology, and sensualism, in philosophy, are two sides of the same theory of human nature (Marciano 2004). Associationism, of course, was not just an eighteenth-century phenomenon. In the twentieth century, associationism can be found in the work of Friedrich Hayek. Indeed, Hayek is usually presented as the first, and one of the rare, twentieth-century economists who attempted to explain that the human mind functions on an associative basis. References are also made to the insights economic theory could gain from modern associationist psychology (Witt 1998, 1999; Rizzelo and Turvani 2000, 2002). No doubt that associationism has evolved since its "origins." However, most features that characterize human psychology were already present in Hume's theory of human nature. One can find the same analysis of cognition viewed as the classification and selective perception of the external stimuli the senses continuously carry to the human mind; similarly, the importance of environment and the role of path-dependence are also emphasized. These are the traits that we are now going to analyze.

Hume thus identifies the principles or rules that, according to him, explain the association among impressions and between impressions and ideas. These principles that explain how impressions and ideas are joined, united, and associated with each other are "RESEMBLANCE, CONTIGUITY in time and place, and CAUSE and EFFECT" (*THN*, 11; see also *EHU*, 24). More precisely, these principles involve the two crucial faculties involved in human cognition, memory and imagination. Hume thus sums up human cognition as follows: "These are therefore the principles of union or cohesion among our simple ideas, and in the imagination supply the place of that inseparable connection, by which there are united in our memory" (*THN*, 12). The respective roles of memory and imagination can be described as follows: memory stores and "repeats impressions in the first manner" (8), then imagination separates ideas and unites "them again in what form it pleases" (10). To be more precise, impressions and ideas combine with each other in a given sequence such that "an impression first strikes upon our senses. . . . Of this impression there is a copy taken by the mind, which remains after the impression ceases; and this we call an idea. The idea . . . produces the new impressions. . . . These again are copied by the memory and imagination, and become ideas; which perhaps in their turn give rise to other impressions and ideas" (8).

Therefore, if one recalls that an object is perceptible through an impression or an idea, perception can thus be considered as an operation that associates impressions and ideas with each other and attributes them to an object. That is, an object can be described as a set, a class, or a network of impressions and ideas related to each other and attributed to this object. But how are perceptions attributed to an object? Hume argues that the ability to associate a perception with an object depends on the fact that the connection already exists in the memory—a connection that itself rests on an original experience. Perception consists in assigning the incoming perceptions to already existing classes, that is, to relate ideas to impressions and then impressions or ideas of one object to the same object or to another object. Hume clearly argues in this direction when he states that perception rests on the existence of perceptions already received from the environment: "When ev'ry individual of any species of objects is found by experience to be constantly united with an individual of another species, the appearance of any new individual of either species naturally conveys the thought to its usual attendant" (93).

Through the repetition of perceptions, habits are created that permit and fuel further perceptions. The role of habits in perception of the environment is reinforced by Hume's insistence on the fact that the transformation of impressions into ideas and the attribution of impressions or ideas to objects is spontaneous and immediate. This reveals that cognition does not involve any reasoning or understanding. Human reason does not play any role in the cognitive process that consists in associating impressions and ideas to objects. It depends on the habits of perception, the classes past perceptions have created in the mind. This is confirmed by Hume's analysis of the two major problems (human) cognition has to face. The first problem relates to the transfer of impressions from one object to another object, that is, from one class of perceptions to another. This question is difficult because Hume rejects the dualism that characterizes rationalist theories. Therefore, reason cannot be mobilized to distinguish between the essence of an object and its material occurrence. Or, in the terms used by Hume, "Reason can never satisfy us that the existence of any one object does ever imply that of another" (97). Hume is then more precise: "When the mind, therefore, passes from the idea or impression of one object to the idea or belief of another, it is not determin'd by reason, but by custom or a principle of association"

(92). Human beings can thus be considered to depend on the information provided by customs. A second problem arises in attributing a continued existence to objects, even when they are not present to the senses. When senses cease to operate, impressions are no longer transmitted to the mind, but objects do not disappear; the classes of perceptions still exist in the individual's mind. But which faculty allows the maintenance of such a class of perceptions? Once again, reason cannot play this role; it would grant reason functions it cannot perform, namely, the possibility to overcome, to go beyond individual experience: "Upon the whole our reason neither does, nor it is possible it ever shou'd, upon any supposition, give us the assurance of the distinct contin'd existence [individuals] feel or see" (193). On the contrary, Hume argues that the "sentiment" that things have a distinct and continued existence "is entirely unreasonable [and] must proceed from some other faculty than understanding" (192). Hume then refers to imagination to explain that objects still exist even in the absence of any sensory perception: "This opinion must be entirely owing to the IMAGINATION" (192). Thus, imagination plays a similar role as memory (to link impressions and ideas to objects) but in different circumstances (when the object is no longer present to our senses). This perspective implies that imagination is a faculty that consists in combining the impressions and ideas stored in the memory. Once again, we are drawn to the sensory experience of the world.

We can now see that Hume's conception of cognition is not different from Hayek's description of "sensory perception" as "an act of classification" (1952, 142). Perception depends on habit of cognition and, although passive, always consists in the selective classification of incoming impressions. That is, perception can be considered as an act of interpretation of external stimuli according to the cognitive frames that past experiences of the world have contributed to build. From this perspective, one may even say that the human mind functions according to a "winner take all" strategy (Gifford 1996). If a connection is already memorized, then the incoming impression is immediately conveyed to the existing class. However, when an impression cannot be classified, the object or phenomenon that corresponds to this impression is not "perceptible" (Hayek 1952, 142–43). Impressions are received only when and because they can be associated with past experiences, that is, recognized and identified as belonging to an existing class. As a consequence, perception is clearly path-dependent, driven not only by the already accumulated and structured knowledge but also by our tacit expectations about incoming impressions. Thus, as noted by Steve Horwitz (2000, 25) about Hayek's theory of perception, "based on previous sensory experience, the mind gives us a model of the present environment that serves as the backdrop for classifying incoming sensory information in the current context." This also corresponds to Hume's theory.

Perception is thus necessarily biased for being highly dependent on our preceding experiences of the external world. This result is consistent with a phenomenon that psychologists name "curse of knowledge": once an individual knows something, he or she cannot imagine thinking otherwise. Along the same lines, Timur Kuran (1995, 173) notes that individuals "perceive selectively, noticing facts consistent with our beliefs more readily. This bias imparts resistance to our beliefs by shielding them from counter-evidence." This also means that human rationality cannot but be limited: individuals do not rationally compute the data they receive from their environment. They (more or less) unconsciously classify and reclassify impressions following established preconceptions or perception-filters. Thus the process of knowledge acquisition conveys the image that the human mind functions as a screening device or what Ludwig Lachmann calls a "filter of experience" (quoted in O'Driscoll 1977) but also that "each individual's filter is different from every other filter" (Lachmann's words again [O'Driscoll 1977]). Each individual is thus a unique example of a human being because he or she develops a subjective appraisal of the environment. However, even if subjective, individual perception depends on other individuals or, more precisely, depends on how others perceive each individual's actions.

Benevolence, Sympathy, and Communication with Others

New political economists argue that egoism is a feature of human nature general enough to be used as a basis for a model of government. As Geoffrey Brennan (1992, 13) puts it, "The central feature of that [Enlightenment] tradition is the searching out of invisible hand institutions, arrangements that achieve benign results without *undue* reliance on benevolent motivations . . . because . . . it does not make sense to assume that everyone will act out as duty requires." This line of reasoning contradicts what Hume asserts about human nature. Hume reverses the "hierarchy" between benevolence and egoism or self-love, granting to the former—namely, to the willingness to take another's welfare into consideration—a fundamental part in his theory of human nature. Benevolence—and not egoism—is thus identified as an "original" feature of human nature. Indeed, Hume argues, there are principles of human nature; these principles are the basic characteristics of human nature, and benevolence is the most fundamental of these principles:

> It is needless to push our researches so far as to ask, why we have humanity or a fellow-feeling with others. It is sufficient, that this is experienced to be a principle in human nature. We must stop somewhere in our examination of causes; and there are, in every science, some general principles, beyond which we cannot hope to find any principle more general. No man is absolutely indifferent to the happiness and misery of others. (*EPM*, 109 n. 19)

Or as he also puts it,

> If we consider the principles of the human make, such as they appear to daily experience and observation, we must, *a priori*, conclude it impossible for such a creature as man to be totally indifferent to the well or ill-being of his fellow-creatures. (116)

Thus, concern for others is more profoundly anchored in human nature and thus precedes self-love and egoism. As a consequence, Hume explains that our capacity to be concerned by others cannot be considered a consequence of egoism, self-interest, or self-love (see, for instance, *EPM*, 164–69). To "comprehend the force of humanity and benevolence" (109), to be convinced of the precedence over egoism and self-love, no philosophical investigation seems to be required. As it appears from the preceding quotations, "daily experience and observation" are sufficient. There are so many instances in which individuals express their concerns for others; instances in which an increase in the happiness and well-being of other individuals increases our own happiness and well-being that it is not reasonable to doubt that there exists such a principle in our nature as the "benevolent principle" (117–18).

Interestingly, the capacity to be affected by others, or to take their situations into account, is not independent from the theory of human nature depicted above. Indeed, within a sensualist-associationist framework, the domain of individual knowledge is determined by the subjective and thus necessarily limited individual perception. Both the dependence of ideas on impressions and the cognitive sequence that links individual perceptions to objects is restricted to an individual's own experience. Obviously, individual knowledge goes beyond the limits of personal experience and includes others' experiences and others' perceptions, under the form of customs and habits, which represent knowledge accumulated by other individuals. Because an individual's environment necessarily includes other individuals, interactions with others are at the same time an important source of knowledge and a cause of influence on the way knowledge is structured. That is, "other individuals' actions and reactions or, ultimately, preferences" (Witt 1998, 164) shape and change the individual's preferences. Thus, Hume acknowledges the existence of an interactive learning process through which opinions are formed and changed by communication with others. Moreover, the faculty or operation on which communication with others rests is also the source and the vehicle of benevolence among individuals.

The principle that explains how individual or private knowledge increases and is refined through interactions with others is *sympathy*. However, sympathy must not be confused with a particular sentiment, for instance, with altruism or benevolence. Sympathy is a psychological capacity—a "very powerful principle" (*THN*, 577)—that characterizes human beings, and even animals, and which allows a certain form of communication between individuals. "No quality of human nature is more remarkable in itself and its consequences, than the propensity we have to sympathise with others, and to receive by communication their inclinations and sentiments, however different from, and even contrary to our own" (316). More precisely, even if sympathy has a cognitive dimension, sympathetic communication cannot be equated to a "cognitive process" (see, for instance, Pitson 1996, 262). Indeed, Hume argues that an individual who feels sympathy toward others participates in the same experiences: human minds are

> similar in their feelings and operations, nor can any one be actuated by any affection, of which all others are not in some degree susceptible. As in strings equally wound up, the motion of one communicates itself to the rest; so all affections readily pass from one person to another, and beget correspondent movements in every human creature. (*THN*, 575–76)

Therefore, because of sympathy, knowledge is not restricted to one individual but is shared by all the individuals feeling sympathy toward one another. Sympathy extends individual knowledge beyond the limits of personal experience, by providing information about experiences that have not yet been experienced but that have been experienced by others. Thus, sympathy allows individuals to receive information about others' experiences.

Furthermore, besides the quantity of information transmitted, sympathy also *qualitatively* increases individual experience by permitting tacit communication about the sentiments and opinions of other individuals. Thus, through sympathy individuals attribute to objects qualities that would otherwise—namely, by pure perception—be impossible to attribute to these objects. For instance, as Hume writes, "our sense of beauty depends very much on this principle" (576). Indeed, "in every judgement of beauty, the feelings of the person affected enter into consideration, and communicate to the spectator similar touches of pain or pleasures. . . . What association of ideas would ever operate, were that principle here totally unactive" (*EPM*, 113). Beauty is not a quality that corresponds to an object only. Beauty does not depend on the geometrical relations that exist between the different parts of these objects. What makes an object beautiful is the fact that the object pleases its owner and that we perceive this pleasure through sympathy:

> Where any object has a tendency to produce pleasure in its possessor, it is always regarded as beautiful. . . . Whenever an object has a tendency to produce pleasure in the possessor . . . it is sure to please to the spectator, by a delicate sympathy with the possessor. (*THN*, 576–77)

Therefore, what individuals know about an object not only depends on their own perceptions of the object but also rests on the way others perceived the same object.

Sympathy not only transmits quantity of data and qualitative information on others' tastes. It also conveys feelings and plays an important role in the definition of which actions are virtuous or, one may say, valuable. Hume indeed extends to the domain of the moral the argument that "what pleases to others also induce pleasure in the observer." Virtue is thus defined with respect to approbation: "Virtuous" is used to designate "whatever mental action or quality gives to a spectator the pleasing sentiment of approbation" (*EPM*, 160). More precisely, from Hume's perspective, an action or a quality is made valuable through our powers of approval. Therefore, evaluation of an action or a quality depends on the possible approbation by others and does not rest only on a private decision; in particular, this means that these are not only private benefits that make an action, a quality, valuable or virtuous. Hume thus does not envisage that individuals could consider as valuable and rewarding only those actions that serve their self-interests. Hume then combines this argument with the importance that motives such as generosity, benevolence, or concern for others play in human behavior. Among many virtuous actions or qualities, some are susceptible to being approved because they serve the public good, the good of humanity, or the welfare of others: "A *sympathy* with public interest is the source of *moral approbation*" (*THN*, 499–500). These actions or qualities that are valuable for the whole society are then named "social" virtues. This means that when human beings are benevolent, they tend to consider as valuable—and thus to approve—those actions and qualities that promote the public good.

Certainly, this does not rule out private interest as a possible motive for acting; as I show in the next section, in certain circumstances an individual may deliberately and egoistically look for the approbation of others. However, Hume insists that this type of behavior does not correspond to the basic condition of human nature. Spontaneously, individuals tend to favor those actions and qualities that are approved by others and that contribute to the welfare of others. Part of Hume's argument rests on the role sympathy plays in the development of social virtues. Indeed, from Hume's perspective, interestingly, sympathy creates these social virtues: "Sympathy is the source of esteem, which we pay to all the artificial virtues" (577). By this Hume means that the "pleasing sentiment of approbation," which gives birth to virtuous and valuable actions, springs from and is conveyed by sympathy. That is, we esteem all the artificial or social virtues; we approve the behaviors or qualities of virtuous individuals because and when we sympathize with these individuals.

Therefore, sympathetic communication is not different from what the associationist psychologist Albert Bandura calls "vicarious learning," which can be characterized as "a mechanism of learning rooted in the social dimension of learning according to which humans are able to learn not only from direct experience, but also from the observation of others" (Rizzelo and Turvani 2002, 205). One cannot dissociate the two aspects, individual and social, of cognition. Sympathy not only explains communication, it also explains the origins and existence of social beliefs about another's behavior. Sympathy explains why, "although subjective in nature, the individual's cognitive development . . . is moulded in social process" (Witt 1998, 164). As Hume notes, sympathy contributes to the homogenization of knowledge: "To this principle, we ought to ascribe the great uniformity we may observe in the humours and turn of thinking of those of the same nations" (*THN*, 316). This creates an "emotional commitment" (Frank 2001), which is a necessary condition for cooperation. That is, sympathy gives birth to the common background necessary to repeat interactions and allows for the emergence of rules.

The Limitation of Benevolence and Sympathy

Hume thus considers that the most remarkable, and most important, qualities and capacities of human nature are benevolence and sympathy. These are the basic features upon which rests human behavior: individuals take into account the way their actions are perceived by others and, reciprocally, are concerned by the welfare of others (Fontaine 1997). Certainly, human beings are also susceptible to acting out of egoist motives. Hume does not neglect the fact that individuals may behave egoistically, favoring their private interest; hence the reference to human knavery. Knavery can characterize the behaviors of politicians, legislators, or judges and may also undoubtedly extend to those who are governed.[6] Therefore, Hume acknowledges the possible mixture in the motives out of which individuals act. As he notes, "There is some benevolence . . . some spark of friendship for human kind; some particle of the dove, kneaded into our frame, along with the element of the wolf and serpent" (*EPM*, 147). A question then arises as to the conditions under which moral and immoral motives, sympathetic benevolence and malevolence, can coexist. Hume provides an explanation based on the limitation of humanity and benevolence, and on the *scarcity* of sympathy.

The limitation in generosity, benevolence, and sympathy is justified by the explanation given as to how sympathetic communication proceeds between individuals. As said earlier, sympathetic communication rests on the transmission of information about others. That is, through sympathy, individuals receive perceptions about the behaviors of others, their feelings and sentiments. Therefore, the "functioning" of sympathy rests on the same principles as the perception of any other object: when we sympathize with another individual, we first receive an impression

6. As noted by Daniel M. Hausman (1998, 67), even if Hume had in mind officeholders, the quotation about knaves used as a motivational axiom by new political economists "is stated in a perfectly general way, and one can take it to apply equally to those who govern and those who are governed."

as to his or her situation, behavior, or feelings. Next, the strength and the durability of the "information" conveyed by sympathy depends on the transformation of this impression into an idea. When the impression, received by sympathy, is transformed into an idea, it is stored—possibly transformed by imagination—into the spectator's memory and, as a consequence, may be recalled even when the "subject" of our sympathy is "remov'd from our senses." As mentioned above, an individual transforms an impression into an idea when the impression is received many times. Thus, sympathy promotes communication if what is transmitted from one individual to another is repeated through many interactions. That is, sympathy can be viewed as a principle that functions only between individuals who are close enough to allow repeated interactions. Thus, as Hume notes, "when they [men] extend their concern beyond themselves, 'tis not to a great distance; nor is it usual for them, in common life, to look farther than their nearest friends and acquaintance" (*THN*, 534). More precisely, sympathy decreases when the distance that separates individuals increases: "Sympathy, we shall allow, is much fainter than our concern for ourselves, and sympathy with persons remote from us, much fainter than with persons near or contiguous" (116). As a corollary, it is highly unlikely, if not impossible, to observe sympathy between strangers. Indeed, the communication, and the feelings thus conveyed, between strangers will not have enough strength to last beyond the interaction. That is, these feelings will not be as strong as those that take place between individuals accustomed, for whatever reason, to feel sympathy toward each other.

> When the present misery of another has any strong influence upon me, the vivacity of the conception is not confin'd merely to its immediate object, but diffuses its influence over all the related ideas, and gives me a lively notion of all the circumstances of that person, whether past, present, or future; possible, probable or certain. By means of this lively notion I am interested in them; take part with them; and feel a sympathetic motion in my breast, conformable to whatever I imagine in his. If I diminish the vivacity of the first conception, I diminish that of the related ideas; as pipes can convey no more water than what arises at the fountain. By this diminution I destroy the future prospect, which is necessary to interest me perfectly in the fortune of another. I may feel the present impression, but carry my sympathy no farther, and never transfuse the force of the first conception into my ideas of the related objects. (386)

Therefore, even if benevolence, generosity, and sympathy are universal characteristics, in the sense that all human beings as well as animals "possess" such "qualities" and "capacities," this does not imply that everyone must feel sympathy, and behave with generosity, toward anyone else. Thus, while Hume insists on the importance of the "moral" virtues of human beings, he also acknowledges that these are limited. Hume always insists on the weaknesses or the frailties of human nature: "The qualities of the mind are selfishness and limited generosity" (494); "men being naturally selfish, or endow'd only with a confin'd generosity, they are not easily induc'd to perform any action for the interest of strangers, except with a view to some reciprocal advantage, which they had no hope of obtaining but by such a performance" (519); "we are naturally very limited in our kindness and affection" (519).

These limitations or, more precisely, the combination of benevolence and sympathy, on the one hand, and of malevolence, on the other, determine the origin, principles, and functions of governments. How do these features translate into Hume's account of the proper role of government? And what does it imply that is different from a rationalist theory of government? These questions are addressed in the next section.

The Nature of Institutions and Hume's Theory of Human Nature

Although new political economists suppose that their conception of institutions is similar to that of Hume, because they stem from the same assumptions about human behavior, there are indeed differences to take into consideration. More precisely, Hume's conception of institutions and the characteristics of the governments of civil societies differs from what new political economists assume because it directly results from his theory of human nature. Two sets of major differences can be put forward.

The Origin of Societies

The first difference comes from the weakness of rationality. Indeed, as shown above, Hume rejects the idea that individuals could be rational in the same way as new political economists assume they are. From Hume's perspective, human beings cannot go beyond their sensible experience of the world; to reason consists of building on the materials gathered by the senses. Individual knowledge is path- and past-dependent and decisively depends on customs and habits.

The limitation of rationality that characterizes human cognition has important institutional consequences. Indeed, because of their weak rationality, individuals are not able to envisage and then build institutions that they have not experienced. Hume cannot but reject the idea that a social contract could be viewed as a real or even a fictitious foundational event of civil societies. At the same time, Hume nonetheless considers that the lack of government is a nonsustainable institutional arrangement. He thus notes that "men cannot live without society, and cannot be associated without government" and adds, "men are utterly incapable of society without government" (*THN*, 539). There obviously exists a tension between the capacities individuals display and the necessity of an institutional apparatus and of specific rules—which Hume names "conventions."[7] This tension resolves because Hume assumes that human beings have always lived in social states: "His [man's] very first state and situation may justly be esteem'd social" (493). This contrasts with what many new political economists, using the rationality assumption, have stated about individuals living in situations without rules. This also contradicts the idea, accepted by most new political economists, that the establishment of a civil society could result from a radical and voluntary constructivist decision. On the contrary, a long and gradual process has driven individuals out of the state of nature into civil societies. Hence the decisive institutional role played by customs: rules and institutions inherited from the past embody more wisdom and knowledge than any single individual is able to grasp. Any constructivist and rational attempt to replace long-established rules by newly devised ones is risky. Such behavior may endanger peace and the stability of a civil society and a government "establish'd for many centuries":

> A government is establish'd for many centuries on a certain system of laws, forms, and methods of succession. The legislative power, establish'd by this long succession, changes all on a sudden the whole system of government, and introduces a new constitution in its stead. I believe few of the subjects will think themselves bound to comply with this alteration, unless it have an evident tendency to the public good: But will think themselves still at liberty to return to the antient government. (561)

7. Interestingly, the same kind of tension characterizes Smith's analysis of the state's role (see Young, this volume).

This position, stemming from an assumption on human capacities, is reflected in Hume's methodology. Indeed, since the lessons that can be drawn from these past "experiences" are of the utmost importance, Hume adopts an approach that consists in the historical description of past societies and rejects the philosophical reconstructions based on imaginary situations. He thus criticizes the analyses that discuss the origins of civil societies and, in particular, those that rest on an imaginary state of nature. The state of nature is viewed as a "mere" and "idle" "philosophical fiction, which never had, and never cou'd have any reality" (493) and whose analysis cannot lead to particular insight as to the origins and the actual functioning of civil societies. In fact, Hume compares the state of nature to the "golden age of poets" (493; *EPM*, 87). This reference to poetry indicates that Hume does not grant much credit to philosophical speculations; he even argues that the fictions poets invented are preferable to those of the philosophers: "Philosophers may have been bewilder'd in those speculations," while "poets have been guided more infallibly" (*THN*, 493). This is explained by the fact that poets have understood what philosophers have neglected: in the state of nature, "if every man had a tender regard for another, or if nature supplied abundantly all our wants and desires, that the jealousy of interest, which justice supposes, could no longer have place" (494). That is, as in poetic descriptions, the state of nature can be viewed "as the most charming and most peaceable condition, that can possibly be imagin'd" (492). The state of nature is not a situation of war against all in which malevolent and rational individuals understand the necessity of rules.

Thus, Hume obviously admits that the "very first state and situation" of man is a "social state" in which "cordial affection, compassion, sympathy, were the only movements, with which the human mind was yet acquainted" (494; *EPM*, 87). As a consequence, and despite the strength that characterizes his assertions about the necessity of governments, Hume put forward the possibility that societies exist, on a quite durable basis, *without* the help of a government. "The state of society without government is one of the most natural states of men," explaining that this may occur "with the conjunction of many families" and last "long after the first generation" (*THN*, 451). Within families, between "friends and acquaintances," sympathy operates and individuals are naturally benevolent toward each other. This is the reason that one may envisage the absence of government. No government is required on a small scale, that is, within small groups because the virtues of human nature are sufficient to give birth to peaceful societies: "This we find verified in the American tribes, where men live in concord and amity among themselves without any establish'd government and never pay submission to any of their fellows" (540). Under these conditions, if one person treats another unjustly, the negative reactions of actual spectators, and its echo (by sympathy) in the mind of the perpetrator of the injustice, or that person's response to the imagination of how spectators would react, discourage injustice. However, as shown above, sympathy and benevolence are restricted to small societies. Sympathy explains why spontaneous order societies are "nearness societies" in the geographic space or in the space of preferences (Josselin and Marciano 2001). When benevolence disappears and sympathy ceases to operate, a government is a necessity. This argument obviously contrasts to what new political economists put forward: malevolence is not the general feature of human nature that has to be taken into account to decide *that* a government is required. According to Hume, a government is required only in certain circumstances: "Though government be an invention very advantageous, and even in some circumstances absolutely necessary to mankind; it is not necessary in all circumstances, nor is it impossible for men to preserve society for some time, without having recourse to such an invention" (*THN*, 539).

Civil Societies, Constitutions, and Governments

Let us turn now to the functioning of the institutions and governments that have been established in civil societies. New political economy builds on the idea that constitutions have to be established to control the behaviors of rational and potentially malevolent individuals—of citizens as well as of officeholders.[8] This is supposedly included in the most celebrated sentences mentioned above and used by new political economists as a motto. The paragraph in question is usually presented as revealing Hume's opinions about the condition that has to be fulfilled to establish a government. Interestingly, Hume discusses a "maxim" that has been established by "political writers":

> *Political writers* have established it as a *maxim*, that, in contriving any system of government, and fixing the several checks and controuls of

8. For instance, Geoffrey Brennan (2000, 1) writes that the "familiar classical question—who guards the guardians?—is *the* central normative question in the public choice approach to politics and to institutional design more generally" (emphasis in the original).

> the constitution, every man ought to be supposed a *knave*, and to have no other end, in all his actions, than private interest. By this interest we must govern him, and, by means of it, make him, notwithstanding his insatiable avarice and ambition, co-operate to public good. Without this, *say they*, we shall in vain boast of the advantages of any constitution, and shall find, in the end, that we have no security for our liberties or possessions, except the good-will of our rulers; that is, we shall have no security at all. (*Essays*, I.IV; emphasis added, except on "knave")

When he proposes his own evaluation of this "maxim," Hume then writes that "it is, therefore, a just *political* maxim, *that every man must be supposed a knave*: Though at the same time, it appears somewhat strange, that a maxim should be true in *politics*, which is false in *fact*" (I.IV). We propose to explain this seeming paradox as follows.

As to the control of citizens, Hume certainly insists on the weakness and frailty of human nature as well as on the fact that the natural virtues that characterize individual psychology are (spatially) limited. These limitations, one may say, render conventions and governments necessary. However, one cannot neglect the fact that Hume also stresses that the most important and remarkable characteristic of human nature is benevolence and not malevolence. This leads to another, and complementary conclusion: politicians, officeholders, or members of governments have to take benevolence and sympathy as the basis for establishing conventions or legal rules. They have to take into consideration the natural capacity of human beings to be benevolent toward other human beings: "Any artifice of politicians may *assist nature* in the producing of those sentiments, which she suggests to us, and may even on some occasions, produce alone an approbation or esteem for any particular action" (*THN*, 500; emphasis added). As a corollary, politicians who ignore the natural virtues of human beings, focusing only on the limitations and weaknesses of human nature, will not be able to rule a civil society. The explanation is that it will be impossible to define what a good rule consists of: "If nature did not aid us in this particular, 'twou'd be in vain for politicians to talk of honourable or dishonourable, praiseworthy or blameable" (500). That is, it is not only the knowledge embodied in customs that has to be privileged by politicians when establishing constitutions, but also the virtues of human nature: "The utmost politicians can perform, is, to extend the natural sentiments beyond their original bounds; but still nature must furnish the materials, and give us some notion of moral distinctions" (500). The role of constitutions is to build on these features, to extend their domain of validity rather than to neglect and, as a consequence, to contradict them: "Encrease to a sufficient degree the benevolence of men, or the bounty of nature, and you render justice useless, by supplying its place with much nobler virtues, and more valuable blessings" (494). This assumption obviously contrasts with the assumption that underlies the theories developed by new political economists. Politicians must not consider systematically that individuals are knaves but must also take into account that human beings are fundamentally benevolent and, in certain circumstances, benevolent toward each other. That is, because he envisages that benevolence and sympathy are general (although limited) characteristics of human nature, Hume considers this virtue and this capacity as the necessary and unavoidable basis for establishing and ruling civil societies.

As to the control of governments, Hume stresses, as Andrew Farrant and Maria Pia Paganelli (this volume) remind us, the decisive role that specific constitutional provisions have to play: "In pure republics, where the authority is distributed among several assemblies or senates, the checks and controuls are more regular in their operation [than in a monarchy]; because the members of such numerous assemblies may be presumed to be always nearly equal in capacity and virtue; and it is only their number, riches, or authority, which enter into consideration" (*Essays*, I.VI.7). He even adds that "a republican and free government would be an obvious absurdity, if the particular checks and controuls, provided by the constitution, had really no influence, and made it not the interest, even of bad men, to act for the public good" (*Essays*, I.III.2). From this perspective, one may be tempted to conclude that Hume's conception of institutions is not different from that promoted by new political economists: constitutional provisions only guarantee that officeholders "act for the public good"; otherwise, the latter are only motivated by their personal interest and behave as *knaves*. However, such a conclusion is only partially exact because it neglects the fact that Hume does not put officeholders on the same footing as other citizens. In particular, Hume notes that

> the persons, whom we call civil magistrates, kings and their ministers, our governors and rulers, who being indifferent persons to the greatest part of the state, have no interest, or but a remote one, in any act of

> injustice; and being satisfied with their present condition, and with their part in society, have an immediate interest in every execution of justice, which is so necessary to the upholding of society. (*THN*, 537)

So if a knave is an individual who acts unjustly, then it appears that officeholders cannot be considered as such. More precisely, in the *Essays*, Hume explains why it is important that magistrates be different from other individuals: "The persons, who first attain this distinction by the consent, tacit or express, of the people, must be endowed with superior personal qualities of valour, force, integrity, or prudence, which command respect and confidence" (*Essays*, I.V.4). Thus, these qualities, which are granted to certain individuals, are those that found the authority of magistrates and legitimate government.

This opinion reflects Hume's description of the primary, and secondary, principles of government. As to the first, Hume notes that "all governments [are] founded, and all authority of the few over the many [depend] upon these three opinions . . . of public *interest*, of *right to power*, and of *right to property*" (*Essays*, I.V.4). Other principles of governments, such as self-interest, fear, and affection, are not a primary but only secondary source of authority. They are susceptible to generate obedience only if the magistrate's authority is already established: "The magistrate's authority must be antecedently established, at least be hoped for, in order to produce this expectation" (*Essays*, I.V.4).

Certainly, Hume does not go as far as Richard Musgrave (or even James M. Buchanan; see Farrant and Paganelli, this volume) and does not consider that a constitution works well because and when it relies on angelic behavior. Indeed, Hume still insists that everyone is subject to the same weaknesses and that to be chosen as officeholder does not change human nature: "As this imperfection is inherent in human nature, we know that it must attend men in all their states and conditions; and that these, whom we chuse for rulers, do not immediately become of a superior nature to the rest of mankind, upon account of their superior power and authority" (*THN*, 552). Hume also adds that a government is "compos'd of men subject to all human infirmities" and that "what we expect from them depends not on a change of their nature" (539, 552). However, Hume nonetheless insists on the differences that have to exist between common people and government members. This also contrasts with what new political economy assumes.

Conclusion

Although new political economy usually presents itself as "the natural *heir* of an Enlightenment tradition that begins with Hume and Smith" (Brennan and Buchanan 1985, 101), it seems that, as we have demonstrated in this essay, in assuming rationality and egoism, new political economy does not really assume the heritage of the classical political economy tradition. Indeed, Hume's theory of human nature is notably different from the conception of humanity adopted by new political economists. While the latter focus on rationality and egoism or malevolence, Hume stresses the limitations of human rationality and insists on benevolence as a natural virtue and sympathy as a basis for communication between individuals. This is not to say that Hume never considers that human beings may behave as knaves, rationally and egoistically. However, it is assumed that human beings behave as *knaves* only when benevolence no longer applies and sympathetic communication is not possible. To adopt such a conception of humanity implies change as to the way institutions can be envisaged and governments modeled. Thus, Hume's model of government is quite different from that of new political economists.

It may be considered, as neoclassical economists do, an important point to assume that individuals are indeed rational and egoist. But these assumptions do not correspond to Hume's theory of human nature. Hume's theory is close to the refined conceptions of human beings that have been recently proposed by economists and psychologists in the debates about the necessity to go beyond *homo economicus*, to move from *homo economicus* to *homo sapiens* (see, among others, Anderson 2000; Thaler 2000). The reference to Hume is all the more important, in that this literature either sharply criticizes (see, for instance, the analyses in terms of "collective agency" in Gilbert 1989) or, at best, ignores classical political economists, who are still considered as precursors of rational choice theories and neoclassical analyses. Economics, it is argued, has to be supplemented with concepts derived from other social sciences, in particular, cognitive theory and psychology (Frey 1997a, 1997b; Frey and Stutzer 2001; Frey and Benz 2004; Rabin 1998; Rizzelo 1999; Rizzelo and Turvani 2000, 2002; Rosenberg 1991; Witt 1998, 1999). Even Austrian economists, who claim that the spontaneous order tradition goes from Hume and Smith to Carl Menger and Hayek, rarely discuss the theory of human nature of the economists of the Scottish

Enlightenment (see, however, Horwitz 2000, 2001). Rather, Austrian standard public choice or new Austrian political economy refers to authors such as G. L. S. Shackle, Ludwig Lachmann, and Hayek (Boettke and Lopez 2002; Buchanan and Vanberg 2002; Wolgemuth 2002). Once again, no or very few references are made to the founders of political economy, although one can find the same elements about human nature and behavior. To keep these references to Hume in mind helps us to view in what meaning these analyses are rooted in political economy. It also reveals that Hume's model of government is closer to more heterodox forms of economic thought than to orthodox, neoclassical economics. Finally, it reminds us that most of the recent developments made by economists about human psychology were already present in the writings of classical political economists.

References

Anderson, Elisabeth. 2000. Beyond Homo Oeconomicus: New Developments in Theories of Social Norms. *Philosophy and Public Affairs* 29:170–200.

Boettke, Peter J., and Edward J. Lopez. 2002. Austrian Economics and Public Choice. *Review of Austrian Economics* 15.2–3:111–19.

Brennan, Geoffrey. 1992. Taking Political Economy Seriously. *Methodus* 4.1:11–15.

———. 2000. Trust, Adjudication, and the *Quis Custodiet* Problem. Mimeo, Research School of Social Sciences, Australian National University.

Brennan, Geoffrey, and James M. Buchanan. 1985. *The Reason of Rules: Constitutional Political Economy*. Cambridge: Cambridge University Press.

Brunner, Karl. 1987. The Perception of Man and the Conception of Society: Two Approaches to Understanding Society. *Economic Inquiry* 25.3:367–88.

Buchanan, James M. 1987. Constitutional Economics. In *The New Palgrave: A Dictionary of Economics*, edited by John Eatwell, Murray Milgate, and Peter Newman. London: Macmillan.

———. 1990. The Domain of Constitutional Economics. *Constitutional Political Economy* 1.1:1–19.

Buchanan, James M., and Victor J. Vanberg. 2002. Constitutional Implications of Radical Subjectivism. *Review of Austrian Economics* 15.2–3:121–29.

Davis, John B. 1995. Personal Identity and Standard Economic Theory. *Journal of Economic Methodology* 2.1:35–52.

Fontaine, Philippe. 1997. Identification and Economic Behaviour: Sympathy and Empathy in Historical Perspective. *Economics and Philosophy* 13.2:261–80.

Frank, Robert. 2001. Cooperation through Emotional Commitment. In *Evolution and the Capacity for Commitment*, edited by R. M. Nesse. New York: Russell Sage Foundation.

Frey, Bruno S. 1997a. *Not Just for the Money*. Aldershot, U.K.: Elgar.

———. 1997b. Constitutions for Knaves Crowd Out Civic Virtues. *Economic Journal* 107:1043–53.

Frey, Bruno S., and Alois Stutzer. 2001. Economics and Psychology: From Imperialistic to Inspired Economics. *Revue de philosophie economique* 2.2:5–22.

Frey, Bruno S., and Matthias Benz. 2004. From Imperialism to Inspiration: A Survey of Economics and Psychology. In *The Elgar Companion to Economics and Philosophy*, edited by John Davis, Alain Marciano, and Jochen Runde. Cheltenham, U.K.: Elgar.

Gifford, Adam, Jr. 1996. Subjectivity, Bounded Rationality, and Rule Following Behavior. Mimeo, Department of Economics, California State University, Northridge.

Gilbert, Margaret. 1989. *On Social Facts*. Princeton, N.J.: Princeton University Press.

Hausman, Daniel M. 1998. Rationality and Knavery. In *Game Theory, Experience, Rationality: Foundations of Social Sciences, Economics, and Ethics in Honor of John C. Harsanyi*, edited by Werner Leinfellner and Eckehart Köhler. Dordrecht: Kluwer.

Hayek, Friedrich. 1952. *The Sensory Order: An Inquiry into the Foundations of Theoretical Psychology*. London: Routledge & Kegan Paul.

Horwitz, Steven. 2000. From *The Sensory Order* to the Liberal Order: Hayek's Nonrationalist Liberalism. *Review of Austrian Economics* 13:23–40.

———. 2001. From Smith to Menger to Hayek: Liberalism in the Spontaneous-Order Tradition. *Independent Review* 4.1:81–97.

Hume, David. [1748] 1975. *An Enquiry concerning Human Understanding*. Oxford: Clarendon Press.

———. [1742] 1987. *Essays, Moral, Political, and Literary*. Indianapolis, Ind.: Liberty.

———. [1739] 1992. *A Treatise of Human Nature*. Reprint, Buffalo, N.Y.: Prometheus.

———. [1751] 1998. *An Enquiry concerning the Principles of Morals*. Oxford: Oxford University Press.

Josselin, Jean-Michel, and Alain Marciano. 2001. Public Decisions in the Scottish Enlightenment Tradition. *Journal of Economic Studies* 27.6:5–13.

Kuran, Timur. 1995. *Private Truths, Public Lies: The Social Consequences of Preference Falsification*. Cambridge, Mass.: Harvard University Press.

Marciano, Alain. 2004. The Philosophical and Historical Foundations of New Political Economy. In *The Elgar Companion to Economics and Philosophy*, edited by John Davis, Alain Marciano, and Jochen Runde. Cheltenham, U.K.: Elgar.

Medema, Steven G. 1998. Wandering the Road from Pluralism to Posner: The Transformation of Law and Economics in the Twentieth Century. In *From Interwar Pluralism to Postwar Neoclassicism*, edited by Mary S. Morgan and Malcolm Rutherford. *HOPE* 30 (supplement): 202–24.

O'Driscoll, Gerald P., Jr. 1977. Spontaneous Order and the Coordination of Economic Activities. *Journal of Libertarian Studies* 1.2:137–51.

Pitson, Antony E. 1996. Sympathy and Other Selves. *Hume Studies* 22.2:255–71.
Rabin, Matthew. 1998. Psychology and Economics. *Journal of Economic Literature* 36:11–46.
Rizzelo, Salvatore. 1999. *The Economics of the Mind.* Cheltenham, U.K.: Elgar.
Rizzelo, Salvatore, and Margherita Turvani. 2000. Institutions Meet Mind: The Way out of an Impasse. *Constitutional Political Economy* 11:165–80.
———. 2002. Subjective Diversity and Social Learning: A Cognitive Perspective for Understanding Institutional Behaviour. *Constitutional Political Economy* 13:197–210.
Rogers, G. A. J. 1993. Locke, Anthropology, and Models of the Mind. *History of the Human Sciences* 6.1:73–87.
Rosenberg, Shawn W. 1991. Rationality, Markets, and Political Analysis: A Social Psychological Critique of Neoclassical Political Economy. In *The Economic Approach to Politics: A Critical Reassessment of the Theory of Rational Action*, edited by Kristen R. Monroe. New York: HarperCollins.
Thaler, Richard H. 2000. From Homo Oeconomicus to Homo Sapiens. *Journal of Economic Perspectives* 14:133–41.
Witt, Ulrich. 1998. Imagination and Leadership: The Neglected Dimension of an Evolutionary Theory of the Firm. *Journal of Economic Behaviour and Organisation* 35:161–77.
———. 1999. Do Entrepreneurs Need Firms? A Contribution to a Missing Chapter in Austrian Economics. *Review of Austrian Economics* 11.1–2:99–109.
Wolgemuth, Michael. 2002. Democracy and Opinion Falsification: Towards a New Austrian Political Economy. *Constitutional Political Economy* 13.3:223–46.
Young, Robert. 1985. *Darwin's Metaphor: Nature's Place in Victorian Culture*. Cambridge: Cambridge University Press.

Are Two Knaves Better Than One? Hume, Buchanan, and Musgrave on Economics and Government

Andrew Farrant and Maria Pia Paganelli

> You must only take care to remove all the vices. If you remove part, you may render the matter worse. . . . For whatever may be the consequence of such a miraculous transformation of mankind, as would endow them with every species of virtue, and free them from every species of vice; this concerns not the magistrate, who aims only at possibilities. He cannot cure every vice by substituting a virtue in its place. Very often he can only cure one vice by another; and in that case, he ought to prefer what is least pernicious to society.
>
> —David Hume, "Of Refinement in the Arts" (1752)

We may think of a problem in at least two ways. We may ask what the best-possible scenario is, or we may ask what the worst-possible scenario is. We may therefore base our theories on the best-possible assumptions or on the worst-possible assumptions. Thinking in terms of the former is generally considered best-case theorizing. Thinking in terms of the latter is generally considered worst-case theorizing.

Worst-case theorizing about government has a long and distinguished history in political economy (Levy 2002; Toma and Toma 1984).[1] David

The authors thank the participants at the 2004 *HOPE* conference, the 2004 History of Economics Society meeting, and the 2004 Summer Institute for the Preservation of the History of Economics, as well as David M. Levy, Tyler Cowen, Doug Den Uyl, Jerry Evensky, Mark Yellin, and *HOPE*'s reader for useful comments and discussion. All remaining mistakes are ours.

1. Toma and Toma (1984, 93) note, "[The] Leviathan assumption appears to be at the heart of the classical conception of constitutional government." Brennan and Buchanan ([1980] 2000, 220) acknowledge that their Leviathan model of government marks a return to "the [worst-case] spirit of the classical liberal political economists." James Mill's 1820 model of

Hume provides the classic statement of worst-case thinking in political economy: "Political writers have established it as a maxim, that, in contriving any system of government, and fixing the several checks and controuls of the constitution, every man ought to be supposed a *knave*, and to have no other end, in all his actions, than private interest" ([1742] 1985a, 42–43). Hume models public choosers as self-interested knaves pursuing their private interests, rather than as angelic public-spirited creatures (best case).

Reference to Hume's worst-case model of government is commonplace in the contemporary constitutional political economy literature (see, e.g., Brennan and Buchanan [1985] 2000; Sutter 1998; Faria 1999). James M. Buchanan—a founding father of that literature—is considered responsible for the revival of worst-case thinking about government in modern political economy (Levy 2002).[2] Buchanan argues that one ought to model both the private chooser and the public chooser symmetrically (see, e.g., Buchanan 1987, 85, 89–90; Buchanan and Musgrave 2001, 127). If private interest is pervasive in private choice, then it is also likely to prove pervasive in public choice. What generates market failure in one context will similarly generate government failure in the other (Buchanan and Musgrave 2001, 126–27).[3]

In stark contrast, however, Richard Musgrave (1997, 156) models private and public chooser asymmetrically. Private choosers are akin to Hume's knaves, whereas public choosers, by contrast, are rather more akin to public-spirited angels (Buchanan and Musgrave 2001, 82).

In this essay, we argue that Buchanan's analysis of government has more in common with that of Musgrave than it does with that of Hume. Despite the proclivity in the constitutional political economy literature to point to Hume as an inspiration for modern-day worst-case theorizing, we suggest that modern constitutional political economy is another example of best-case thinking; its analysis ultimately relies on angelic

government as slave driver writ large is remarkably similar to the Leviathan model of government provided by Brennan and Buchanan in the late 1970s. Indeed, the suggestion that one should model government as slave driver was not unique to Mill: "Every Monarch is a Slave-holder upon the largest scale" (Bentham [1822] 1989, 171). Toma and Toma (1984, 93) suggest that the Brennan-Buchanan Leviathan model "seems to apply naturally to a monarchial form of government."

2. "If the purpose is one of drawing the constitutional limits on the taxing power, would it not be meaningful to utilize a worst-case scenario and to see model governments, anywhere and everywhere, as revenue-maximizing? That is, given any revenue source, would it not be best to assume maximal exploitation?" (Buchanan 1992, 105).

3. "The economist who utilizes *homo economicus*, who can identify market failure . . . is under an obligation to identify government or political failure" (Buchanan 1979, 77).

behavior—even if on a rather different level than that of Musgrave. Hume instead is consistent in his worst-case theorizing about government, thinking that the only feasible solution to political knavery is yet more knavery.

Whether contemporary political economy is an example of best-case or worst-case modeling is relevant because the performance of a model depends on whether its underlying suppositions hold in reality or not. If the rules of the game governing both private (market) and public (government) choice alike are structured in accordance with the assumption that all men are knaves, and if men are indeed knaves, nobody is worse off. If men are angels, the institutional arrangements will either simply prove unnecessary (assuming they are not binding) or, if binding, will generate some loss in efficiency. Similarly, if institutions are designed in accordance with the supposition that men are angels, and if that supposition proves accurate, the first-best outcome will result. But if all men are knaves, large suboptimality will surely reign.

The essay is organized as follows: in section 1 we review Hume's worst-case model of government. For Hume, knavery (private interest) checks knavery in the context of public choices. We suggest that one ought to read Hume as providing a second-best-type argument. The first-best outcome, the wholesale elimination of knavery is, Hume argues, utterly unattainable. Knavery is simply part of the backdrop provided by human nature. Thus the partial elimination of knavery is likely to make matters far worse, as the partial removal of knavery only weakens any existing checks against whatever knavery still remains. As Hume puts it in a slightly different context—two vices are better than one, in that each tempers the ill effects resulting from the other. Section 2 describes the Buchanan-Musgrave debate. Buchanan argues that knavery checks knavery within a private choice scenario typified by high-quality rules of the game (e.g., the logic of entry and exit within a competitive market, and the rule of law and security of property rights). The knavery of public choosers is constrained by high-quality rules of the game as well (e.g., constitutional rules). On the other hand, Musgrave relies on angelic government agents to check the excesses of private-choosing knaves, thereby correcting for market failure and the like. Musgrave requires no constitutional checks on the said angels' uses of discretionary power: as angels are not knaves, in the realm of public choice there is no need for any checks. Thus Musgrave's view suggests that first-best efficiency obtains in both the private- and public-choosing spheres. The antidote to private-choosing knavery is angelic public spirit. In section 3 we claim that

Buchanan implicitly sidesteps the question of how knavery is checked within a public choice context. He sides with Musgrave on "the constitution based on public spirit" side of the barricade. Buchanan argues for constitutional constraints to check the knavery of public choosers, thus implicitly abandoning the assumption of motivational symmetry at the constitutional level—and we argue—thereby supposing angels both write and enforce the constitutional rules of the game. In this respect Buchanan differs from Hume. Hume relies exclusively on knavery even at the constitutional level. The example of a successful constitution that Hume provides is the British constitution, a constitution that no angel wrote, but which emerged from centuries and centuries of knavery clashing against knavery.

1. Hume's Second-Best Theory of Constitutional Equilibrium

David Hume, like the modern constitutional political economist, argues for the fixity of agent-type.[4] Knavery and pervasive self-interest are descriptive of humanity's "present depraved state" (Hume [1742] 1985a, 609). Private interest is, for Hume ([1742] 1985b, 38), a "great weakness," but a weakness that is "incurable in human nature." Hume ([1742] 1985a, 42) argues that "in contriving any system of government and fixing the several checks and controuls of the constitution, every man ought to be supposed a *knave*, and to have no other end, in all his actions, than private interest."[5] Plans of government that assume otherwise or that

4. Hume ([1772] 1999, 150): "There is a great uniformity among the actions of men, in all nations and ages, and that human nature remains still the same, in its principles and operations. The same motives always produce the same actions: the same events follow from the same causes. . . . Would you know the sentiments, inclinations, and course of life of the Greeks and Romans? Study well the temper and actions of the French and English. . . . Mankind are so much the same, in all times and places, that history informs us of nothing new or strange in this particular. Its chief use is only to discover the constant and universal principles of human nature, by showing men in all varieties of circumstances and situations, and furnishing us with materials from which we may form our observations, and become acquainted with the regular springs of human action and behavior." On constitutional equilibrium, William Paley ([1785] 2002, 337) writes, "This security is sometimes called *the balance of the constitution*: and the political equilibrium, which this phrase denotes, consists in two contrivances—a balance of power, and a balance of interest."

5. While Hume does not deny human benevolence, he does stress that it weakens with social distance. As society increases in size and complexity, such benevolence becomes increasingly attenuated: "Men being naturally selfish, or endow'd only with a confin'd generosity, they are not easily induc'd to perform any action for the interest of *strangers*, except with a view to some reciprocal advantage, which they had no hope of obtaining but by such a performance" (Hume

suppose any "great reformation in the manners of mankind, are plainly imaginary. Of this nature, are the *Republic* of PLATO, and the *Utopia* of Sir THOMAS MORE" ([1752] 1985a, 514).

Given the inadequacy of modeling with any supposition of dramatically changed agent-type or angelic-type men (514), Hume proposes to use institutions (or rules) to align private interest with public interest. Good rules of the game serve to induce even those agents who are "knaves" to act such as to further the public good. Indeed, "republican and free government would be an obvious absurdity, if the particular checks and controuls, provided by the constitution, had really no influence, and made it not the interest, even of bad men, to act for the public good" ([1742] 1985c, 15–16; see also 24).

Thus it is by private "interest [that] we must govern him [man], and, by means of it, make him, notwithstanding his insatiable avarice and ambition, cooperate to public good. Without this, say they [political writers], we shall in vain boast of the advantages of any constitution, and shall find, in the end, that we have no security for our liberties or possessions, except the good-will of our rulers; that is, we shall have no security at all" ([1742] 1985a, 42). Elsewhere, Hume ([1742] 1985c, 15) laments that were it otherwise, were rules an inadequate substitute for agent-type, he "should be sorry to think, that human affairs admit of no greater stability, than what they receive from the casual humours and characters of particular men."

Assuming knavery in both private- and public-choosing spheres implies that in both spheres the "allurement of present, though often very frivolous temptations" ([1742] 1985b, 38)—namely, what Buchanan calls the lure of the "off-diagonal" in any canonical prisoner's dilemma (PD) scenario (see Buchanan and Congleton 2003, 35–54)—will induce pervasive suboptimality whenever individuals interact within a poor-quality incentive structure.

Immediately on having stated the maxim that one ought to model political agents as if they were knaves, Hume ([1742] 1985a, 43) suggests

---

1978, 519; emphasis added; see also Yellin 2002, 378–79). While suggesting that benevolence reigns within the family, thus explaining why property is held in common within the family, Hume argues that any theory of government resting on an idealized assumption of benevolent public officials is "plainly imaginary" (514). On benevolence and Hume's theory of property, see Levy 1992, 92–106. On Hume and benevolence, see Marciano, this volume, and Yellin 2002. On the role of social distance, see, among others, the experimental results of Elisabeth Hoffman, Kevin McCabe, and Vernon Smith (1996). We thank *HOPE*'s reader for drawing our attention to the possible role of benevolence in government in Hume.

"it appears somewhat strange, that a maxim should be true in *politics*, which is false in *fact*. But to satisfy us on this head, we may consider, that men are generally more honest in their private than in their public capacity, and will go greater lengths to serve a party, than when their own private interest is alone concerned." Thus the way in which knavery rears its ugly head is not invariant to institutions. Why might the prevalence of knavery systematically differ in private and public choice contexts? Hume's argument rests on the insight that approbational incentives systematically differ in politics and everyday life.

Hume's argument, couched in modern economic language, is more or less the following: a knave (whether engaging in public or private choice) maximizes his utility subject to his constraints. His utility depends on both material income and good reputation. In a private choice context (an exchange) his constraint is transparency, meaning a nonnoisy signal of one's behavior. Transparency ensures that one's cheated trading partner knows *ex post* by whom he was cheated (see Levy 1992), though income increases if one cheats. One's defection in any simple PD situation will generate material income, but at the cost of a loss of reputational utility, and perhaps, in a repeated game, potential future income. Hume ([1742] 1985a, 43) notes that, indeed, "honour is a great check upon mankind."

In any large numbers–type situation, however, the tight connection between personal cheating and reputation may weaken. Where opacity rather than transparency prevails (where any signal of individual cheating is noisy), "this check is, in a great measure, removed" (43).[6] Thus Hume argues that "men are generally more honest in their private than in their public capacity" (43). In the public choice context Hume envisages, reputational utility accrues to the individual as a member of a group (party or faction) rather than as an individual per se. Group reputation is thus akin to a public good and suffers from a public good–type problem. Free riding will occur as the reputational costs otherwise fully borne by an individual who cheats are largely externalized onto others. Therefore one's own loss of reputational utility is subject to a 1/*n*-type problem: with large numbers, defection generates reputational externalities—all

6. Madison's discussion of "respect for character" as an inadequate check against faction draws heavily on Hume: "However strong this motive may be in individuals, it is considered as very insufficient to restrain them from injustice. *In a multitude its efficacy is diminished in proportion to the number which is to share the praise or blame*" (emphasis added; see Adair [1974] 1998, 145). On Hume and Madison, see Adair [1974] 1998, 132–51. The possible links with the federalist literature is an important potential future development of the present essay.

members of one's own party or faction suffer the loss of a fraction of their own reputational utility when any single member cheats—thus every individual (only bearing a $1/n$ share of any subsequent reputational loss) has the incentive to cheat. Hume argues, indeed, that where self-interest prevails wholly unchecked by rules or where its workings are actively encouraged by poor-quality rules, as where any large numbers–induced opacity prevails, "the whole senate . . . [will act] . . . as if it contained not one member, who had any regard to public interest and liberty" (43). Hume concludes that where the rules of the game are inadequately aligned with self-interest, they guarantee suboptimality: where "separate interest be not checked . . . we ought to look for nothing but faction, disorder, and tyranny from such a government. In this opinion I am justified by experience, as well as by the authority of all philosophers and politicians, both antient and modern" (43).

Hume proposes a surprising but viable solution to the weakening of the constraints caused by large-group situations: a mixed government similar to the British system. This mixed government differs from the ancient conceptions of mixed government proposed by figures like Cicero or Tacitus because here "one rank [house of commons], whenever it pleased, might swallow up all the rest, and engross the whole power of the constitution. . . . For so great is the natural ambition of men, that they are never satisfied with power; and if one order of men, by pursuing its own interest, can usurp upon every other order, it will certainly do so, and render itself, as far as possible, absolute and uncontroulable" (43–44). And this odd form of mixed government works, for Hume, by a logic similar to that at play in any large numbers PD situation: individual knavery checks collective knavery. Just as it is human nature (knavery) that generates the original problem, so it is human nature (knavery) that provides the solution.[7]

Hume's theory of constitutional equilibrium makes use of the tension between individual and collective self-interest. No single institutional power alone will prevail because the institutional powers are "balanced" against each other. The knavery of one institution will hit the wall of the knavery of another institution. Tyranny will not emerge, and individual liberty can therefore prevail. Similarly, within each institutional

7. Hume ([1742] 1985a, 44–45) asks "by what means is this member of our constitution [house of commons] confined within the proper limits; since from our very constitution, it must necessarily have as much power as it demands, and can only be confined by itself? How is this consistent with our experience of human nature?"

power, competing knaveries play a self-checking role. We would expect that politicians would realize the benefits of collusion. By colluding they may generate enough power to prevail against a competing institutional power. But knavery weakens collusion (see Cowen and Sutter 1999). Thus one PD game helps trump another. The self-interest of any single parliamentarian helps check the self-interestedness of Parliament as a whole. Though the self-interest of Parliament viewed as a collective body or unitary entity lies in engrossing all power (and concomitantly, all available surplus or rents) to itself, the self-interest of any single parliamentarian lies in defecting: voting against Parliament in support of the Crown for a suitable reward. Self-interested knavery, defection, or what Tyler Cowen and Daniel Sutter (1999) term "cooperative inefficacy," is the very glue that ensures that the "antient constitution" sticks. Hume ([1751] 1985, 45) argues therefore that corruption has a beneficial albeit unintended consequence: "Some degree and kind of it are inseparable from the very nature of the constitution, and necessary to the preservation of our mixed government." We can read Hume as suggesting that political knavery (cooperative inefficacy) has second-best efficiency properties.[8]

2. "Politics without Romance"? The Buchanan-Musgrave Debate

The Buchanan-Musgrave debate centers on whether to follow Hume, when Hume claims that public choosers ought to be modeled as pursuing their private interests.

James M. Buchanan characterizes public choice as the study of politics without romance (see, e.g., Buchanan 1979, 211) by endorsing

8. Hume's worst-case essay had an immense influence on James Mill's ([1820] 1978) slave-driver model of government. Mill utterly rejects Hume's pregnant theory of constitutional equilibrium on worst-case grounds. Mill simply treats it as axiomatic that any single party (Crown, Lords, or Commons) will ultimately enjoy supremacy—subjugating the other two parties to the constitutional settlement. The unitary polity thus extracts all surplus above subsistence from the hapless populace. Where self-interest (political knavery) short-circuits the logic of cooperative efficacy, however, the populace retain a greater than subsistence share of the social surplus. T. B. Macaulay's famous attack on Mill's worst-case theorizing argues, just like Hume, that it is the very self-interest of the relevant parties that makes the British constitution stick. Any single party is willing to defect from any agreement made with another party to cooperate toward the end of weakening the power (and ultimately subjugating) the remaining party. Macaulay argues that any such agreement is highly unstable in the face of incentives to cheat. Paley ([1785] 2002, 339–40) similarly argues that any collusion between parties to the constitutional settlement is highly unstable in the presence of incentives to defect.

Hume's view that all people are to be presumed knaves in politics. Richard Musgrave, on the other hand, openly rejects Hume's views when he claims, "I do not join Hume's proposition that in viewing government 'everyone ought to be considered a knave.' . . . I would rather draw on people's capacity to serve as responsible members of the community, so that government may do its important tasks and do them well" (Buchanan and Musgrave 2001, 82).

The debate may be summed up by Buchanan himself:

> Sometime after *The Power to Tax* was published . . . Richard Musgrave and I were at a conference somewhere, and I raised this question: Don't you feel that under certain circumstances, you would want to constrain the government? And I said, for example, suppose you had a tiger, a pet tiger. Wouldn't you want to have a muzzle on that pet tiger in case that he might bite somebody? So you put him on a muzzle. And Richard Musgrave said, oh I wouldn't want to do that because I might want the tiger to eat the grass.[9] (Buchanan and Musgrave 2001, 89)

Geoffrey Brennan and James Buchanan's *Power to Tax* ([1980] 2000) is a classic in worst-case political economy, modeling government as a revenue-hungry Leviathan.[10] Brennan and Buchanan suggest that constitutional rules will constrain Leviathan's taxing proclivities, placing a constitutional "muzzle" on government's discretionary power. Buchanan's position could not perhaps appear any further removed from that of Musgrave. Indeed, Buchanan suggests that "politically, there is a dramatic difference between the way we [Buchanan and Musgrave] implicitly model what politics can do" (Buchanan and Musgrave 2001, 251).

David M. Levy (2002) argues that Buchanan's worst-case philosophy of constitutional political economy is similar to J. W. Tukey's worst-case philosophy of mathematical statistics: they both focus on worst-case thinking rather than best-case thinking, and they both look at how to

9. "Important contributions have been made by public-choice analysis. But too much of its work—especially in the United States—has been in the Hobbesian image of Leviathan with an ever-growing and abusive government. Such need not be the case. . . . bureaucrats (why not civil servants?) may be public-spirited as well as selfish, and political leadership may be constructive as well as destructive" (Musgrave 1997, 156).

10. See also, among others, Forbes and Zampelli 1989, Ross 1983, Shapiro and Sonstelie 1982, and Oates 1985.

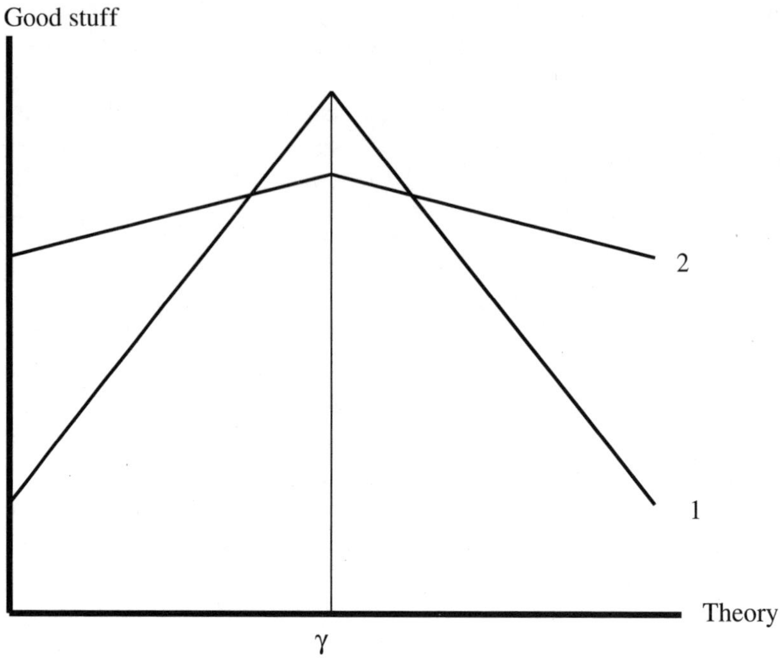

Figure 1 Fragile and robust political economy

avoid disasters rather than at how to achieve the best theoretical (even if not necessarily feasible) outcome. "The use of heavy-tailed distributions as paradigm—without worrying overly much about descriptive accuracy *as well as the 'unrealistic' use of Leviathan models*—are defended by the desire to avoid disaster" (Levy 2002, 131; emphasis added).[11]

Levy translates "worst-case" thinking in political economy (especially worst-case theorizing about government) into the "*lingua franca* of robust statistics" (131). Figure 1 maps the performance of two institutional frameworks (sets of "rules of the game," to invoke a favored public choice term) as a function of the putative state of the world, for example, one's assumptions with regard to agent-type.

Let us suppose that the state of the world is that represented by γ. Where γ represents the state of the world (or supposition of the model), institution 1 generates a greater amount of the metric "good stuff"

11. See, for example, Brennan and Buchanan [1985] 2000, 35, 62–63.

(Levy's terminology) than does institution 2. If γ holds, then 1 outperforms 2 in terms of generating our desirable metric "good stuff."

Levy's analytical machinery allows insights into the (Hume)-Buchanan-Musgrave debate. Institution 1 represents Musgrave's position—roughly akin to what Buchanan calls "benevolent despot" public finance theory (see, e.g., Buchanan 1987, 56, 303). Institution 1 may represent Hume's absolute monarchy as well. Institution 2 represents Buchanan's worst-case philosophy of constitutional political economy, as well as Hume's "antient constitution." Supposition γ represents the "benevolent despot" assumption—the assumption that some individuals (particularly those in government) are not knaves.

Levy (2002, 131) notes that "von Neumann's minimax loss approach to decision making is absolutely central to robust [worst-case] thinking." The maximax approach to decision making, however, is utterly central to best-case thinking about government, leading us to favor 1 over 2: The possible failure of γ does not impact on the choice between 1 and 2. Indeed, traditional public finance theory (1 in the graph) is superior to "public choice" (2 in the graph) where the envisaged "despot" is wholly public-spirited (where γ holds). Similarly, for Hume "absolute monarchy" (1) is superior to "mixed government" (2) where the monarch is wholly public-spirited. Weaken the supposition of public-spiritedness (γ), however, thereby modeling the monarch as more akin to Hume's "knave," or the government as more "despot" than "benevolent," and deadweight losses are utterly pervasive, or, in Hume's framework, tyranny inevitably results.

Worst-case thinking (minimax), however, necessitates that we take the possible failure of γ rather more seriously. Robust institutions (2) are designed to place a bound on the loss of "good stuff" that results on supposition γ's failure (Levy 2002, 134). And therein, or so we argue, lies a problem.

3. Robust Institutions: Romance by the Backdoor?

Gordon Tullock (1987, 87) identifies a problem in constitutional political economy: "The view that the government can be bound by specific provisions [constitutional rules] is naïve. Something must enforce those rules, and whatever enforces them is itself unbounded." Is the constitutional political economist à la Buchanan ultimately something of a best-case thinker? Does constitutional political economy allow romance back into the analysis?[12]

We suggest that Buchanan and Musgrave are both best-case thinkers of a sort. Hume is a consistent worst-case thinker. Buchanan differs from Musgrave simply as to at which stage of the analysis he allows best-case theorizing to enter the picture. Musgrave (1997, 156) allows best-case thinking to enter the analysis center stage when suggesting that government intervene to rectify market failures. Buchanan allows best-case thinking to rear its head at the constitutional stage—implicitly suggesting that angel-designed and -enforced constitutional rules mitigate government failure. This is not to say that best-case thinking per se is to be avoided at all times, but simply that political economists ought to readily admit to themselves that best-case thinking is perhaps inescapable within their models.

In terms of figure 1, we suggest that constitutional political economy implicitly makes something akin to a maximax (best-case) assumption when drawing institution 2. Constitutional political economy readily limits the supposition of γ (public-spiritedness) to one point for institution 1 (e.g., government discretion) while making a tacit supposition that γ (or some very close approximation to γ) holds true at all points when drawing institution 2 (e.g., constitutional constraints).

Levy's analogy between constitutional political economy and robust statistics allows us to pinpoint the difference between robust estimators and robust institutions. The robustness of any estimator, while contingent in a certain sense—namely, the presence or absence of certain technical conditions—is a noncontingent feature of statistical reality. Rules of the game, however, may be contingent. The properties of estimators are simply what they are irrespective of human wishes or desires that they prove otherwise (Levy 2002, 132). The robustness (or otherwise) of sets of rules of the game, are, by contrast, not simply akin to a datum to which agents passively adjust. Yet it is in precisely just such a fashion that we suggest worst-case political economy views sets of rules of the game: constitutional political economy appears to presuppose that constitutional rules are akin to a kind of noncontingently robust "enforcement technology." Brennan and Buchanan's ([1980] 2000, 240) remark that "we *need not predict that each child will fall off the cliff to justify*

12. On the presence of romance or knavery in politics, see, among others, Frey 1997 and Brennan and Hamlin 2000.

the installation of railings" (emphasis added) is especially apposite. The noncontingent rules analogy is further illustrated as follows:

> "It is costly to build a fence or to purchase a chain. It is possible to prove that the *no-fence, no-chain* solution is more efficient than either, *provided* that we model the behavior of our dog in such a way that respects the boundaries of our property" [γ]. . . . [Is the example] really very different from that procedure which argues that tax structure *X* is more "efficient" than tax structure *Y* provided that we model the behavior of government in such a way that it seeks only to further efficiency in revenue collection? (225; emphasis added)

Railings, fence, and chain, however, just like Buchanan's "tiger muzzle" (Buchanan and Musgrave 2001, 89) are all examples of a purely noncontingently robust "enforcement technology." All are physical technologies, which, once actually put in place, *do* provide a highly effective constraint against whatever particular undesirable behavior it is that we wish to reduce or otherwise eliminate. The rules of the game are, as such, wholly binding: agent-type (γ or otherwise) is irrelevant.[13] The "robustness" of any constitutional constraints, however, is utterly predicated on their design and enforcement by human agents.[14] We suggest that as interpreted from figure 1, institution 2 involves the acceptance of some γ-type supposition about constitutional design and enforcement. It presumably ill suits the constitutional political economist (of all people) to invoke a supposition of public-spiritedness (γ) regarding the agent ultimately charged with the task of designing and enforcing the constitutional rules of the game. Without such an assumption, however, we suggest that it is unclear—at least in terms of Levy's "insurance" metaphor—why the constitutional "insurance" will actually pay off when "worst-case" disasters threaten.[15] We suggest that constitutional

13. Constitutional political economy emphasizes "setting up rules or constraints within which politicians must operate, rules that will make it a *relatively trivial matter as to the personal characteristics of those who happen to be selected as governors*" (Buchanan [1981] 2001, 47; emphasis added).

14. "There is . . . one *crucial assumption* which clearly underlies the whole constitutional construction—that of *enforceability*" (Brennan and Buchanan [1980] 2000, 13; emphasis added). "Faith in rules [cannot] replace the exercise of responsible policy choice" (Musgrave 1997, 159).

15. Levy (2002, 131) argues that constitutional rules provide "insurance" against the potential "worst-case" disaster (loss of "good stuff") that results when supposition γ fails. Constitutional norms may "prove acceptable as embodying a minimax strategy aimed at securing protection against the worst-case outcomes that might emerge" (Brennan and Buchanan [1985] 2000, xxiii).

economics—like Musgrave's advocacy of governmental intervention—has at its very foundation a best-case supposition.

Buchanan has overtly sought to distance his own worst-case constitutional political economy from the implicit best-case theorizing pervasive in others' writings, such as in libertarian anarchist writings (e.g., Rothbard 1996): "My practical society . . . moves one stage down from the ideal [anarchy] and is based on the presumption that individuals could not attain the *behavioral standards* required for such an anarchy to function" (Buchanan 1977, 11; emphasis added). In recognition of this "frailty in human nature," individuals agree to "enact laws, and to provide means" for their enforcement (11). Buchanan's apparent prima facie insistence that the rules of the game adequately substitute for agent-type is illuminated by his analysis of a "Two-Stage Utopia" (11–12). "Stage 1" order (anarchy) is only feasible if we envisage an appropriate "modification of human nature" (12). On this point, Buchanan agrees with Hume ([1752] 1985a, 514) that the "plainly imaginary" nature of any plan of government necessitating "great reformation in the manners of mankind" is particularly applicable to the case of libertarian anarchy. The attainment of "Stage 2" order, namely, that represented by constitutionally constrained government, however, only requires a change in the rules of the game (institutions of governance) rather than any remaking of agent-type. Thus rules apparently substitute for agent-type (e.g., Buchanan [1981] 2001, 47). But the original problem, however, reappears: how can we assure that the constitutional rules are the "right" ones? And how do we assure that the "right" rules will be enforced?

Buchanan is aware that agent-type might prevent any change in the rules of the game from sticking *ex post*. Where the populace are clearly "incapable of adopting the requisite set of constitutional attitudes," they are "incapable of evaluating their long-term interests" (Buchanan 1977, 12–13). The public is thus unwilling to engage in nonconvex optimization, unwilling to exchange their current rents (thus reducing their current utility) in return for a higher payoff at a future date (Levy 1992).[16]

16. Elsewhere, Buchanan ([1981] 2001, 42) argues for the necessity of a "widespread adoption of a 'constitutional attitude,' a proclivity or tendency to examine issues from a constitutional perspective, as opposed to the pragmatic, short-run, utilitarian perspective that seems to characterize . . . day-to-day political discussion and action." How, though, does constitutional political economy propose to mitigate the PD-type logic intrinsic to large-numbers politics? A simple example is illustrative. Envisage politics as a simple 2 × 2 matrix. The lure of the off-diagonal (Buchanan's term) is pervasive. The situational logic intrinsic to the matrix as drawn (namely, row and column dominance) suffices to generate suboptimality (envisage the

At this juncture, Buchanan (1977, 14) cedes that anarchist and constitutional political economist alike face the same dilemma. Brennan and Buchanan ([1985] 2000, 166) are refreshingly candid in admitting to their hope that something akin to a "new civic religion" will emerge, one placing great emphasis on the "skepticism of the eighteenth century concerning politics and government." The hope for a new "civic religion," however, belies Buchanan's ([1981] 2001, 46) remark that constitutional political economy displays little "or no concern with replacing 'bad,' 'evil,' or 'incompetent' politicians with others who may be 'good.'"[17] Even if Buchanan works with the presumption of universal knavery at the postconstitutional level (everyday politics), he seems to reintroduce best-case thinking and its "angelic" or public-spiritedness assumptions at the preconstitutional and constitutional level, to generate the solution to government failure.

Moreover, what assurance do we have that the rule designers will not provide constitutional rules that will enhance their personal interests at the expense of societal well-being? Buchanan seems unable to avoid relying on the angelic nature of the constitutional writers.

---

loss of potential value as rent-seeking waste). Buchanan suggests that a constitutional "generality norm" be implemented, thereby eliminating the lure of the off-diagonal and restricting the potential outcomes to cell 1 or cell 4. Thus suboptimality (cell 4) is eliminated. Unfortunately, however, little attention is paid to why any such norm is binding *ex post*. The rules are envisaged as akin to a physical constraint *or* they are more akin to a potential constraint—any such potentiality only being realized when the rule is actually enforced. Enforcement, however, is subject to precisely the same situational logic as the original predicament for which such enforcement is thought to provide a potential solution. Enforcement is a public good—society is made better off when cells 2 and 3 are simply not available options (even though if chosen they are never actually realized). Public goods are classic nonconvexities. Thus enforcement is privately costly—one is made worse off at least initially. Why suffer any short-term "pain" for long-term "gain"? Constitutional political economy, while prima facie appearing a political economy decrying any reliance on preaching as a means of social salvation, appears to ultimately have no recourse to any alternative other than preaching: namely, attempting to inculcate what Buchanan elsewhere refers to as a "constitutional attitude."

17. "Formal constraints on behavior, as laid down in legal and constitutional structures, can *never alone* be sufficient to insure viability in social order. An underlying set of ethical norms or standards seems essential, although we recognize that formal and informal constraints become substitutes at some margins of adjustment" (Buchanan and Musgrave 2001, 25). "Perhaps more *important than formal constitutional changes are changes in ethical attitudes that would make attempted reforms workable*" (Buchanan [1996] 2001, 275; emphasis added). Elsewhere, Buchanan intriguingly remarks that economists neglect "the 'constitution of private man,' which roughly translates as 'character,' as well as the 'constitution of public men,' which translates into the necessary underpinning of a free society, the 'character' of society, if you will" (1979, 102).

Constitutional political economy makes creative use of Rawlsian-type "veil of ignorance" arguments. No good explanation is provided, however, as to why the rules chosen behind any such veil are binding *ex post*. Moreover, a knave has no incentive to go behind any veil (real or imagined). Using the Buchanan-Musgrave metaphor of tiger and muzzle, why would any knave volunteer to muzzle his or her own self-interest? Only angels would sacrifice themselves for the well-being of others.

Hume, on the other hand, offered a solution that consistently assumes knavery at all levels. Hume does not need to rely on angels writing the British constitutional rules, as the "antient constitution" was not written by anybody. The "antient constitution" emerged from centuries of compromise, bargaining, and negotiations between rival parties and political bodies, which is to say, the constitution seemed to have emerged from centuries of clashing knavery.

Hume, therefore, avoids Buchanan's problem at its root. The British system works, and works rather well, according to Hume, because it does not rely at *any* level on angelic behavior. The constitutional rules allow knavery to check knavery by maintaining a multiplicity of competing self-interested parties both at the enforcement level and, especially, at the rule-writing stage. Having only one person writing the constitution would be a disaster. The knavery of the constitutional writer would be unchecked by other knavery, thereby resulting in tyranny.

> If any single person acquire power enough to take our constitution to pieces, and put it up a-new, he is really an absolute monarch; and we have already had an instance of this kind [Oliver Cromwell], sufficient to convince us, that such a person will never resign his power, or establish any free government. (Hume [1742] 1985d, 52)

Knavery offers enough incentives to have constitutional rules that allow for knavery to check knavery. In fact, the British constitution does not have any single individual or body as its author. It is the unintended result of centuries of experience with self-interested behaviors. William Paley ([1785] 2002, 328) describes how the

> constitution of England, like that of most countries of Europe, hath grown out of occasion and emergency; from the fluctuating policy of different ages; from the contentions, successes, interests, and opportunities, of different orders and parties of men in the community. It

> resembles one of those old mansions, which, instead of being built all at once, after a regular plan, and according to the rules of architecture at present established, has been reared in different ages of the art, has been altered from time to time, and has been continually receiving additions and repairs suited to the taste, fortune, or conveniency, of its successive proprietors.

It is exactly this patchwork product of chance, rather than the wisdom of one or a few public-spirited angel-like individuals, that, for Hume, generates rules robust enough to keep decentralized and competing self-interests in check. Rules formed by the experience of knavery playing against knavery, rather than by the experience of one knave or a few colluding ones, are more robust examples of worst-case thinking because they are better able to cope and to learn how to prevent the knavery of one group from prevailing. Relying on one constitutional author implies that his knavery would go unchecked. On the other hand, if the players are many, there is a multiplication of knavery that would prevent any single knavery from wholly prevailing.[18]

For Hume, assuming angels write constitutional rules is just as much a mistake as assuming that angels would enforce a perfect constitution and rule a country. Knavery is for Hume the most efficacious check on knavery, given human nature. And the rules that allow knavery to play against knavery must be generated by the same unintentional and "accidental" process of competing knavery rather than by a self-proclaimed public-spirited mind.[19]

For Hume, therefore, knavery offers enough incentives to write, enforce, and maintain the rules. This of course does not imply that the checks which knavery provides against knavery are going to work every single time (as the Cromwell episode teaches), but that such checks as exist are the best we have available, given that attempting to remake man is not feasible.

18. For an exposition of the role of decentralization in forming robust rules, see Paganelli 2005.

19. "By a balance of power is meant, that there is no power possessed by one part of the legislature, the abuse or excess of which is not checked by some antagonist power, residing in another part" (Paley [1785] 2002, 337). Where "power is distributed among several courts, and several orders of men, we should always consider the separate interest of each court, and each order; and if we find that, by the skilful division of power, this interest must necessarily, in its operation, concur with public, we may pronounce that government to be wise and happy" (Hume [1742] 1985a, 43).

Conclusion

Buchanan argues that Musgrave's favored institutional structure is highly nonrobust in the presence of nonangelic public choosers. Buchanan's model, however, while providing a relatively robust institutional structure for private choosers, appears to leave humanity in the hand of blind hope in the public-choosing sphere. Hume, by contrast, while thinking consistently in terms of the worst-case (universal knavery in politics) offers a second-best solution. In Hume's view, because of the reciprocal check—or mutual antagonism—that multiple knavish agents provide on one another, two knaves are better than one.

References

Adair, Douglas. [1974] 1998. *Fame and the Founding Fathers*. Indianapolis, Ind.: Liberty Press.

Bentham, Jeremy. [1822] 1989. *First Principles Preparatory to Constitutional Code*. Edited by P. Schofield. Oxford: Clarendon.

Brennan, Geoffrey, and James M. Buchanan. [1980] 2000. *The Power to Tax*. Indianapolis, Ind.: Liberty Press.

———. [1985] 2000. *The Reason of Rules*. Indianapolis, Ind.: Liberty Press.

Brennan, Geoffrey, and Alan Hamlin, eds. 2000. *Democratic Devices and Desires: Theories of Institutional Design*. Cambridge: Cambridge University Press.

Buchanan, James M. 1977. *Freedom in Constitutional Contract: Perspectives of a Political Economist*. College Station: Texas A&M University Press.

———. 1979. *What Should Economists Do*? Indianapolis, Ind.: Liberty Press.

———. 1987. *Economics: Between Predictive Science and Moral Philosophy*. College Station: Texas A&M University Press.

———. 1992. *Better Than Plowing*. Chicago: University of Chicago Press.

———. [1981] 2001. Constitutional Restrictions on the Power of Government. In *Choice, Contract, and Constitutions*. Indianapolis, Ind.: Liberty Press.

———. [1996] 2001. Distributional Politics and Constitutional Design. In *Choice, Contract, and Constitutions*. Indianapolis, Ind.: Liberty Press.

Buchanan, James M., and Roger Congleton. 2003. *Politics by Principle, Not Interest*. Indianapolis, Ind.: Liberty Press.

Buchanan, James M., and Richard A. Musgrave. 2001. *Public Finance and Public Choice: Two Competing Visions of the State*. Cambridge, Mass.: MIT Press.

Cowen, Tyler, and Daniel Sutter. 1999. The Costs of Cooperation. *Review of Austrian Economics* 12.2:161–73.

Faria, J. R. 1999. Is There an Optimal Constitution? *Constitutional Political Economy* 10:177–84.

Forbes, Kevin, and Ernest Zampelli. 1989. Is Leviathan a Mythical Beast? *American Economic Review* 79.3:568–77.

Frey, Bruno. 1997. A Constitution for Knaves Crowds Out Civic Virtues. *Economic Journal* 107.443:1043–53.

Hoffman, Elisabeth, Kevin McCabe, and Vernon Smith. 1996. Social Distance and Other-Regarding Behavior in Dictator Games. *American Economic Review* 86.3:653–60.

Hume, David. 1978. *A Treatise of Human Nature*. Edited by P. H. Nidditch. Oxford: Oxford University Press.

———. [1742] 1985a. Of the Independency of Parliament. In *Essays, Moral, Political, and Literary*, edited by Eugene F. Miller. Indianapolis, Ind.: Liberty Press.

———. [1742] 1985b. Of the Origin of Government. In *Essays, Moral, Political, and Literary*, edited by Eugene F. Miller. Indianapolis, Ind.: Liberty Press.

———. [1742] 1985c. That Politics May Be Reduced to a Science. In *Essays, Moral, Political, and Literary*, edited by Eugene F. Miller. Indianapolis, Ind.: Liberty Press.

———. [1742] 1985d. Whether the British Government Inclines More to Absolute Monarchy or to a Republic. In *Essays, Moral, Political, and Literary*, edited by Eugene F. Miller. Indianapolis, Ind.: Liberty Press.

———. [1752] 1985a. Idea of a Perfect Commonwealth. In *Essays, Moral, Political, and Literary*, edited by Eugene F. Miller. Indianapolis, Ind.: Liberty Press.

———. [1752] 1985b. Of Refinement in the Arts. In *Essays, Moral, Political, and Literary*, edited by Eugene F. Miller. Indianapolis, Ind.: Liberty Press.

———. [1772] 1999. *An Enquiry concerning Human Understanding*. Oxford: Oxford University Press.

Leoni, Bruno. 1972. *Freedom and the Law*. Los Angeles: Nash.

Levy, David M. 1992. *The Economic Ideas of Ordinary People*. London: Routledge.

———. 2002. Robust Institutions. *Review of Austrian Economics* 15.2–3:131–42.

Mill, James. [1820] 1978. Essay on Government. In *Utilitarian Logic and Politics: James Mill's "Essay on Government," Macaulay's Critique, and the Ensuing Debate*, edited by J. Lively and J. Rees. Oxford: Clarendon Press.

Musgrave, Richard. 1997. Reconsidering the Fiscal Role of Government. *American Economic Review* 87.2:156–59.

Oates, Wallace E. 1985. Searching for Leviathan: An Empirical Study. *American Economic Review* 75.4:748–57.

Paganelli, Maria P. 2005. Adam Smith: Why Decentralized Systems? *Adam Smith Review*. Forthcoming.

Paley, William. [1785] 2002. *The Principles of Moral and Political Philosophy*. Indianapolis, Ind.: Liberty Press.

Ross, Robert J. S. 1983. Facing Leviathan: Public Policy and Global Capitalism. *Economic Geography* 59.2:144–60.

Rothbard, Murray. 1996. *For a New Liberty*. San Francisco: Fox & Wilkes.

Shapiro, Perry, and Jon Sonstelie. 1982. Did Proposition 13 Slay Leviathan? *American Economic Review* 72.2:184–90.

Sutter, Daniel. 1998. Leviathan at Bay: Constitutional versus Political Controls on Government. *Economic Inquiry* 36 (October): 670–78.

Toma, E., and M. Toma. 1984. Constitutional Tax Constraints within a Classical Model of Leviathan. *HOPE* 16.1:89–105.

Tullock, Gordon. 1987. The *Calculus* after 25 Years. *Cato Journal* 7.2:313–21.

Yellin, Mark E. 2002. Indirect Utility, Justice, and Equality in the Political Thought of David Hume. *Critical Review* 14.4:375–89.

Unintended Order and Intervention: Adam Smith's Theory of the Role of the State

Jeffrey T. Young

Is it possible to give a coherent account of Smith's theory of the role of the state in a system of natural liberty? If by "coherent" we mean reducible to a single principle or even slogan such as "laissez-faire," then the answer, of course, is "No." Ever since Jacob Viner (1928, 153–54) pointed out at the occasion of the celebration of the sesquicentennial of the publication of the *Wealth of Nations* (*WN*) that "Adam Smith was not a doctrinaire advocate of laissez faire," scholars have come to appreciate that Smith actually advocated "a wide and elastic range of activity for government." As a catalog of all the specific policies Smith is seen to support somewhere in the pages of *WN*, Viner's article is still the locus classicus. However, Viner made no attempt to provide a coherent account of the principles that might be seen to underpin and perhaps unify Smith's agenda. Indeed, he seems to have thought that such a project would be impossible, as he suggests that Smith must have forgotten, for example, that he advocated certain regulations of interest rates and banks when he came to write book 5 on the duties of the sovereign (139).

Notwithstanding Viner's authority in the history of economics, the question of Smith's views on the state remains controversial. Robert Heilbroner (1996), for example, emphasizes the significant list of things Smith thought government should do, while E. G. West (1990) and George Stigler (1976) champion Smith as an advocate of economic liberty and the limited state.

I wish to thank Vivienne Brown, David Levy, John Maloney, Warren Samuels, and Andrew Skinner for helpful comments on previous versions of this essay. The usual disclaimer applies.

Other commentators in the modern era have concentrated on underlying principles and policy norms. Andrew Skinner (1996, 204), for example, sees certain general principles informing Smith's agenda for state action, and he argues that these, not the specific agenda itself, are what is important and of general application. Another significant modern approach is that associated with Donald Winch (1978, 1983, 1992, 1996) and Knud Haakonssen (1981, 1996). They focus on the science of the legislator of which Smith considers political economy to be a branch. In this view natural jurisprudence provides the normative foundation for Smith's theory of the role of the state. Many, such as T. D. Campbell and I. S. Ross (1981), have focused on the utilitarianism of Smith's approach to policy, and there is now a growing recognition of Smith's concern for distributive equity as another distinct policy norm (Young and Gordon 1996; Witztum 1997; Verburg 2000).

The problem, as Viner has so well identified, is that *WN* reveals a fundamental tension in Smith's treatment of the state. On the one hand, we have the famous passages that extol the virtues of natural liberty and unintended order pointing toward a policy of laissez-faire. But, on the other hand, Smith, throughout the text, endorses a significant laundry list of specific government interventions in addition to those public works he assigns to the government outright in book 5. However, while at one level it may be entirely appropriate to view this list as ad hoc, it is not without philosophical underpinning. Indeed, this dialectical tension runs throughout Smith's thought and is inherent in his Humean epistemology.

At a deeper level we may express this tension as one between the "standpoint of ordinary life," to use Charles Griswold's (1999, 13) expression, and the perspective of the philosopher, "whose trade it is, not to do anything, but to observe everything" (*WN*, I.i.9). Agents, who are assumed to learn solely from empirical experience (including the experience of their own passions) unintentionally generate and perpetuate orderly patterns of social life. They make decisions and moral judgments on the basis of what Haakonssen (1981, 79) calls "contextual knowledge." In *Essays on Philosophical Subjects*, Smith (1980, II.12) calls philosophy "the science of the connecting principles of nature," and as such it represents to the imagination "invisible chains which bind together . . . disjointed objects." The philosopher's trade, then, is to produce what Haakonssen (1981, 79) calls "system knowledge." A defining attribute of philosophy, then, is that it in some sense reveals what is hidden to agents in ordinary life. (Although anyone could become a philosopher.)

Take the division of labor as an example. While Smith declines to offer a positive explanation of its origins, he categorically states it "is not originally the effect of any human wisdom, which foresees and intends the general opulence to which it gives occasion" (*WN*, I.ii.1).[1] The "propensity to truck, barter, and exchange" (I.ii.1) leads agents in ordinary life to spontaneously engage in division of labor. Only when one of them, after the fact, takes a philosophical, systematic point of view will humans make the connection between it and "general opulence." Yet Smith is frequently critical of philosophy's tendency to create systems of thought far removed from empirical human experience. Without going into the specifics of Smith's critique of the Stoics, we might note as an example, from *The Theory of Moral Sentiments* (*TMS*), that "the plan and system which Nature has sketched out for our conduct, seems to be altogether different from that of the Stoical philosophy" (VII.iii.i.43). Here is a clear tension between standards of virtue and conduct arising out of ordinary human experience and those that arise out of purely philosophical speculation. There is also the "man of system" who imagines "that he can arrange the different members of a great society with as much ease as the hand arranges the different pieces upon a chess-board" (VI.ii.2.17). Quoting Griswold (1999, 13) again, Smith qua philosopher was "a devoted and resourceful defender of the standpoint of ordinary life." The philosopher who respects and defends this standpoint will continually rein in the tendency of the mind to create metaphysical systems divorced from human experience and only offer suggestions for improvement consistent with that perspective.

Following Skinner's suggestion that we concentrate on principles, in this essay I show that once we understand the complexities of Smith's overall philosophical position, it is possible to give a coherent account of his position on the role of the state in terms of two dialectical tensions between competing policy norms. These are, first, the relation between justice, understood as commutative justice, and utility, understood as the common good, and, second, the relation between commutative justice and distributive justice, understood as equity. His general position on both of these relationships is not difficult to discern. He states it clearly early on in *TMS*, and he sticks with it throughout *WN*. It is a theory of unintended order in which the passions inherent in human nature, not a perception of utility, are the original source of justice that is

1. Elsewhere (Young 1997, 2001), I have attempted to fill in a Smithian explanation of the origins of the division of labor.

responsible for establishing social order, the good of the whole. Utility is an unintended consequence. Similarly, distributive equity emerges spontaneously as an unintended consequence of individual behavior rooted in the passions. The characteristic feature of this track of the dual relation is that justice serves as both a necessary and a sufficient condition for public utility. Justice emerges out of the interactions of ordinary life, based on agents acting on contextual knowledge. The same general pattern emerges again in *WN* where the natural sentiments of humanity—for example, self-interest, the propensity to truck and barter, the virtue of prudence, desire to be admired—become the efficient causes of increasing population and national wealth, the main indicators of public utility, the final cause. The standard of living of the lowest members of society is raised in the process above that of an African king, and so distributive equity is served as well.

However, once the perspective of the philosopher appears on the scene (not necessarily in the form of a specialist, at least not at first), the central problem we must address is that the general model does not work in all contexts. Someone, the first true Smithian philosopher, will notice that from a systemic point of view, spontaneous, unintended orders are not always beneficial, nor is equity always guaranteed as an outcome of market processes. Along this second track of the dialectical relationship, justice is a necessary but not a sufficient condition for public utility. In such instances it becomes the philosopher's job to offer the statesman advice to correct the problem. Utility will be the primary policy norm, but, as I will argue, even when offering utilitarian advice the philosopher (and statesman who implements policy) must not stray from the perspective of the sympathetic impartial spectator. This produces a tension between unintended order and intervention, which recurs throughout both *TMS* and *WN*. The instances of tension between commutative justice, utility, and equity in *TMS* map into parallel instances in *WN*. Smith's position on the role of the state is, thus, complex. He has at least three policy norms, and he has two models of their interrelationship. However, since these models are both grounded in the same philosophical system at this level, there is both consistency and coherence in Smith's theory taken as a whole.

This essay is divided into three parts plus a brief conclusion. I present the general model as it appears in both *TMS* and *WN* in the first part. In the second, I show how the general principles of intervention on both utilitarian and equity grounds are set out in *TMS* and then followed through in *WN*. The upshot is that in *WN* Smith would retain some of the laws of police as necessary to protect public utility, and he would perhaps favor some others on equity grounds. The third part begins with the three duties of the sovereign first laid out at the end of book 4 and shows how they support commutative justice, distributive equity, and public utility. Both tracks, or models, are evident in these duties and in Smith's treatment of taxation.

The Theory of Unintended Order

In a recent book James R. Otteson (2002) has argued that the theory of unintended order, which he aptly describes as a "market place" model, is the central feature of Smith's thought in both *TMS* and *WN*. For lack of anything better, I refer to this simply as Smith's "general" model. Smith sets out this model and applies it to an analysis of the interplay between justice and utility in part 2, section 2 of *TMS*. Having first contrasted the virtues of justice and benevolence, Smith defines the laws of justice as those that guard a person against injury in the form of loss of life, health, possessions, estate, or personal rights (*TMS*, II.ii.2.2).[2] Such injuries arouse the resentment of the impartial spectator and cause him to sympathize with the victim's desire for revenge. The sense of justice arises out of the unsocial passions: "Resentment . . . is the safeguard of justice and the security of innocence" (II.ii.1.4). Remorse is the sentiment that arises in the heart of the perpetrator when he "reflect[s] on the sentiments which mankind must entertain with regard to him," that is, he views his action from the perspective of the impartial spectator. Then he will sympathize with the sense of resentment other men feel for him (II.ii.2.3). The desire to be approved of leads him to "humble the arrogance of his self-love and bring it down to something which other men can go along with" (II.ii.2.2).

In this way the natural desires and moral sentiments of individuals lead ultimately to the evolution of the rules of justice, the only rules of virtue capable of exact specification and breaches of which are to be punished. There is, of course, more to the story than this. The point, though, is that Smith derives these rules from the supposed interactions of ordinary people functioning in a society. The people themselves are assumed

2. It is perhaps worth noting that this is a broader, more common, conception of justice than Hume's. As is well known, Hume virtually equated justice with property, while for Smith justice protects persons, health, and character as well as possessions.

to have no knowledge of the larger social consequences of their actions. A person is injured, and the observer immediately feels resentment toward the perpetrator and sympathy for the victim. These actions are not the result of reasoned reflection, although the process of achieving mutual sympathy does require some significant mental activity, at least until it is thoroughly learned. The agents are essentially operating on natural feelings about the actions that they observe among others. The pleasure of mutual sympathy alone leads to the proper degree of self-command and of fear of remorse necessary to generate just behavior as the norm.[3]

The scene shifts in the next chapter when Smith points out that this "constitution of Nature" has utility. From looking at justice from the perspective of the natural desires and knowledge of the individual agents involved, Smith asks us to step back and take a larger, philosophical perspective on the same set of actions. From this perspective we learn that "it is thus that man, who can subsist only in society, was fitted by nature to that situation for which he was made" (II.ii.3.1). Indeed, we learn that justice is the sine qua non of society itself: "Beneficence . . . is less essential to the existence of society than justice. Society may subsist, though not in the most comfortable state, without beneficence; but the prevalence of injustice must utterly destroy it" (II.ii.3.3). Justice is a necessary condition for the existence of society.[4]

3. The administration of justice is, of course, one of Smith's three primary duties of the state. As such I discuss it in the third part of the essay. However, since I am drawing a contrast between the unintended order arising out of ordinary life and the intended order arising from government action, a point of clarification may be useful. In using the term *intervention* to describe such government action, I do not mean to imply that Smith has some other sort of story to tell about the origin of formal governmental institutions or about the functions those institutions perform in society. In that sense government institutions are endogenous to Smith's general model. A case in point here is justice, as is money and the role of the mint. Even though these formal institutions are assigned the role of administering justice, this does not change the fact that the first origin of the rules of justice would be an unplanned, spontaneous process. The same story could be told about the origin of the institutions of government itself, the courts, parliament, monarch, etc. In using the term *intervention* I mean to imply that these institutions are well developed, especially the legislative function, and that "system knowledge" (whether true or not is not the question here) is being employed to intentionally promote social utility.

4. Smith's view of justice is incremental. The existence of society does not require "perfect justice," as we may infer from a comment Smith makes in the context of criticizing François Quesnay: "If a nation could not prosper without the enjoyment of perfect liberty and perfect justice, there is not in the world a nation which could ever have prospered. In the political body, however, the wisdom of nature has fortunately made ample provision for remedying the bad effects of the folly and injustice of man; in the same manner as it has done in the natural body, for remedying those of his sloth and intemperance" (*WN*, IV.ix.28). There will be other instances when public utility, the good of society, may override justice in particular instances. Thus, when Smith says that justice is a necessary condition for society to exist, I take him to

There follows immediately a lengthy paragraph on the importance of being able to distinguish between efficient and final cause in a world where "we observe the means adjusted with the nicest artifice to the ends which they are intended to produce" (II.ii.3.4). In particular, when it comes to understanding social life, phenomena produced by the actions of the mind, we are likely to confuse ends and means and to suppose that knowledge of the ends is the explanation for the emergence of the means.

> But though, in accounting for the operations of bodies, we never fail to distinguish in this manner the efficient from the final cause, in accounting for those of the mind we are very apt to confound these two different things with one another. When by natural principles we are led to advance those ends, which a refined and enlightened reason would recommend to us, we are very apt to impute to that reason, as to their efficient cause, the sentiments and actions by which we advance those ends, and to imagine that to be the wisdom of man, which in reality is the wisdom of God. (II.ii.3.4)

Apparently Smith is specifically thinking here of Hume's theory of justice, which Smith interprets as doing precisely what he says one should not do: derive the laws of justice from a perception of their utility. Smith then goes on to refute this view by offering "many obvious observations" such as the fact that our concern for society arises from and is compounded of our concern for specific individuals in the society (II.ii.3.10).

Here now is the general pattern: utility, seen as the good of society, is the unintended, beneficial outcome of numerous individual actions. Smith explains these actions and the institutions that result (the laws of justice) on the basis of natural reactions of individual agents to specific events. Their knowledge of each is "contextual," because it is confined to the event itself. They have no knowledge of—and, therefore, no intent to promote—the good of society, neither its existence nor its preservation.

Justice in the sense of refraining from injuring another is the same as "what Aristotle and the Schoolmen call commutative justice" (VII.ii.1.10). There is another sense of the word *justice* in which

> we are said not to do justice to our neighbour unless we conceive for him all that love, respect, and esteem, which his character, his situation, and his connexion with ourselves, render suitable and proper for

mean that the "usual strain of men's conduct" must be to follow the rules of natural justice and to refrain from injuring each other (*TMS*, V.2.16).

> us to feel, and unless we act accordingly. It is in this sense that we are said to do injustice to a man of merit who is connected with us, though we abstain from hurting him in every respect, if we do not exert ourselves to serve him and to place him in that situation in which the impartial spectator would be pleased to see him. (VII.ii.1.10)

This is distributive justice, and for Grotius it entailed the proper practice of the virtue of benevolence. It is this meaning of the term that became standard in the natural jurisprudence tradition. In the *Lectures on Jurisprudence* (*LJ*), we find that Smith treats distributive justice as an imperfect right, the same as charity, or benevolence. These duties are part of morals, not jurisprudence properly speaking (*LJ*[A], 1.14–15). Thus, Smith confines justice to its commutative sense only, and this is his meaning whenever he uses the term. He does not, however, ignore distributive equity as a matter of ethical concern for the distribution of income and wealth, particularly the standard of living of the poorest members of society.[5]

The general model of unintended order that Smith develops to explain the relationship of commutative justice to public utility reappears in the relation between commutative justice and distributive equity. This is the invisible hand's one appearance in *TMS*:

> The produce of the soil maintains at all times nearly that number of inhabitants which it is capable of maintaining. The rich only select from the heap what is most precious and agreeable. They consume little more than the poor, and in spite of their natural selfishness and rapacity, though they mean only their own conveniency, though the sole end which they propose from the labours of all the thousands whom they

5. In previous work Barry Gordon and I attempted to argue that Smith did use distributive justice understood in its jurisprudential sense of an imperfect right as a governmental policy norm, and as such he, implicitly at least, elevated it to nearly the same status as justice (Gordon and Young 1996; Young 1997). However, Gloria Vivenza (2001, 198), speaking from a deep knowledge of the classical roots of the concept, has argued that "it is wrong to associate the latter [Smith's concept of fairness] with distributive justice." Moreover, in his most recent book, D. D. Raphael (2001, 114) asserts that "it is certainly mistaken . . . [to suppose] that Smith regards the needs of the poor as a claim of justice." Amos Witztum and I (2003) have recently attempted to counter these arguments, but pursuing this is beyond the scope of the present essay. There is broad agreement that Smith was concerned about the distribution of income and wealth, although, as I shortly show, he spoke in terms of "equity" rather than "justice" per se. Thus, to avoid unnecessary controversy or misunderstanding, in this essay, I refer to the third policy norm as "distributive equity," or "equity" for short, rather than as "distributive justice." Following Smith, I use "justice" in its commutative sense only.

> employ, be the gratification of their own vain and insatiable desires, they divide with the poor the produce of all their improvements. They are led by an invisible hand to make nearly the same distribution of the necessaries of life, which would have been made, had the earth been divided into equal portions among all its inhabitants, and thus without intending it, without knowing it, advance the interest of the society, and afford means to the multiplication of the species. (IV.1.11)

Commutative justice, which protects the property rights of the rich, is here the guarantor of distributive equity, the welfare of the poor. This in turn promotes the common good by providing a means for population growth. The general model applies to both securing the good of the society and caring for the poor. Even though the example here of that "rustick hospitality" of the "great proprietors" refers to the precommercial state of society (*WN*, III.iv.5), we will see that the model holds for commercial society as well, at least in its progressive state.

The general model of unintended social order maps quite readily from *TMS* into *WN*. The principle of unintended beneficial social outcomes pervades the book, beginning with the division of labor "from which so many advantages are derived" but which is "not originally the effect of any human wisdom, which foresees and intends that general opulence to which it gives occasion" (*WN*, I.ii.1). The invisible hand metaphor is repeated once more, this time without any reference to distributive effects, and the foundational role of the rules of justice in the economy is brought out in the famous penultimate paragraph of book 4:

> All systems of preference or of restraint, therefore, being thus completely taken away, the obvious and simple system of natural liberty establishes itself of its own accord. Every man as long as he does not violate the laws of justice, is left perfectly free to pursue his own interest his own way, and to bring both his industry and capital into competition with those of any other man, or order of men. The sovereign is completely discharged from a duty, in the attempting to perform which he must always be exposed to innumerable delusions, and for the proper performance of which no human wisdom or knowledge could ever be sufficient; the duty of superintending the industry of private people, and of directing it towards the employments most suitable to the interest of the society. (*WN*, IV.ix.51)

As justice functions to make society possible in *TMS*, it functions here to make the economy function. It stands in the same relation to public utility here as it does in *TMS*, and in both the general pattern prevails of final causes emerging as the unintended consequences of the efficient causes. The latter are based in principles inherent in human nature.

The same may be said of the relation between commutative justice and distributive equity. In a commercial society "the produce of labour constitutes the *natural recompence* or wages of labour" (*WN*, I.viii.1; emphasis added). This is a matter of commutative justice, as failure to pay the recompense would result in an injury to the laborer. However, with the establishment of commutative justice there is security of possession, the prerequisite for capital accumulation. Thus, commercial society, even the imperfect one of Smith's contemporary world, had generated a long-term trend of economic growth that produced a sustained rise in the "real recompence" of labor, as the accumulation of capital led to the demand for labor growing faster than the supply (I.viii.35).

> Is this improvement in the circumstances of the lower ranks of the people to be regarded as an advantage or as an inconveniency to the society? The answer seems at first sight abundantly plain. Servants, labourers and workmen of different kinds, make up the far greater part of every great political society. But what improves the circumstances of the greater part can never be regarded as an inconveniency to the whole. No society can surely be flourishing and happy, of which the far greater part of the members are poor and miserable. It is *but equity besides*, that they who feed cloath and lodge the whole body of the people, should have such a share of the produce of their own labour as to be themselves tolerably well fed, cloathed and lodged. (I.viii.36; emphasis added)

The improvement in the real standard of living of the lower ranks of the people that Smith sees having taken place over the previous century is beneficial to society, that is, public utility, but it is also beneficial as a matter of equity. The clear indication in the passage is that equity is a distinctly different norm from public utility.

The normal functioning of commercial society not only has the utilitarian property of maximizing the value of the annual product, it also supports equity by enriching the poor. What rustic hospitality did in the precommercial society the market accomplishes in commercial society. The general model applies to both public utility and equity, and Smith deploys it in both books. In short, commutative justice is both a necessary and a sufficient condition for both public utility and distributive equity.

The Theory of Intervention

In *TMS*, once he has established the general model, Smith immediately raises a possible objection:

> Upon some occasions, indeed, we both punish and approve of punishment, merely from a view to the general interest of society, which, we imagine, cannot otherwise be secured. Of this kind are all punishments inflicted for breaches of what is called either civil police, or military discipline. (II.ii.3.11)

In the case of military discipline

> a centinel, for example, who falls asleep upon his watch, suffers death by the laws of war, because such carelessness might endanger the whole army. This severity may, upon many occasions, appear necessary, and for that reason, just and proper. When the preservation of an individual is inconsistent with the safety of a multitude, nothing can be more just than that the many should be preferred to the one. (II.ii.3.11)[6]

As D. D. Raphael (1972–73, 95) has shown, though, this is the exception that proves the rule, because the spectator feels differently about this case compared with the norm, even though the spectator approves of the punishment. As Smith explains:

> Yet this punishment, how necessary soever, always appears to be excessively severe. The natural atrocity of the crime seems to be so little, and the punishment so great, that it is with great difficulty that our heart can reconcile itself to it. Though such carelessness appears blamable, yet the thought of this crime does not naturally excite any such resentment, as would prompt us to take such dreadful revenge. A man of humanity must recollect himself, must make an effort, and exert his whole firmness and resolution, before he can bring himself either to inflict it, or to go along with it when it is inflicted by others. (*TMS*, II.ii.3.11)

6. Raphael (1972–73, 96) claims that in the sentinel case Smith concedes too much to Hume by asserting that the utility of the punishment makes it just. I agree with Raphael; Smith should not have claimed that the utility of the punishment makes it just. Justice and utility are distinct principles of ethical judgment, which can come into conflict with each other, and normally Smith himself treats them as distinct. It would have been more consistent with his theory to simply say that sometimes a greater public good overrides justice, as I have also argued elsewhere (Young 1997). This is the sense in which I interpret the sentinel case in this essay.

Nonetheless, the case represents a counterinstance to the general model. Left to their own volition, the natural sentiments of humanity would not punish the sentinel so severely. Consequently, sentinels would become lazier and armies would be lost. The general model breaks down. The natural sentiments do not lead to utilitarian results.

As is well known, Smith goes on, in part 4, to mount an extended defense of his theory against Hume's utilitarianism. In part 7, following Hume's and Hutcheson's empiricism, Smith claims:

> But though reason is undoubtedly the source of the general rules of morality, and of all the moral judgments which we form by means of them; it is altogether absurd and unintelligible to suppose that the first perceptions of right and wrong can be derived from reason, even in those particular cases upon the experience of which the general rules are formed. These first perceptions, as well as all other experiments upon which any general rules are founded, cannot be the object of reason, but of immediate sense and feeling. . . . If virtue, therefore, in every particular instance, necessarily pleases for its own sake, and if vice as certainly displeases the mind, it cannot be reason, but immediate sense and feeling, which, in this manner, reconciles us to the one, and alienates us from the other. (VII.iii.2.7)

However, contrary to Hume, these "first perceptions" are not perceptions of the utility of the sentiments:

> But still I affirm, that it is not the view of this utility or hurtfulness which is either the first or principal source of our approbation and disapprobation. These sentiments are no doubt enhanced and enlivened by the perception of the beauty or deformity which results from this utility or hurtfulness. But still, I say, they are originally and essentially different from this perception. (IV.2.3)

Rather, the "sentiment of approbation always involves in it a sense of propriety quite distinct from the perception of utility" (IV.2.5). Smith has already shown, in part 1, that judgments of the propriety of sentiments precede those of the consequences of actions. He then goes on to show that many virtues, which are normally thought to be virtuous because they are useful, either to society or to individuals, arise out of a perception of their propriety, not their utility. Among these is the virtue of public spirit, putting the interest of society ahead of one's own.

Smith is clear that utility cannot be the origin of moral judgment, but nonetheless it is a principle of moral judgment.

> This utility, *when we come to view it*, bestows upon them [public-spirited men], undoubtedly, a new beauty, and upon that account still further recommends them to our approbation. This beauty, however, is chiefly perceived by *men of reflection and speculation*, and is by no means the quality which first recommends such actions to the natural sentiments of the bulk of mankind. (IV.2.11; emphasis added)

We note here two significant aspects of utility as a principle of moral judgment. First, it is an *ex post* judgment, and, second, it is philosophers who make it. It is the philosopher, adopting a systematic, holistic perspective, who notices after the fact that public-spirited behavior is praiseworthy because of its beneficial social consequences. This further suggests that what the "man of humanity" is doing when he "recollects himself" is rendering a philosophical judgment of the sleeping sentinel, and that in this case philosophical argumentation, not "immediate sense and feeling," is needed to obtain moral approbation of the punishment.

However, even in the case of rendering judgments on the basis of social utility, the philosopher will still refer to the sympathetic judgment of an impartial spectator. The impartial spectator views the interests of the many as superior to the interests of a single individual or small group:

> The patriot who lays down his life for the safety . . . of this society, appears to act with the most exact propriety. He appears to view himself in the light in which the impartial spectator naturally and necessarily views him, as but one of the multitude, in the eye of the equitable judge, of no more consequence than any other in it, but bound at all times to sacrifice and devote himself to the safety, to the service, and even to the glory of the greater number. (VI.ii.2.2)

When the impartial spectator puts himself or herself in the position of the philosopher, he or she adopts the utilitarian ethic that the good of the whole trumps the good of the individual.

The *ex post*, holistic judgments of the philosopher are ultimately rooted in Smith's general model in that an impartial spectator would approve of invoking utilitarian standards when viewing the system holistically instead of contextually. There are three significant implications of this. First, there is a definite role for discovering and implementing rules, laws, or general policy purely from a utilitarian perspective if they can be shown to truly promote the good of the whole. Second, those in governmental authority should exhibit that sort of public spirit which is "founded upon the love of humanity, upon the real fellow-feeling with the inconveniencies and distresses to which some of our fellow-citizens may be exposed" (VI.ii.2.15). The best leaders will put themselves in the position of "fellow-citizens." Thus, the same kind of process that Smith uses to explain the origin of social order is used here to guide the rulers of the government to motivate them to rule in the public interest. Third, if the ruler engages in this imaginative change of place with his subjects he will

> respect the established powers. . . . He will accommodate, as well as he can, his public arrangements to the confirmed habits and prejudices of the people; and he will remedy as well as he can, the inconveniencies which may flow from the want of those regulations which the people are averse to submit to. . . . like Solon, when he cannot establish the best system of laws, he will endeavour to establish the best that the people can bear. (VI.ii.2.16)

In a sort of ironic twist, Smith's general model guides the philosopher and the lawgiver even in those cases where it seems to break down. In this way Smith can construct a theory of intervention that maintains the integrity of the perspective of common life and the daily interactions of individuals following their natural sentiments and interests.

Smith's theory of intervention, then, brings philosophical speculation, which discovers the need for utilitarian rules promulgated by governmental authority, as well as governmental authority itself under the authority of the judgments of the impartial spectator. Smith identifies two broad areas where this would apply: civil police (or more broadly the laws of police that include the regulation of economic activity) and military discipline. In considering those governmental rules, intentionally instituted to promote public utility, I identify three distinct cases. First, as in the case of the sentinel, the spontaneous results of people following their natural sentiments may produce results that all reasonable people (people of humanity) will agree after reflection are destructive of the common good and are, therefore, pathological. In this case legislation, or governmental authority of some type, must intervene to regulate individual behavior.

Second, there may be practices, or laws, that have emerged over time that violate justice to promote a larger public good. However, in this case customs and traditions may preserve such practices and allow them to live on beyond their original justification, hindering people's abilities to perceive their essential injustice. This is the case of infanticide and euthanasia in the ancient and savage societies:

> The extreme indigence of a savage is often such that he himself is frequently exposed to the greatest extremity of hunger, he often dies of pure want, and it is frequently impossible for him to support both himself and his child. We cannot wonder, therefore, that in this case he should abandon it. One who, in flying from an enemy, whom it was impossible to resist, should throw down its infant, because it retarded his flight, would surely be excusable; since by attempting to save it, he could only hope for the consolation of dying with it. That in this state of society, therefore, a parent should be allowed to judge whether he can bring up his child, ought not to surprise us so greatly. In the latter ages of Greece, however, the same thing was permitted from views of remote interest or conveniency, which could by no means excuse it. Uninterrupted custom had by this time so thoroughly authorised the practice, that not only the loose maxims of the world tolerated this barbarous prerogative, but even the doctrine of philosophers, which ought to have been more just and accurate, was led away by the established custom, and upon this, as upon many other occasions, instead of censuring, supported the horrible abuse, by far-fetched considerations of public utility. (V.2.16)

There is no indication here that the conditions that render the practice "excusable" also render it just. Thus, the practice can be sanctioned only on grounds of utility. Once it has outlived its utility, the injustice should become obvious, and it would, if the natural sentiments had not been dulled by custom.

That infanticide continues to be sanctioned by "far-fetched considerations of public utility" brings us to the third possible case. Some laws may be instituted contrary to the natural sentiments of justice for reasons of public utility that turn out on close inspection to be false. In the *Lectures on Jurisprudence* Smith included the case of wool smugglers in the same paragraph with that of the sentinel.

> Thus some years ago the British nation took a fancy (a very whimsicall one indeed) that the wealth and strength of the nation depended entirely on the flourishing of their woolen trade, and that this could

> not prosper if the exportation of wool was permitted. To prevent this it was enacted that the exportation of wool should be punished with death. This exportation was no crime at all, in natural equity, and was very far from deserving so high a punishment in the eyes of the people; they therefore found that while this was the punishment they could get neither jury nor informers. No one would consent to the punishment of a thing in itself so innocent by so high a penalty. They were therefore obliged to lessen the punishment to a confiscation of goods and vessel. (*LJ*[A], ii.91–92; also *LJ*[B], 182)

This case is similar to the sentinel case in that reasons of public utility are thought to override and justify a violation of justice in the form of a punishment disproportionately severe compared with the crime. However, it differs in that the reasons of public utility are said to be whimsical, such that they cannot overcome the people's natural inclination to view the smuggler as innocent.

To summarize, Smith's theory of intervention as it appears in *The Theory of Moral Sentiments* and in the *Lectures on Jurisprudence* is based on those cases where justice does not appear to entail utility as an unintended outcome. This introduces space within which the law can operate to regulate individual behavior for the good of the whole. These cases appear in three variations depending on whether the reasons of public utility are legitimate for all times and places, legitimate in some stages of society but not in others, or simply false. These are respectively the cases of the sentinel, infanticide in ancient Greece, and wool smuggling.

The infanticide case also touches on distributive equity in an interesting way. Recall that in the *TMS* passage quoted above (V.2.16) Smith notes that, in the savage state, society allowed the parent to decide whether to rear the child. In that age the parent's responsibility toward the child was treated as a matter of benevolence, not justice:

> We may observe . . . that in the early and more rude periods of society men were not conceived to be bound to aliment their children (or maintain them). It was not supposed that one was bound to do any thing for those who did not do their part to their own maintenance. As now men are only bound not to hurt one another and to act fairly and justly in their dealings, but are not compelled to any acts of benevolence, which are left intirely [*sic*] to his own good will, so in the ruder times this was extended to the nearest relations, and the obligation they were under to do for one another was supposed to be binding only

> by their inclination; and all kindnesses betwixt them were reckon'd as acts of benevolence and not as what they were bound in justice to perform. . . . This was extended at first much farther, and a parent was considered as at liberty either to maintain and educate his children or to leave them at the mercy of the weather and the wild beasts. (*LJ* [A], iii.78–79)

It was only with the establishment of Christianity that the practice of exposing children was finally eliminated, but not as a matter of justice. Rather, it was a case of legally compelling acts of beneficence:

> A superior may, indeed, sometimes, with universal approbation, oblige those under his jurisdiction to behave, in this respect, with a certain degree of propriety to one another. The laws of all civilized nations oblige parents to maintain their children, and children to maintain their parents, and impose upon men many other duties of beneficence. The civil magistrate is entrusted with the power not only of preserving the public peace by restraining injustice, but of promoting the prosperity of the commonwealth, by establishing good discipline, and discouraging every sort of vice and impropriety; he may prescribe rules, therefore, which not only prohibit mutual injuries among fellow-citizens, but command mutual good offices to a certain degree. . . . Of all the duties of a law-giver, however, this, perhaps, is that which it requires the greatest delicacy and reserve to execute with propriety and judgment. To neglect it altogether exposes the commonwealth to many gross disorders and shocking enormities, and to push it too far is destructive of all liberty, security, and justice. (*TMS*, II.ii.8)

Even though Smith excludes benevolence, which entails distributive justice and equity, from jurisprudence, there is still some justification for the sovereign to intervene by establishing laws that go beyond strict commutative justice. As in the case of intervention to promote public utility, such benevolent interventions also receive the approval of the impartial spectator. Just as we saw certain exceptions to the general model of the relation between commutative justice and public utility, commutative justice does not always ensure distributive equity. In such cases, it is legitimate for the sovereign to intervene and command acts of beneficence. The parents' obligation to support and educate their children is one such example.

We thus end up with four cases of intervention on utilitarian or distributive grounds.[7] Each has its counterpart in *WN*. First, the sentinel case, where reasons of public utility overrule justice, appears in the form of market failure. The general pattern that unites these two cases is that the spontaneous behavior of individuals following their natural sentiments fails to secure the common good. In terms of a modern prisoner's dilemma game, the sentinel clearly has an incentive to choose the noncooperative strategy of falling asleep. Similarly, market failure entails individuals choosing noncooperative behavior in the absence of any legal or social sanction. In *WN* this means that the pursuit of self-interest does not maximize public utility, the case of market failure. There are two well-known examples of this in the book: regulations of interest rates and regulations on banknote issues.

With respect to interest rates the problem is what we now call asymmetric information leading to adverse selection. If interest rates were allowed to rise to clear the market of a credit shortage, for example, then only high-risk borrowers would be left in the market:

> If the legal rate of interest in Great Britain, for example, was fixed so high as eight or ten per cent., the greater part of the money which was to be lent, would be lent to prodigals and projectors, who alone would be willing to give this high interest. Sober people, who will give for the use of money no more than a part of what they are likely to make by the use of it, would not venture into the competition. A great part of the capital of the country would thus be kept out of the hands which were the most likely to make a profitable and advantageous use of it, and thrown into those which were most likely to destroy it. Where the legal rate of interest, on the contrary, is fixed but a very little above the lowest market rate, sober people are universally preferred, as borrowers, to prodigals and projectors. (*WN*, II.iv.15)

Clearly in the context of this particular market the spontaneous pursuit of self-interest leads to the destruction of society's capital. As in the case of the sentinel, a utilitarian standard must be intentionally imposed. In this sense the regulation of the interest rate parallels the sentinel case of *TMS*.

7. The natural sentiments that establish the rules of commutative justice can come into conflict with either distributive equity or public utility. However, it would appear from the passages cited on distributive equity that public utility and distributive equity do not conflict. Thus, the liberal reward of labor is good on both utilitarian and equity grounds, as is the requirement that parents maintain their children.

The regulation of banknotes is a similar example of market failure causing adverse selection in banking. In the absence of regulations against issuing small denomination banknotes, "many mean people are both enabled and encouraged to become bankers" (*WN*, II.ii.90). The result is a system that is less secure, more prone to bank failure with attendant harm to the general public. Shortly thereafter Smith lays down a general rule for intervening to correct market failure:

> Such regulations may, no doubt, be considered as in some respect a violation of natural liberty. But those exertions of the natural liberty of a few individuals, which might endanger the security of the whole society, are, and ought to be, restrained by the laws of all governments; of the most free, as well as of the most despotical. The obligation of building party walls, in order to prevent the communication of fire, is a violation of natural liberty, exactly of the same kind with the regulations of the banking trade which are here proposed. (II.ii.94)

Unlike the discussion of the sentinel in *TMS* there is no indication here that the social good of the regulation makes it just. As a violation of the natural liberty of the few to protect the many, it represents a clear case of overruling considerations of justice for the common good.[8] Since the general rules of justice originate unintentionally in the interactions of ordinary life where agents possess only contextual knowledge, such regulations as these require the perspective of the philosopher and must be implemented intentionally through governmental authority.

Second, the laws of primogeniture and entails, leftover from precommercial society, were once useful, though contrary to natural justice, but the circumstances that made them such have now passed. Consequently, their present effects constitute a net loss to society. The law of primogeniture, although a violation of the natural law of succession, came into being, "that the power, and consequently the security of the monarchy, may not be weakened by division." Thus, "in those disorderly times," it had its usefulness (*WN*, III.ii.3). However,

> laws frequently continue in force long after the circumstances, which first gave occasion to them, and which could alone render them reasonable, are no more. In the present state of Europe, the proprietor of

8. Recall that Smith's conception of justice is incremental. Thus, in cases where we see the rules of justice being superseded by considerations of public utility, it is really only a marginal loss of justice that is involved. The general system of the laws of justice must remain intact for society to continue to exist.

> a single acre of land is as perfectly secure of his possession as the proprietor of a hundred thousand. The right of primogeniture, however, still continues to be respected, and as of all institutions it is fittest to support the pride of family distinctions, it is likely to endure for many centuries. (III.ii.4)

The same applies to entails, "the natural consequences of the law of primogeniture" (III.ii.5).

The harmful social consequences of these laws operating together arise out of the fact that they contribute to maintaining large tracts of land in an unimproved state. "It seldom happens, however, that a great proprietor is a great improver" (III.ii.7; see also *LJ*[B], 163). The improvement of the land is like a commercial project. It therefore requires the attention of those in the habit of undertaking such projects. "Merchants are commonly ambitious of becoming country gentlemen, and when they do, they are generally the best of all improvers" (III.iv.3). Entails prevent merchants from buying up all the land they might want, and the result is that large tracts of land remain unimproved.

These laws fit closely the pattern of our second case, infanticide in the rude state. They were useful in precommercial society, but they impede improvement in commercial society. Moreover, being of long standing, they have become embedded in the customs and habits of the people. Tradition, therefore, stands in the way of abolishing the practices. The parallel in these examples is not exact, however, as infanticide requires the sovereign to enact positive law requiring parents to care for their children. In the present example, the offending practices are already embodied in positive laws, and all that is called for is their removal. Once this is effected the pattern would become that of the general model. The laws of justice would cause people following their self-interests to promote the common good, as land would then flow to its highest-valued use, and the large estates would be broken up into smaller holdings.

This brings us to the third case, wool smuggling. The sort of intervention called for here goes to the heart of what Smith was trying to do in *WN*, his "very violent attack" on the mercantile system (1987, 208). Although some of the regulations and special privileges he criticized would fit into the pattern of the previous case in that they may have been useful at one time, the general pattern of Smith's attack is that they arise from a false conception of public utility.

> It is by this superior knowledge of their own interest that they [merchants and manufacturers] have frequently imposed upon his [landlord's] generosity, and persuaded him to give up both his own interest and that of the publick, from a very simple but honest conviction, that their interest, and not his, was the interest of the publick. The interest of the dealers, however, in any particular branch of trade or manufactures, is always in some respects different from, and even opposite to, that of the publick. (*WN*, I.xi.p.10)

This sincere confusion, the mean spirit of monopoly, and the prejudices of the people coupled with the sophistries of the mercantile system resulted in a whole system of law that sacrificed justice for a fallacious conception of the common good. Again, from the perspective of an impartial spectator, the interests of the many overbalance the interests of one or a few. So it is from this perspective that Smith, the philosopher, condemns the mercantile system.

Specific examples of such laws are so numerous as to prevent any exhaustive treatment. The example of the laws against wool smuggling and the injustice of the severe punishments they meted out appears twice in *WN* (IV.viii.17; V.ii.k.64). Indeed, all the laws that Smith cites as supporting the system fit the pattern. Apprenticeship laws violate the "property which every man has in his own labour" in order to protect the public from incompetence, but the interest of the employer would be more effective in judging the ability of a workman (I.x.c.12). The Corn Laws, which prohibit the exportation of corn, essentially "sacrifice the ordinary laws of justice to an idea of publick utility, to a sort of reasons of state" (IV.v.b.39). Exclusive privileges of corporations establish monopolies against the public, and so on. Smith calls for the dismantling of the entire system at the end of book 4 (see *WN*, IV.ix.51, quoted above). This is actually a far-reaching policy of intervention into the existing economy. Another way of looking at it is to say that the laws of justice must replace the laws of police.[9] As in the second case, once this is accomplished the general model will prevail. Commutative justice will serve to promote public utility.

9. In treating of systems of political economy in book 4, Smith never called the system of natural liberty a system of political economy. The fact that he viewed the central message of the book as a call to eliminate the laws of the mercantile political economy so that the laws of justice would be the primary regulators of economic activity may shed light on why he might not have viewed natural liberty as a system of political economy. I have argued this point more extensively elsewhere (Young 2001).

There is some indication in Smith's denunciation of the mercantile system that he also views it as offending against equity. The domestic manufacturers of linen cloth, for example, "by extorting from the legislature" bounties on the exportation of the cloth coupled with encouragements to the importation of the linen yarn, the raw material, are able to profit at the expense of the domestic spinners of the yarn. But the domestic spinners are "poor people, women commonly, scattered about in all different parts of the country, without support or protection." Smith concludes: "It is the industry which is carried on for the benefit of the rich and the powerful, that is principally encouraged by our mercantile system. That which is carried on for the benefit of the poor and the indigent, is too often, either neglected, or oppressed" (IV.viii.4). The elimination of the system will bring about greater distributive equity. Thus, to the extent that the system creates inequities, its abolition will allow commutative justice to promote greater equity.

There are, however, also some instances in *WN* parallel to the fourth case of intervention where commutative justice cannot alone function as the guarantor of distributive equity. In Smith's attack on the Corn Laws and the regulations that have the unintended consequence of turning a scarcity of corn into a famine, there is at least a hint of concern about equity.

> The freedom of the corn trade is almost every where more or less restrained, and in many countries, is confined by such absurd regulations, as frequently aggravate the unavoidable misfortune of a dearth, into the dreadful calamity of a famine. . . . In a Swiss canton, or in some of the little states of Italy, it may, perhaps, sometimes be necessary to restrain the exportation of corn. In such great countries as England and France it scarce ever can be. To hinder, besides, the farmer from sending his goods at all times to the best market, is evidently to sacrifice the ordinary laws of justice to an idea of publick utility, to a sort of reasons of state; an act of legislative authority which ought to be exercised only, which can be pardoned only in cases of the most urgent necessity. The price at which the exportation of corn is prohibited, if it is ever to be prohibited, ought always to be a very high price. (IV.v.b.39)

This passage, in conjunction with the entire digression in which it is found, is sometimes taken to show that Smith's commitment to the primacy of the laws of justice is absolute (Hont and Ignatieff 1983, 19–22;

Rashid 1998, 117). This position is understandable, since Smith is clearly attempting to make a strong case, against popular superstition, that the laws of justice, not legislative authority, ought to govern the corn trade. However, he does suggest that in emergencies legislative authority would be justified in intervening to prevent starvation. As it would be the poorest members of the state who would be most exposed, there is a basis for intervention on equity grounds. Seen in this light, the passage is at least reminiscent of the paragraph quoted above from *TMS* (II.ii.8), which also supports a similar agenda—benevolent intervention in extreme cases. Thus, famine might be one of those "shocking enormities" that the legislator is authorized to prevent, even at the expense of laws of justice. As in the case of utilitarian intervention, such benevolent intervention also receives the support of the impartial spectator.

We can also detect some concern for distributive equity in Smith's critique of the herring buss bounty. Being a tonnage bounty, it tends to increase the number and size of the boats, but it does not necessarily actually increase the catch. Thus we find that

> in many parts of Scotland, during certain seasons of the year, herrings make no inconsiderable part of the food of the common people. A bounty, which tended to lower their price in the home market, might contribute a good deal to the relief of a great number of our fellow-subjects, whose circumstances are by no means affluent. But the herring buss bounty contributes to no such good purpose. (*WN*, IV.v.a.34)

Smith has not necessarily endorsed such a bounty, but he has suggested that it might be beneficial. This would, then, be another example of a regulation in the state of natural liberty designed to help the poor.

In this section I have identified four cases or types of interference that Smith is seen to authorize (or condemn) in his moral philosophy and jurisprudence. These were the cases of the sentinel, infanticide, the wool smuggler, and the care for children. Each was shown to have its counterpart in *WN*. The abolition of laws that have either outlived their usefulness or are based on false conceptions of public utility, while requiring an extensive agenda of interference into the contemporary system, presents no fundamental difficulty for the general model. Once these issues have been addressed, commutative justice will promote public utility and distributive equity even more extensively. The remaining two cases, however, imply a role for intervention even in the state of natural liberty on both utilitarian and distributive grounds.

The Duties of the Sovereign

In the first two parts I have attempted to give an account of Smith's theory of the role of the state in terms of the interrelationships among three policy norms: commutative justice, distributive equity, and public utility. The theory results in a dual, two-track model of unintended order and intervention. In each case I hope to have shown that we can map quite readily from the principles of the moral philosophy to the application of those principles in *WN*. My task in this section is to do the reverse: namely, to take Smith's statement of the duties of the sovereign and trace them back to the policy norms. Superficially, this is an easy task, since justice and utility are explicitly stated norms. It is also easy to account for all three norms in Smith's maxims of taxation.

The presumption now is that the system of natural liberty has been established. Laws based on a false conception of public utility and those that are no longer useful have all been eliminated (unless they serve to promote a legitimate end, such as national defense).

> According to the system of natural liberty, the sovereign has only three duties to attend to; three duties of great importance, indeed, but plain and intelligible to common understandings: first, the duty of protecting the society from the violence and invasion of other independent societies; secondly, the duty of protecting, as far as possible, every member of the society from the injustice and oppression of every other member of it, or the duty of establishing an exact administration of justice; and thirdly, the duty of erecting and maintaining certain publick works and certain public institutions, which it can never be for the interest of any individual, or small number of individuals, to erect and maintain; because the profit could never repay the expence to any individual or small number of individuals, though it may frequently do much more than repay it to a great society. (*WN*, IV.ix.51)

Aligning these three duties with the two of the three policy norms is immediately obvious. Defense and justice support the norm of commutative justice. Without national defense there would be no system of justice to maintain; similarly, without the administration of justice there would be no justice. These duties are the necessary counterpart to the general model. Public utility justifies the third duty, which rests on the recognition that certain types of works, such as investments in infrastructure, and institutions, such as schools, would not spontaneously arise without government encouragement even though they are of great public benefit. Government must provide what the market will not. This marks the appearance of the second track of the model in the sovereign's duties.

It is not too hard to also account for at least some concern for distributive equity. The corruption of the majority of the people, the loss of the martial virtues, and the mutilation of the mind are well-known consequences of the division of labor: "In every improved and civilized society this is the state into which the labouring poor, that is, the great body of the people, must necessarily fall, unless government takes some pains to prevent it" (V.i.f.50). Society can establish schools modeled on the Scottish parish schools, and it can impose on the public the necessity of acquiring a basic education. It can subsidize the pay of the teachers, offer "badges of distinction" to encourage the common people to send their children to the schools, and require an examination as a prerequisite for practicing a trade (V.i.f.55–57). Since the poor are the beneficiaries of these subsidies and encouragements, the state's attention to education serves the norm of distributive equity as well as public utility.

Distributive equity should also be an attribute of the system of taxation, as the first maxim of taxation states the ability to pay principle (V.ii.b.3). This is further refined to entail the principle of progressive taxation when Smith discusses the inequality of taxes on house-rents: "It is not very unreasonable that the rich should contribute to the publick expence, not only in proportion to their revenue, but something more than in that proportion" (V.ii.e.6). Moreover, all the maxims of taxation are of "evident justice and utility," thus indicating that the same three norms underpin Smith's evaluation of the system of taxation in a system of natural liberty (V.ii.b.7).

The three norms are quite evident in the sovereign's duties and in the maxims of taxation, as are the two tracks of unintended order and intervention. Along the latter, for example, Smith is quite willing to use the tax system to alter behavior "in the name of the public interest" (Skinner 1996, 186), and Skinner concludes that this opens a field of intervention of "wide application" (187). Moreover, the provision of public works and institutions, "which it can never be for the interest of any individual, or small number of individuals, to erect and maintain," opens a wide range of activities, where markets will not of themselves provide public utility (*WN*, IV.ix.51; see also V.i.c.1). While Smith does not revisit issues, such as the regulation of interest rates and banknotes, the third duty of the sovereign rests on the same underlying principles. The system knowledge of the philosopher is required to promote public utility in cases of market failure.[10]

However, with respect to distributive equity Smith may well have thought that the natural growth-enhancing properties of commercial society, attention to the education of the poor, and equity in the tax system would largely suffice to establish distributive justice, at least to the extent that he was concerned about it. Intervention to prevent starvation in an emergency I think Smith would condone, but given his conception of a properly functioning grain market, such instances would be rare.

Conclusion

As Viner persuasively argued many years ago, Smith endorsed a wide range of government involvement in the economy, much of which was uncodified and outside the three duties of the sovereign. The complexity and inchoate nature of Smith's treatment continues to generate controversy. In this essay I have attempted to offer a coherent account of Smith's theory of the role of the state, which incorporates not only the three duties but also the specific regulations Smith proposed elsewhere in *WN*. To do so I have identified three interacting policy norms in his moral philosophy: commutative justice, distributive equity, and public utility.

These three interact in different ways depending on the context. In recognition of this I have identified a two-tiered approach in the theories of unintended order and of intervention. The former is Smith's general model; the latter recognizes breakdowns either in the general model or in the existing society. At both levels there is a very close, if not exact, correspondence between the moral philosophy and *WN*. The general model runs throughout, but we can also discern throughout the workings of the theory of intervention. The salient feature of the general model is that commutative justice is both necessary and sufficient to ensure both distributive equity and public utility via the theory of beneficial unintended consequences.

10. It is interesting to note that just as Smith's theory of the spontaneous emergence of justice informs the way he would apply a utilitarian standard to making *ex post* judgments of public utility, his theory of the beneficial unintended results of market processes is used to suggest that market principles and incentives be used wherever possible in the provision of public services. Thus, for example, he advocates a competitive market for religion in preference to a state monopoly church.

In the general model, utility is an unintended consequence. It is a by-product of agents interacting in ordinary life, and it points to the need to establish the system of natural liberty. However, utility is an *ex post* philosophical judgment, not the origin of the fundamental rules of social order. Having established the systematic perspective of the philosopher, we see that it is possible *ex ante* to generate rules, which also promote public utility, but will not emerge spontaneously. Such is the case of the sentinel, and, I have argued, it is the case of market failure. This is the basis of what I have been calling the interventionist track. While the two norms of justice and utility dominate Smith's thought on governmental intervention, he does not lose sight of distributive equity, rooted in the virtue of benevolence, as another policy norm.

There is a fundamental unity and coherence to the whole in that the utilitarian norm of the philosopher, which evaluates systems of law and government, is itself a product of the impartial spectator theory of the general model, as is the benevolence norm of distribution. The dialectical tension between the perspective of ordinary life and that of the philosopher creates a similar tension between laissez-faire and intervention. To use the Boettke-Horwitz (this volume) dichotomy we can also see this as a tension between economist as student and economist as savior. While Smith would certainly be critical of attempts to remake society in the image of some philosophically generated plan, there is no a priori presumption against government intervention in specific cases. As I have shown, these tensions run throughout Smith's works. They carry over into his economics where the pursuit of self-interest frequently, but not always, serves the public interest, and commutative justice may not always guarantee distributive equity. Seeing Smith's program as the varied interaction of three norms along the two tracks gives us a greater appreciation of the complexity of what he was trying to do. In this essay I hope to have given this complexity a greater degree of coherence than has yet appeared in the Smithian literature.

References

Campbell, T. D., and I. S. Ross. 1981. The Utilitarianism of Adam Smith's Policy Advice. *Journal of the History of Ideas* 42:73–92.

Griswold, Charles L., Jr. 1999. *Adam Smith and the Virtues of the Enlightenment*. Cambridge: Cambridge University Press.

Haakonssen, Knud. 1981. *The Science of a Legislator: The Natural Jurisprudence of David Hume and Adam Smith*. Cambridge: Cambridge University Press.

———. 1996. *Natural Law and Moral Philosophy: From Grotius to the Scottish Enlightenment*. Cambridge: Cambridge University Press.

Heilbroner, Robert. 1996. *Teachings from the Worldly Philosophy*. New York: Norton.

Hont, Istvan, and Michael Ignatieff. 1983. Needs and Justice in the *Wealth of Nations*. In *Wealth and Virtue: The Shaping of Political Economy in the Scottish Enlightenment*, edited by Istvan Hont and Michael Ignatieff. Cambridge: Cambridge University Press.

Otteson, James R. 2002. *Adam Smith's Market Place of Life*. Cambridge: Cambridge University Press.

Raphael, D. D. 1972–73. Hume and Adam Smith on Justice and Utility. *Proceedings of the Aristotelian Society*, n.s., 73:87–103.

———. 2001. *Concepts of Justice*. Oxford: Clarendon Press.

Rashid, Salim. 1998. *The Myth of Adam Smith*. Cheltenham, U.K.: Elgar.

Skinner, Andrew S. 1996. *A System of Social Science: Papers relating to Adam Smith*. 2nd ed. Oxford: Clarendon Press.

Smith, Adam. 1976a. *An Inquiry into the Nature and Causes of the Wealth of Nations*. Edited by A. S. Skinner and R. H. Campbell. Oxford: Clarendon Press.

———. 1976b. *The Theory of Moral Sentiments*. Edited by D. D. Raphael and A. L. Macfie. Oxford: Clarendon Press.

———. 1978. *Lectures on Jurisprudence*. Edited by R. L. Meek, D. D. Raphael, and P. G. Stein. Oxford: Clarendon Press.

———. 1980. *Essays on Philosophical Subjects*. Edited by W. P. D. Wightman and J. C. Bryce. Oxford: Clarendon Press.

———. 1987. *The Correspondence of Adam Smith*. Edited by Ian Simpson Ross. Oxford: Clarendon Press.

Stigler, George. 1976. Adam Smith's Travels on the Ship of State. In *Essays on Adam Smith*, edited by Andrew S. Skinner and Thomas Wilson. Oxford: Clarendon Press.

Verburg, Rudi. 2000. Adam Smith's Growing Concern on the Issue of Distributive Justice. *European Journal of the History of Economic Thought* 7.1:23–44.

Viner, Jacob. 1928. Adam Smith and *Laissez Faire*. In *Adam Smith, 1776–1926*, edited by J. M. Clark et al. Chicago: University of Chicago Press.

Vivenza, Gloria. 2001. *Adam Smith and the Classics: The Classical Heritage in Adam Smith's Thought*. Oxford: Oxford University Press.

West, E. G. 1990. *Adam Smith and Modern Economics*. Cheltenham, U.K.: Elgar.

Winch, Donald. 1978. *Adam Smith's Politics: An Essay in Historiographic Revision*. Cambridge: Cambridge University Press.

———. 1983. Science and the Legislator: Adam Smith and After. *Economic Journal* 93 (September): 501–20.

———. 1992. Adam Smith: Scottish Philosopher as Political Economist. *Historical Journal* 35.1:91–113.

———. 1996. *Riches and Poverty: An Intellectual History of Political Economy in Britain, 1750–1834*. Cambridge: Cambridge University Press.

Witztum, Amos. 1997. Distributive Considerations in Adam Smith's Conception of Economic Justice. *Economics and Philosophy* 13:241–59.

Witztum, Amos, and Jeffrey T. Young. 2003. The Neglected Agent: Ethics and Power in Adam Smith. Paper presented at the annual meeting of the History of Economics Society, Duke University, North Carolina, July.

Young, Jeffrey T. 1997. *Economics as a Moral Science*. Cheltenham, U.K.: Elgar.

———. 2001. Justice versus Expediency: The *Wealth of Nations* as an Anti-Political Economy. In *Reflecting on the Canon*, edited by Evelyn Forget and Sandra Peart. London: Routledge.

Young, Jeffrey T., and Barry Gordon. 1996. Distributive Justice as a Normative Criterion in Adam Smith's Political Economy. *HOPE* 28.1:1–26.

The Theory of Economic Policy in British Classical Political Economy: A Sympathetic Reading

David M. Levy and Sandra J. Peart

> How selfish soever man may be supposed, there are evidently some principles in his nature, which interest him in the fortune of others, and render their happiness necessary to him.
>
> —Adam Smith, *Theory of Moral Sentiments* (1759)

> Bentham's followers . . . may have been led by Bentham's incautious use of the phrase ["greatest happiness of the greatest number"] into exaggerating the democratic or isocratic tendencies implicit in *Utilitarianism*.
>
> —F. Y. Edgeworth, *Mathematical Psychics* (1881)

In his 1952 *Theory of Economic Policy in English Classical Political Economy*, Lionel Robbins rightly maintained that the English classical economists were reformers in a utilitarian tradition.[1] To make utilitarianism operational, they needed to specify the weights for individuals' capacities for happiness. Classical economists held that everyone counted as one. And although Robbins (1938) himself accepted that as a *norm*,

An earlier version of this article received helpful comments from Warren Samuels, Richard Wagner, Steve Meardon, Roger Backhouse, and Andrew Farrant. Any mistakes that remain are our responsibility.

1. Although there are later studies of classical economic policy (e.g., Samuels 1966), we focus on Robbins's because his criticism of the scientific status of classical economic policy is a criticism of all economic policy recommendations. "The criterion the English Classical Economists found in the principle of utility, the principle that the test of policy is to be its effect on human happiness. . . . This attitude is common to all the English Classical Economists. We get the picture badly out of focus if we conceive that reliance on the principle of utility was confined to Bentham and his immediate circle" (Robbins 1952, 177–78).

the strictures that he advanced in his *Nature and Significance* against such weights as *science* spoke against the scientific status of classical policy.[2] In this essay, we add one significant element to Robbins's account: we argue that the economic policy of the classical economists constitutes a variation of the theory of exchange.[3] What we find missing in Robbins's discussion is an appreciation of the role of sympathy in the classical economists' theory of economic policy because Robbins supposes that utilitarianism is bereft of appeals to sympathetic motivation. On the contrary, we argue that motivation through a sympathetic process is a vital component of the classical utilitarian tradition that helps both motivate and constrain economic policy as a type of exchange.

Sympathy allows complicated exchanges to proceed through the political process. By restraining individuals from injustice, it allows the well-being of majorities, utilitarianism by counting (Peart and Levy 2005a), to have a semblance of plausibility. Sympathy connects spectators with actors in such a way that spectators might be willing to trade something of theirs to prevent harm to actors. Adam Smith's ([1759] 2004, III.i.46) account of a European without a personal stake in the matter who is willing to give up a little finger to save China is well known. The trade that concerns us was the payment by British taxpayers to make slavery disappear from the empire.

2. "It is a fundamental difficulty of utilitarian ethics that it appears to involve the comparability and summation of the satisfactions of different individuals. . . . the weighting which is given to the satisfactions of different individuals is another element which partakes of the nature of an ethical postulate rather than a principle established by observation or introspection. Among the English utilitarians the assumption was that each man's capacity for happiness to be counted as equal. But it is easily possible to think of other assumptions which might be held to be equally binding" (Robbins 1952, 180). F. Y. Edgeworth's hedonic calculus made Robbins uneasy (Robbins 1938; Peart and Levy 2005c). Edgeworth's consideration of people with such a low capacity for happiness that their total happiness might integrate out as zero or even negative is discussed in Peart and Levy 2004. His eugenic conclusion is blocked by the "weak" Pareto principle that, as Robbins (1981) recognized, is not a value-free foundation for economics.

3. "I had not thought it necessary to observe that, in speaking of exchanges, I did not mean to limit myself to *voluntary* exchanges;—those in which the whole transaction takes place with the full consent of both parties to all the terms of it. Most exchanges, indeed, are of this character; but the case of taxation,—the revenue levied from the subject in return for the protection afforded by the sovereign, constitutes a remarkable exception; the payment being compulsory, and not adjusted by agreement with the payer. Still, whether in any case it be *fairly* and reasonably adjusted, or the contrary, it is not the less an exchange. And it is worth remarking, that it is just so far forth as it is an exchange,—so far forth as protection, whether adequate or not, is afforded in exchange for this payment,—that the payment itself comes under the cognizance of this science. There is nothing else that distinguishes *taxation* from *avowed robbery*" (Whately [1831] 2002, lecture 1, n. 5).

To make our assertion that later classical economists see reforms as akin to sympathetic exchanges, we need to provide evidence at the outset that sympathy was viewed as important by the later classical economists in the utilitarian tradition. In *Utilitarianism* John Stuart Mill claimed that education and "a complete web of corroborative association" serve to extend sympathy. In the process of a moral education, the well-being of others becomes akin to the "physical conditions of our existence":

> Not only does all strengthening of social ties, and all healthy growth of society, give to each individual a stronger personal interest in practically consulting the welfare of others; it also leads him to identify his *feelings* more and more with their good, or at least with an even greater degree of practical consideration for it. He comes, as though instinctively, to be conscious of himself as a being who *of course* pays regard to others. The good of others becomes to him a thing naturally and necessarily to be attended to, like any of the physical conditions of our existence. (Mill [1861] 1969, 231)

Mill's phrase, "the contagion of sympathy," locates his notion of sympathy in a tradition older than Smith's, one that emphasizes the unreflective, automatic aspects of sympathy:[4] "Consequently the smallest germs of the feeling are laid hold of and nourished by the contagion of sympathy and the influences of education; and a complete web of corroborative association is woven round it, by the powerful agency of the external sanctions" (232).

In our understanding, the 1833 Act of Emancipation is an important example because Mill viewed it as the paradigm of reform. As such, we begin with a discussion of the exchange that abolished slavery. As Robbins does not discuss the role of economists in the antislavery movement, we quote some unfamiliar texts at length.[5]

4. The difference between Hume's and Smith's treatment is discussed in Levy and Peart 2004 and Fleischaker 2004. Fleischaker's use of "contagion" to describe Hume's sympathetic machinery to distinguish it from Smith's "projection" machinery is most helpful.

5. The topic of antislavery seems absent from Robbins's book on Robert Torrens, as Buxton's name is not found, although Wakefield's position on slavery and colonial development is discussed at some length (Robbins 1958, 155–60). Torrens's role in the antislavery debates is featured in the new specialist account of the debates leading up to emancipation. Here is an instance both of the importance of sympathetic compensation and of the race-neutral procedure of classical economists for which we have argued elsewhere (Peart and Levy 2005b): "Torrens drew his [evidence] from the new experiments in colonization by Britons in the South Pacific. He asked the House of Commons to base its expectations on the actual behavior of 'men

Second, if policy is viewed as exchange, then the notion of a quid pro quo is obvious. As Richard Whately says, one trades taxes for protection against murder and theft.[6] He left unsaid that the governmental protection agency would insist that the taxpayer contribute to the cause by, say, putting valuables inside the house and not on the lawn. We consider how the classical analysis of poor relief relies upon the quid pro quo of sumptuary controls in exchange for protection against extreme destitution.

Third, if policy is an act of exchange, then one might insist upon having a representative at the table when deals are done. Thus, political representation would be an important component of an economic theory of policy. In our third section, we provide testimony for the importance of political representation in Mill.[7] Mill was a member of Parliament during the Eyre controversy and the Fenian violence, and Mill was often caricatured in *Punch* during these years. As far as we can see, the only policy issue given visual form is that of political representation.

Finally, we close with the natural question. What happened to the view of politics as exchange? We have argued elsewhere that sympathy collided with the theological interpretation of natural selection (Peart and Levy 2003a, 2004). Although W. H. Hutt revived politics as exchange in his 1943 *Plan for Reconstruction*, the idea was not recognized until decades later. Hutt drew upon a tradition, lost to the rest of the profession, of sympathy and the well-being of majorities, to explain what

---

of the British race,' already placed in circumstances quite similar to those in which Buxton contended, freed Africans would work for wages. On any frontier, Englishmen 'immediately ceased to work for wages' and sought to cultivate on their own" (Drescher 2002, 134). In the 1840 *Prospectus of the Society for the Extinction of the Slave Trade*, we find the name "Colonel Torrens" as a member of the "Provisional Committee" (Buxton [1840] 1968, 13). Torrens also appears in the *Anti-Slavery Reporter*'s list of the famous who gathered at the great Exeter Hall meeting in preparation for the final push for passage of the Act of Emancipation.

6. "Many are apt to think Taxes quite a different kind of expense from all others, and either do not know, or else forget, that they receive any thing in *exchange* for the Taxes. But, in reality, this payment is as much an exchange as any other. You pay money to the baker and butcher for feeding you, and to the tailor for clothing you; and you pay the King and Parliament for protecting you from being plundered, murdered, or cheated. Were it not for this, you could be employed scarcely half your time in providing food and clothing, and the other half would be taken up in guarding against being robbed of them; or in working for some other man, whom you would hire to keep watch and to fight for you. This would cost you much more than you pay in Taxes" (Whately 1833, 66–67).

7. We have elsewhere (Peart and Levy 2003b) discussed how J. E. Cairnes emphasized the importance of the political representation of the freed American slaves as a way to ensure their interests were protected; and how Mill in *Representative Government* viewed a minimal amount of sympathy as a necessary condition for a representative form of government (Peart and Levy 2005a).

he called "consumer sovereignty."[8] In the collision with the theology of natural selection, utilitarianism lost its majoritarian interpretation. Perhaps the last great economic theorist who saw the majoritarianism in utilitarianism, if only to oppose it in service to Darwinian science, was F. Y. Edgeworth.[9]

Abolishing Slavery by Exchange

We have noticed that Richard Whately viewed taxation as an exchange for the government enforcement of justice. The text we quoted from (see note 6) is titled *Easy Lessons on Money Matters; For the Use of Young People* (1833). In the instance Whately considers, protection from violence, the resources provided for taxation more than pay for themselves in terms of output gained. This is indeed an easy problem.

Now let us consider how he addressed a hard problem where the policy is costly in the sense that it is not self-financing. This we view as a signature of a sympathetic exchange, what we might say reveals a willingness "to do the right thing" even if one receives nothing in return for doing so. On 28 February 1833 Whately, then archbishop of Dublin, wrote a letter to the Anti-Slavery Society in which he considered how to get rid of slavery. As this has not been widely discussed, we quote large extracts with references to the account given by Seymour Drescher in his *Mighty Experiment: Free Labor versus Slavery in British Emancipation*.

Whately begins with a moral claim and the illusion of freedom from culpability of those who are not slave owners:

> I perfectly concur with you in thinking the existence of slavery in our empire a national sin, and that justice demands, therefore, that we

8. "Because the moral principle of 'sympathy for the greater number at the expense of sympathy for the lesser number' formed the essence of their teaching, the Utilitarian economists have, moreover, been brought into a permanent clash with reformers and philanthropists. For the latter are commonly aware of and moved by the interests of the few only with whom they are in direct contact" (Hutt 1936b, 131–32). Hutt's shaky command of the texts was noted by Viner (1938), who missed Hutt's insight into the majoritarian aspect of the utilitarian tradition that may well have come via Graham Wallas (e.g., 1898). Testimony from Malthus ([1798] 2004, XVI.1) shows that Smith was read by his contemporaries as a majoritarian.

9. "Bentham's followers . . . may have been led by Bentham's incautious use of the phrase ["greatest happiness of the greatest number"] into exaggerating that democratic or isocratic tendencies implicit in *Utilitarianism*" (Edgeworth 1881, 117). Robbins's strictures in *Nature and Significance* block the scientific status of Edgeworth's appeal to differential capacity for happiness and prepare the way for the Paretian interpretation of utilitarianism (Peart and Levy 2005c).

should be ready to bear our fair proportion of the evils consequent upon it.

Though this, however, is the case *really*, the persons most closely connected with the sinful act will often *appear* the chief or the sole perpetrators. One who has planned, for instance, and authorised a murder, will often fancy himself innocent, compared with him whose hands were actually imbrued with blood. (E. J. Whately 1866, 183)

Drescher (2002, 108) reports discussions of the importance of habitual behavior. Whately stresses this at the outset: "Most of those who swell the cry for immediate emancipation are ignorant of the chief evil of slavery—viz., its making and keeping the slave unfit for freedom, by completely separating in his mind the two ideas habitually associated in the minds of free labourers, properly so called (not parish paupers), of labour and maintenance" (E. J. Whately 1866, 184).

As is common in classical economics, Whately appeals to proverbial wisdom (Peart and Levy 2005b): "The greatest of the ancient moralists lays it down, that a man is *naturally* a slave as long, and *only* as long, as he is unfit for freedom,—*i.e.*, incapable of taking care of himself, and requiring to be guided like a child."[10] Then Whately refers to his teaching on fallacies from *Logic* (1827, 145–56), in which he explains how difficult it is to separate inference from desire: "Unhappily for the *application* of this excellent principle, the person who alone is well qualified both to *know* when a slave is fit for freedom, and to train him to that fitness, is the very person who is interested in keeping him as slave" (E. J. Whately 1866, 184).

Leaping a century ahead to discussions of self-assessed taxation, Whately proposes a truth-revealing process:

If any way can be devised which can make it the *master's* interest to free his slaves, that, it appears to me, and that alone, will solve the difficulty. And the only way I can conceive in which this can be effected is, to take off a portion of the duties on colonial produce, to be replaced by an equivalent tax on slaves; that the tax to be *ad valorem*, the price of each slave to be fixed by the *master*, and each slave to be redeemable at the price fixed. (184)

10. W. H. Hutt—who introduced the term *consumer sovereignty*—tells us how it came to be: "I am not sure whether I coined the term myself. Marketing literature contains phrases like 'the customer is always right,' and I am told that a proverbial expression in High Dutch is 'De klant is koing' (the customer is king)" (1940, 66).

One can trust homeowners to truthfully assess their own home's value for tax purposes—"Why my tiny Georgetown town house couldn't possibly be worth more than $5,000!"—if and only if that assessment is an offer to sell: "Oh, never mind."

> Thus the slaves best *qualified* to become independent labourers for wages, being the most costly, would be those the master would, for his own interest, be the most anxious to set free; and it is probable he would be ready himself to *lend* such a slave the price of his freedom, allowing him to *work out* the debt at a stipulated rate of wages. Such an intermediate state between slavery and freedom would, I think, prove the best preparatory to an independence advantageous to both parties. (185)

A test for sympathetic compensation is whether the reform would be self-financing in any short time horizon. If it were, then there might as well be only two parties to the transaction. For Whately, it was clear that emancipation will not be self-financing:

> Of course, in proportion as this plan succeeded, the revenue from the West Indian Islands would for the present diminish. This I would reckon as one of its advantages, as relief would thus be afforded to a class peculiarly in need of it. And if the English people grudged a trifling and temporary defalcation of revenue for the accomplishment of such an object as the gradual extinction of slavery, in the only way in which it can be effected without cruelty to the negroes themselves, it is plain their clamour in the cause of humanity must be the grossest hypocrisy. (185)

Thus, the compensation to be paid in exchange for freedom was from the spectator/consumer who benefited from slavery past. The slave was not supposed to provide compensation for his freedom. The emancipation would not be self-financing.

Thomas Fowell Buxton was the parliamentary wizard who, as floor manager later in the year, negotiated the Act of Emancipation for William Wilberforce and the antislavery movement. As such, Buxton crafted the complicated compensation package that ended imperial slavery (Drescher 2002). In *The African Slave Trade and Its Remedy*, Buxton ([1839] 1968, 11–12) found the sympathetic compensation embodied there, a "sublime" act by the "disinterested":

> One noble sacrifice in behalf of the negro race has already been made. In the words of the most eloquent citizen of another nation [Dr. Channing]—"Great Britain, loaded with an unprecedented debt, and with a grinding taxation, contracted a new debt of a hundred million dollars, to give freedom, not to Englishmen, but to the degraded African. I know not that history records an act so disinterested, so sublime. In the progress of ages England's naval triumphs will shrink into a more and more narrow space in the records of our race. This moral triumph will fill a broader, brighter page."

This principle would later become embodied in John Stuart Mill's *Principles* as the doctrine of compensation for reform. In Mill's statement of the principle of compensation, the paradigm was the 1833 Act of Emancipation, "whether the object be education; a more efficient and accessible administration of justice; reforms of any kind which, like the Slave Emancipation, require compensation to individual interests" ([1848] 2004, bk. 5, chap. VI, sec. V.6.2).

The obvious question, to which we have no answer, is whether Whately's views on the matter had an impact on the discussions in Wilberforce's circle.

Poor Laws

Protection against violence is not the only protection discussed in the period. Protection against the vagaries of life in a commercial society is much discussed by Robbins. A defining characteristic of a sympathetic agent is a willingness to share. The natural policies one might expect from sympathetic agents would be akin to what we would call a "safety net."[11] We glance at the discussion of poor relief in British economics with an eye toward conditionality. What sort of responsibilities do those asking for assistance bear? If policy is an exchange, each party has to expect to give up something in order to get something else. Without giving up something valuable, there is no exchange; the policy is a gift. What the taxpayers give up is easy enough. Perhaps their rewards are sympathetic; perhaps not. Our authorities have different views on that matter. What is the person who applies for charity expected to give up?

11. Thus, Hutt's *Plan for Reconstruction* (1943, 8) begins with the safety net: "The Board shall, with the advice and assistance of the Trustee, determine a guaranteed minimum income for every person from whom a form . . . is received."

The idea that a minimum existence, a protection against extreme distress, can be guaranteed, occurred to Thomas Robert Malthus in the paragraph immediately following his 1798 argument that the poor laws of Britain had the perverse consequences of helping create the poor that they maintained. One could, however, solve this unintended consequence by attaching conditions:

> Lastly, for cases of extreme distress, county workhouses might be established, supported by rates upon the whole kingdom, and free for persons of all counties, and indeed of all nations. The fare should be hard, and those that were able obliged to work. It would be desirable that they should not be considered as comfortable asylums in all difficulties; but merely as places where severe distress might find some alleviation. A part of these houses might be separated, or others built for a most beneficial purpose, which has not been infrequently taken notice of, that of providing a place, where any person, whether native or foreigner, might do a day's work at all times and receive the market price for it. Many cases would undoubtedly be left for the exertion of individual benevolence. (Malthus [1798] 2004, V.25)

When Nassau W. Senior reviewed European experience with the safety net, he paid close attention to these conditions. What were the terms of trade?

> We have now given a very brief outline of the institutions of those portions of the Continent which appear, from the returns, to have adopted the English principle of acknowledging in every person a right to be supported by the public. It will be observed that in no country, except, perhaps, the Canton de Berne, has compulsory relief produced evils resembling, either in intensity or in extent, those which we have experienced; and that in the majority of the nations which have adopted it, the existing system appears to work well. (Senior 1835, 84)

There are several cases to consider that are not germane to the existing British situation. First, there are quasi-slave societies:[12]

12. Senior (1841, 2:46–47) would later argue that the old poor law of England was an attempt by the masters to reintroduce a system akin to slavery: "We believe that the English poor laws originated in selfishness, ignorance, and pride. Better motives, without doubt, though misdirected by almost equal ignorance, dictated the changes which were made in the laws during the eighteenth century—the fourth which elapsed from their commencement; but we are convinced that the origin was an attempt substantially to restore the expiring system of slavery." This view of older policy is akin to that of Smith ([1776] 2004, III.iv.10): "All for ourselves

> Among some of the nations in question villenage still exists. Now where slavery, in any of its forms, prevails, the right of the slave or villein to support is a necessary and a safe consequence. I[t] is necessary, because a person who is not a free agent cannot provide for himself. It is safe, because one of the principal evils of pauperism, improvidence, can scarcely exist among slaves. (84)

Second, there are countries in which the compulsory system has just started (84–85). Third, there are countries where people would lose a good deal, either in property or in social standing by applying for public relief (85–87).

Then Senior turns to the remaining cases, which are comparable. There is no cost of applying for public assistance in Britain:

> But the conditions on which parochial assistance is afforded in the countries in question, form perhaps the principal difference between their systems and that which we have adopted. In England, where the scale and allowance system prevail, no condition whatever can be said to be imposed on the pauper. What he receives is a mere gratuitous addition to his income. Even where work is required, the hours are in general fewer, and the labour less severe than those of the independent labourer. And the workhouse, the most powerful of our instruments of repression, affords, in general, food, lodging, clothing, and warmth, better than can be found in the cottage, *and may be quitted at a day's notice*. (87–88)

On the Continent, by contrast, there is a real cost of being a pauper, so this is an exchange: "But in all the countries which we have been considering, except the Canton de Berne and perhaps Denmark, the great object of pauper legislation, that of the rendering the situation of the pauper less agreeable than that of the independent labourer, has been effectually attained" (88). Senior then reviews the various conditions that different countries attach to the right of assistance, such as restrictions on marriage and the like (88–94).

Famously, when Mill reviewed Harriet Martineau's *Illustrations of Political Economy*, he found only "one point of importance" with which to differ. Her work on population was behind the times: "The recent investigation of the poor-law commission, with which Miss Martineau is

and nothing for other people, seems, in every age of the world, to have been the vile maxim of the masters of mankind."

familiar, seem to us as conclusive in support of the *principle* of a poor-rate, as they are in condemnation of the existing practice" (Mill [1834] 1967, 227–28).

A View from *Punch*

We have discussed elsewhere how *Punch* opposed the classical economists' views of human homogeneity during the 1850s and 1860s (Peart and Levy 2005b).[13] There were many issues upon which *Punch* took issue with Mill. The verse, "A Fenian on His Friends," printed 7 March 1868, blames the Fenian violence on Mill's support of the former slaves in Jamaica in his failed attempt to bring Governor Eyre to justice.[14] Racial cartoons are impossible to miss in *Punch* at the time. Images refer to Mill's *On Liberty*, *Logic*, and *Political Economy*. He is often pictured in the company of John Bright. Nonetheless, we have not found a single one in which Mill is pictured in a racial context.

When there is a political issue pictured in association with Mill, it invariably concerns the extension of the franchise. If policy were viewed as an act of exchange, then political representation would be required to protect one's interests.[15] This suggests that, from the point of view of a well-informed opposition, what is most important about Mill's policy is the extension of the franchise.

The role of sympathy in self-government is explained in Mill's *Representative Government*. Mutual sympathy plays a critical role in the argument, being a necessary condition for representative self-government.[16]

13. While the race-neutral accounts in Adam Smith and John Stuart Mill are clear, the position of Senior is debated. This statement from his *Outline of the Science of Political Economy* suggests that he is in line with Smith and Mill: "Almost all the differences between the different races of men, differences so great that we sometimes nearly forget that they all belong to the same species, may be traced to the degree in which they enjoy the blessings of good government" (Senior [1836] 1938, 76). Here is his application of that principle to poor-law reform: "The able-bodied pauper is the result of art; he is not the natural offspring of the Saxon race" (Senior [1841] 1865, 2:98).

14. Mill's statement of the role of sympathy in the enforcement of justice in *Utilitarianism* ought to be read as the explanation for his actions as the head of the Jamaica Committee. Packe's discussion (1954, 470–71) is unhelpful. Robbins's (1957) unhappiness with Packe is well merited.

15. James Mill's ([1820] 1978, 79) view of virtual representation—the interests of a woman being represented by the men in her life—was criticized by Macaulay ([1829] 1978, 116) four decades before.

16. "Among a people without fellow-feeling, especially if they read and speak different languages, the united public opinion, necessary to the working of representative government, cannot exist" (Mill [1861] 1977, 547).

As a source of moral obligation, sympathy constrains people and forms a barrier to injustice (Mill [1861] 1977, 547). Mutual sympathy creates the boundaries of successful association.[17] Government must take people "as they are," but some sympathy with others is requisite for representative government.[18] Competition and a sufficient number of disinterested sympathetic individuals to influence the election will prevent factional injustice.[19]

As evidence of how well *Punch* was informed on these matters, it provided testimony that a test for representation was the efficacy of sympathetic motivation, the ability to cooperate: "One of the reasons, Mr. Mill, why the working classes ought to have the elective franchise, is said to be the capacity which they evince for organization" (8 April 1867, 144).

Figures 1–8 are the images of Mill that we have found in *Punch*. We reproduce sections of the caricatures that feature Mill.[20] Figure 1 (10 February 1866) has Mill, the author of *On Liberty*, with the dancing bear of reform, John Bright, on a chain.[21] Figure 2 (2 February 1867) is a double page imagining of the parliamentary debaters as gladiators. It shows Mill again, but now with *Logic* in conjunction with Bright as the great adversaries of aristocracy. Figure 3 (16 February 1867) shows Mill and Bright now in the role of seconds in the debates to come. Figure 4 (30 March 1867) reacts to Mill's proposal to make men and women equal persons in the eyes of the law. It now gives Mill a cartoon of his own.

17. "To render a federation advisable, several conditions are necessary. The first is, that there should be a sufficient amount of mutual sympathy among the populations. The federation binds them always to fight on the same side" (Mill [1861] 1977, 553).

18. "Governments must be made for human beings as they are, or as they are capable of speedily becoming: and in any state of cultivation which mankind, or any class among them, have yet attained, or are likely soon to attain, the interests by which they will be led, when they are thinking only of self-interest, will be almost exclusively those which are obvious at first sight, and which operate on their present condition. It is only a disinterested regard for others, and especially for what comes after them, for the idea of posterity, of their country, or of mankind, whether grounded on sympathy or on a conscientious feeling, which ever directs the minds and purposes of classes or bodies of men towards distant or unobvious interests" (Mill [1861] 1977, 445).

19. "The reason why, in any tolerably constituted society, justice and the general interest mostly in the end carry their point, is that the separate and selfish interests of mankind are almost always divided; some are interested in what is wrong, but some, also, have their private interest on the side of what is right: and those who are governed by higher considerations, though too few and weak to prevail against the whole of the others, usually after sufficient discussion and agitation become strong enough to turn the balance in favour of the body of private interests which is on the same side with them. The representative system ought to be so constituted as to maintain this state of things" (Mill [1861] 1977, 447).

20. The full versions are available in digital form from the authors on request.

21. We owe the "dancing bear" reading to Andrew Farrant.

Figure 1 *Punch*, 10 February 1866

Continuing the theme on 1 June 1867, figure 5 remarks on the defeat of Mill's proposal with another such cartoon. Figure 6, the two-page plate of 15 July 1867, marking the triumph of the reform bill, deserves to be reproduced in full because even in this small scale, we can appreciate Mill's central role in the reform. (See detail in figure 7.) Here is the image of Mill himself. Figure 8 (21 March 1868) shows the author of *Political Economy* with a new baby in his arms.

Hutt's Politics as Exchange

When James Buchanan revived the theory of politics as exchange, he proceeded from Knut Wicksell's nineteenth-century work. As far as Buchanan recognized, there was nothing in the English-language discussion that made this suggestion. Hutt's descent to obscurity explains why it was not until 1988 that the 1943 *Plan for Reconstruction* was recognized as in the politics as gains from trade tradition (Buchanan 1988).[22]

22. Buchanan notes that F. A. Hayek called his attention to Hutt's connection with Buchanan's larger project (Buchanan 1988, 135–52).

Figure 2 *Punch*, 2 February 1867

Figure 3 *Punch*, 16 February 1867

MILL'S LOGIC; OR, FRANCHISE FOR FEMALES.

"PRAY CLEAR THE WAY, THERE, FOR THESE—A—PERSONS."

Figure 4 *Punch*, 30 March 1867

There are several components to democratic politics as exchange framework. First, one must suppose something akin to competition inside the political process. Second, one must have a way to deal with the possibility of majoritarian taking. We argue elsewhere that the classics supposed sufficient sympathy (Peart and Levy 2005a); the modern Rawls-Buchanan approach supposes the constraint of impartiality at the constitutional level. It is not clear whether these approaches are fundamentally different, although one emphasizes imagination across people and the other emphasizes imagination across time.[23] Third, one must be comfortable with the outcome of a majority-rule process. Here Buchanan and Tullock (1962) are clearly not, since majority rule is only

23. "The cosmopolitanism of the early orthodox writers is in itself evidence of a certain scientific aloofness; for whilst it might be unjust to regard nationalism as springing from the struggle for political and economic power and prestige, the universal exploitation of the national and racial feeling in the cause of vested interests are clearly responsible for the repulsion which the economist felt towards the expression of nationalistic aspirations" (Hutt 1936b, 56). "The 'bloated capitalist' with his cigar and diamond rings, or the 'sweater' with foreign or Semitic features, were essential creations" (59).

one of many decisions rules that might be selected at the constitutional stage.[24]

Hutt's larger work, in particular his disagreement with Joan Robinson about the efficiency of price discrimination, is revealing in this context. Robinson's defense of discrimination depends upon the utilitarian tradition in which one counts units of utility, and not people being helped or harmed. This is siding with Edgeworth against Spencer and the classical utilitarians (Peart and Levy 2005b). Robinson developed Edgeworth's mean-utilitarianism via A. C. Pigou, for whom an income transfer from producer to consumer is of no social consequence.

Hutt proposes to reformulate welfare judgments based on the well-being of consumers, who are of course the *majority* in any choice. Consumer sovereignty was intended by Hutt to continue the tradition of the classical economists, to make explicit what they took for granted. For Hutt (1936b, 130), this tradition explains their unpopularity:

> It cannot be denied that if economists had confined themselves to the purely formal or logical side of their science they would have been less unpopular in society. But all along, orthodox writers in this field have, in fact, been concerned with "the general good" or "the social welfare." They have been constantly stressing the opposition between social advantage and the benefits accruing to particular individuals or particular groups.

So what is this "general good"?

> There was nothing subtle about the notion in the economists' minds. It was pure common sense to them. They knew that a tariff on corn would benefit farmers but spread a diffused burden on consumers. There was nothing question-begging about it. The notion of the conflict of interest had been understood by several eighteenth-century pamphleteers and economists. They regarded it in terms of the opposition between organized groups and the community as consumers. It

24. Hutt's review of *Calculus of Consent* is wonderfully interesting in this regard. "It is at the 'operational' level, however (in the process of legislating within the limits of the constitution), that it may be the most important to prevent blocking by minorities. But if the constitution (a) forbids discrimination *except after some form of unanimous consent* . . . and (b) enshrines the principle of compensation (when legislation—assumed to be for the common gain—harms the few in favouring the many), there seems to be no other surviving purpose for the unanimity principle at the 'operational' level. Given the entrenchment of these two qualifying rules, it seems to us that simple majority decisions would be acceptable" (Hutt [1966] 1975, 28). We owe our knowledge of this review to Richard Wagner.

THE LADIES' ADVOCATE.

MRS. BULL. "LOR, MR. MILL! WHAT A LOVELY SPEECH YOU *DID* MAKE. I DO DECLARE I HADN'T THE SLIGHTEST NOTION WE WERE SUCH MISERABLE CREATURES. NO ONE CAN SAY IT WAS *YOUR* FAULT THAT THE CASE BROKE DOWN."

Figure 5 *Punch*, 1 June 1867

Figure 6 *Punch*, 15 July 1867

Figure 7 *Punch*, 15 July 1867 (detail)

Figure 8 *Punch*, 21 March 1868

was reflected in the attacks of Turgot and his contemporaries on "the spirit of monopoly," it was stated forcibly by Tucker, it was found in the *Wealth of Nations*, it was implied in subsequent economic writings, and it again crystalized clearly in the mind of Ricardo, who held that the consumers' interests should be paramount. (130–31)

To see the difference between median- and mean-based utilitarianism, consider the now-familiar argument that perfect price discrimination and competition are equally efficient. This supposes that a transfer from consumer to producer is of no social concern. But what if one regards an income transfer from one person to another as injustice? Hutt is perhaps the last exemplar of median-based utilitarianism who makes a social decision by counting those helped and those harmed; the many consumers or the few producers:

The existence of most of the differential charging that we find is based either (in the short run) on the exploitation of co-operant producers

> possessing immobile resources; or else (in the long run) at the consumers' expense through bringing about an unfavourable distribution of investment of productive resources. It is an arbitrary private benefit that is obtained from discrimination in the majority of classes. There are no grounds for assuming that produces an ideal distribution of investment adjusted to the existence of different scales of preferences on the part of consumers. It represents a pricing system developed in the interests of private profit and based mainly on chance facts arising out of the relations of many co-operating agents in the productive process. (1936a, 77–78)[25]

Hutt (1936b, 131) asserts that this insistence on distinguishing the interests of the few from the interests of the many caused the great attacks on classical economics:

> We need to look no further than this for the causes of that attitude of mind which has so early seized on Carlyle's condemnation of economics as "the dismal science"; which enabled Kingsley's unscrupulous caricature of an economist [*Alton Locke*, chap. 10] to be accepted as authentic by the public opinion of his day; which led Napoleon to say that if an empire were built of granite, political economy would grind it to powder; which has led to that general dislike and misrepresentation of the Classical economists lasting right down to the present day. "No real Englishman," said Bagehot, "in his secret soul was ever sorry for the death of an economist."[26]

Hutt knew much that has been lost.

25. Thus in Hutt's *Plan for Reconstruction*, price discrimination was outlawed except in the Joan Robinson case where the commodity would not exist at all without discrimination (Hutt 1943, 34–39).

26. So much is right with this paragraph—the Jewish "sweaters" that Hutt has mentioned are featured in *Alton Locke* (Levy 2001; Peart and Levy 2005b). But the line from Bagehot is misquoted. It reads: "No real English gentleman, in his secret soul, was ever sorry for the death of a political economist: he is much more likely to be sorry for his life" (Bagehot 1858, 22). "English gentleman" is more to Hutt's point than the "Englishman" that Hutt misremembered.

References

Bagehot, Walter. 1858. *Estimates of Englishmen and Scotchmen*. London: Chapman and Hall.

Buchanan, James M. 1988. Economists and the Gains-from-Trade. In vol. 19 of *The Collected Works of James M. Buchanan*. Indianapolis, Ind.: Liberty Fund.

Buchanan, James M., and Gordon Tullock. 1962. *The Calculus of Consent*. Ann Arbor: University of Michigan Press.

Buxton, Thomas Fowell. [1839] 1968. *The African Slave Trade and Its Remedy*. London: Dawsons of Pall Mall.

———. [1840] 1968. *Prospectus of the Society for the Extinction of the Slave Trade and of the Civilization of Africa*. London: Dawsons of Pall Mall.

Drescher, Seymour. 2002. *The Mighty Experiment: Free Labor versus Slavery in British Emancipation*. Oxford: Oxford University Press.

Edgeworth, F. Y. 1881. *Mathematical Psychics*. London: Kegan Paul.

Fleischaker, Samuel. 2004. Hume and Smith on Sympathy. Paper presented at the Summer Institute for the Preservation of the History of Economics, George Mason University, Virginia, July.

Hutt, W. H. 1936a. Discriminating Monopoly and the Consumer. *Economic Journal* 46 (March): 61–79.

———. 1936b. *Economists and the Public*. London: Cape.

———. 1940. The Concept of Consumers' Sovereignty. *Economic Journal* 50 (March): 66–77.

———. 1943. *Plan for Reconstruction: A Project for Victory in War and Peace*. London: Kegan Paul, Trench, Trubner, & Co.

———. [1966] 1975. Unanimity versus Non-discrimination (as Criteria for Constitutional Validity). In *Individual Freedom: Selected Writings of William H. Hutt*, edited by Svetozar Pejovich and David Klingaman. Westport, Conn.: Greenwood.

Levy, David M. 2001. *How the Dismal Science Got Its Name: Classical Economics and the Ur-Text of Racial Politics*. Ann Arbor: University of Michigan Press.

Levy, David M., and Sandra J. Peart. 2004. Sympathy and Approbation in Hume and Smith: A Solution to the Other Rational Species Problem. *Economics and Philosophy* 20:331–49.

Macaulay, T. B. [1829] 1978. *Mill's Essay on Government: Utilitarian Logic and Politics*. In *Utilitarian Logic and Politics*, edited by Jack Lively and John Rees. Oxford: Clarendon Press.

Malthus, T. R. [1798] 2004. *An Essay on the Principle of Population, As It Affects the Future Improvement of Society, with Remarks on the Speculations of Mr. Godwin, M. Condorcet, and Other Writers*. 1st ed. http://www.econlib.org/library/Malthus/malPop.html.

Mill, James. [1820] 1978. *On Government*. In *Utilitarian Logic and Politics*, edited by Jack Lively and John Rees. Oxford: Clarendon Press.

Mill, John Stuart. [1834] 1967. Miss Martineau's Summary of Political Economy. *In Essays on Economics and Society*, vol. 4 of *Collected Works*, edited by John M. Robson. Toronto: University of Toronto Press.

———. [1861] 1969. *Utilitarianism*. In vol. 10 of *Collected Works*, edited by John M. Robson. Toronto: University of Toronto Press.

———. [1861] 1977. *Considerations on Representative Government*. In vol. 19 of *Collected Works*, edited by John M. Robson. Toronto: University of Toronto Press.

———. [1848] 2004. *The Principles of Political Economy with Some of Their Applications to Social Philosophy*. 7th ed. Edited by William J. Ashley. http://www.econlib.org/library/Mill/mlP.html.

Packe, Michael St. John. 1954. *The Life of John Stuart Mill*. New York: Macmillan.

Peart, Sandra J., and David M. Levy. 2003a. Denying Human Homogeneity: Eugenics and the Making of Post-classical Economics. *Journal of the History of Economic Thought* 25.3:261–88.

———. 2003b. Post-Ricardian Political Economy, 1830–1870. In *The Blackwell Companion to the History of Economic Thought*, edited by Warren J. Samuels, John Davis, and Jeff Biddle. Oxford: Blackwell.

———. 2004. Sympathy and Its Discontents: "Greatest Happiness" versus "General Good." *European Journal of History of Economic Thought* 11.3:453–78.

———. 2005a. A Discipline without Sympathy: The Happiness of the Majority and Its Demise. *Canadian Journal of Economics* 38.3:937–54.

———. 2005b. *The "Vanity of the Philosopher": From Equality to Hierarchy in Post-classical Economics*. Ann Arbor: University of Michigan Press.

———. 2005c. From Cardinal to Ordinal Utility Theory: Darwin and Human Capacity for Happiness. *American Journal of Economics and Sociology* 64.3.

Robbins, Lionel. 1938. Interpersonal Comparisons of Utility: A Comment. *Economic Journal* 48 (December): 635–41.

———. 1952. *Theory of Economic Policy in English Classical Political Economy*. London: Macmillan.

———. 1957. Packe on Mill. *Economica*, n.s., 24 (August): 250–59.

———. 1958. *Robert Torrens and the Evolution of Classical Economics*. London: Macmillan.

———. 1981. Economics and Political Economy. *American Economic Review* 71 (May): 1–10.

Samuels, Warren J. 1966. *The Classical Theory of Economic Policy*. Cleveland: World.

Senior, Nassau W. 1835. *Statement of the Provision of the Poor*. London: B. Fellows.

———. [1841] 1865. English Poor Laws. In *Historical and Philosophical Essays*. London: Longman, Green, Longman, Roberts & Green.

———. [1836] 1938. *An Outline of the Science of Political Economy*. London: Allen & Unwin.

Smith, Adam. [1759] 2004. *The Theory of Moral Sentiments*. 6th ed. http://www.econlib.org/library/Smith/smMS.html.

———. [1776] 2004. *An Inquiry into the Nature and Causes of the Wealth of Nations*. 5th ed. Edited by Edwin Cannan. http://www.econlib.org/library/Smith/smWN.html.

Viner, Jacob. 1938. Review of *Economists and the Public: A Study of Competition and Opinion*. *Journal of Political Economy* 46.4:571–75.

Wallas, Graham. 1898. *The Life of Francis Place: 1771–1854*. London: Longmans, Green.

Whately, E. J. 1866. *Life and Correspondence of Richard Whately, D.D.* London: Longmans, Green.

Whately, Richard. 1833. *Easy Lessons on Money Matters; For the Use of Young People*. London: Parker.

———. [1827] 1975. *Elements of Logic*. 2nd ed. Delmar, N.Y.: Scholars' Facsimiles & Reprints.

———. [1831] 2002. *Introductory Lectures on Political Economy*. 2nd ed. http://www.econlib.org/library/Whately/whtPE.html.

Part 2

Aspects of the American Experience

How TRIPs Got Legs: Copyright, Trade Policy, and the Role of Government in Nineteenth-Century American Economic Thought

Stephen Meardon

The cause of free trade was advanced successfully in Britain to achieve the repeal of the Corn Laws in 1846, the removal of other tariffs in Gladstone's budget of 1853, and the Cobden-Chevalier treaty of 1860. It was advanced much less successfully in postbellum America, where protection reigned until 1913. The cause is advanced today in the Doha-round negotiations of the World Trade Organization (WTO) and, in the Western Hemisphere, in the proposed Free Trade Area of the Americas (FTAA) and several subregional and bilateral preferential trade agreements. Or is it not?

The WTO and FTAA negotiations have stalled repeatedly—and spectacularly at the failed Cancún WTO talks of September 2003, if less conspicuously before and since—because of the vastly different agendas of developing and developed countries. Developing countries press for the dismantling of rich countries' antidumping laws and of their protection of agriculture and cotton goods. Developed countries, particularly the United States, press not only for access to poor countries' markets but also for their acceptance of stricter definitions and greater enforcement of intellectual property rights. The chapter on TRIPs (*t*rade-*r*elated aspects of *i*ntellectual *p*roperty rights) was included in the WTO agreement at the conclusion of the Uruguay round of the GATT; since that time

I am grateful to the organizers of and participants in the 2004 *HOPE* conference and the 2004 conference "A Decade of Development Thinking" at the Research Department of the Inter-American Development Bank, where I presented earlier versions of this essay. I also benefited from discussions with Michael Perelman and from the research assistance of Whitney Walker. The usual disclaimer applies.

the United States has been seeking tougher provisions. While the United States relented in Cancún (Bhagwati 2004, 57), it did so while simultaneously pursuing more forceful regional and bilateral agreements.

Intellectual property provokes the ire of globalization's critics: it entails monopoly rents that accrue to producers of pharmaceuticals, of genetically engineered agricultural goods, and of entertainment and media products, most of whom reside in rich countries. Proponents view the rents as the just returns to innovation and as a necessary incentive for progress. Critics see the rents as evidence of "corporate-led globalization" and "profit over people."

The criticisms have spurred a reassessment of the appropriateness of intellectual property chapters in trade agreements. Why is intellectual property trade-related? In any case, should it be? The reassessment has been undertaken by advocates as well as skeptics of globalization. It has followed various lines of argument and employed different methods, some rooted in contemporary theory, some in politics, some in history. Jagdish Bhagwati (2004, 57), one of globalization's chief advocates, writes that "intellectual property protection is a matter of collecting royalties, and including them in a trade institution such as the WTO seriously distorted what that organization should accomplish." Ha-Joon Chang (2002), a skeptic, considers international agreements for the enforcement of intellectual property rights to be among the methods by which rich countries (which promoted their own development in the nineteenth century precisely by pirating the intellectual property of foreigners) are now "kicking away the ladder" from poor countries. TRIPs, therefore, "needs a serious overhaul, if not an outright abolition" (Chang 2001, 303). B. Zorina Khan analyzes historical data from the U.S. book trade to determine whether the country's refusal throughout most of the nineteenth century to enter into an international copyright agreement produced net welfare benefits or costs for Americans. Ultimately, her conclusion is similar to Chang's in substance, if not in tone: "Strong measures by the state to counter piracy may lead to social overinvestment in property rights enforcement." Specifically, "the U.S. experience during the nineteenth century suggests that appropriate intellectual property institutions are not independent of the level of economic and social development" (Khan 2004, 30).

Notwithstanding the use by Chang, Khan, and others of historical argument to criticize the marriage of trade and intellectual property rights, the *intellectual* history of that marriage has been given scant attention.

The perceived connections between trade and one particular form of intellectual property—copyright—is especially worthy of historical scrutiny. Khan (2004, 5) notes that copyright has not generated nearly as much scholarly interest as patents. Yet the question of international copyright in the nineteenth-century United States was controversial and sustained through generations, while the question of international patent recognition was neither.[1] Inasmuch as copyright does receive scholarly attention, historical arguments for legislation tend to be neglected in favor of basic historical facts of the contents of legislation or historical data manifesting the economic effects of legislation. Chang (2002, 57), for example, surveys some of the principal ideas in nineteenth-century America supporting trade restrictions, but where his subject turns to copyright his historical observations are limited to broad-brush characterizations of policies: "Even the most advanced countries were still routinely violating the [intellectual property rights] of other countries' citizens well into the twentieth century. . . . Even the USA, already a strong advocate of patentee rights, did not acknowledge foreigners' copyrights until 1891." The observation is true. It is even important. But it does not convey the ideas that maintained the nineteenth-century copyright status quo nor those that resisted and ultimately toppled it. Nor does it contribute to an understanding of how any of them related to protection or free trade.

Khan (2004, 9) offers at least a sketch of the opposing sides of the controversy: she writes that international copyright was kept at bay in the United States until 1891 because of the efforts of "publishers, printers, and representatives of the Democratic Party." But the sketch requires some revision and much elaboration. Although it is true that the votes for the Platt-Simonds Copyright Act of 1891 were made mostly by Republicans, and the votes against mostly by Democrats, there was much voting across party lines. More to the point, and notwithstanding the roll calls, the arguments that kept international copyright at bay for most of the half century leading up to the vote were formulated mainly not by Democrats, but by Republicans—specifically, Republicans (and, prior to

1. In 1837 Henry Clay ([1837] 1896, 35), who engineered the first concerted legislative push toward international copyright, stated in his Senate Select Committee report on the subject that "already the principle has been adopted, in the patent laws, of extending their benefits to foreign inventions or improvements. It is but carrying out the same principle to extend the benefits of our copyright laws to foreign authors" (see also Barnes 1974, 61–74). At the very beginning of the half-century wrangle over international copyright, the corresponding dispute over patents had already been settled.

1854 and less consistently, Whigs) of a common protectionist stamp. On the other hand, the arguments in favor of international copyright were devised by the minority of Republicans of Jacksonian Democrat lineage (and, in the preceding twenty years, of liberal Republican and mugwump affinities).[2]

Why, one might ask, do the arguments and the identities of their exponents matter at all? Why not attend just to the details of legislation and their economic consequences? My premise is that the political and doctrinal allegiances of authors of arguments on both sides of the international copyright controversy matter because they reflect how, in the nineteenth century, intellectual property was "trade related." Those who were at the vanguard of the movement for international copyright were also the leading advocates of free trade—and their ambivalence about the Republican Party after the Civil War was due above all to that party's adherence to protectionist principles. Likewise, the principal articulators

2. Khan's sketch of political alignments is consistent with the chapter-length account of Meredith L. McGill (2003, 84–85), who writes that "in Congress, active support of international copyright tended to be Whig, northern, and avowedly protectionist," in contrast to the "largely Democratic opposition." The advocacy of international copyright by Henry Clay, a staunch protectionist Whig, would appear to seal the case. I contend instead that Clay's advocacy highlights the fundamental ambiguity of international copyright as a matter of free trade or protection—but it does not overturn the rule of thumb that I advance about the political and ideological alignments on both sides of the debate. What is more, I disagree with McGill's characterization of those alignments. Unfortunately one cannot settle the matter simply by tallying votes, in part because until 1890–91 the several treaties and bills to establish international copyright did not come to a vote: they were tabled or died in committee. But even a glance at the final roll calls for the Platt-Simonds Act in 1890–91 is not sufficient to discern the political and ideological commitments of those in favor and those opposed. Like the earlier international copyright initiatives that failed, the act included a "manufacturing provision": the stipulation that U.S. copyright for a foreign work was contingent on its being typeset and printed in the United States. But Platt-Simonds went further: to give teeth to the manufacturing provision, it also prohibited commercial importation of books securing U.S. copyright that were not typeset and printed in the United States. The leaders of the opposition, Senators John Warwick Daniel and John Henninger Reagan, Jacksonian Democrats from Virginia and Texas, and Senator John Sherman, a liberal Republican from Ohio, understood themselves to be voting not against international copyright, but rather against the equivalent of a prohibitive tariff (Putnam 1891, 395; *Congressional Record*, 51st Cong., 2nd sess., 2607, 2385–86, 2608, 2610). On the other side, a large majority of Republicans who supported international copyright did so because it was bundled with a substantial increase in protection, and declined to do so otherwise. When Sherman sponsored, and Daniel and Reagan supported, an amendment to preserve the international copyright part of the bill while scrapping nonimportation, Republicans rejected the amendment by a large margin. In the final analysis, therefore, even the 1890–91 debate, as lopsided as it turned out to be with Republicans in favor of Platt-Simonds and Democrats opposed, is consistent with the general rule that opponents of international copyright per se were protection-minded Republicans, while advocates were Jacksonian Democrats and free-trade Republicans.

of the case against international copyright were also the foremost advocates of protection—and they were at home in the Republican Party mainly for that reason.

My purpose is to lay bare the intellectual connections between free trade and international copyright, on one side of the debate, and protection and opposition to international copyright, on the other. The connections, I will argue, were the different roles of government favored by the two sides' doctrines. Free-trade doctrine maintained that the principal role of government was to protect the natural right of individuals to appropriate the fruits of their own labor. The salient protective doctrine affirmed an active role of government in fostering certain industries, ensuring industrial diversification, and actively promoting productivity growth. The champions of each side of the tariff controversy believed that their favored role of government necessitated their chosen position on international copyright.

To show why, I will recall the arguments and advocacy of two such champions. Each was the single most respected figure on his side of the tariff debate, and each was deeply involved in the question of international copyright. Each, moreover, was directly interested in the publishing industry.

The first, William Cullen Bryant (1794–1878), was, with Emerson and Longfellow, one of the most revered men of letters in mid-nineteenth-century America. His reputation owed much to his poetry, but it was due also to his work as editor and publisher for a half century of the *New York Evening Post* and to his leadership of many political causes, including that of the American Free Trade League (of which he was the first president). The second, Henry C. Carey (1793–1879), is well known to historians of economic thought as America's leading protectionist thinker. He was also, until he retired in 1838 to devote himself to political economy, partner in the publishing firm founded by his father and maintained as Carey & Lea (later Carey, Lea & Blanchard) of Philadelphia (Kaser 1957, 62).

In the remainder of the essay I will review the contributions of Bryant and Carey to the nineteenth-century U.S. debate over international copyright, and I will try to show why, in the mind of each, international copyright was trade related. I will conclude by considering the relevance of history to the present. Economic history may suggest, as Chang has argued and Khan implied, that the present-day link between tighter international copyright agreements and trade liberalization may not be in the best interest of poor countries. But that is not the thrust of this essay. Intellectual history suggests a different conclusion. The consequence of the trade relatedness of international copyright in nineteenth-century America should put rich countries on guard as well.

William Cullen Bryant, Free Labor, and Free Trade

William Cullen Bryant was already a widely read and acclaimed free trader at the age of thirteen. His father, Dr. Peter Bryant, served for several years in the Massachusetts legislature, so the family's house was abuzz with political discussion. Dr. Bryant was also a lover of poetry who cultivated young Cullen's aptitude for versification. The boy's abilities in politics and poetry coalesced in 1807, when, with Britain and France embroiled in war and each country pressing a naval blockade of the other's American commerce, Congress passed and President Jefferson signed the Embargo Act. The act was intended to compel the combatants to end their dispute, or at least those of their practices that caused the most collateral damage to the United States. But it provoked fierce antipathy in the commercial centers of New York and New England. Cullen inveighed against the act in a satirical poem, originally of 244 lines, which impressed his father so much that he sought out a publisher for it in early 1808. Published as "The Embargo; or, Sketches of the Times, A Satire; by a Youth of Thirteen," the work was sufficiently popular in Boston to warrant a second edition with an additional 175 lines (Brown 1971, 24–27).

Mandeville aside, opportunities to cite free-trade poetry are infrequent. Bryant's is worth citing less for the sublimity of the genre than for its containing the kernel of the idea motivating his leadership of the free-trade cause for most of the following seventy years. After his opening lines Bryant implored the muse of satire to lend him poetic strength to aid the cause:

> Satiric Muse, shall injured Commerce weep
> Her ravish'd rights, and will thy thunders sleep;
> Dart thy keen glances, knit thy threat'ning brows,
> Call fire from heaven to blast thy country's foes.
> Oh, let a youth thine inspiration learn—
> Oh give him "words that breathe and thoughts that burn"!

Neither at this moment nor afterward were Bryant's arguments against commercial barriers original. His importance to economic thought would be as an influential advocate and opinion maker, not a theorist. His arguments warrant examination nonetheless because his influence was great. Bryant's defense in "The Embargo" of unimpeded international trade includes traces, as in the second cited line above, of the natural rights tradition. It also includes, more distinctly, the related conviction that government restrictions of trade bear unintended consequences—of poverty, namely, and even starvation. "Th' Embargo rages, like a sweeping wind, / Fear lowers before, and famine stalks behind," he wrote. He continued,

In vain Mechanics ply their curious art,
And bootless mourn the interdicted mart;
While our sage *Ruler's* diplomatic skill,
Subjects our councils to his sovereign will;
His grand "*restrictive energies*" employs,
And wisely regulating trade—destroys.

As he matured, Bryant continued writing, but he did not expect to do so as a vocation. Through most of his third decade and into his early thirties he tried his hand at the law in Plainfield and Great Barrington, Massachusetts, while making occasional literary contributions to such publications as the *United States Literary Gazette* and the *North American Review*. In Great Barrington his association with the Sedgwicks, a prominent family in Massachusetts politics and society, provided companionship, conversation, and connections. With one of their number Bryant studied political economy, taking up Smith, Say, Thornton, and Ricardo (Godwin 1883, 1:184–85). With two others, who had moved to New York to practice law, Bryant was introduced into the intellectual and social circles of the city (Brown 1971, 112–13, 135).

Weary of the law and enticed by the prospect of making a living in letters in New York, Bryant quit his practice and moved to the city in 1825. In mid-1826 the founding editor of the *New York Evening Post* was injured and required a temporary replacement. Bryant, by then a recognized critic and poet, was hired to the position. He proved to be an adept manager and an able and eloquent editorial writer. His particular passion was the question of the tariff, which he considered "legal robbery" (Brown 1971, 150, 159). When the editor died in 1829, Bryant took over fully the position and over time acquired controlling ownership of the business (173).

In the early years of Bryant's editorship Henry Clay was the principal voice of the "American system" of protection. Clay, therefore, was the paper's chief foe, and Andrew Jackson its champion, even several years after the two contested the presidency in 1832. In an editorial of 31 March 1834, Bryant made clear the reasons for the paper's stance. Clay, he wrote,

> is the parent and champion of the tariff and internal improvements; of a system directly opposed to the interests and prosperity of every merchant in the United States, and devised for the purpose of organizing an extensive scheme through which the different portions of the United States might be bought up in detail. By assuming the power of dissipating the public revenue in local improvements, by which one portion of the community would be benefited at the expense of many others, Congress acquired the means of influencing and controlling the politics of every State in the Union, and of establishing a rigid, invincible consolidated government. By assuming the power of protecting any class or portion of the industry of this country, by bounties in the shape of high duties on foreign importations, they placed the labor and industry of the people entirely at their own disposal, and usurped the prerogative of dispensing all the blessings of Providence at pleasure. They could at any time decide what class of industry should be enriched, and what class impoverished; whether commerce should flourish or decay; whether the manufacturer of cotton, wool, or iron should become a king, while the common laborer sank into a pauper. Out of this system grew those great manufacturing establishments which have monopolized almost all the pursuits of simple mechanics, and converted them from independent men presiding over their own homes, masters of their own shops, and proprietors of their own earnings, into the pale, sickly, and half-starved slaves of companies and corporations. (Bryant 1994, 20)

Bryant believed the protective tariff to be class legislation favoring the few at the expense of many. It was also, as he had expressed in verse long before, ruinous to industry. Eight years later he restated the point in an editorial titled "How to Destroy a Commercial Town," written in response to Clay's tariff of 1842, which raised the average duty by roughly

50 percent.[3] "There are several methods of bringing ruin upon a city which owes its prosperity to its flourishing commerce with foreign nations," Bryant warned. One could obstruct its harbors. One could, as during the late embargo, forbid by law the passage of vessels to and from the port. Or one could follow Clay, establishing "a law laying, upon merchandize imported from abroad, duties so enormously high that they cannot be paid, amounting to a prohibition of foreign commerce" (Bryant 1994, 176).

To Bryant, the unfairness of protection and the likelihood that it would "bring ruin" on a populace were reasons enough to renounce the policy. But one could say more. It was unfair and ruinous because it was contrary to the legitimate role of government. At its core the government's role was to secure "free labor," in all the term's meanings. Specifically, a government functioning in its legitimate role would ensure the following: (1) that individuals could sell their labor for whatever wages an unencumbered market would allow; (2) that they could keep for themselves all of their wage earnings except those required to finance a small and stripped-down government; and (3) that with those earnings they could purchase goods for the best price an unencumbered market would offer. Free labor therefore demanded, to the minds of Bryant and his readers, a consistent stand on three of the day's most controversial issues. For individuals to be able to sell their labor freely demanded opposition to slavery. For individuals to be as free as possible from taxation demanded not only a minimalist government, but, in particular, a government averse to the financing of internal improvements (contra Henry Clay) and the resulting spoils of patronage. And for individuals to be able to trade their wages for goods at the best price they could get demanded free trade. When Bryant pressed in 1843 for "commercial emancipation" from "the practice of confining trade by the invisible, but potent chains of law" (Bryant 1994, 187), therefore, his language was not just metaphorical. He considered restrictions on international trade to be a violation of the principle of free labor—and, in the same manner as slavery, a contravention of the legitimate role of government.

Bradley Bateman (this volume) acknowledges the importance of the free labor ideal to salient conceptions of the role of government, but identifies the ideal too much with "republicanism," especially in the

3. Import duties were 36.9 percent of the value of dutiable imports in 1844, up from 25.8 percent in 1842; and 30.5 percent of the value of all imports in 1844, up from 19 percent in 1842. See U.S. Census Bureau 1975.

years prior to the Civil War. To the editor and most readers of the *Evening Post*, free labor was the basic principle of *democratic* government—even (albeit with a small "d") after the founding in 1854 of the Republican Party. In an 1853 editorial, Bryant wrote,

> In the first place we shall abide by the democratic party, because it is our party, because it is the party with whose principles, as laid down by Jefferson and as expounded by many enlightened men both of his time and ours, we fully agree. We recognize the great basis of the democratic party, simplicity in government—as little government, as little patronage, as little expenditure as the structure of civil polity can subsist with, and a strict construction of the constitution. (Bryant 1994, 270)

Shortly afterward, in 1855, when the Democratic Party's willingness to accommodate slavery finally outweighed all else, provoking the defection of Bryant and numerous other northern Democrats to the Republican Party, Bryant still insisted that "true democracy" would not yield. He maintained that, under the circumstances, their defection served the cause more effectively than would party loyalty. After all, "living principles are better worth fighting for than dead heroes" (Bryant 1994, 288).

Bryant on International Copyright

The same principles demanded an additional policy. The United States already had a copyright law: an act of 1790 that granted to U.S. citizens, residents, and their heirs a fourteen-year copyright for new books, maps, and charts, and offered authors still alive after the first fourteen years the right to renew for another fourteen. An act of 1831 extended copyright to twenty-eight years for citizens, residents, and heirs, with the possibility of renewal for an additional fourteen (Clark [1960] 1973, 24–25). But no U.S. copyright protection whatsoever existed for citizens and residents of foreign countries—and that, Bryant believed, was unjust.

For once Clay and Bryant agreed. The efforts to secure international copyright began in 1836, when a partner in a London publishing firm moved to New York in an effort to issue a simultaneous American edition, under copyright, of a British work. The effort failed, the work was pirated, and the firm's New York branch was ruined. But the partner had influential supporters, including Clay and Bryant (Clark [1960] 1973,

41–42). The American International Copyright Association was established by George P. Putnam in 1837, with Bryant prominent among its members. The association presented numerous petitions to Congress, and a bill was drawn up with Clay's sponsorship that would accomplish the association's ends. Senate bill no. 223, titled "An Act to amend the several acts respecting copyright," was concise and simple:

> *Be it enacted, etc.,* That the provisions of the act to amend the several acts respecting copyrights, which was passed on the third day of February, eighteen hundred and thirty-one, shall be extended to, and the benefits thereof may be enjoyed by, any subject or resident of the United Kingdom of Great Britain and Ireland, or of France, in the same manner as if they were citizens or residents of the United States, upon depositing a printed copy of the title of the book, or other work for which a copyright is desired, in the clerk's office of the district court of any district in the United States, and complying with the other requirements of the said act: *Provided,* That this act shall not apply to any of the works enumerated in the aforesaid act, which shall have been etched or engraved, or printed and published, prior to the passage of this act: *And provided, also,* that, unless an edition of the work for which it is intended to secure the copyright shall be printed and published in the United States simultaneously with its issue in the foreign country, or within one month after depositing as aforesaid the title thereof in the clerk's office of the district court, the benefits of copyright hereby allowed shall not be enjoyed as to such work. (Clay [1837] 1896, 38–39)

The cause of international copyright was a natural one for Bryant to pick up. His first editorial on the subject, on 27 September 1836, was titled "Copyright and Patent Right Are Natural Rights." Bryant asserted that if international recognition of patents were granted (as it had been), then international copyright should be granted for the same reason. But as his title indicates, the argument involved more than just that:

> In all ages and all nations of the world, the rights of an individual to the creations of his own labour or skill have always been considered sacred. . . . On the same basis rests an author's right of property in the book which he draws from the resources of his mind, and prepares with labour both of the hand and the head. On the same basis, also, rests the right of the inventor to the productions of his own ingenuity.

> These are natural rights, not rights created by law; not rights growing out of kingly grants, or the preponderance of might over justice. (Bryant 1994, 57–58)

The consistency, to Bryant's mind, of international copyright with the other applications of the free labor ideal hardly requires comment. What is worth remarking is how constant remained Bryant's support for the measure through all the years of debate over it. Senate bill no. 223 was laid on the table, and no other bill made any further progress until Congress's ultimate acceptance of international copyright in 1891—by which time Bryant and the other original proponents were long dead. From 1836 until the end of his life in 1878, however, Bryant made several more attempts. More editorials followed. Bryant organized the American Copyright Club in 1842, and he remained in the forefront of the movement through an unratified copyright treaty with Britain in 1853, several unsuccessful bills, and numerous memorials presented to Congress (see, e.g., Bryant 1848). Table 1 lists the main initiatives for international copyright leading up to the ultimate success of 1891.

The length of the list testifies to the determination of Bryant and his allies. Of course it demonstrates the same of his opponents—to whom we now turn.

Henry C. Carey: Publisher and Political Economist

Throughout most of the nineteenth century, opposition to international copyright and advocacy of protection was not built on disavowal of the natural law tradition that underlay procopyright and free trade. Instead, protectionists and copyright opponents turned the very same rhetorical tables used by Bryant and his allies against them. The master of the art, and by far the most influential of Bryant's adversaries, was Henry C. Carey.

Early in his career and until his fifth decade, Carey, like his father, Matthew, was a Philadelphia publisher. Henry and a brother-in-law bought out Matthew Carey's interest on his retirement in 1822; in that year M. Carey & Sons became the house of Carey & Lea. Thanks to Carey's industriousness, the firm "ruled the Philadelphia booktrade" and sustained the city's rivalry with New York as center of the nation's publishing industry (Kaser 1957, 63; Lehmann-Haupt 1951, 120). Carey &

Table 1 International Copyright: Early Initiatives and Final Attainment

Year	Initiative	Content	Special Provisions
1837	Clay Bill[1]	National treatment in copyright for authors of U.K. and France	Remanufacture and publication in the U.S. required within one month after publication abroad
1853	Everett (Anglo-American) Treaty[2]	Reciprocal copyright with U.K.: National treatment in each country for authors from the other	No international price discrimination allowed
1858	Morris Bill[3]	National treatment in copyright for foreign authors	Remanufacture by a U.S. publisher required within thirty days after publication abroad
1868	Baldwin Bill[4]	National treatment in copyright for foreign authors	Foreign books with copyright must be wholly manufactured in U.S. and published by an American citizen
1870	Clarendon Treaty[5]	Reciprocal copyright with U.K.: National treatment in each country for authors from the other	Registration and deposit of book sample required within three months after publication in country of origin
1871	Cox Bill[6]	National treatment in copyright for foreign authors	Conditional on foreign author's country granting *equal* copyright to U.S. authors. Republication by U.S. publisher required within three months after publication in country of origin
1872	Beck/Sherman Bills[7]	"International copyright" implying a share of reprinting proceeds for foreign authors	Any domestic publisher has the right to reprint foreign works, but must pay 10% (Beck) or 5% (Sherman) royalty to foreign author
1878	Harper draft of Clarendon Treaty[8]		Like the Clarendon Treaty, but registration and deposit of book sample are required *before* publication in country of origin

Table 1 continued

Year	Initiative	Content	Special Provisions
1884	Dorsheimer Bill[9]	Reciprocal copyright with any country that agrees: National treatment in each country for authors from the other	Conditional on foreign author's country granting *equal and similar* copyright to U.S. authors. No manufacturing provisions
1885	Hawley Bill[10]	Amended version of Dorsheimer Bill	Applies to all copyright articles, not only books
1886	Chace Bill[11]	National treatment in copyright for foreign authors	Registration required within fifteen days of publication in country of origin. Deposit of U.S. edition required within six months. *As soon as the U.S. edition ceases to be published, copyright for foreign authors is void.* Prohibition of imports of books securing U.S. copyright
1891	Platt-Simonds Act[12]	Amended version of Chace Bill, followed by Chace-Platt Bill	Exception to prohibition of imports for newspapers and magazines, and for books if *no more than two copies* of a foreign edition are imported for personal, not commercial, use

1. S 32, 25th Cong., 2nd sess.
2. Sen. Confidential Ex. Doc. No. 6, 32nd Cong., 2nd sess.
3. Bowker 1886, 28.
4. H. Rept. No. 16, 40th Cong., 2nd sess.
5. Bowker 1886, 29.
6. HR 470, 42nd Cong., 2nd sess.
7. HR 1667, 42nd Cong., 2nd sess.; S 688, 42nd Cong., 2nd sess.
8. Bowker 1886, 31.
9. H. Rept. No. 189, 48th Cong., 1st sess.
10. S 191, 49th Cong., 1st sess.
11. S 1178, 49th Cong., 1st sess.
12. Clark [1960] 1973, 194–99.

Lea published a variety of books: the copyrighted works of American authors, like James Fenimore Cooper's *The Last of the Mohicans*, for which Carey paid Cooper $5,000 in 1826; and reprints without copyright of foreign books, including the tremendously popular works of Sir Walter Scott (Kaser 1957, 79, 95).

Most of the 930 books published by the firm from 1822 until Carey's retirement in 1838 were reprints without copyright (Kaser 1957, 72, 115)—but that fact does not explain his opposition to international copyright. The reprint trade was sometimes lucrative, but it was always risky. The "courtesy of the trade" called for publishers to refrain from reprinting a foreign work once another publisher had made a newspaper announcement of intention to print it—but such courtesy was unenforceable by law and violated by habit (McGill 2003, 105). The business was a frenzied one in which publishers jockeyed for the first copies of British books to cross the ocean and then raced without rest to typeset the works, print sufficient copies, and get them to the shops of Philadelphia, New York, Boston, and other northern towns. Mere hours could make the difference between spectacular success and utter failure, and "small fortunes could be made or lost in a single day" (Kaser 1957, 149). One strategy for success was to position agents wherever necessary along the route from London to the U.S. publishing house, and from there to the local bookshop, to ensure a speedy transfer of the first available copies and rapid distribution of the reprints. Another was to invest in faster printing equipment or to hire other printers. Yet another was to buy an advance copy from the British publisher or to buy it directly from the author. And if all else failed, one could just steal the advance copy. American publishers, not least Carey & Lea, used all of these methods (Kaser 1957, 25, 95, 103). The firm was generally successful, but it also suffered several losses and faced a fierce battle of encroachment from the upstart Harpers (Kaser 1957, 150–52).

If Carey's narrow personal and financial interests determined his political proclivities, one might expect him to have favored international copyright, not opposed it. The pace of business under an international copyright regime would have been less frenetic. One could also argue, as advocates of international copyright often did, that copyright of foreign works would stimulate demand for American substitutes—which Carey & Lea already produced, and which, presumably, they would have produced in greater numbers. If indeed production of American substitutes grew, Carey would have yet another reason to support international copyright: he was an unapologetic Anglophobe who deplored Americans' slavish imitation of, and preference for, British works. "We are bound up in the chains of intellectual slavery," he scolded, "to a people far inferior to ourselves" (Carey 1853, 231). Finally, legislative initiatives for international copyright, beginning with Henry Clay's bill of 1837, were routinely bundled with "manufacturing provisions" that, at a minimum, made copyright of foreign works contingent on having them reprinted and published in the United States within a few months of their publication abroad (Barnes 1974, 63; Clark [1960] 1973, 44). More stringent provisions could have included, as they later did in the Chace Bill of 1886 and the Platt-Simonds Act of 1891, an outright prohibition of commercial imports of copyrighted books. A practical approach for a publisher was to voice opposition to international copyright if stringent manufacturing provisions were absent, and at least tepid support so long as they were included. Henry C. Lea, scion of Carey's former business partner, took exactly that position (Clark [1960] 1973, 136–43). But Carey made no such hedge.

To understand Carey's opposition to international copyright requires more than recognition of his financial stake in the reprint trade early in his career. It requires inspection of his argument. At the root of the argument was a vision of the government's role that differed markedly from that of his intellectual opponents. Carey expounded that role most clearly in his rationale for tariff protection, which he advocated tirelessly and passionately from a few years after his retirement until the end of his life.

Carey on Protection and Productivity

The first work that Carey published, immediately after his retirement in 1838, was *Principles of Political Economy*. The book contains Carey's main theoretical contribution, on which he founded all the work in his remaining four decades: a detailed refutation of David Ricardo's theory of land rent. But in 1838 the theory did not yet lead him to protection. That happened in 1847, when, distressed by the Walker tariff reduction, Carey wrote in three months *The Past, the Present, and the Future* ([1847] 1872; Elder [1880] 1883, 26). It was a justification of protection built on a self-contained system of historical and economic laws; it benefited from a young nation's experience of having watched the laws unfold in the compressed time of generations instead of centuries or millennia.

Carey's ([1847] 1872, 311) system implied a harmony of interests between labor and capital that would exist but for "the interference of the laws of man with those of the Deity." In later books, *Principles of Social Science* (Carey [1858] 1883, 1:iii) and *The Unity of Law; as Exhibited in the Relations of Physical, Social, Mental, and Moral Science* (Carey 1872, ix), he claimed priority for the ideas articulated by Frédéric Bastiat, whose opposition to protection was founded similarly on a system of economic harmonies. To Carey, though, the protective tariff was not necessarily an interference with the laws of the Deity. In some places and times, and certainly in the United States, it was necessary to preserve their natural harmony.

The crux of his argument was to show that what was "natural," particularly in the settlement of land and the concentration of population, was not what political economists had theretofore believed. Here is where Carey took issue with Ricardo. Ricardo had proposed that the most fertile lands were settled first, and that as the population grew, less fertile lands came under cultivation while more rent accrued to the better lands' owners. "Mr. Ricardo's system is one of discords," Carey argued: if people married and multiplied, rents were raised and wages depressed; if the rights of property were respected, undeserved rewards accrued to the few and misery to the many. "His book," he pronounced, "is the true manual of the demagogue, who seeks power by means of agrarianism, war, and plunder" (Carey [1847] 1872, 74–75). But Ricardo's system was not only worrisome, it was wrong: "Mr. Ricardo's proposition is diametrically opposed to all the facts presented by the history of the United States: of England: and of the World" (56). The proof was in the way that land settlement and population growth had proceeded naturally in the past, and the way it still proceeded. Ricardo, he claimed, was too far removed from the process to discern it (24).

To read Carey one must think of pyramids. The pyramid is the abstract form of a mountain, Carey's point of reference for showing how settlement proceeds through time. It is also the abstract form of the proper relationships among families, communities, and nations.

Human settlement in any region, Carey explained, does not begin on the most fertile lands, as Ricardo had assumed, but on the lands that are easiest to clear with a minimum of technology. The first settlers of Massachusetts settled at rocky Plymouth and eked out a living as best they could; in New York settlers first chose land high above the Hudson River instead of the fertile land at its bank (25–26). The more fertile is the land, the denser are its forests and swamps and the harder they are to clear. A community of early settlers who are sparsely concentrated and produce little surplus food is hardly able to tame wild forests and swamps with scant time and primitive techniques. Nor do the settlers have the luxury to study new techniques. Therefore they choose sites that are midway or near the top of a mountain or hill, not in the river valley below.

Few people can concentrate on unfertile land, but as those few make halting improvements in their techniques of clearance and cultivation, they can move down the mountain to the superior land and also support a greater population. As the population grows, a smaller proportion of it is needed for cultivation—so many more minds can be employed in devising better techniques (25). Techniques improve not only because more minds are devoted to their improvement, though, but also because each mind is made more productive by collaboration with a growing number of others. Better techniques of clearance and cultivation allow the community to move on to still better soil, and even to improve the inferior soils—which permits more population growth, and so on. Rent increases with population growth, but not as Ricardo imagined. More rent is paid for the newly cultivated land, not the old: it is the reward to its cultivators of its greater fertility, made possible by the community's accumulated improvements in techniques (62).

Further improvements make the community still more concentrated and wealthy. Its citizens move back up the side of the mountain from which they descended, cultivating with improved techniques the land they once abandoned and diversifying their occupations and trade with one another. As they grow wealthier, they begin to profit from intercourse with other communities—primarily those nearby, and gradually and to a lesser extent those more distant. Each mountainside community now resembles spatially a pyramid, at the base of which the most land is cultivated most intensively. As each becomes more concentrated in terms of population, intensiveness of cultivation, and diversification of activities, so too does the group of them.

> If, now, we take a bird's-eye view of these various communities, we shall see in each an infinite number of little pyramids, with heights proportioned to their breadth and depth. With the extension of the breadth of cultivation we have seen it rising in its height until it has advanced far up the steep hill-side; and on all sides we see it rising higher as it sinks deeper into the fertile soils of the valley below. . . . With the

> establishment of intercourse among these little communities, the tendency to union, so well begun in each, is seen to spread. Each grows in wealth and population, and intercourse becomes more frequent; and next we find them all combining for the making of roads, or canals, the founding of colleges, and other works calculated to promote the common good. The union becomes more complete: . . . General laws now embrace the whole of the various societies constituting this pyramid, which now surmounts the whole. (286)

In the last sentence the pyramid of the mountainside community transfigures into a pyramid of social organization. The rationale of protection lies in both. At the base of the social pyramid are each community's many family units. Each family, organizationally, is a pyramid in itself—and each, crucially, is inward looking. Husbands, wives, and children are more concerned with the welfare of their familial pyramid than they are with that of the larger organizational pyramids comprising it (287–89). Nevertheless, to build local roads, schools, libraries, and churches, families will combine to form a community, which is similarly concerned principally with the welfare of its constituents. Communities, too, in order to build highways and canals, will combine to form a state; states will form nations; and, presumably, nations will form alliances. But the natural tendency of each organizational unit is to look primarily inward (downward from its apex, as it were), and the natural order of authority demands that the larger the unit, the less authority it has over its constituent units.

Each unit derives advantages from, but does not concern itself disproportionately with, the larger union of which it is a member. Concentration—of productive power, in geographic space—Carey favored. Centralization—of authority, in organizational space—he condemned (289–90).

To Carey, any inversion of the relations within and among the pyramids would be an interference in the natural order and would erode the wealth of the whole. Exactly such an inversion, he argued, would result in the United States without tariff protection. Europe's demand for produce, combined with the abundance of land in the United States, already encouraged people to disperse too widely. Too many Americans cultivated poor soils and traded their produce with distant buyers instead of concentrating on rich soils, diversifying their activities within smaller geographic areas, and trading with their neighbors. To illustrate he pointed to the rich meadows of Pennsylvania, between the manufacturing centers of Pittsburgh and Philadelphia, which remained covered wastefully with timber while pioneers migrated west to cultivate dry prairies (298). It might appear that the pioneers moved en masse because manufactures were acquired cheapest by interregional and international specialization and trade. But the appearance is deceptive, Carey held, and the relation unnatural. "In a natural state of things, the people of the United States can manufacture more cheaply than any nation of the world. . . . All that is wanted is that the shoemaker with his lapstone shall be *permitted* to take his place by the side of the hides and the food, as he would long since have done but for the existence of a disturbing force of prodigious power" (470). If people are concentrated and their activities diversified, they will have more of both manufactures and produce, shoes and food. Their concentration ensures that they will have the techniques and the impetus to cultivate the most fertile soil; its fertility will feed a diverse manufacturing community that develops the techniques. If unnatural commercial opportunities encourage them to settle differently, they will have fewer shoes and less food.

Hence the need for tariff protection. "Concentration, even to its present extent, cannot be maintained without protection. . . . we must arrest the progress of depopulation and promote concentration upon rich soils, and that can be done only by increased protection" (469). And to those who would complain about the negation of "free trade," Carey responded that far from negating it, protection enabled it. By permitting the farmer to stand side by side with the shoemaker, protection sustains the natural geographic, commercial, and social order, without which "every attempt at the establishment of freedom of trade must be a failure" (470).

Protection was perhaps the most important function that a government would serve in Carey's system while filling its appropriate role, but there were several others. Among them were constructing turnpikes and even footpaths; building aqueducts; coining money; establishing standards of measurement; surveying land; studying and giving public notice of the weather; keeping records of births, marriages, and deaths; levying property taxes to provide public schools; regulating the city's suppliers of gas; caring for the blind, deaf, and dumb; draining marshes; establishing a postal service; and disseminating new technologies of agriculture (Carey [1858] 1883, 3:410–14). How were all these functions related? Given the "identity of physical and social laws" (1:vi), it was possible to state the unifying principle in physical terms—and to do so not just metaphorically. The appropriate relation of the state to the populace was identical to the relation of the head to the body:

> In all these cases, the political head does exactly that which, as we have seen, has been provided to be done by the physical one—co-ordinating the movements of the various members of the society in such manner as to remove the obstacles which stand in the way of association, and prevent that diversification of the employments of society which is required for adding value to land and labor, and giving freedom to man. The more perfect that co-ordination, whether in the physical or social body, the more complete must be the development of all the parts, and the more harmonious that action of the whole. (3:414)

In brief, the legitimate role of government—in trade policy, as in all else—was to ensure concentration without centralization, and to ensure consequently the diversification of industry, thus enabling "people of all ages and sexes to combine their efforts for increasing the productiveness of labor" (3:441).

Peter Boettke and Steve Horwitz (this volume) ascribe to Friedrich List a vision of the role of government similar to Carey's. The correspondence is no coincidence: List and Carey were near contemporaries, were fellow Pennsylvanians during List's periods of residence in the United States from 1825 to 1830 and 1831 to 1832, and were both influenced by Carey's father (O'Connor 1944, 29–36). Their common vision, based on a "stages" philosophy of history, held that the advancement of society from one stage to the next requires active government policies to foster industrialization. Such a role of government implies a role for the economist. The economist, as Boettke and Horwitz put it, becomes "savior"—designing, articulating, and even advocating policies to foster economic development. Carey played precisely that role, as accounts of his life and work acknowledge.[4]

Rarely acknowledged and less understood is how Carey viewed the government's role to be circumscribed, and how he continued to fill the role of economist as savior while articulating the limits rather than the expanse of appropriate government policy.[5] "Are there, then," Carey asked rhetorically, "no proper limits to the sphere of action of those

4. See, for example, Morrison 1986, 36, 81–83.

5. Again see Morrison (1986, 37), who concedes the difficulty of demarcating the sphere of government in Carey's system.

who guide and direct the commerce of the State?" He answered: "There are—*their whole duty being found in the removal of the obstacles to perfect combination.* Going beyond that point, government leaves its proper sphere—doing then mischief in place of good" ([1858] 1883, 3:441; emphasis in original). One departure from the proper sphere of government—and to Carey, one of the most mischievous—was international copyright.

Carey on International Copyright

Increasing the productiveness of labor, Carey believed, required tariff protection. To be precise, it required the dissemination of knowledge, and tariff protection was an indirect means of fomenting the dissemination. But even as protection served its function, bad policies in other areas could inhibit the transfer of knowledge. International copyright was one such policy.

Peter Temin (2000, 110–11, 116–19), quoting a British visitor to New England factories in the mid-nineteenth century, recalls the astonishment with which such visitors viewed the quality of industrial machinery in what was primarily an agricultural nation. The United States was advancing on and even surpassing Britain technologically. The American system of manufactures, comprising interchangeable parts manufactured by gauged and replaceable machine tools, figures importantly in Temin's explanation of America's technological advancement. So too does stable government, clear laws, a cleverly designed protective tariff, a general commitment to public education, and the incentive to innovate provided by patents. His explanation might be distilled to this: there existed in nineteenth-century America the incentive to create and apply new ideas and the facility of disseminating them (with his emphasis placed, perhaps, on the former).

Carey would not have disputed Temin's explanation. In fact, nearly a century and a half before Temin, Carey inquired similarly into the causes of America's technological progress—even quoting an amazed British visitor to highlight the extent of the country's advancement. But the quotation Carey chose packed greater punch. Always endeavoring to turn his opponents' own words against them, Carey quoted the great free-trade luminary of the era, Richard Cobden. Cobden described an America "where the people are more educated" than in Britain; he also described the anxiety of another Manchester manufacturer that "if we are to hold our own, if we are not to fall back in the rear of the race of nations we must educate our people to put them upon a level with the more educated artisans of the United States" (Carey [1853] 1868, 84).

To Cobden, his manufacturer friend, and their American acolytes, Carey responded, "let them next ask themselves what have been the causes of this vast change in the relative positions of the two countries" (84). Like Temin, Carey avowed the importance of incentives to create and apply ideas and the ease of disseminating them—but he reversed the emphases, concentrating on the latter. "Will not the answer be," he asked, "common schools, cheap school-books, cheap newspapers, and cheap literature?"

Carey might have suggested at least one amendment to Temin's explanation, though. American technological progress, Carey believed, was due in no small part to the particular form of U.S. copyright law. By granting copyright to U.S. residents but denying it to foreigners, the law cheapened ideas in printed form and ensured greater access to them.

The manifest reason for Carey's opposition to international copyright was expediency. He estimated the additional cost, under international copyright, of the books read throughout the country would be at least seven million dollars per year. But consistency demanded that Carey's objection to international copyright should not be founded on expediency alone. It had to be founded on natural law; it had to be built on the same fundamental principles that underlay his advocacy of protection. In 1837 Henry Clay ([1837] 1896, 34) had defended international copyright on principle, reporting that "we should be all shocked if the law tolerated the least invasion of the rights of property in the case of merchandise, whilst those which justly belong to the works of authors are exposed to daily violation." Carey had conversely to demolish it on principle. He needed to demonstrate that the rights of property, and the system of "physical and social laws" more generally, did *not* justly require international copyright but rather its absence. Expediency without principle would not do, he admitted (Carey [1853] 1868, 21).

Carey justified his position by arguing that the rights of the property owners and the rights of authors, equated by Clay, were in truth not equal at all. Ideas could never be legitimately considered individual property: individuals made only marginal and incremental improvements to prior authors' ideas, which were the common property of all.

> The question is often asked: Why should a man not have the same claim to the perpetual enjoyment of his book that his neighbor has

> in regard to the house he has built? The answer is, that the rights of the parties are entirely different. The man who builds a house quarries the stone and makes the bricks of which it is composed, or he pays another for doing it for him. When finished, his house is all, materials and workmanship, his own. The man who makes a book uses the common property of mankind, and all he furnishes is the workmanship. Society permits him to use its property, but it is on condition that, after a certain time, the whole shall become part of the common stock. (32–33)

Because intellectual property is legitimately owned by the entire community, the "copyright" of an individual to his written work, Carey averred, is a misnomer. He did not deny that the community may find it expedient to guarantee an author a temporary monopoly in the reproduction of his work in order to give him added incentive to produce it. But the monopoly was not to be construed as a right. It was a privilege. "The day has passed, in this country," Carey wrote, "for the recognition of either perpetuity or universality of literary *rights*." He insisted, instead,

> that literary *privileges* exist in virtue of grants from the people who own the materials out of which books are made; that those privileges have been perhaps already too far extended; that there exists not even a shadow of reason for any further extension; and that to grant what now is asked would be a positive wrong to the many millions of consumers, as well as an obstacle to be now placed in the road towards civilization. (13; emphasis in original)

Beyond denying that international copyright was prescribed by the system of physical and social laws, Carey asserted that the *absence* of international copyright was *required* by the system. But here a question nags. Why did Carey inveigh against international copyright with such vehemence while speaking in such a muted tone ("perhaps already too far extended") against domestic copyright? Put differently: Why did he consider impediments to the transfer of foreign knowledge so particularly pernicious that they warranted discrimination against foreign authors and publishers? Absent an answer, his agitation over international copyright would appear overwrought, and perhaps just a veil for special interests.

Carey did have an answer, and it lay once more in his distinction between the (beneficent) concentration of productive resources in geographic space and the (baneful) centralization of authority in organizational space. "Centralization," he held, "tends towards taxing the people for building up great institutions at a distance from those who pay the taxes" (58). The "taxes" supporting the institution of the literary marketplace were paid in the form of monopoly rents to copyright holders. To Carey, international copyright, which would subject the citizens of America and Britain to copyright laws that encompassed them all, was a perfect example of centralization: monopoly rents would be paid disproportionately by Americans in a literary marketplace dominated by the British. Decentralization, conversely, would entail each country regulating its literary institutions independently: "English authors are already secured in a monopoly for forty-two years among a body of people so large that a contribution of a shilling a head would enable each and all of them to live in luxury; and if British policy prevents their countrymen from paying them, it is to the British Parliament they should look for redress, and not to our Executive" (57–58).

Centralization, moreover, would be attended by its doppelgänger, deconcentration—just as decentralization was attended by concentration, and all of its concomitant benefits. Specifically, Carey maintained that "the rapid advance that has been made in literature and science is the result of the *perfect protection* afforded by decentralization" (85; emphasis in original). Thus was the absence of international copyright, and the resulting discrimination against *foreign* authors, requisite to the role of government. The particular exclusion of foreign literary and scientific works from domestic copyright—like the particular exclusion of foreign goods from domestic markets—promoted the combination of efforts and sharing of knowledge, thereby fostering technological progress and growth of the productivity of labor. The analogy is not perfect: Carey neither anticipated nor hoped that discrimination against foreign authors would keep out foreign ideas in the manner that tariff protection would keep out foreign goods. Rather the opposite. What matters is that for the intended ends of both policies, national discrimination was vital, not merely collateral.

Having advanced his ideas, Carey was in a position to answer the concerns of those of his allies who, like Clay, might be led erroneously to believe that the bedrock principles of protection demanded an international copyright agreement. On the Anglo-American International Copyright Treaty of 1853, which provided for national treatment in each country of copyright holders from the other, Carey wrote:[6]

6. The treaty is found in U.S. Congress 1853 and is the culminating subject of Barnes 1974, chaps. 11–12.

> [The treaty's] confirmation is, as I understand, urged on some senators on the ground that consistency requires it. Being in favor of protection elsewhere, they are told that it would be inconsistent to refuse it here. In reply to this, it might fairly be retorted that nearly all the supporters of international copyright are advocates of the system called, in England, Free Trade; and that it is quite inconsistent in them to advocate protection here. To do this would however be as unnecessary as it would be unphilosophical. Both are perfectly consistent. Protection to the farmer and planter in their efforts to draw the artisan to their side, looks to carrying out the doctrine of decentralization by the annihilation of the monopoly of manufactures established in Britain; and our present copyright system looks to the decentralization of literature by offering to all who shall come and live among us the same perfect protection that we give to our own authors. What is called free trade looks to the maintenance of the foreign monopoly for supplying us with cloth and iron; and international copyright looks to continuing the monopoly which Britain has so long enjoyed of furnishing us with books; and both tend towards centralization. (85)

Carey's opposition was pivotal in sinking the treaty (Barnes 1974, 252–61). In an attempt to quell the opposition that Carey stirred up, the American negotiator proposed a manufacturing provision requiring republication in each country of works copyrighted in the other.[7] But it proved to be either too little or too late. (Whether too little or too late for the U.S. Senate is unclear because of delays in transatlantic communications. To Carey, certainly, the provision was too little.)

In at least one fundamental respect, Carey and Bryant agreed. International copyright was trade related—and regardless of whether one was a free trader and international copyright supporter or a protectionist and opponent, each pair of positions was, as Carey affirmed, "perfectly consistent." But the differences between the two partisans were manifold. The most conspicuous was that Carey's positions enjoyed the sympathies of the majority in Congress throughout Bryant's and Carey's lives and beyond. For over a half century preceding 1891, through dropped or deferred legislation such as the Clay Bill of 1837, the Anglo-American Treaty of 1853, and the Chace Bill of 1886 (among others), the interests of readers and printers, wedded to the prevailing protectionist doctrine by the ideas of Carey and his allies, kept international copyright at bay.

7. The proposed amendment is found in U.S. Congress 1854.

Conclusion

The recent surge of concern over TRIPs has produced ripples of interest in the history of intellectual property institutions and their consequences for the development of emerging economies. Economists have asked whether the premise that intellectual property is trade related—and the consequent incorporation of intellectual property chapters into bilateral, regional, and multilateral/nonpreferential trade agreements—works to the benefit or detriment of developing countries. By investigating the evolution of intellectual property rights and their economic consequences in the now-developed countries, economic historians have attempted to provide answers.

The historical interest has not extended, however, to the *intellectual history* of the trade relatedness of intellectual property rights. My purpose has been to show how, in the United States, one form of intellectual property was perceived to be trade related a century and a half before TRIPs. The debate over international copyright, sustained from the mid-1830s to 1891, ran parallel to the tariff controversy, which preceded and outlasted it.

I have argued that advocacy of free trade generally implied support for international copyright, while advocacy of protection implied opposition to international copyright. There were numerous exceptions to the rule—but many of the apparent ones could more accurately be said, on closer scrutiny, to confirm it. Democrats opposed the Platt-Simonds Copyright Act of 1891, for instance, and protectionist Republicans supported it. Attention to their debate, however, reveals that opponents voted against the act, despite their advocacy of international copyright, because they perceived one of its manufacturing provisions to be a highly protectionist measure. Supporters voted for the act precisely because they shared that perception, and declined to vote for it at all if the provision was removed.

The connections between the free trade and pro-international copyright positions, on the one hand, and protection and anti-international copyright, on the other, are manifest in the arguments of William Cullen Bryant and Henry C. Carey. Both men were prolific thinkers, authors, publishers, and advocates, and each was in the vanguard of his chosen side in both debates. Each man's position was cemented by the role of government in his system of thought. To Bryant, free trade and international copyright were policies consistent with a government whose role was to secure free labor. To Carey, protection and opposition to international copyright were policies consistent with a government whose role was to promote the diversification of industry and advancement of the productivity of labor.

What is the relevance of all this to the present? While the economic history of TRIPs may be of use in prescribing beneficial intellectual property institutions for developing countries, the intellectual history of TRIPs is more likely to be useful for different ends. The ideas proffered by the likes of Bryant and Carey influenced the course of policy at once by giving voice to political and economic interests and influencing popular perceptions of those interests. Intellectual history thus offers a way to consider the political and ultimately the economic consequences of economic rhetoric—in the nineteenth century, certainly, and perhaps by analogy today. The questions that I would like to pose are, what may be the political and ultimately the economic consequences in developed countries of TRIPs? What is to be gained or lost by pressing vigorously for the inclusion of more rigorous intellectual property provisions in multilateral, regional, and bilateral trade forums, as the United States has sought to do from the GATT and WTO to the NAFTA, the U.S.-Chile Free Trade Agreement, the Central America–Dominican Republic–U.S. Free Trade Agreement, and the proposed Free Trade Agreement of the Americas? History reminds that the intellectual bundling of free trade and intellectual property has been done before. What might be its repercussions?

Free traders failed repeatedly for sixty years after the end of the Civil War to reduce the average tariff to its immediate prewar level. They failed despite making a case that, by comparison with the one made for free trade today, was compelling. Specifically, the principles of free labor engendered an antimonopoly argument for trade. Free trade, its advocates argued, would eliminate the special privileges granted to producers in specific industries, most notably cotton goods, iron, and steel. It would promote competition, lower prices, and raise consumers' real incomes.

In the quotation just preceding this conclusion, Carey attempted to turn the tables on the free traders: he argued that free trade promoted monopoly, and protection mitigated it. His conviction was sincere—but that particular part of his argument was unpersuasive, and relatively few of his followers bothered to repeat it. He was much more persuasive in arguing that international copyright promoted monopoly.

In the face of the latter argument, the proponents of free trade and international copyright were put on the defensive. Bryant retorted that it was "a very erroneous view of the matter":

> A copy-right law instead of being a monopoly, is the very reverse. A monopoly is a legislative grant, to an individual or association, of exclusive or peculiar privileges or immunities denied to the rest of the community. A copyright law, on the other hand, confers no new privilege or immunity, but absolutely takes away a portion of an author's right of property in a work of his own creation, and renders no equivalent, except the mere guarding the remainder with some special provisions. (Bryant 1994, 57)

Here Bryant's argument is the less persuasive one. One wonders whether the tireless advocacy of international copyright by free traders like Bryant—who framed the cause as one inextricably related to free trade—hindered the advancement of their principal cause. The long-awaited sweeping tariff reductions were deferred until 1913. Might the wait have been shorter if the antimonopoly credentials of the free-trade advocates had not been called into question?

References

Barnes, James J. 1974. *Authors, Publishers, and Politicians: The Quest for an Anglo-American Copyright Agreement, 1815–1854*. Columbus: Ohio State University Press.

Bhagwati, Jagdish. 2004. Free Trade after Cancún. *Foreign Affairs* 83.1:52–63.

Bowker, R. R. 1886. *Copyright: Its Law and Literature*. New York: Office of the Publishers' Weekly.

Brown, Charles H. 1971. *William Cullen Bryant*. New York: Charles Scribner's Sons.

Bryant, William Cullen. 1848. Memorials of John Jay and of William C. Bryant and Others in Favor of an International Copyright Law. House Misc. Doc. No. 76, 30th Cong., 1st sess., 29 April.

Bryant, William Cullen, II, ed. 1994. *Power for Sanity: Selected Editorials of William Cullen Bryant, 1829–1861*. New York: Fordham University Press.

Carey, Henry Charles. 1853. Note from Henry C. Carey. *Putnam's Monthly Magazine of American Literature, Science, and Art* 2.8:229–31.

———. [1853] 1883. Letters on International Copyright. In vol. 1 of *Miscellaneous Works of Henry C. Carey*, edited by William Elder. Philadelphia: Henry Carey Baird & Co.

———. [1847] 1872. *The Past, the Present, and the Future*. Philadelphia: Henry Carey Baird & Co.

———. 1872. *The Unity of Law; as Exhibited in the Relations of Physical, Social, Mental, and Moral Science*. Philadelphia: Henry Carey Baird & Co.

———. [1858] 1883. *Principles of Social Science*. Philadelphia: J. B. Lippincott & Co.

Chang, Ha-Joon. 2001. Intellectual Property Rights and Economic Development: Historical Lessons and Emerging Issues. *Journal of Human Development* 2.2:287–309.

———. 2002. *Kicking away the Ladder: Development Policy in Historical Perspective*. London: Anthem Press.

Clark, Aubert J. [1960] 1973. *The Movement for International Copyright in Nineteenth Century America*. Westport, Conn.: Greenwood Press.

Clay, Henry. [1837] 1896. Henry Clay's Report in Favor of International Copyright. In *The Question of Copyright*, edited by George H. Putnam. New York: G. P. Putnam's Sons.

Elder, William. [1880] 1883. A Memoir of Henry C. Carey. In vol. 1 of *Miscellaneous Works of Henry C. Carey*, edited by William Elder. Philadelphia: Henry Carey Baird & Co.

Godwin, Parke. 1883. *A Biography of William Cullen Bryant, with Extracts from His Private Correspondence*. New York: D. Appleton & Company.

Kaser, David. 1957. *Messrs. Carey & Lea of Philadelphia: A Study in the History of the Booktrade*. Philadelphia: University of Pennsylvania Press.

Khan, B. Zorina. 2004. *Does Copyright Piracy Pay? The Effects of U.S. International Copyright Laws on the Market for Books, 1790–1920*. Cambridge, Mass.: National Bureau of Economic Research.

Lehmann-Haupt, Hellmut. 1951. *The Book in America: A History of the Making and Selling of Books in the United States*. New York: R. R. Bowker Company.

McGill, Meredith L. 2003. *American Literature and the Culture of Reprinting, 1834–1853*. Philadelphia: University of Pennsylvania Press.

Morrison, Rodney J. 1986. Henry C. Carey and American Economic Development. *Transactions of the American Philosophical Society* 76.3:1–91.

O'Connor, Michael Joseph Lalor. 1944. *Origins of Academic Economics in the United States*. New York: Columbia University Press.

Putnam, George H. 1891. *The Question of Copyright: A Summary of the Copyright Laws at Present in Force in the Chief Countries of the World*. New York: G. P. Putnam's Sons.

Temin, Peter. 2000. The Industrialization of New England, 1830–1880. In *Engines of Enterprise: An Economic History of New England*, edited by Peter Temin. Cambridge, Mass.: Harvard University Press.

U.S. Census Bureau. 1975. *Historical Statistics of the United States: Colonial Times to 1970*. Series U211-12. Washington, D.C.: U.S. Government Printing Office.

U.S. Congress. 1853. Senate Confidential Ex. Doc. No. 6, 32nd Cong., 2nd sess., 24 February.

———. 1854. Senate Confidential Ex. Doc. No. 6, 33rd Cong., 1st sess., 24 January.

Bringing in the State? The Life and Times of Laissez-Faire in the Nineteenth-Century United States

Bradley W. Bateman

The stylized facts of when and how the federal government became directly involved with the economy in the United States are reasonably well known. Although the Progressives in the early twentieth century had advocated a strong role for the state in regulating the economy, their successes in "bringing in the state" were largely limited to the state and municipal level.[1] Not until the Great Depression and the election of Franklin Delano Roosevelt did the federal government become more fully involved in regulating and stabilizing the American economy.[2]

This essay was first presented to the History of Economic Thought Workshop at the University of Toronto, 12 March 2004. Avi J. Cohen, Alan Hines, David Laidler, and Don Moggridge each provided helpful comments in the revision of this essay. I also received several helpful comments at the 2004 *HOPE* conference. I especially appreciate the comments and prodding from Roger Backhouse, Tim Leonard, Steve Meardon, Steve Medema, and Warren Samuels. Bill Barber provided useful comments on this essay at the History of Economic Society meetings at Victoria College, University of Toronto, 28 June 2004. My research assistant, Anh Trinh, read the penultimate draft of the essay and made several helpful suggestions. I, alone, retain responsibility for any errors that remain.

1. The phrase "bringing in the state" comes from Evans, Rueschemeyer, and Skocpol 1985. It is of central importance to understand that many Progressives were ideologically comfortable with state intervention in the economy only at the state and local level, but not at the federal level. Because this essay deals only with the federal level of economic intervention, many of the Progressives' efforts were taking place in another arena.

2. The least-hagiographic account of how economic management was introduced in the New Deal is Barber 1996. Bradford Lee (1989) provides a compelling account of the restraints that held Herbert Hoover back from expanding the federal government's role in the economy, despite the potential for electoral success if he undertook such an expansion.

Likewise, the stylized facts of when and how American economists first moved beyond the precepts of a minimalist state, and their arguments for "bringing in the state" to help manage the economy, are a reasonably well-known story. When Richard T. Ely, Henry Carter Adams, John Bates Clark, and their colleagues founded the American Economic Association in 1885, one part of their intention was to counter arguments for laissez-faire and to develop arguments in favor of the importance of the state to a well-functioning economy. These "ethical economists" failed in their ambition to create a forum for actively advocating the state's role in the economy, for the AEA very quickly became the home for economists of all stripes, and several of the most prominent of the ethical economists who had founded the organization were forced through academic trials to pull back during the 1890s from public positions in favor of labor unions and the right to strike.[3]

What success the "ethical economists" were to enjoy in influencing economic policy came later, in the first two decades of the twentieth century, when the Progressive movement began to realize some electoral success. Virtually all of those who kept their academic positions in the last two decades of the nineteenth century eventually gained prominence in the Progressive movement and were able to make important contributions then to the debate of such emerging issues as child labor and unemployment insurance.[4] In their many fights, they won a moral battle in establishing the first beachhead for academic expertise in questions of economic management, and they were successful at helping to shape the first pieces of labor legislation (at the state and local level); but the establishment of a viable federal welfare state and a serious notion of economic stabilization were still two decades away at the time that the Progressive project collapsed following World War I and the social sciences in America retreated into scientism.[5]

3. The standard accounts of the early life of the AEA are Furner 1975 and Ross 1991.

4. The best treatment of the role of the ethical economists in early Progressive Era policymaking is Moss 1996, which discusses the formation and work of the American Association of Labor Legislation. One of Moss's important contributions is in pointing out that the contemporaneous conception of federalism limited the ethical economists' success in getting legislation passed.

5. There is certainly more than one way to interpret the stylized facts about the first efforts at "bringing in the state." Richard Vietor (2000) says that during 1914–32 the economic regulation in the American economy outside the bounds of the Federal Reserve Act (1913), the Clayton Antitrust Act (1914), and the Transportation Act (1920) was decentralized and not at the federal level. "Regulatory responsibilities in most other areas of the economy were still decentralized" (973). Of the areas covered by these three landmark pieces of legislation, he says, "none of

The purpose of this essay is to scrutinize the cultural background to the rise of the "ethical economists" in the nineteenth century and so to explore the contexts in which they tried to introduce economic management to the modern American economy. This background helps explain both the style and spirit in which they attempted to make their stand as well as the structural barriers to their success. While the fate of the ethical economists is not completely determined by this background, it is impossible to understand the material on which chance and circumstance operated without understanding these cultural elements.[6]

A New Country, a New Idea, and a New Church

Following the Revolution, American society took several unexpected turns. In a popular, largely uncoordinated effort to make good on the promises of the Revolution, citizens turned against many of the leaders and institutions that had shaped the American Revolution. No sooner had Washington been inaugurated than the populace began to turn against the idea of a ruling elite that would control politics and the evolution of the new nation. In particular, the arguments of Alexander Hamilton and the Federalists became increasingly unpopular. Although Washington's cabinet was composed of the good and the great from the ranks of the revolutionary leaders, he was unable to keep them together and above partisanship. The Federalists had argued persuasively during the period of constitutional negotiation that "faction" and "interest" should not be a part of the national government, but now, in the breach, "party" seemed to be an inevitable result of power and governing. Hamilton and the Federalists argued for "energetic" government, but Jefferson was dubious: "I am not a friend to a very energetic government."

---

the three proved sufficient for coping with the problems that developed a decade later" (972). Jonathan Hughes (1977), however, sees a vast network of economic regulation that derived first in the colonial period and led to an interventionist mind-set that he believes never relented.

6. I have created an easier task, but one that is at least manageable in the space provided, by treating only the federal state in this essay. It is certainly true, as both Alan Hines and Don Moggridge were quick to point out to me, that some individual states had a somewhat different experience with efforts to regulate and stimulate the economy during the years of the early republic. Whereas there was little support then for federal intervention in the economy, some states such as Pennsylvania were much more experimental. Louis Hartz (1948) provides a complete story of state efforts to stimulate and regulate the Pennsylvanian economy. The redeeming fact of these experiments, for the purposes of this essay, is that while they represent a contrary trend in some states during the first eighty to ninety years of the republic, they culminated in a widespread disgruntlement by the time of the Civil War so that the appeal of the laissez-faire arguments was widespread at both the state and federal levels by 1860, or earlier.

In the public mind, and in public rhetoric, the issue was the meaning of republicanism. The Federalists' conceptions of an educated elite who would rule disinterestedly over the rest of society came from Aristotle and European philosophy; theirs was classical republicanism in which civic duty was being exercised by an elite.[7] Now, however, in a way that no one was able to control, the American public was redefining republicanism to mean the control of the government by the common people. Rather than accept that some people were better suited through birth, wealth, or education to lead the new nation, so-called democratic societies sprang up in every state, and in most large cities, espousing a new conception of republicanism; instead of focusing on the importance of cultivating civic virtue in the ruling class, the rhetoric of republicanism quickly adapted itself to a new focus on individual autonomy and public sovereignty. There was also an explosion of newspapers in the two decades after ratification of the Constitution, most of which espoused the new theory of republicanism.[8] One might say that the idea of a new "democratic republicanism" was being forged at the grassroots level.

It is, of course, ironic that the "founding father" most sympathetic to the new republican movement should be one of the best educated and one with a clear claim to a position in the "natural aristocracy" of the new nation. But Thomas Jefferson was, nonetheless, to emerge as the representative of this populist movement. Joyce Appleby (1984, 84) has accused Jefferson of being "sly" when he wrote that "the introduction of this new principle of representative democracy has rendered useless almost everything written before on the structure of government, and in a great measure relieves our regret, if the political writings of Aristotle, or any other antient have been lost." The simple fact is, however, that Jefferson was a serious student of the Scottish Enlightenment and knew his Adam Smith well. Although his statement was certainly deliberate, it was not necessarily sly or opportunistic. Smith rejected Aristotle's argument that civic virtue resided in a disinterested elite, and likewise Jefferson.[9]

7. Richard Bushman (1979) offers an excellent survey of the issues at stake in public discourse about republicanism at the time of the Declaration of Independence.

8. James Kloppenberg (1987) offers a convincing explanation of the transformation of republican rhetoric in light of three contending threads in American discourse: religious, political, and moral. Joyce Appleby (1984) provides a useful survey of the democratic societies and of the changing nature of newspaper publishing in the early republic.

9. The best account of Jefferson's relationship to the Scottish Enlightenment generally, and Adam Smith specifically, is Wills 1978. More comprehensive treatments of the influence of

Smith's teachings jibed with the new republicanism in another important way. In addition to insisting that common men could speak and vote for themselves, the new republicans based an important part of their optimistic assumptions about America's future on their belief that economic prosperity would flow from the initiative of common men such as themselves. They believed that the wealth of the nation would emerge from the work of their hands, and they wanted to be let free to pursue their own self-interests.

But while Jefferson could square his elite education with the political and economic impulses of the new republicans, there is little reason to think that the men who drove this grassroots movement were themselves influenced by Smith.[10] In fact, while the members of the democratic societies and the bulk of the new newspaper publishers were avidly republican, and were quite sophisticated in their uses and adaptations of the republican idea, they distrusted formal education and abjured European philosophy. In short, they were anti-intellectual.[11]

Nowhere was this anti-intellectualism more apparent than in the grassroots revolution that transformed American Protestantism in the early republic. America had not been a particularly religious country before the Revolution, but in the years immediately following the Revolution there was a swelling of religious fervor that was unmatched in the Atlantic world.[12] Men and women who had lived through the successful establishment of the new nation, and who now watched a wholesale

Scottish Enlightenment philosophy on the American Revolution can be found in May 1976 and White 1978.

10. William Barber (1988, 5) states that Smith was not popular in college curricula in the early republic because he was thought to be "unsound on matters of religious doctrine." Martin Burke (1995, chap. 3) points out that Smith's dichotomy between productive and unproductive labor made him suspect to educated ministers who disliked being seen as "unproductive." It is worth noting in this context that most professors in the early decades of the republic were ordained ministers.

11. The standard reference on the origins and development of anti-intellectualism in American life is Hofstadter 1962. Nathan Hatch (1989, 11) suggests that because the evangelicals who were so central to the rise of republican thinking published many tracts, we should rethink Hofstadter's characterization of them as anti-intellectual. This is surely an error, however, for the use of print media does not qualify one as an intellectual. The constant denigration of formal education and the populist insistence on the wisdom of the uneducated must surely count as anti-intellectual, whether the argument is made orally or in print. Hofstadter (1962, 7) perhaps makes the point best when he says, "The common strain that binds together the attitudes and ideas which I call anti-intellectual is a resentment and suspicion of the life of the mind and those who represent it; and a disposition constantly to minimize the value of that life."

12. Jon Butler (1990) tells the story of how Christianity spread after the Revolution.

movement out of settled communities and onto the frontier, believed that they were living in a special time in human history. Their belief in the uniqueness of the new history that they were creating fed an "enthusiastic" interest in evangelical Protestantism. Just as the common people felt themselves empowered to make political decisions and rejected the wisdom of an educated political elite, they felt empowered to make religious decisions and rejected the authority of an educated clergy. So deep was the revulsion against educated clergymen that the national church organizations were unable to control the flow of new literature, the rise of itinerant preachers, and the establishment of new congregations. Just as political leaders such as John Adams and Alexander Hamilton found themselves unable to control or influence popular political sentiment, religious leaders found themselves unable to control the surge of religious "enthusiasm" erupting around them.

Thus, the anti-intellectualism that shaped the emerging democratic impulse of the early republic influenced both political and religious life. By 1800 the majority of white Americans had embraced Jefferson's Republican Party, and Methodists and Baptists were spreading across the nation at an unprecedented speed.[13] "The eighteen hundred Christian ministers serving in 1775 swelled to nearly forty thousand by 1845. The number of ministers per capita more than tripled; the colonial legacy of one minister per fifteen hundred inhabitants became one per five hundred. . . . The Congregationalists, which had twice the clergy of any other American Church in 1775, could not muster one tenth the preaching force of the Methodists in 1845" (Hatch 1989, 4).[14]

A Political Economy without Economists

The heyday of nineteenth-century American use of the term *laissez-faire* to denote the argument for a minimalist state was undoubtedly in the decades following the Civil War. The term came into widespread use then through the influence of the social Darwinism of Herbert Spencer

13. Perhaps nowhere is the relationship of Jefferson to the people who voted for him as ironic as in the case of the evangelical Christians. Jefferson himself was a committed deist, who did not believe in the divinity of Jesus; but in the eyes of the evangelicals he was heroic for work to disestablish the church in Virginia following independence. The evangelicals saw disestablishment as the key to their own rise in popularity.

14. This reduction in the number of ministers per capita is even more impressive when it is considered against the swelling population of the period.

and William Graham Sumner (Fine 1956, 29).[15] But while the term *laissez-faire* was not as widely used in the first half of the nineteenth century, the idea that the government had little or no constructive role to play in the economy dominated American life through the cultural influence of republicanism.[16] "In the early nineteenth century, to be an American was by definition to be a republican, the inheritor of a revolutionary legacy in a world ruled by aristocrats and kings" (Wilentz 1984, 61). And these republicans believed that left to their own devices, Americans could build a vibrant economy.[17]

When Alexis de Tocqueville visited the United States in 1829–31, his observations seemed to bear out the truth of the republicans' belief. "In democracies nothing is greater or more brilliant than commerce; it is what attracts the regard of the public and fills the imagination of the crowd; all energetic passions are directed toward it. . . . They are therefore all brought into commerce, not only because of the gain it promises them, but for love of the emotions that it gives them" ([1840] 2000, 528). True to their word, the republicans who had spread out onto the frontier were avid to make a success of themselves.

But the economic ideal that animated the republicans was not taken from a textbook; it was a popular idea turned into a cultural more. While men like Jefferson may have been well versed in their Adam Smith, the ordinary people whose thoughts and arguments made the republican movement were not taking their cues from learned treatises in economics or politics.[18] In fact, the American soil was so barren for scholarship

15. There had always been a more limited use of the term *laissez-faire* to characterize the position of the free traders who opposed tariffs. I am interested here only in the larger sense of the term in its broader meaning of minimal state intervention in the national economy. As Tim Leonard points out in his essay in this volume, it would have been more accurate to use the term *social Lamarckians* rather than the term *social Darwinists*. For a nuanced treatment of the complications in interpreting nineteenth-century interpretations of Darwinism and its application to human society, see Paul 2002.

16. In focusing on the extent to which arguments were made for active government involvement in managing the economy, I am skirting one of the largest debates in the historiography of nineteenth-century American ideas; namely, whether republican thought is correctly characterized as liberal thought. This literature is simply too large to address adequately in the space available.

17. Appleby 1984 contains an explanation of the degree to which the reality of this vision was underpinned by changing European populations and the sudden increases in demand for American wheat after 1757.

18. Burke (1995, 80, 90–91) points out that in the 1830s, texts written for the express purpose of popularizing Smith's teachings for workingmen began to be published. Some texts supported his teachings, some argued against them.

and formal learning that no economic treatises were produced in the first two decades of the nineteenth century. In this sense, republicanism was an idea that animated a populace of anti-intellectuals.

When economic texts and treatises did begin to appear, they were neither original nor particularly analytical. The analytical texts were largely the efforts of men like Daniel Raymond or George Fitzhugh who tried to rework Ricardian themes to explain why the American case was so different from the British. The greatest success, however, and the author of the best-selling textbook was Francis Wayland, an ordained Baptist minister and the president of the Baptists' college in Rhode Island, Brown University. Wayland's *Elements of Political Economy* (1837) contained an amalgam of moral edicts about the importance of capital to economic growth, the sanctity of private property, and the harmony of interests that existed between the various classes of American society. The harmony of interests drew directly from Frédéric Bastiat's work, the commitment to minimalist government was purely republican, and the moral tone was set by evangelical Protestantism.[19]

At this time, the capstone course of American undergraduate education was taught by the college president and consisted of lessons in moral philosophy. In a pragmatic nation suspicious of intellectuals and animated by evangelical Protestantism, Wayland's text represented a workable compromise for such a course. It was a safe book from which young men could be taught the verities of entrepreneurial capitalism.

Wayland's book was also popular, however, because by the 1830s the various evangelical sects on the frontier were entering a second generation, and many of these people felt a desire for education and professional opportunity for their children as communities once again began to become more settled. Hofstadter (1962) argues that anti-intellectualism always lies latent in American culture, but that it tends to ebb and flow. Desiring to educate their children for the professions, the citizens of the frontier states (and territories) built hundreds of small, church-supported colleges. A book such as Wayland's was a nonthreatening way to educate those youth. Until the Civil War, this was to be the measure of formal American economic thought; it was largely a vehicle for propagating the shared values of the Protestant ethic, self-determination, and

19. A. W. Coats (1988, 358) terms these thinkers the "clerical Ricardians." The term is perfectly apt, as long as one keeps in mind that they were trying to adapt Ricardo's theory to a different end than Ricardo had; they were Ricardian in method, though not in result.

republicanism.[20] America had gotten economists, but the basic premises of American economic thought had not been changed; it was a reflection of the popular discourse on economic life.

A Party of Republicans

This is not to say that there were not differences of opinion between American economists. The foremost difference was between those who supported a tariff and those who did not. But in the first half of the nineteenth century, the tariff was an issue that split republicans, not republicans and antirepublicans.[21] The most famous advocate of tariffs to protect American industry (as opposed to those who wanted nominal tariffs to raise revenue), Henry Carey, was a republican, as was Daniel Raymond, for whom Carey had tried to obtain an appointment at the University of Maryland. Those who advocated a protective tariff argued that the American impulse to hard work and entrepreneurship would be able to play out more fully without the threatening competition of the large monopolistic capital accumulations of Europe. Theirs was largely an argument for creating a set of institutional arrangements under which the republican ideal could be most fully realized. American republicanism in the early republic was antimonopolistic and egalitarian, and these influences carried through strongly in the entire antebellum period.

But unlike the tariff, the issue of slavery did eventually cause republicans to choose sides. By the 1830s, when Jackson's Democracy and the Whigs had become the two leading parties, republicanism had become a plank of both parties' ideologies. Through the many party splits and the realignments in party politics in the early nineteenth century, autonomy and popular sovereignty remained at the core of the American national ethos, and republicanism was the banner under which they flourished.

But as slavery moved from a moral, religious issue to a political issue in the two decades before the Civil War, the "political abolitionists" came increasingly to use and shape republican rhetoric to make their arguments. As a moral issue, abolition was unable to move a majority of

20. Two of Wayland's competitors in the early market for economic textbooks, Thomas Cooper (South Carolina College) and Thomas Roderick Dew (College of William and Mary), were also college presidents. In different ways, their texts addressed the special economic and social conditions of the South.

21. It is true, of course, that the Whigs generally supported the tariff and that Jackson's Democracy did not. But there were prominent strands of republican thought in each party.

Americans. In fact, many who disliked slavery would have no truck with the group of Christians who formed the "moral abolitionist" camp. Men like Salmon P. Chase and William H. Seward, who became leaders of the political abolitionists, found the tool they needed to move the public to the cause of abolition when they turned to republicanism. Drawing on the ideas of autonomy, self-determination, and public sovereignty, they were able to fashion a series of arguments that appealed to the public in terms that were at once familiar and fresh. They subjected issues such as whether to extend slavery into the territories and the practice of holding humans as slaves to detailed republican analysis. As their arguments were spread and elaborated, the slaveholders (the "Slave Power") came to be depicted as the kind of aristocratic, elite power that was thought to have been the pinnacle of classical republicanism. Thus, the political abolitionists were able to shape a public rhetoric that appealed to small farmers and independent artisans without using "learned" arguments. They were brilliantly inventive in a way that did not trigger anti-intellectual reaction.

The crux of the argument about the need to keep slavery out of the territories was an economic argument. From firsthand reports and widespread newspaper coverage of the South, the political abolitionists formed the opinion that "slavery would have to be abolished as an intolerable obstacle to regional and national development" (Foner 1970, 41). The vitality and drive that the republicans attributed to "free labor" was widely seen to be absent in the slaveholding South because of the servile condition of the laboring population. Slaves, of course, were said to have no incentives to work hard because they lacked the ability to improve their status. But the political abolitionists also believed that slavery caused the position of white small farmers and artisans in the South to be degraded. Without easy access to land, without access to high-wage farm work, without fundamental respect for those who labor, and without a thriving laboring class to support shopkeepers and artisans, there was no chance for economic development. At the same time, the political abolitionists saw Northern society as dynamic and fast developing into a new kind of capitalist society. "The ideal of equal opportunity for social mobility and economic independence seemed to them to be not dreams but living realities" (29).

This distinction between a slow, debilitated South and a vibrant North formed the basis of the republican argument against allowing slavery into the territories. On the one hand, the political abolitionists wanted to diminish the reach of the stagnation that they saw in the South; on the other hand, they believed that the success of their ideology depended on eventual access to the land in the territories by Northern laborers. The 1850s were the period of the most rapid movement out of established farms and towns in the East onto the frontier, and so this argument reached people in a way that the moral antislavery argument had not. Each month in the 1850s saw thousands of families depart for the territories, and these people were receptive to the newly packaged argument for abolition.

The broad outline of the arguments against slavery can be seen in these arguments against its extension into the territories. Slavery was demeaning and kept slaves from becoming hardworking contributors to the nation's economic development. But it is undoubtedly the case that the weight of this argument still fell on the effects of slavery on the white populace. The fact that the nation was not growing and developing as fast as it might was more compelling for many people than was the degraded condition of the slaves. Likewise, the argument that the Slave Power was taking over American democracy and instituting a native aristocracy was repugnant to those who held the basic American ideals of autonomy and public sovereignty. Racism and racial misunderstanding were still the order of the day; slavery was largely a problem in the abstract for white Northerners (Foner 1970, chaps. 8, 9).

The white Northerners who eventually supported the broad republican position against slavery were drawn, of course, from both the Whigs and the Democracy. Factions within each party opposed slavery, and the efforts of the Southern slaveholders to control national politics created bitter resentment in each party. When a name for the new party that would shelter these various factions had to be found, an obvious choice was the Republican Party, since so many Americans conceived of themselves within the rhetorical framework of the new republicanism that had been created at the time of the nation's founding.

But the name was more than just a ploy or a rhetorical spin. Not only was the party built on the shell of the Free Soil Party, which had fought to keep the territories free of slavery, but its second major plank was "free labor," drawn from the republican ideal that American society should be shaped by small farmers, shopkeepers, artisans, and mechanics. The party staunchly espoused the antislavery position in 1856 and 1860, but it espoused the free labor position with equal fervor. In principle, this meant that the party stood not just for the abolition of slavery but for something positive, as well, "the affirmation of the superiority of the social system of the North—a dynamic, expanding capitalist society, whose achievements and destiny were almost wholly the result of the dignity and the opportunities which it offered the average working man" (Foner 1970, 11). It is crucial to understand, however, that this concept of American labor entailed the peculiarly American concepts of equality and classlessness: the laborers of the Republican ideology were not a propertyless, wage-earning class. Abraham Lincoln always defined capital as accumulated labor, and Horace Greeley (1850, 9) defined labor as "useful doing in any capacity or vocation." Thus, most all Northerners were thought to fit under this rubric. Being in support of "labor" was actually the opposite of class warfare; it was part of an explicit effort to erase class lines by equating the work of virtually all people, making it all dignified, and giving warrant to the success of anyone who was "self-made."

In practice, the economic policies of the antebellum Republicans were negotiated over a range of options that continued to fit the republican outlook of the previous half century. The most well-remembered Republican economic policy is probably Carey's advocacy of the tariff, but, as pointed out above, his position was predicated on the assumption that a tariff would create more opportunities for small artisans and mechanics and so make republican society more robust. Carey's argument was about the *framework* for supporting a dynamic republican society. Likewise, the right to strike was a key part of Republican economic policy. Striking, however, meant only the right to leave a job; the accumulated labor in a capitalist's plant and equipment was his by his rights to the product of his own labor, and his employees were argued to have no right to "strike" in the modern sense. "Strikers" were men who left an employment that they did not like and who would move west and make an effort to raise their own capital by homesteading.[22]

Thus, the antebellum Republican Party had an idea of the economy and economic policy that called for some role for the government, but not an active one. The government should set the rules that would unleash

22. To fully understand this concept of striking, it is helpful to consider that in the eighteenth century it had been illegal in many states to leave one's employment before the end of a contract. The history and widespread practice of indentured slavery for whites also is important to seeing this "free labor" concept of striking in its full context. For a discussion of the actual practice of indentured slavery and statistics on its prevalence in colonial America, see Hughes 1977.

the small entrepreneur, and this would, in turn, free up the initiative and hard work of the population. What they expected to achieve with this policy was not unlike what Tocqueville saw when he had visited thirty years earlier.

But while the party's slogan "Free Soil, Free Labor, Free Men" was an effective rallying cry and appealed to the instincts of a generation of Northerners who were highly mobile and relocating to the Northwest Territory, it was also a rhetoric that was being eclipsed as it was being uttered. Even before the Civil War, the size of the wage-earning population was expanding rapidly. Lincoln claimed in 1859 that no more than one-eighth of the working population was engaged in wage labor, but estimates in the twentieth century have placed the percentage of workers in 1860 earning wages, not "independently employed," as closer to 60 percent.[23]

Now All Change

But whatever the fit of the republican's free labor ideology before the war, it became completely outdated after the war. During the last thirty-five years of the century, as the nation underwent industrialization, urbanization, and mass immigration, the ideal of the independent man able to earn his way in the world through dint of hard labor, and thus to accumulate a small capital for himself, became obsolete. The vertical integration of American industry simply overwhelmed the possibility of widespread success through small entrepreneurship; now workingmen were wage laborers, and they were not likely to become anything else.[24]

But American industry was not the only institution in American society that was changing. As the nation struggled with, and failed to reconcile, the fate of the freed men, modernity settled over every aspect of American culture.

One of the first places that this happened was Protestantism. The effects of Darwin's *On the Origin of Species* (1859), together with the

23. The 60 percent figure comes from Eric Foner (1970, 32), who is citing David Montgomery (1967, 26–30). Bushman (1979, 92) claims that the number was closer to 40 percent. Robert Margo (2000, 214) reports that 37 percent of American labor was employed in manufacturing in 1860, to which would have to be added (at a minimum) employment in mining, construction, trade, and transportation. In addition, some agricultural labor would also be wage earning but not "independent." In any case, the figure is large and far exceeds Lincoln's modest estimate.

24. Rowland Berthoff (1979) questions whether the republican ideal had become impractical for Americans as an actual guide to their economic lives at a much earlier date.

Higher Criticism from Germany, unsettled the Protestant churches as they struggled with their traditional belief in the literal truth of the Bible. Before the Civil War, virtually all denominations and sects of Protestantism believed in the literal truth of Hebrew and Christian scripture; now they faced serious arguments from different quarters that it was perhaps only a symbolic text. This would eventually lead to a split in the last decades of the century between a "private" party of Protestants who continued to insist on the literal truth of the Bible and to emphasize individual salvation, and a "public" party working instead on the reform of social problems.[25]

The private party of Protestants focused on the denial of scientific and humanistic scholarship and thus drew heavily on the native traditions of anti-intellectualism. Not unlike the republicans during the first half of the century who had embraced an idea but rejected intellectual culture and scholarly achievement, the private party Protestants embraced the Bible as a text but rejected any scholarly exegesis that did not fit their arguments of inerrancy.

The public party, on the other hand, drew from a long tradition of Christian reform, dating at least from the Second Great Awakening, and which had always been comfortable with scholarship and higher learning. For instance, late in his career, Charles Gradison Finney, perhaps the most high-profile minister in the Second Great Awakening, became closely identified with Oberlin College. Thus, it is not surprising that the leaders of the public party were often excellent writers and that many were college administrators or professors.[26]

Their attachment to colleges and universities meant that opportunities for public party Christians were rapidly expanding at the end of the nineteenth century. University enrollments in the United States increased four times faster than the rate of population growth between 1870 and 1910 (Schmidt 1957, 182).[27] And, likewise, the number of faculty positions was increasing quickly. A. W. Coats (1988, 34) reports that while there is no truly reliable guide, the number of teaching hours for

25. This description of a two-party Protestantism comes from Marty 1986. Ferenc Szasz (1982) has shown that the tension between Darwinism and evangelical Christianity was relatively mild until the 1920s; the Higher Criticism was actually much more disturbing to evangelical Christians in the decades at the end of the nineteenth century.

26. See, for instance, Handy 1950, 97–115.

27. Coats (1988, 439 n. 9) reports that the number of degrees granted increased at the rate of 450 percent, twice the rate of population growth in the same period.

economics increased about sixfold between 1876 and 1890. Thus, there was room for new professors in a rapidly growing field.

But despite these impressive numbers, the going was not easy for members of the public party who wanted to work in academe rather than in the ministry. There was actually no common name for the many varieties of public party Protestants at this time; they were called, among other things, social Christians and the Kingdom movement. Early in the twentieth century, however, they became labeled as followers of the Social Gospel, the term that is still most commonly used (retrospectively) by church historians and social historians. Not surprisingly, given the rapidly changing industrial conditions, the most prominent advocates of the Social Gospel in the academy were the "ethical economists." When they looked at the condition of white workingmen, or at the life of immigrants in the rapidly growing cities, they were repulsed. Thus, they wanted to address issues such as the working conditions in factories, child labor, and urban poverty. They felt a Christian impulse to help the poor and the oppressed, and saw the plight of the less fortunate as an economic problem. It was exactly this impulse that made their entrance into university life so difficult.

Although there was an acute need for more professors in the classroom, the power structure of American universities was firmly in the hands of the industrial capitalists. Whether the university was private or public, the captains of industry controlled the boards of trustees. In this environment, it became virtually impossible in the 1870s and 1880s to be an advocate of the rights of labor or of an active role for the state in controlling the economy and to also work in an American university.

Although American universities were quickly developing toward their twentieth-century positions of world academic leadership, they were still hobbled by the cultural mores of the early nineteenth century. Widely seen as an appropriate site for practical learning, universities were expected to train people for professional careers and to develop technical expertise, but they were not valued by the larger public as a location for scholarly or intellectual achievement. Professors sought and found a certain degree of autonomy if they did work that did not have social implications; but if it did, they found themselves under close scrutiny. Throughout the last two decades of the nineteenth century, prominent young ethical economists were put on "academic trial" for their beliefs; they were all either dismissed or changed their views.[28]

28. Furner 1975, Ross 1991, and Coats 1988 all provide good coverage of the extent of these trials and their outcomes.

Even before these trials, it had not been practical to be an academic economist after the Civil War unless one advocated the absolute right of corporate capital to do as it pleased. Francis Amasa Walker, the president of MIT and the first president of the American Economic Association, said in one of his AEA presidential addresses that when he had entered the profession that laissez-faire "was not made the test of economic orthodoxy, merely. It was used to decide whether a man were an economist at all" (quoted in Coats 1988, 362).

This dominance of laissez-faire in university economics departments merely reflected the situation in the larger culture. As Sidney Fine (1956, 29) has shown, "in the period between Appomattox and the accession of Theodore Roosevelt to the presidency in 1901, laissez-faire was championed in America as it never was before and has never been since." This dominance of an explicit laissez-faire ideology was novel in many regards, most notably in that it drew on the social Darwinist ideas of Herbert Spencer and William Graham Sumner. Their reworking of the idea of the survival of the fittest filled a need for an explanation of why so many people were being pushed down in the new industrialization: they deserved it.[29]

The More Things Change, the More They Stay the Same

But if the argument that the laborers in American industry deserved no more than they received was a novel idea, there was little else that was new about the nature of how this idea was spread and sustained. Sumner was a distinguished Yale professor, but his ideas were bad popularizations of what Darwin had written. And as economic ideas, they have had no lasting influence on economic analysis; they were devoid of analytical content. But they were extremely popular, nonetheless. Their popularity rested not on their closeness to Darwin's ideas but rather on the convergence of several traditional elements in American culture: republicanism, evangelical Christianity, and anti-intellectualism. Sumner presented evolutionary ideas in a form that appealed to people whose thinking was already shaped by these forces in American culture.

29. Sidney Fine details how Spencer's and Sumner's works were embraced in popular culture. Diane Paul (2002) explains the extent to which social Darwinism actually drew from Darwin's work, a point also discussed by Tim Leonard in his essay in this volume.

Nancy Cohen (2002) has recently shown how republican ideology changed in the decades after the Civil War. Frustrated on the one hand with the failure of Reconstruction and the abject state of the freedmen, and impressed on the other hand with the efficiency and immensity of industrial explosion, several of the most prominent antebellum republicans developed a "new Liberalism" in the decades after the war.[30] Edwin Godkin, the editor of the *Nation*, was a staunch advocate of the republican arguments against slavery before the war; after the war, he became an apologist for the new economic inequality and the efficiency of large-scale corporations. David Wells was Lincoln's special commissioner of the national revenue; after the war, he became a leading propagandist for the argument that workingmen now needed to accept their new position in industrial capitalism. Free labor and free men were a thing of the past, as republicanism reshaped its rhetoric of economic development and industrial dynamism, and shed its concern for the status of independent workingmen. Now, instead of judging policies on the opportunities they afforded for free labor, policies were to be judged on how much they increased consumption or lowered prices.

The private party of American Protestantism also developed a close, popular bond with the new industrialists. Virtually all the great "captains of industry," including Vanderbilt, Cornell, Rockefeller, Wannamaker, and Carnegie, nurtured their earlier ties with evangelical Christianity. In turn, the private party of Christianity developed and preached the "gospel of wealth." Whereas the republicanism of the early republic and the antebellum years had depended on the idea of small farmers, mechanics, and artisans whose hard work would make them and the country economically successful, now the republican dream became the attainment of great riches through vertical integration and capital accumulation. But whereas the republicanism of the Gilded Age simply gave up on the glorification of the small businessman and "free labor," the evangelical churches continued to offer a rhetoric of salvation that allowed these same people the chance to find personal meaning and social importance in their new roles. Evangelical Christianity and republicanism had been yoked together since the 1790s, and they continued to work in the same direction; but now their roles were shifted. Both republicans and evangelicals praised and honored the new industrial leaders, and claimed that

30. It must be noted that I am talking here about republican thought, not Republican Party thought. Many members of the Democracy who had broken off to help form the Republican Party, such as David Wells, left the party after the Civil War and became Democrats.

their contributions to society warranted whatever condition the workers now found themselves in. But only evangelical Protestantism continued to offer workingmen a vision of their own fundamental dignity.

Anti-intellectualism played the same supporting role in this new configuration that it had since the days of the early republic. On the one hand, it continued to allow evangelical Christians to ignore the scholarly world and especially the emerging scientific knowledge of the late nineteenth century. On the other hand, it allowed businessmen to shape and control the new universities with impunity. If there were professors with "bad" or "unacceptable" ideas, then it was fine to have them censured or fired, since they obviously did not really know very much. Or worse, they had ideas that might disturb what was most important in American life: corporate growth and economic progress. The fear of anarchy after the Haymarket murders in 1886 lent popular legitimacy to this marginalization of the ethical economists' ideas and meant that there was little or no public outcry against their fate. Anti-intellectualism, public opinion, and corporate power fit nicely together at this moment in American history.

Against this background, it is easier to understand both the plight and the tactics of the Social Gospelers. It seems hard to imagine that they ever had a chance during the nineteenth century to seriously affect public attitudes and economic policy. The two denominations with the greatest concentration of ministers preaching a Social Gospel in the nineteenth century were the Congregationalists and the Episcopalians. Each was large, but each had shrunk relative to the other mainline denominations throughout the nineteenth century. Neither commanded a large enough following on the national level to influence national politics. And there is no evidence that a majority of the people in the pews of either church were ever actively committed to the ideas they heard preached on Sunday mornings by ministers who advocated the Social Gospel.

Likewise, the Social Gospelers stood little chance of success in the emerging research universities, since these were dependent on corporate money (private universities) or were under immense political pressure from boards controlled by industrialists who were political contributors (public universities). The steady stream of academic trials and firings bore this reality out all too well.

But the tactics of the Social Gospelers drew from the same cultural currents that the laissez-faire economists depended on. Unlike the republican revisionists, the Social Gospelers held onto the traditional republican rhetoric of the importance of the workingman in American society. More to the point, they railed against gross inequalities of income and the political power that accrued to the wealthy. In their devotion to fundamental equality and the dignity of human labor, they were quintessentially American.

The Christian basis of their program was also an aspect of the American culture that had developed in the early republic. Economists such as Richard T. Ely and John R. Commons wanted to redeem the nation through a well-articulated jeremiad. Unfortunately for them, Protestantism was no longer united in the same ways that it had been ninety years earlier, and the anti-intellectual strain of the private party kept the message of the ethical economists safely out of bounds for Protestant workers. And for the growing number of Catholic and Jewish workers, emigrating from southern and central Europe, the Christian nationalism of the ethical economists had no appeal.

The Life and Times of Laissez-Faire

As William Barber (2003, 231) has recently written, "When the country's centennial was celebrated in 1876, American economists had an inferiority complex. Writing on this occasion, Harvard's Charles Dunbar—the first American to be accorded the title of Professor of Political Economy—observed that American scholarship as yet contributed nothing to fundamental economic knowledge. In his reading, American economics to date had been derivative, stagnant, and sterile. He further stated that most of the domestic restatements of doctrines formulated abroad were flawed. Foreign observers tended to echo his appraisal."[31] Against this background, it is not surprising to find that economists' writings on laissez-faire throughout the nineteenth century largely reflected larger cultural mores. The public rhetoric on government involvement in the economy by the end of the century had evolved considerably from its republican form early in the century, and economists such as William Graham Sumner contributed to this metamorphosis with their popularizations of evolutionary ideas.

But it was not until the end of the nineteenth century that analytical ideas about laissez-faire began to be developed by American economists. With the publication of John Bates Clark's *Philosophy of Wealth: Economics Principles Newly Formulated* (1886) and *Distribution of Wealth:*

31. Barber is referring to Dunbar 1876.

A Theory of Wages, Interest, and Profits (1899), Americans were to have their first native, analytical treatments of market forces and the potential and desirability for (or lack of) government intervention. Because so much of American debate in the last decades of the century depended on the changing status of the workingman as an element of American economic growth, it is not surprising that Clark chose to focus his marginal analyses on labor markets.

What is perhaps surprising is that this nascent analytical tradition in American economics sprang from within the ranks of the same ethical economists who had founded the AEA. Like many of the AEA's founding members, Clark had studied in Germany and returned home an advocate of Christian socialism and a national approach to ameliorating economic dislocation. There has been a tendency to lump Clark with the old-school advocates of laissez-faire against whom the AEA's founders were ranged in 1885, but this characterization is incorrect. He was one of the early advocates of Christian socialism and a prominent member of the new school of ethical economists.[32]

But while the exact nature of Clark's trajectory from Christian socialism to marginal productivity theorist is still to be fully explained, the elements of his analytical development should not be surprising. Ely and Clark both studied with Karl Knies at Heidelberg, and both were introduced to marginal thinking in Knies's seminar. And although we tend to focus on Clark's arguments about labor's marginal productivity, the truth is that Ely had already introduced marginal analysis to his popular textbook(s) in the 1880s.[33] Thus, the question is not how Clark became a marginalist, or how marginalism came into American economics; we know the answer to both of those questions. The more interesting and unanswered question is how Clark's use of marginal thinking evolved in the American context.

But whatever the answer to that question is, it is clearly wrong to argue, as Dorothy Ross (1991) and Nancy Cohen (2002) have done, that the appearance of Clark's work at the end of the century marks the triumph of neoclassicism in American economics. That triumph, when it came, was not until sometime after World War II. Mary Morgan and Malcolm Rutherford (1998), among others, have shown conclusively that through the interwar period, American economics continued to be a

32. This is a point made in chapter 2 of Yonay 1998.

33. See Bateman 2004, 193–201, for an early argument along these lines, with more references.

plural enterprise, one not dominated by neoclassical economics. There is, in fact, a serious question of whether Clark's work can be properly called neoclassical. It is clearly marginal, but it does not rise to the same level of being an "engine for analysis" that Alfred Marshall's *Principles of Economics* achieved.[34] Joseph Dorfman (1955) has noted that the German influence in American economics always contained an "Austrian" element, and this is an obvious reference to the simple marginal analytics that Ely and Clark brought home with them. But as in the case of Eugen von Böhm-Bawerk and Friedrich Wieser, who were also Knies's students, there is a long way from Clark to Marshall.

What Ross and Cohen have mistaken for a triumph of neoclassicism is actually a conflation of the early interest in Clark's analytics, which the long quotation from Barber above makes clear was long sought after, with the popular dominance of laissez-faire. As Cohen's work makes clear, there are strong similarities between neoclassicism and some of the revisionist republican arguments about industrial capitalism. In particular, the revisionists moved away from a focus on producers (laborers) and toward a focus on consumption. When the grounding for popular economic arguments moved away from their previous basis in labor output and to a basis in the quantity and price of consumer goods, the ethical basis of popular discourse was, indeed, moving squarely onto the ideological grounds of neoclassical economics.

But this similarity should not be mistaken for a triumph of neoclassicism. There was also a nascent tradition of historical analysis developing at the same time, and it would have widely respected adherents, such as E. R. A. Seligman, at the turn of the century. In fact, the nature of American economics at the turn of the century was very plural, not only in the sense that different schools existed (were emerging) but in the sense that one economist might work in different styles, or different methods (Bateman 1998). And despite the keen interest in the work of Marshall and Clark, it is much more accurate to describe the period as one of détente between the historicists and marginalists of the new school and clerical Ricardians and the laissez-faire advocates of the old school. After the initial ruckus over the founding of the AEA, both sides quieted down and looked for ways to coexist.[35] The main sense of the 1890s

34. A useful discussion on this larger point and the place of Marshall's *Principles of Economics* in the history of neoclassicism is Ekelund and Hebert 2002.

35. This rapprochement is nicely described in Coats 1988. It is explained on a somewhat different basis in Bateman 1998.

might best be described as a search for common ground in which several methods of analysis were tolerated; the common ground that emerged entailed a cautious and uncertain consideration of the nature of the new economic society.

The similarity between some of the popular arguments for laissez-faire at the end of the century and some of Clark's work at the same time raises several interesting questions. Was he, like his predecessors throughout much of the first 125 years of the republic, drawing from popular economic arguments and adapting his analytical interests to fit them? Was Clark as influenced by the contemporary cultural milieu as his less-distinguished predecessors? To what extent was Clark merely replicating what he had learned from Knies, and to what extent was he extending it?

Whatever the answers to these questions, it is difficult to credit Clark with any widespread influence on popular ideas if for no other reason than popular ideas about the role of the state after the publication of his two great works had not perceptibly changed. Laissez-faire dominated before and after.

Thus the role of economists in the evolution of nineteenth-century American ideas about "bringing in the state" was neither original nor profound. To a large extent, they merely reflected the ideas of the popular culture. To the extent that their work became widely read and used in college courses, it served mainly to buttress existing ideas that derived from the republican ideology that had developed at the end of the eighteenth century in the early republic. Evangelical Protestantism and anti-intellectualism served to support and propagate those republican ideas, and American economists seem to have been hemmed in by these same two forces; a bias against speculative thought and an adherence to a basic Protestant ethic characterized most nineteenth-century American economic thought. In fact, when a native intellectual tradition devoted to making an argument against laissez-faire finally emerged, it drew heavily from the republican tradition and the force of American Protestantism. The failure of this movement in the nineteenth century is closely tied into the prevalence of anti-intellectualism and into the movement's inability to find allies willing to defend academic freedom and the value of free inquiry.

The emergence of academic economics as a large-scale enterprise in the final decades of the nineteenth century set the stage for the analytically driven battles over laissez-faire in the twentieth century, and it points to several of the main elements of those battles. But the analytical fight over laissez-faire was still to come.

References

Appleby, Joyce. 1984. *Capitalism and a New Social Order: The Republican Vision of the 1790s*. New York: New York University Press.

Barber, William J., ed. 1988. *Breaking the Academic Mould: Economists and American Higher Learning in the Nineteenth Century*. Middletown, Conn.: Wesleyan University Press.

———. 1996. *Designs within Disorder*. Cambridge: Cambridge University Press.

———. 2003. American Economics to 1900. In *A Companion to the History of Economic Thought*, edited by Warren Samuels et al. Oxford: Blackwell.

Bateman, Bradley W. 1998. Clearing the Ground: The Demise of the Social Gospel and the Rise of Neoclassicism in American Economics. In Morgan and Rutherford 1998.

———. 2004. Why Institutional Economics Matters as a Category of Historical Analysis. In *Research in the History of Economic Thought and Methodology* 22–A:193–201.

Berthoff, Rowland. 1979. Independence and Attachment, Virtue and Interest: From Republican Citizen to Free Enterpriser, 1787–1837. In *Uprooted Americans: Essays in Honor of Oscar Handlin*, edited by Richard L. Bushman et al. Boston: Little Brown.

Burke, Martin J. 1995. *The Conundrum of Class: Public Discourse on the Social Order in America*. Chicago: University of Chicago Press.

Bushman, Richard L. 1979. "This New Man": Dependence and Independence, 1776. In *Uprooted Americans: Essays in Honor of Oscar Handlin*, edited by Richard L. Bushman et al. Boston: Little Brown.

Butler, Jon. 1990. *Awash in a Sea of Faith: Christianizing the American People*. Cambridge, Mass.: Harvard University Press.

Coats, A. W. 1988. The Educational Revolution and the Professionalization of American Economics. In *Breaking the Academic Mould: Economists and American Higher Learning in the Nineteenth Century*, edited by William J. Barber. Middletown, Conn.: Wesleyan University Press.

Cohen, Nancy. 2002. *The Reconstruction of American Liberalism, 1865–1914*. Chapel Hill: University of North Carolina Press.

Dorfman, Joseph. 1955. The Role of the German Historical School in American Economic Thought. *American Economic Review* 45:17–28.

Dunbar, Charles. 1876. Economic Science in America, 1776–1876. *North American Review* 122:124–54.

Ekelund, Robert B., Jr., and Robert F. Hebert. 2002. The Origins of Neoclassical Economics. *Journal of Economic Perspectives* 16.3:197–215.

Evans, Peter B., Dietrich Rueschemeyer, and Theda Skocpol, eds. 1985. *Bringing the State Back In*. Cambridge: Cambridge University Press.

Fine, Sidney. 1956. *Laissez Faire and the General Welfare State: A Study of Conflict in American Thought, 1865–1901*. Ann Arbor: University of Michigan Press.

Foner, Eric. 1970. *Free Soil, Free Labor, Free Men: The Ideology of the Republican Party before the Civil War*. New York: Oxford University Press.

Furner, Mary O. 1975. *Advocacy and Objectivity: A Crisis in the Professionalization of American Social Science*. Lexington: University Press of Kentucky.

Greeley, Horace. 1850. *Hints toward Reform*. New York.

Handy, Robert T. 1950. George D. Herron and the Kingdom Movement. *Church History* 19:97–115.

Hartz, Louis. 1948. *Economic Policy and Democratic Thought: Pennsylvania, 1776–1860*. Cambridge, Mass.: Harvard University Press.

Hatch, Nathan O. 1989. *The Democratization of American Christianity*. New Haven, Conn.: Yale University Press.

Hofstadter, Richard. 1962. *Anti-Intellectualism in American Life*. New York: Knopf.

Hughes, Jonathan R. T. 1977. *The Governmental Habit: Economic Controls from Colonial Times to the Present*. New York: Basic Books.

Kloppenberg, James T. 1987. The Virtues of Liberalism: Christianity, Republicanism, and Ethics in Early American Political Discourse. *Journal of American History* 74.1:9–33.

Lee, Bradford A. 1989. The Miscarriage of Necessity and Invention: Proto-Keynesianism and Democratic States in the 1930s. In *The Political Power of Economic Ideas: Keynesianism across Nations*, edited by Peter A. Hall. Cambridge, Mass.: Harvard University Press.

Margo, Robert A. 2000. The Labor Force in the Nineteenth Century. In *The Cambridge Economic History of the United States*, edited by Stanley L. Engerman and Robert E. Gallman. Cambridge: Cambridge University Press.

Marty, Martin. 1986. *Pilgrims in Their Own Land*. New York: Viking.

May, Henry F. 1976. *The Enlightenment in America*. New York: Oxford University Press.

Montgomery, David. 1967. *Beyond Equality*. New York: Knopf.

Morgan, Mary S., and Malcolm Rutherford, eds. 1998. *From Interwar Pluralism to Postwar Neoclassicism. HOPE* 30 (supplement).

Moss, David A. 1996. *Socializing Security: Progressive-Era Economists and the Origins of American Social Policy*. Cambridge, Mass.: Harvard University Press.

Paul, Diane B. 2002. Darwinism, Social Darwinism, and Eugenics. In *The Cambridge Companion to Darwin*, edited by Jonathan Hodge and Gregory Radick. Cambridge: Cambridge University Press.

Ross, Dorothy. 1991. *The Origins of American Social Science*. Cambridge: Cambridge University Press.

Schmidt, George P. 1957. *The Liberal Arts College: A Chapter in American Cultural History*. New Brunswick, N.J.: Rutgers University Press.

Szasz, Ferenc M. 1982. *The Divided Mind of Protestant America, 1880–1930*. University, Ala.: University of Alabama Press.

Tocqueville, Alexis de. [1840] 2000. *Democracy in America*. Vol. 2. Translated by Henry Mansfield and Delba Winthrop. Chicago: University of Chicago Press.

Vietor, Richard H. K. 2000. Government Regulation of Business. In vol. 3 of *The Cambridge Economic History of the United States*, edited by Stanley L. Engerman and Robert E. Gallman. Cambridge: Cambridge University Press.

White, Morton. 1978. *The Philosophy of the American Revolution*. New York: Oxford University Press.

Wilentz, Sean. 1984. *Chants Democratic: New York City and the Rise of the American Working Class, 1788–1850*. New York: Oxford University Press.

Wills, Garry. 1978. *Inventing America: Jefferson's Declaration of Independence*. Garden City, N.Y.: Doubleday.

Yonay, Yuval. 1998. *The Struggle for the Soul of Economics: Institutionalist and Neoclassical Economics in America between the Wars*. Princeton, N.J.: Princeton University Press.

Mistaking Eugenics for Social Darwinism: Why Eugenics Is Missing from the History of American Economics

Thomas C. Leonard

American economics came of age as an expert policy science during the Progressive Era (roughly 1890–1920), which was also the high-water mark of biological approaches to social and economic problems. Eugenic and other biological thought deeply influenced American economics and the other newly professionalizing social sciences, especially sociology and psychology. The roster of anglophone economists (and other social scientists) who embraced eugenic ideas and policies is impressive, in both its breadth and its ideological diversity.

The progressive social scientists, those who led the Progressive Era movement for labor reform, were especially attracted to eugenic ideas. Scholars like Irving Fisher, Francis Amasa Walker, Henry Rogers Seager, Edward Alsworth Ross, John R. Commons, Sidney Webb, Charles Richmond Henderson, and Charlotte Perkins Gilman, and journalists like Paul Kellogg of the *Survey* and the *New Republic's* Herbert Croly, all invoked eugenic ideas, especially to justify the exclusionary labor and immigration legislation that is a central legacy of the Progressive Era.

I make the case that eugenic thought influenced the reform ideas and legislation of the Progressive Era in Leonard 2003a and Leonard 2005. The present essay is historiographical in emphasis. It asks, if eugenic thought influenced reform economics and legislation of the Progressive

I wish to thank Brad Bateman, Bill Barber, David Levy, Steve Medema, Sandy Peart, Malcolm Rutherford, and the other participants at the *HOPE* 2004 conference, the 2004 George Mason University Summer Institute, and the 2004 History of Economics Society conference session on the Progressive Era. I also wish to acknowledge two helpful referee reports. As explained in detail below, I adopt the old-fashioned term *progressive* (with a lowercase *p*).

Era, why has that influence gone largely unremarked? Why is eugenics more or less missing from the history of American economics?

This is a complex and unavoidably controversial question, so the first four sections provide some historical context. In section 5, I try to unpack the complexities of Progressive Era biological thought to argue that eugenics has been misplaced and thus overlooked. In particular, I criticize an influential historiographical tradition that treats eugenics as a mere continuation of Gilded Age social Darwinism, and that treats social Darwinism as a kind of synecdoche for what, in retrospect, progressivism is seen to oppose: individualism, laissez-faire economics, imperialism, racism, and militarism.

1. The Progressive Era and American Economics

American economics became a professional policy discipline during the Progressive Era—so called for its reform spirit and for its reform legislation—an era that begins a vastly more expansive state relationship to the economy. By the First World War, the U.S. government had created the Federal Reserve, amended the Constitution to institute a personal income tax, established the Federal Trade Commission, applied existing antitrust laws to industrial combinations and to labor unions, restricted immigration, regulated food and drug safety, and supervised railroad rates.[1] State governments regulated working conditions, banned child labor, capped working hours, and set minimum wages. By the 1910s more than forty states had instituted inheritance taxes. Local governments municipalized gas and water companies. Professional economists, especially the progressives among them, played a leading role in the Progressive Era transformation of the state's relationship to the American economy.

Less well known is the influence on that transformation of a biologically based movement for social and economic reform—eugenics. Progressive Era economics, like the regulatory state it helped found, came of age at a time when biological approaches to social and economic reform were at (or near) their apex.

1. U.S. efforts to tax wealthy and high-income persons predate the passage of the Sixteenth Amendment in 1913. A temporary federal inheritance tax was passed to finance the Spanish-American War, and, in 1894, Congress passed legislation, later ruled unconstitutional, taxing (at 2 percent) all annual incomes above $4,000. By 1906 President Roosevelt was agitating for a federal personal income tax.

In justifying labor legislation, progressive economists joined eugenic thought to their theories of wage determination to argue that the superior, deserving poor could be uplifted only by removing from the labor force groups deemed biologically unfit—groups they called "unemployable." Blacks, immigrants, and those defective in character or intellect were regarded by progressives active in labor legislation less as victims of industrial capitalism than as threats to the health and well-being of the worthy poor and of society more generally. Progressive Era reform economics ultimately argued that eugenic treatment of the biologically unfit—the so-called industrial residuum—was necessary to uplift the worthy poor (Leonard 2003a). Many reformers also included women in the class of "unemployable," if for somewhat different reasons (Leonard 2005).

2. The Influence of Eugenic Thought

It is hard to overestimate the influence of Darwinian and eugenic ideas in the Progressive Era. I believe one cannot fully understand the economic ideas that underwrote labor and immigration reform without also understanding the biological thought that crucially informed them. If the relationship between American labor reform and the biology of human inheritance seems to the modern reader unexpected, it is, in part, because eugenics, new scholarship notwithstanding, is still widely misunderstood—regarded as an aberrant, pseudoscientific, laissez-faire doctrine, a kind of twentieth-century successor to Gilded Age social Darwinism that was wholly abandoned after the eugenic atrocities of German National Socialism. In short, eugenics was everything the progressives are seen to have opposed.

But the progressives were not that progressive, and eugenics was, in actual fact, the broadest of churches. Eugenics was not aberrant; it was not seen as a pseudoscience; it was not laissez-faire; it rejected social Darwinism; and it was not abandoned after Nazi atrocities. Eugenics was mainstream; it was popular to the point of faddishness;[2] it was supported by leading figures in the still-emerging science of genetics;[3] it appealed

2. Eugenic ideas were faddish enough to become a staple at country fairs, where "fitter family" competitions were held and even made their way into the funny pages. See this Buster Brown cartoon, from circa 1903: www.geneseo.edu/~easton/humanities/busterbrown.html.

3. Diane Paul and Hamish Spencer (1995, 302) argue that, before the 1930s, Thomas Hunt Morgan was the only Mendelian geneticist to reject the eugenicist idea that socially undesirable traits were the product of bad heredity.

to an extraordinary range of political ideologies, not least to the progressives; it was—as state control of human breeding—a program that no proponent of laissez-faire could consistently endorse; and it survived the Nazis.[4]

Histories of eugenics traditionally have focused upon movements in the United States, the United Kingdom, and in Third Reich Germany; but we now know that eugenic thought was commonplace elsewhere, influencing scholars, writers, scientists, and policymakers in virtually all non-Catholic Western countries and in many others besides: there are scholarly treatments of the eugenics movements in Canada, France, Japan, Russia, Denmark, Sweden, Norway, Finland, Romania, China, Latin America, and elsewhere.[5] By 1933, the American demographer and eugenicist Paul Popenoe could boast that eugenic sterilization laws obtained in jurisdictions comprising 150 million people (Kevles 1995, 115).[6]

Eugenic thought not only crossed national borders; it also crossed political ideologies, traversing an extraordinary range of political views. Ideologically, the eugenics movement could attract reactionaries, such as Madison Grant, author of *The Passing of the Great Race*. But eugenics also won proponents of a quite different politics, including Margaret Sanger, the birth control advocate who began intellectual life as a radical anarchist (a protégée of Emma Goldman's); national socialists such as Karl Pearson, Sidney Webb, and George Bernard Shaw; social conservatives such as Francis Galton, founder of modern eugenics, and Charles Davenport, head of the Eugenics Record Office at the Cold Spring Harbor Laboratory; and the sui generis feminist and economist Charlotte Perkins Gilman. Writing a monograph-length survey of eugenics for the *Quarterly Journal of Economics*, James A. Field (1911, 1–2) opined that

4. Sweden, for example, greatly expanded its eugenic sterilizations during the Second World War. More than sixty thousand Swedes, over 90 percent of them women, were sterilized from 1941 to 1975 (Broberg and Tydén 1996, 109–10). The other Scandinavian countries also expanded eugenic sterilization programs after the Second World War, as part of what the historian Daniel Kevles (1999, 437) calls "the scientifically oriented planning of the new welfare state."

5. On Canada, see McLaren 1990; France, Schneider 1990; Japan, Suzuki 1975; Russia, Adams 1990; Scandinavian countries, Broberg and Roll-Hansen 1996; Romania, Bucur 2002; Latin America, Stepan 1991; China, Dikötter 1992.

6. Eugenic sentiments can even be found among scholars from traditionally black colleges. Kelly Miller (1917) worried about the lower fertility of the Howard University professoriate—"the higher element of the negro race"—when compared with the average African American. See also Hasian 1996.

"eugenics is [one of the most] hopeful application[s] of science in social reform."

Biological justifications for social and economic reform naturally appealed to those, such as Irving Fisher, a founder of the American Eugenics Society, who served as officers in eugenic organizations. One is not surprised to find leading eugenicists proselytizing, as when Karl Pearson ([1887] 1901, 307–8) suggested that "Socialists have to inculcate that spirit which would give offenders against the State short shrift and the nearest lamp-post," or when Sidney Webb (1907, 17) devised a novel term, "adverse selection," to describe what he saw as English "race suicide," a Progressive Era term of art for the process by which the unfit outbreed their biological betters: "Twenty-five percent of our parents, as Professor Karl Pearson keeps warning us, is producing 50 percent of the next generation. This can hardly result in anything but national deterioration; or, as an alternative, in this country gradually falling to the Irish and the Jews." But the influence of eugenic ideas extended well beyond the organizations dedicated to eugenic research and proselytizing.[7]

Justices Louis Brandeis and William Howard Taft joined the infamous *Buck v. Bell* Supreme Court decision, where Oliver Wendell Holmes, a proponent of eugenics, opined that "the principle that sustains compulsory vaccination is broad enough to cover cutting the Fallopian tubes." "Three generations of imbeciles," they agreed, "is enough."[8] President Theodore Roosevelt (1907, 550) called race suicide—"the elimination instead of the survival of the fittest"—the "greatest problem of civilization," and he regularly returned to the theme.[9] President Calvin Coolidge, in 1921, warned of the perils of race mixing: "Biological laws tell us that certain divergent people will not mix or blend. The Nordics propagate themselves successfully. With other races, the outcome shows deterioration on both sides. Quality of mind and body suggests that observance of ethnic law is as great a necessity to a nation as immigration law" (14). Coolidge said, "America must remain American" when he signed the Immigration Restriction Act of 1924, which imposed racial quotas advocated by Irving Fisher and which radically curtailed immigration from eastern and southern Europe.

7. I owe to Dan Rodgers this distinction between the professional eugenicists, who founded and staffed the eugenics organizations, and the vastly larger number of scholars, writers, and policymakers influenced by eugenic ideas.

8. *Buck v. Bell*, 274 U.S. 200, 208 (1927).

9. For the leading role of economists in promoting race-suicide arguments in the context of immigration, see Leonard 2003a, 714–21.

The intellectual influence of eugenics extended well beyond the public sphere.[10] Virginia Woolf confided to her diary that "imbeciles" "should certainly be killed." T. S. Eliot favorably reviewed eugenic articles from journals such as *Eugenics Review*. In 1908 D. H. Lawrence indulged in an extermination fantasy:

> If I had my way, I would build a lethal chamber as big as the Crystal Palace, with a military band playing softly, and a Cinematograph working brightly, and then I'd go out in back streets and main streets and bring them all in, all the sick, the halt, and the maimed; I would lead them gently, and they would smile at me. (cited in Childs 2001, 10)

Not all proposed eugenic remedies were as extreme as lethal chambers or compulsory sterilization for the unfit. But few disagreed with the diagnosis—that some races (and other groups) were biologically inferior, and these unfit races (and other groups) were the root cause of social and economic problems. And few opposed the eugenic prescription—that the state can and should plan human breeding so as to reduce the proportion of the unfit.

Thus does the new scholarship in the history of eugenics now adopt a broader perspective on eugenics, understanding it as "a biologically based movement for social reform" (Schneider 1990, 4), one that eventually "belonged to the political vocabulary of virtually every significant modernizing force between the two world wars" (Dikötter 1998, 467). Seen this way, it is perhaps less surprising that the fledgling economists who blueprinted and began erecting the key structural elements of what would become the American welfare state readily made recourse to biological explanations of economic problems.

3. Who Were the Progressives?

Progressive Era historiography employs a sometimes bewildering variety of labels to describe the Left-liberal social theorists and reformers who promoted the idea that an activist state, as guided by social-scientific expertise, should reform markets in the name of advancing a social welfarist vision of the common good (Fried 1998, ix). The diverse

10. I owe the following examples to Donald Childs's (2001) fascinating volume, *Modernism and Eugenics: Woolf, Eliot, Yeats, and the Culture of Degeneration*.

terminology among historians reflects, in part, the scope and heterogeneity of American reform movements in the Progressive Era: nativists, Social Gospelers, temperance advocates, muckrakers, birth-control advocates, eugenicists, charity reformers, settlement house workers, pacifists, good-government advocates, city-beautiful advocates, and conservationists.

I adopt the old-fashioned term *progressive* (with a lowercase *p*), in recognition of the reformers' (rare) agreement on the cause of labor reform through legislation and their shared belief in what Linda Gordon (1992, 36) calls the "progressive traditions of statism and . . . expertise." Labor reform was the very heart of the progressive agenda, as was the belief in the virtues of an expert technocratic vanguard to justify and to promote the labor-reform agenda.

Perhaps no group better embodied this progressive ethos than American reform economists. The reform economists' impulses to set the world to rights were powered by a potent combination—the German academic social activism they had admired as graduate students and the Protestant Social Gospel's evangelical will to remake society.

When, soon after its founding, the reform-minded American Economic Association (AEA) transformed itself from an agency of Christian social reform into a more scholarly and scientific professional organization (Coats 1960), the progressive economists' creed of activism through expertise—what Mary Furner (1975) calls "advocacy"—did not disappear; it relocated. Perhaps wiser after the academic-freedom trials at the end of the nineteenth century, the progressive economists founded organizations outside universities to conduct research on the labor question and to lobby, advocate, and rake muck.

Academic economists traded not just on the relatively newfound authority of their professorial chairs but also on the specialized knowledge they could offer to those writing reform legislation. As Daniel Rodgers (1998, 108) puts it: "Expert policy counsel, in fact, turned out to be the ground on which laissez-faire's professional critics regrouped and refashioned a position of influence. . . . [they] established new forms of authority by colonizing the social space between university professorships and expert government service." In the United States, Progressive Era reform economists essentially invented a role we today take for granted, the academic expert who advises policymaking bodies.

Two of the most influential reform organizations were the American Association for Labor Legislation (AALL) and the National Consumers'

League (NCL). Ann Shola Orloff and Theda Skocpol (1984, 726) call the AALL the "leading association of U.S. social reform advocates in the Progressive Era." Mostly forgotten today, the AALL was a key labor-reform advocacy group, influential in effecting Progressive Era legislation regulating workplace safety, minimum wages, and maximum hours.

The AALL was founded in December 1905 at the Baltimore AEA meetings, principally by two of Gustav Schmoller's students, Henry Farnam of Yale and Adna F. Weber of the New York Bureau of Labor Statistics (Rodgers 1998, 236).[11] The first group meeting was in early 1906. Richard T. Ely was the AALL's first president, and John R. Commons was its first executive secretary. The latter position was soon taken over by Commons's protégé John B. Andrews, who led the organization for many years, overseeing its transformation from scholarly muckraking shop to politically powerful pressure group. Irene Osgood (who became Irene Osgood Andrews), another Commons disciple, served as the AALL's assistant secretary.

Henry Rogers Seager was involved from the very beginning, serving as the third and fifth president (Commons was the second). Princeton's William Willoughby was the fourth president, and Irving Fisher served as the sixth AALL president. The AALL masthead practically mapped the interlocking directorates of American progressivism: Jane Addams of Hull House; Charles Richmond Henderson, a sociologist at the University of Chicago and head of Charities and Corrections; Paul Kellogg, editor of the *Survey*, an influential progressive organ; Louis Brandeis, AALL legal counsel until appointed to the Supreme Court by Woodrow Wilson; and Wilson himself, even after he became president of the United States.[12]

11. Henry Farnam, the Yale economist who cofounded and personally funded the AALL, was an early adopter of eugenic ideas. He argued in 1888 that "every effort . . . to remove what Malthus called the 'positive checks' to populations, without at the same time increasing the preventative checks, must result in an increase of the very classes which are least able to take care of themselves, and render more and more imperative the solution of that exceedingly difficult problem which Mr. Arnold White calls 'sterilization of the unfit'" (295). "We are," said Farnam, "by means of our very improvements, setting forces in operation which tend to multiply the unfit" (295).

12. Many other AALL leaders were progressive economists active in labor reform: Father John Ryan, author of *A Living Wage*; Matthew B. Hammond; Royal Meeker (appointed by Wilson to be commissioner of the Department of Labor). Elizabeth Glendower Evans, Massachusetts minimum wager and a friend of Louis and Alice Brandeis, was affiliated with the AALL. The AALL also attracted some academic economists less obviously reformers, such as Harvard's Frank Taussig. In later years, institutionalists such as Wesley Clair Mitchell, Leo Wolman, and Walton Hamilton were members of the AALL General Administrative Council.

The NCL, led by the indomitable Florence Kelley, was less academic, was run by women, and was more skillful politically (Rogers 1998, 236). Josephine Goldmark, sister-in-law to Brandeis, was active in the NCL leadership and supervised the production of the Brandeis Brief, an annotated compilation of social science reports defending maximum-hours (and in later versions, minimum-wage) legislation for women. The NCL assembled local consumer leagues that, before embracing legislation, emphasized moral suasion: raising the consciousness of genteel consumers of ladies garments produced under sweatshop conditions, using NCL labels to certify satisfactory working conditions. Alice Goldmark Brandeis was an active member of the NCL and secretly paid the expenses of the Washington NCL office (Bary 1972).

The NCL tapped progressive economists for advisers and board members. Commons served as NCL president from 1923 to 1935. Seager, A. B. Wolfe of Oberlin College, and Arthur Holcombe of Harvard were members of the NCL minimum-wage committee as early as 1909 (Hart 1994, 209 n. 94). Ely and Father John Ryan of Catholic University were also active NCL advisers.

No single entity can stand in for the heterogeneous and fractious reform groups that have, at one time or another, acquired the label of "progressive." But, in the realm of labor reform, the AALL economists and their (sometime) allies of the NCL make for excellent exemplars, because of their impeccable reform credentials, their preference for expert statutory reforms over collective bargaining, and their abiding faith in social science, the state, and their own disinterested expertise as reliable guides to the social good.

4. What Drew the Progressives to Eugenics?

Eugenic ideas, which date to Plato's *Republic* at least, were not new in the Progressive Era, but they acquired new impetus with the era's advent of a more expansive state relationship to American society. The modern incarnation of eugenic thought, conventionally dated to Francis Galton's first eugenics publications in the mid-1860s, was essentially ignored for a generation. When in 1868 W. R. Greg (1868, 361), an economics writer and influential early popularizer of eugenics in England, proposed a society in which "paternity should be the right and function exclusively of the élite of the nation," he understood that the prospect was remote in time. Eugenics' moment comes only toward the end of Galton's long life, when the new expansion of state power meant that it was now possible to have not only eugenic thought but also eugenic practice. Eugenic legislation, says the eugenics historian Diane Paul (1995, 6), had to await "the rise of the welfare state."

What drew progressives to eugenics was the same set of intellectual commitments that drew them to labor and other reform legislation. "For progressive reformers," the historian of eugenics Daniel Kevles (1998, 211) writes, "eugenics was a branch of the drive for social perfection that many reformers of the day thought might be achieved through the deployment of science to good social ends."[13] Just as labor and goods markets could no longer be left unregulated, so too must the state take over from "nature" the project of selecting the fittest human beings. Irving Fisher (1907, 20) captured this expansive view of social control when he said: "The world consists of two classes—the educated and the ignorant—and it is essential for progress that the former should be allowed to dominate the latter. . . . once we admit that it is proper for the instructed classes to give tuition to the uninstructed, we begin to see an almost boundless vista for possible human betterment." The progressive intellectual commitments were to the following:

1. the explanatory power of scientific (especially statistical) social inquiry to get at the root causes of social and economic problems;
2. the legitimacy of social control, which derives from an organic conception of society as prior to and greater than the sum of its constituent individuals;
3. the efficacy of social control via expert scientific management of public administration, where
4. expertise is both sufficient and necessary for the task of wise public administration.

Progressives believed deeply in the power of social scientific inquiry. Late Victorian scientists, like Galton, already regarded science (especially the science of society) as a high, even spiritual, calling. In the Progressive Era, especially in the United States, progressive economists and other reformers regarded science as a means for understanding social

13. This is not to suggest that the progressives were utopian; they were not. It is the case, though, that some utopian communities practiced eugenics as part of their philosophy of living. John Humphrey Noyes's Oneida community is an interesting example of social control of human breeding, where "social control" is not equivalent to "state control" (see Karp 1982).

and economic problems, and also as a policy method—via scientific management of public administration—for setting the world to rights.[14]

By "scientific" the progressives meant, roughly, "statistical" in the sense of observation, measurement, tabulation, and, even by the standards of the day, some rudimentary kinds of inference. As with scientific racism or any system that assumes a human biological hierarchy, eugenics required measurement. A hierarchy presupposes that racial or other human types are distinguishable and, if the hierarchy is to be stable, also generally requires a fixity of racial types across generations.[15] It is no accident that the notable proponents of human hierarchy in economics (and in social science more generally) were pioneering statisticians whose social science was founded upon measurement. Galton, Pearson, Francis Amasa Walker, Richmond Mayo-Smith, Irving Fisher, Jeremiah Jenks, and Walter Wilcox were all statisticians—by training or by inclination. They regarded statistical measurement and inference as the method that put the "science" in social science.

The first two of Pearson's (1909, 19–20) "bricks for the foundations of [eugenics]" were announced as follows: "[First] we depart from the old sociology, in that we desert verbal discussion for statistical facts, and [second] we apply new methods of statistics which form practically a new calculus." American progressives regarded statistics as the scientific foundation for legislative reforms. Said the reformer Lester F. Ward (1915, 46): "If laws of social events could be statistically formulated, they could be used for scientific lawmaking."

The progressives also believed strongly in the legitimacy of social control, a catchphrase of Progressive Era reformers, as it was for their

14. The reformers who founded the AEA and later the AALL were empirically minded, and a key selling point of the new reform economics they advocated was its methodological opposition to what they regarded as the excessively abstract, deductive approach of late classical political economy. See Barber 1987.

15. The putative fixity of racial types, most commonly measured by the "cephalic index"—the ratio of skull length to width—was a key concern of eugenicists. Working for the economist Jeremiah Jenks, who headed President Roosevelt's 1907 U.S. Immigration Commission, the pioneering physical anthropologist Franz Boas took biometric measurements of thousands of European immigrants and their American-born and foreign-born children. Boas found the American-born children differed significantly from their immigrant parents and their foreign-born siblings in cephalic index and in other biometric measures, and that the measured differences between the immigrants and their foreign-born children were less than those between the immigrants and their American-born children. Boas concluded that there was no racial fixity but rather "a great plasticity of human type" and that the environmental advantages of the United States explained the greater change among American-born children of immigrants. See Chase 1977.

successors, the institutionalists. "Social control" did not refer narrowly to state regulation of markets. Edward A. Ross (1901), who popularized the term, employed it in a broader, sociological sense, to describe the various ways in which society "can mold the individual to the necessity of the group," which, in the context of eugenics, meant a "program for survival" of the Anglo-Saxon race (cited in Furner 1975, 309).

The legitimacy of social control meant, in practice, the legitimacy of state control. Ward, who coined many neologisms, devised the term *sociocracy* to describe the "scientific control of the social forces by the collective mind of society" (cited in Fine 1956, 263). For progressives, the legitimacy of state control derived from an illiberal and organic conception of the state as an entity prior to and greater than the sum of its constituent individuals. Progressives, who criticized excessive individualism, ordinarily opposed the liberal tradition, which treated the individual as prior to the state and which saw the state's legitimacy as deriving solely from the contractual consent of its creators. Washington Gladden, a leading Social Gospeler and ally of Richard T. Ely, argued that "the idea of the liberty of the individual is not a sound basis for a democratic government." The liberal emphasis on individual freedom, Gladden argued, was "a radical defect in the thinking of the average American" (cited in McGerr 2003, 217).

The progressives' somewhat antidemocratic impulses also informed their views of how reform should be devised and implemented. They believed that academic experts were both sufficient and necessary for the task of wise public administration. Experts were sufficient, because they could and would suspend their own interests to circumvent (or better, transcend) the messy business of interest-group machine politics. As one widely read eugenics text put it: "Government and social control are in the hands of expert politicians who have power, instead of expert technologists who have wisdom. There should be technologists in control of every field of human need and desire" (Albert Wiggam's 1923 *New Decalogue of Science*, cited in Ludmerer 1972, 16–17). Experts were necessary for the task of wise public administration, because the modern conditions of industrial capitalism no longer permitted a quaint liberal individualism, but demanded wise government by expert elites. The idea was that the benignly motivated experts should interpose themselves, in the name of the social good, to better represent the interests of the industrial poor, for whom many reformers felt contempt as much as pity.

Put in historical context, the appeal of eugenics to the progressive mind is clearer. Eugenics necessarily rejects individualism in favor of a collective—"the race" or the nation; eugenics regarded unfettered industrial capitalism as dysgenic, both because improved well-being thwarts natural Malthusian checks and because capitalism promotes the inferior, low-wage races; eugenics boasted an air of scientific authority, especially with its emphasis on statistical measurement; and eugenics opposed laissez-faire values, by substituting an objective, expert determination of the social good for a subjective, individual determination of the social good. Thus were eugenics and progressivism complementary rather than antagonistic trends.[16]

5. Why the Neglect of Eugenics in the History of American Economics?

There are several reasons why Progressive Era eugenics has been unduly neglected in the history of economics. First, "eugenics" remains a dirty word. The atrocities perpetrated by German National Socialism in the name of eugenics have not only tainted the term but have also so colored our view of eugenics that even professional historians have struggled not to indict by association the eugenic ideas of different times and places.[17] Second, and related, contemporary scholarship sometimes inclines to apologize for the now unfashionable enthusiasms of revered ancestors, particularly those who do not fit the traditional profile of a eugenicist (Childs 2001). Third, trends in historical writing are often late in arriving to the history of economic thought. The contemporary understanding of the history of eugenics comes from a revisionist history-of-science literature that dates "only" to the 1980s and 1990s, and, what is more, this recent literature is itself mostly unacquainted with the history of political economy.

Without rejecting any of these hypotheses, the present essay investigates a complementary cause for the amnesia about the influence of eugenics upon the nascent social sciences of a century ago: Progressive Era eugenics is missing because, at least in part, Progressive Era eugenics has been mischaracterized. An influential strain of the era's historiography has tended to treat eugenics as the mere continuation (or more

16. This paragraph is indebted to Searle 1998, 25–26.

17. Daniel Kevles describes his early work as "coming to terms with a dirty word" (cited in Adams 1990, 226).

modern version) of social Darwinism, and it has, moreover, made "social Darwinism" a pejorative that refers to opponents of reform.

American historiography largely understands "social Darwinism" not as the influence of Darwinian ideas upon social science but as an indictment. Indeed, the indictment is so broadly written that even social Darwinism's traditional exemplars, Herbert Spencer and William Graham Sumner, are accused of views they did not hold.

The present essay argues that this influential strand of American historiography misleads with respect to the influence of Darwinian and other biological thought upon the Progressive Era sciences of society, this by treating eugenics as social Darwinism and by treating social Darwinism as a synecdoche for all ideological aspects of Gilded Age American capitalism that progressives are seen to oppose: individualism, laissez-faire economics, imperialism, racism, and militarism. Of the several consequences of this historiographical construct, one is that the influence of eugenics has been obscured. In what follows, I argue that neither social Darwinism nor eugenics are what this influential strand of historiography makes them out be.

5.1. Social Darwinism

The biological and social sciences have been intellectual trading partners for at least two centuries. So, by itself, the notion that biological ideas might influence social science (or vice versa) is neither surprising nor intrinsically objectionable.

But many historians, especially since Richard Hofstadter's influential *Social Darwinism in American Thought* (1944), have tended to reconstruct "social Darwinism" as a bad thing, something that *is* objectionable. "Social Darwinism" is not understood as a description of Darwin's ideas applied to society. It has devolved into an omnibus term of abuse, encompassing the full catalog of capitalist ideologies the progressives are seen to have opposed. In the United States, "social Darwinism" connotes the use of vaguely Darwinian ideas—as reduced to stock phrases such as "survival of the fittest" and the "struggle for existence"—to explain and justify a brutish laissez-faire capitalism of late-nineteenth-century America, and nearly always applies to laissez-faire scholars seen to oppose progressive-minded reform.[18]

18. This paragraph is indebted to Robert Bannister (1979), a leading revisionist critic of Hofstadter's thesis.

There are, broadly, two problems with this influential construct, as several generations of revisionist historians have argued. The first problem is that those who wished to justify late-nineteenth-century laissez-faire rarely made recourse to Darwin. The second problem is that critics of the late-nineteenth-century social order, including the progressives who wished to reform it, *did* make recourse to Darwin and other biological sources, the progressive eugenicists being conspicuous among them. But because the progressives are seen to have opposed individualism, laissez-faire, and the other undesirable attributes American historiography has attached to the term *social Darwinism*, the influence of Darwinian and other biological ideas upon progressive social scientists has been underplayed in American Progressive Era historiography.

American plutocrats who used Darwin to defend the Gilded Age social order were, it turns out, scarcer than hen's teeth (Wylie 1959). Business apologists for laissez-faire more commonly invoked religion, Horatio Alger mythology, the American republican tradition, and even, if less frequently, classical political economy.[19] Darwinian defenses of laissez-faire among scholars, who were more likely to have read Darwin, are not much easier to find. American historiography has made "social Darwinist" into such a broad indictment that even the paradigmatic social Darwinists, Herbert Spencer and William Graham Sumner, fail to fit their standard historiographical profiles perfectly.

Spencer is certainly the historian's prototypical social Darwinian. He defended laissez-faire on evolutionary grounds, and his extraordinary intellectual prominence made him the personal embodiment of what came to be called social Darwinism.[20] Spencer's synthetic philosophy aspired to demonstrate that "social science is not to guide the conscious control of human evolution, . . . [because] such control is an absolute impossibility" (Hofstadter [1944] 1992, 43).

But Spencer would have rejected the label of "Darwinian," in part because his own theory of evolution predated (or at least was published

19. The historian R. J. Wilson (1967, 93) wrote: "It is true that in the last half of the 19th century great numbers of Americans were ideologically committed to the notions of competition, merited success and deserved failure. But it is not true that this commitment was grounded on Darwinian premises. No more than a small handful of American business leaders or intellectuals were 'social Darwinists' in any sense precise enough to have a useful meaning."

20. Both Darwin and Alfred Russel Wallace regarded Spencer as the leading thinker of the late nineteenth century. Hofstadter ([1944] 1992, 33) says of the influence of Spencer: "In the three decades after the Civil War, it was impossible to be active in any field of intellectual work without mastering Spencer."

before) Darwin's *On the Origin of Species*. Spencer also opposed imperialism and militarism, and he resented the use of his phrase, "survival of the fittest," to justify imperial wars waged in the name of preserving the English race.[21]

Spencer was also not Darwinian with respect to biological inheritance. He was, in fact, a leading Lamarckian, so much so that reformers often found themselves in the awkward position of relying upon Spencer's defense of the idea that characteristics acquired during an individual's lifetime can be transmitted to progeny. Indeed, those who opposed Spencer's view of human inheritance were called neo-Darwinians (see section 5.3). Spencer's view was that, in the struggle for existence, self-improvement came from conscious, planned exertion, not from chance variation and natural selection. The biological case Spencer made for laissez-faire rested upon a kind of Lamarckian self-help and not upon Darwinian inheritance. In these important respects, "social Darwinist" is a misnomer even when applied to Spencer.

Sumner serves as the other paradigmatic social Darwinist in Hofstadter (as in many other accounts, such as Sidney Fine's *Laissez Faire and the General Welfare State* [1956]). A disciple of Spencer much more than of Darwin (at least with respect to human society), Sumner also does not completely fit his stock profile of social Darwinist and apologist for American capital (Bannister 1973). Sumner, for example, opposed the tariff, a hot-button apostasy that nearly cost him his academic position. Sumner was also a pacifist, and he openly criticized the American imperial adventure of the Spanish-American War, saying that "my patriotism is of the kind which is outraged by the notion that the United States was never a great nation until [this] . . . petty three months campaign" (Hofstadter [1944] 1992, 195). Sumner, in one of the essays taken to be a classic text of social Darwinism—"What Social Classes Owe to Each Other"—actually defended (open-shop) organized labor and argued that

21. As with John Stuart Mill, the passage of time has seemed to transform once radical ideas into conservative notions. Spencer was considered dangerously radical in the early post-bellum years. Toward the end of his life, Spencer became, for progressives, synonymous with the (Darwinian) defense of laissez-faire. But before the Progressive Era professionalization of American economics, Spencer's anticlerical and antideistic stances were quite controversial in American colleges, which were institutionally Christian, and where clerics taught political economy. This was especially true at conservative Yale, where Sumner's introduction into the curriculum of Spencer's *Study of Sociology* was opposed by the administration and which Sumner fought for on grounds of academic freedom (see Barber 1988, 147–51).

collective bargaining would better serve labor's interests than would the statutory approach ultimately pursued by progressives.[22]

Sumner was an advocate for laissez-faire, not for industry, and when industry benefited from policies opposed to laissez-faire, such as the tariff, Sumner was their enemy. The point here is obvious, but often lost in the stark dichotomies of Progressive Era historiography—not all departures from laissez-faire will serve the cause of progressive reform; indeed, they can work to entrench the status quo that reform seeks to change.

Virtually no Progressive Era scholar consistently described himself or herself as a "social Darwinist." There certainly were no schools of social Darwinism. Though recognizably Darwinian ideas were widespread among Progressive Era social scientists, the term *social Darwinist* seems to have been an epithet from its inception. Though used occasionally by progressive critics of laissez-faire, social Darwinism was made popular and given its more expansive modern meaning by later historians who sympathetically chronicled the progressives' ideas. (Thus Hofstadter's book is concerned more with the progressive critics of social Darwinism than with its proponents.)

For our purposes, what matters is that this influential reading of social Darwinism has become multiply misleading. First, social Darwinism is not only a misnomer; even when applied to its putative paragons, it is also a red herring. Because the label was affixed most prominently to defenders of individualist capitalism, it wrongly implied that their opponents, the progressives, were themselves averse to Darwinian ideas. But the progressive critics of laissez-faire did not object to the use of Darwinian or other biological ideas in social science per se. On the contrary, they themselves routinely made recourse to biological explanations of social and economic phenomena and, arguably, did so more frequently and more intensively than did the scholars they called social Darwinists. What the progressives objected to was laissez-faire itself.

Second, Hofstadter identified other modes of social competition—imperialism and militarism, or competition at the racial (read: national)

22. The question of whether legislation or collective bargaining would better advance the interests of labor divided the progressives from organized labor. Some progressives close to organized labor, such as John R. Commons, were ambivalent. Samuel Gompers, head of the American Federation of Labor, came to believe that organized labor would do better with collective bargaining and became an adversary rather than an ally of the progressive economists who advocated statutory approaches to labor reform. After their falling-out, Gompers derisively referred to the economists' AALL as the American Association for the Assassination of Labor.

level—that he also called "social Darwinism." It is not just that the paradigmatic social Darwinians, Spencer and Sumner, do not deserve the imperialist or militarist labels, or that some progressive reformers, such as Theodore Roosevelt and Karl Pearson, do. By using the same term to describe different phenomena—economic competition among individuals and political competition among races—Hofstadter added more semantic freight to an already overburdened term, pushing toward its current meaning as a pejorative that signals opposition to reform.

Third, and related, Hofstadter ([1944] 1992, 161) sowed further confusion by treating eugenics—what he called "the most enduring aspect of social Darwinism"—as a mere continuation of social Darwinism. Many other historians have followed suit. But not only are eugenics and social Darwinism more different than they are alike, the historiographical association of eugenics with individualism and laissez-faire has obscured the appeal of eugenics to some progressives, thereby helping promote the neglect of eugenics in Progressive Era historiography.

Hofstadter's categories sometimes blind him to the eugenic enthusiasms of reformers, such as the progressive economist-turned-sociologist Edward A. Ross. A mere four pages before acknowledging that the early eugenicists' "biological data . . . were convincing to men like E. A. Ross, who had thoroughly repudiated Spencerian individualism," Hofstadter had claimed that "Ross refused to look upon the poor as unfit or to worship at the shrine of the fittest" (164, 160). Because Hofstadter (wrongly) categorizes eugenic thought with Spencerian individualism, he has difficulty placing Ross. Ross was a notable progressive, who opposed Spencerian individualism, but he also pioneered the race-suicide argument in economics, a view *premised* on the claim that some groups among the poor are unfit.

5.2. Darwinism

Biological theorizing about human variation (of race, of sex, of social position) had a long history in the nineteenth century. Scientific racism, for example, long precedes the modern flowering of eugenic thought circa 1890; it also antedates Darwin's *On the Origin of Species*. But with the advent of the ethically and empirically minded social sciences of the Progressive Era (and with the expansion of social welfare legislation), existing theories of human variation were deployed with a newfound impetus in the social scientific task of determining the root causes of criminalism, poverty, alcoholism, prostitution, and other social and economic pathologies regarded as biologically heritable (Stepan 1986).

As with other intellectuals, progressives mined Darwinian ideas for their various purposes. Darwin could appeal to a wide range of social scientists because the Darwinism of a century ago was so protean—it was able to accommodate quite different attitudes toward social reform. Whether Darwin was influential because of what he said, or in spite of what he said, is a difficult problem in intellectual history, but it is clear that there was something in Darwin for nearly everyone.[23] As the historian Leslie Jones (1998, 7) puts it: "Individualism and socialism, militarism and pacifism, pro-natalism and neo-Malthusianism, organised religion and agnosticism, all have had their Darwinian exegetes." Faithful to Darwin or not, a great range of Progressive Era social scientists worked in a recognizably Darwinian idiom, also importing other biological ideas.

Darwinism has never been more influential than it is today, 145 years since the publication of *On the Origin of Species* (1859). Darwin had worked out his theories twenty years earlier, but, as an establishment figure, he feared his social standing would not withstand publication of them. Darwin also understood the importance of priority to scientific reputation, however. Upon reading a paper by Alfred Russel Wallace, a then obscure naturalist, that independently proposed the theory of evolution by natural selection, Darwin was moved to hasty publication—his introduction calls *On the Origin of Species* an "abstract." Darwin orchestrated, without Wallace's knowledge, the unveiling of both men's work at the same meeting (Raby 2001). While Wallace is sometimes granted codiscoverer credit, it is Darwinism, not Wallacism, that inspires and exercises contemporary scholars.

Darwin and Darwinism start with only two fundamental premises. First, heritable changes occur randomly in individual organisms. Second, some of these changes offer individuals greater fitness than their peers, that is, offer, via natural selection, a greater chance of survival and reproduction. If both premises are true, the population to which the individuals belong will *necessarily* evolve, that is, the population will develop a greater proportion of fitter (with respect to a given environment)

23. The Darwin scholar Morse Peckham (1959, 32) put the question this way: "Is it true that what Darwin said had very little impact, but that what people thought he said, that is, what they already believed and believed to have been confirmed by Darwin, had enormous impact?" This question is still vital and contentious in the Darwin industry.

traits. Darwin never knew what changed or how it was inherited or what caused its changes. He is said to have died with Gregor Mendel's genetics reprint in his library, its pages still uncut. Modern Darwinians know that phenotypes (organisms and their behaviors) are influenced by their genes (collectively, the genotype), and that it is the genotype that changes—via genetic mutation and recombination from sexual reproduction.[24]

But the modern understanding of Darwinism is the product of the evolutionary synthesis begun in the 1930s and 1940s, wherein Darwin's leading idea, natural selection, was joined to the theory of population genetics. Progressive Era biology had no established consensus on matters that are (mostly) settled today. Indeed, genetics and Darwinism, today regarded as inextricably bound together into the modern theory of evolution, were in mostly separate evolutionary camps one hundred years ago.

Progressive Era Darwinism (and sometimes Darwin himself) was ambiguous on aspects of human inheritance that were significant for newly professionalizing social scientists looking to ground their economic and social analyses in biology: particularly on (1) whether the individual or the group is the unit of selection, and (2) whether the environment can affect heredity. These fundamental ambiguities, when added to other unresolved matters in evolutionary thought—(3) whether competition is good or bad, (4) whether fitness consists solely in reproductive success, and (5) whether nature or the state should select the fittest—made Progressive Era biology very accommodating. Social scientists with quite different, even opposed, ideologies could join the project of explaining human variation by recourse to biology because the ambiguity of Progressive Era evolutionary thought, unlike modern Darwinism, could provide support for quite different views of reform.

5.3. Nature or Nurture: What Human Traits Can Be Inherited?

No eugenicist doubted that social and economic pathologies were the product of heredity. The question was whether heredity could be influenced by environmental factors. Reformers especially, well into the 1930s, emphasized environmental effects upon heredity, in the Lamarckian tradition. They believed that characteristics parents acquired during

24. The preceding two paragraphs borrow from Leonard 2003b, 350.

a lifetime could be transmitted to progeny. The drinking of an alcoholic father could, for example, poison his "germ plasm," so that his offspring inherited the affliction. It is not that bad habits acquired during a lifetime are imitated by progeny but that bad habits are genetically (to speak anachronistically) inherited by progeny.

A Lamarckian eugenics was thus possible: improvement of bad homes could also improve bad blood. Indeed, "euthenics" was briefly in use as a neo-Lamarckian term of art describing eugenic improvement through environmental means.[25] Some of the earliest eugenics tracts tended to be Lamarckian in orientation. Richard Dugdale's (1877) famous *The "Jukes": A Study in Crime, Pauperism, Disease, and Heredity*, which considered the family history of a "degenerate" Anglo-Saxon clan, argued that the clan's misfortune was, in part, the product of their degraded environment.

The Lamarckians were opposed by the neo-Darwinians, who argued that human heredity was unaffected by environment.[26] And importantly, Darwin himself was, upon occasion, Lamarckian in his views, especially in *The Descent of Man*. "Habits . . . followed during many generations," wrote Darwin, "probably tend to be inherited" (cited in Degler 1991, 352 n. 29). Thus could Lamarckians find some comfort in Darwin—nurture could affect nature.

The German biologist August Weismann's watershed finding in 1889—that mice with their tails cut off do not bear short-tailed progeny—was seen by many as a refutation of Lamarckism. Some neo-Darwinian eugenicists read Weismann's result as a crucial experiment, conclusive proof that the germ plasm of bad heredity was beyond the reach of environmental reform. Other eugenicists were more cautious. Leonard Darwin, a leader of English eugenics for some years, saw eugenics not as a substitute for ordinary social improvement but as a means of defining the useful limits of environmental social reform (Searle 1976, 47–48).

Karl Pearson and his Galton Laboratory for National Eugenics colleagues were agnostic in principle but hereditarian in practice: "We have

25. "Euthenics" appears to have been coined by Ellen H. (Swallow) Richards, the author of *Euthenics: The Science of Controllable Environment, A Plea for Better Living Conditions as a First Step toward Higher Human Efficiency*, and a founder of home economics; the term *home economics* eventually won out over Richards's preferred label of *human ecology*.

26. Environmental factors can clearly affect phenotypes, as with malnutrition or a broken bone. The question with respect to heredity is whether such changes are transmitted to the genotype. Darwinians argue that environmental changes cannot affect inheritance, barring an environmentally caused change in the genotype, as might be caused, for example, by radiation.

placed our money on environment," said Pearson, "when Heredity wins in a canter" (Searle 1976, 47–48).[27] When in 1909, Pearson published a manifesto, "bricks for the foundation" of eugenic science, he announced that "the relative weight of nature and nurture must not a priori be assumed but must be scientifically measured; and thus far our experience is that nature dominates nurture, that inheritance is more vital than environment. . . . there exists no demonstrable inheritance of acquired characters. Environment modifies the bodily character of the existing generation, but does not modify the germ plasms from which the next generation springs" (1909, 19–20).

Progressive Lamarckians, like Lester Ward, an American sociologist with training in paleontology, took Weismann's results badly. Ward (1891) thought that if Weismann were right—if acquired characteristics cannot be transmitted to progeny—then social reform would be ineffectual. Environmental improvement could be, at best, a temporary palliative, but it could not affect heredity, which he saw as the source of economic and social pathology. Thus did Ward find himself supporting Herbert Spencer—a man whose individualism and laissez-faire economics Ward, like other progressives, loathed—because it was Spencer who led the Lamarckian reply to Weismann's neo-Darwinism.

Other eugenic reformers, such as Wallace and the American economist Charlotte Perkins Gilman, were more sanguine than Ward. They perceived that marriage and mating were important for eugenics and that social reform influencing marriage could therefore have beneficial eugenic effects. The humane Wallace was a reformer but also a stout defender of neo-Darwinian inheritance. Wallace believed that English society was increasingly dysgenic, but he rejected compulsory eugenics as elitist and barbarous, arguing that eugenic ends could better be realized by an expansion of women's education and their political and economic freedom, which would reduce women's economic dependency and thereby reduce the incentive for women to make dysgenic marriages (Leonard 2005).[28]

27. When Edith Elderton's research at the Galton Laboratory claimed that the progeny of alcoholic parents did not inherit their parents' affliction, it was vigorously contested by temperance advocates, such as Alfred Marshall, and by Lamarckian eugenicists, like John Maynard Keynes (Childs 2001, 25).

28. "Progress is still possible, nay, is certain," said Wallace (1892, 156), "by . . . that mode of selection which will inevitably come into action through the ever-increasing freedom, joined with the higher education of women." Wallace (1890, 335) envisioned selection as "effected through the agency of female choice in marriage," leaving "the improvement of the race to the cultivated minds and pure instincts of the Woman of the Future" (337). See also Leonard 2005, 26.

Gilman's sui generis feminist eugenics, what she called "Humaniculture," envisions women as the enlightened society's eugenic agents. Women have a twofold role: they select fitter men for marriage, and they collectively supervise the raising of fitter children. Women select fitter mates with the help of state certification of men's biological fitness. Males are required to be eugenically certified, so that women have better information when selecting a mate and thus are less likely to make a dysgenic match. Gilman also envisioned that all parenting would be given over to a cadre of professionally trained women, what she called "social parentage" (Leonard 2005).[29] On this view, social reform could realize eugenic ends, without invoking "pollution of the germ plasm."

Modern evolutionary biology rejects Lamarckian and other non-Darwinian theories of inheritance. Progressive Era Darwinism could, in contrast, still accommodate a Lamarckian view of inheritance, which offered support to the reform variant of eugenics. The modern view, which sees reformers as partisans of nurture, is belied in the Progressive Era by reformers like Pearson and Wallace, who were staunch proponents of Darwinian inheritance. Similarly, the modern association of laissez-faire with nature is belied by Herbert Spencer, who was a Lamarckian, a vigorous disputant of Weismann and the other neo-Darwinians.

The points are two: first, the modern nature-versus-nurture dichotomy does not map well upon the Progressive Era's laissez-faire-versus-reform dichotomy. Reformers can be found among proponents of Darwinian inheritance (nature) and Larmarckian inheritance (nurture) alike. Today, a eugenicist is invariably Darwinian with respect to inheritance (as are all students of human inheritance). But a century ago, the Lamarckian view of inheritance allowed proponents of ordinary environmental reform to be eugenicists, and many were. Second, and related, whatever one's commitments with respect to the effect of environment upon heredity, he or she could find some support in Progressive Era theories of evolution.

5.4. Unit of Selection: Individual or Group?

Among those who applied biological ideas to social problems, one's stance on the unit of selection better predicted one's view toward reform.

29. These ideas are expressed most compactly in Gilman 1900. "Humaniculture" echoes earlier terminology for eugenics, such as "stirpiculture" and "viriculture." Gilman was a Lamarckian eugenicist; she argued that better (social) parenting could improve the genetic prospects of children born to the unfit (Leonard 2005, 20 n. 28).

Those who thought in terms of collectives or groups, such as Ward, Wallace, and Pearson, were better disposed to reform than were individualists like Spencer. And since eugenics is the species of reform concerned with the collective called "race," eugenics ought to have appealed more to collectivists than to individualists.

Ernst Mayr (1986, 358), dean of American evolutionary biology, has argued that "for most evolutionists, from Darwin on, the individual as a whole, is the principal target of selection." The qualifiers "most" and "principal" are important, for Darwin himself allowed, in places, that human beings, whom he regarded as subject to natural selection, would assist other members of the group in ways that were altruistic—that is, in ways that did not promote (and may even adversely affect) their individual chances of survival and reproduction. Darwin ([1871] 1913, 136) referred to human sympathy for the less fortunate as "the noblest part of our nature."[30] Darwin allowed that species compete with one another to some extent, though he also believed, most clearly for nonhuman animals, that competition among individuals within a species was more intensive and more important for evolution by natural selection.

The question of whether individuals or groups compete clearly mattered for those who would use Darwinian ideas about competition in nature to support or to criticize economic competition (see below). Reformers employing Darwinian ideas could not avoid competition, but they could avert to group rather than individual competition and still be plausibly Darwinian. Most reformers, and certainly the eugenicists among them, saw races and economic classes as the competing groups relevant for selection. Pearson, for example, regarded the English race as an "organized whole"; the idea that races (read: nations) compete is what makes Pearson a *national* socialist and explains why he supported England's imperial wars (1905, 46). We can represent the views of inheritance and the views of the principal unit of selection as a simple matrix. See table 1.

Without yet considering the other unsettled aspects of Progressive Era theories of evolution, we already can see, with only two dimensions, a heterogeneity of views that do not comfortably fit into the Hofstadterian taxonomy and that are, likewise, obscured when viewed through the lenses of modern Darwinism.

30. Modern Darwinism conceives of altruism from the gene's-eye view. An individual may sacrifice itself if that increases the likelihood—by saving kin, those carrying a fraction of the same genes—of the genes surviving, albeit in different phenotypic hosts.

Table 1 Representative Evolutionary Theorists, by Theory of Inheritance and Unit of Selection

	Inheritance	
Unit of Selection	Lamarckian	Neo-Darwinian
Individual	H. Spencer	A. Weismann
Collective	L. Ward	K. Pearson, A. Wallace

5.5. Competing Senses of "Competition"

A third ambiguity of Progressive Era Darwinism concerns what was meant by "competition" and the extent to which competition in nature made an appropriate metaphor for economic competition. Darwin, who insisted upon the descent of man from the "lower" orders of animals, was sometimes read as implying that, thereby, human behavior is animalistic, brutish. On this reading, competition among human beings is akin to competition among animals in nature: the key phrases here are "survival of the fittest" in "the struggle for existence."[31] Both phrases invoked a vision of competition as nature-red-in-tooth-and-claw, an image that provided a vivid critique of the economic competition of the new, raw industrial capitalism. On this account, economic competition is violent, uncooperative, and destructive, implying that nature is a threat, something terrifying to be overcome.

There are two difficulties here. The first is that natural selection can select for cooperative behavior—it in no way entails tooth-and-claw conflict. That cooperative behavior can be adaptive is a commonplace of contemporary evolutionary biology, and it was also known to Progressive Era intellectuals. Petr Kropotkin, a Russian anarchist, made this very argument in his *Mutual Aid: A Factor of Evolution* (1902), where he set out to show how cooperative behavior could be the product of Darwinian natural selection, instancing the social insects and many other examples of cooperation in nature. Kropotkin did not reject Darwin; on the contrary, he found in Darwin's natural selection cooperation rather than competition of the tooth-and-claw variety.

The second difficulty pertains to the ambiguous nature of "competition" in the economic sense. Some Progressive Era economists, particularly those who subscribed to both marginal utility and marginal

31. "Survival of the fittest" is Spencer's phrase; Darwin makes use of it only in the fifth edition of *Origin of Species*. "The struggle for existence" is due to Malthus.

productivity theories, saw economic competition not as destructive conflict but as socially valuable fair play. John Bates Clark, for example, meant by "competition" the refereed rivalry among firms to serve consumers. Clark saw competition as productive and technologically innovative, something policy should promote, whereas progressives saw competition as destructive, something policy should restrain.[32] In Clark's account, unfair economic behavior—such as predatory pricing or exclusive contracting by monopolists—is *anti*-competitive, a departure from fair play and a justification for regulatory intervention.

These competing conceptions of economic competition are virtually opposed: Clark's neoclassical view regards competition as fair play and departures from it as something to be policed, whereas the progressives regarded competition as amoral and destructive—sometimes invoking tooth-and-claw imagery—and departures from it as something to be promoted.

Progressive Era firms did not seek or lobby for competition in Clark's sense. To the contrary, they did all they could to undermine Clarkian competition: they combined in the hope of acquiring monopoly pricing power; they sometimes employed (what antitrust law still calls) anticompetitive practices such as predation and exclusion; and they used political influence to promote and sustain the high tariff that protected them from import competition.

Critics and proponents of reform could thus have entirely different conceptions of economic competition, and both find some support in Darwinism. Progressive critics of laissez-faire could invoke the tooth-and-claw version of Darwin, while neoclassicals like Clark, who, while not laissez-faire, had a more benign view of competitive markets, could appeal to the harmonious, cooperative vision of nature also found in Progressive Era Darwinism.

Thus these very different views of competition in nature—model to be emulated or threat to be overcome—and their implications for economic competition were both plausibly Darwinian. What is more, the progressives' views of natural selection helps us to distinguish social Darwinism, which is modeled on natural selection, from eugenics, which is premised on the failure of natural selection.

32. "Competition" had many different and sometimes conflicting meanings in the Progressive Era. Clark himself used the term in at least four different ways (Leonard 2003c, 539–40). See also Morgan 1993.

5.6. What Is Fitness?

In his influential *The Promise of American Life*, Herbert Croly of the *New Republic* put his case for a vigorous national government in eugenic language, arguing that artificial selection, by which he meant state-guided reform, was superior to natural selection (read: laissez-faire). The state, said Croly (1909, 191), had a responsibility to "interfere on behalf of the really fittest."

Croly required the qualifier "really" because, on the Darwinian account, the fittest are those with greatest reproductive success. For Darwinians, interference with natural selection risks impeding its benefits. "Survival of the unfittest," a phrase attributed to the economics writer W. R. Greg (1868), is thus a contradiction in Darwinian terms. So, when the race-suicide eugenicists proposed that persons of inferior stock were outcompeting their biological betters, they were not making a Darwinian argument, and, in this respect, as in others, the label of Darwinian misleads.[33]

Darwinism calls fit those who have most successfully reproduced, an *ex post* judgment. Eugenicists, on the other hand, tended to regard fitness as a moral or racial attribute, something judged *ex ante*. The social control of human breeding, after all, could not succeed without a prior judgment as to who (that is, which groups) was biologically superior. Indeed, many race-suicide accounts, such as that of Francis Amasa Walker's, argued that the better class of person, by virtue of greater racial refinement, refused to have an adequate number of offspring, allowing the inferior races to outbreed them (Leonard 2003a). Not surprisingly, the eugenicists' biological hierarchy mapped rather well onto traditional prejudices. Races with lower socioeconomic rank routinely found themselves assigned to biological inferiority, their greater relative fecundity notwithstanding.

It is of course true that natural selection could also be—and was—used to explain and justify putative racial hierarchies. The point here is that many eugenicists were non-Darwinian with respect to the nature of fitness. Where Darwinism saw fitness as the outcome of a selection process, eugenics made fitness the basis for initiating a selection process.

33. Two caveats need to be issued here. First, I do not wish to imply opposition between Darwin and Greg, whom Darwin admired. Second, Darwin's worry about the dysgenic effects of law and custom is not limited to reform legislation or charity intended to help the poor. Darwin also warned of the dysgenic effects of primogeniture in *Descent*, saying that it promoted the survival of feeble-minded older sons of the aristocracy (Soloway 1990, 74).

It is no surprise, then, that many promoted eugenics precisely because they believed that natural selection had failed.

5.7. Who Should Select the Fittest: Nature or the State?

Because it was Spencer's coinage, "survival of the fittest" is ordinarily associated with laissez-faire and with biological defenses of laissez-faire. But it is a mistake to identify selectionist sentiment with laissez-faire. The progressive opponents of laissez-faire were also often advocates of survival of the fittest, albeit with a non-Darwinian conception of fitness. What distinguished the progressives' views was their belief that the state, as guided by expert science, could do better than nature in the essential task of weeding out the unfit. The progressives did not reject selection, they rejected *natural* selection.

Laissez-faire theorists who also subscribed to the idea of race degeneration could only argue that ordinary social reform was impeding natural selection and that nature should be allowed to do its job unimpeded by dysgenic social reform. Eugenicists, certainly the progressives among them, typically were skeptical toward natural selection. Some argued that natural selection did not apply to humans. Others, notably the race-suicide theorists—Francis Amasa Walker, Frank Fetter, Edward A. Ross, Sidney Webb, among them—believed that natural selection had ceased to function with the development of industrial capitalism and its higher living standards for the working classes (Leonard 2003a). Still others, such as Lester Ward, believed that natural selection, to the extent it functioned at all, was inefficient. For Ward, nature was profligate and wasteful, so society should not imitate nature but, rather, improve upon it. Thus could Ward promote eugenics, having made his career by attacking social Darwinism.

Eugenics (artificial selection) can be seen as analogous to selection in nature, the similarity that Hofstadter emphasized in presenting eugenics as a continuation of social Darwinism. But, historically, the case actually made for Progressive Era eugenics rarely invoked this analogy, and, in fact, proponents often argued for eugenics on grounds that natural selection did not obtain or, if it did, was undesirable.

So though eugenics and social Darwinism (natural selection) both applied biological ideas to social phenomena, eugenics, by arguing that the course of human evolution must be socially controlled by expert technocrats, offered a vision exactly opposed to Spencer's. The question of whether the state should select the fittest fundamentally divided laissez-faire advocates of survival of the fittest—who argued, "no"—from the eugenicists, who insisted, "yes."[34] It is no accident that, historiographical mislabeling to one side, progressives were drawn to the ranks of eugenics advocacy but cannot be found among social Darwinists.

Among its other problems, the historiography that regards eugenics as a mere continuation of social Darwinism elides what is a most salient division in Progressive Era social thought: the division between the reformers who advocated a more expansive role for the state in society and the economy, and their critics who opposed it.

6. Conclusion

"Social Darwinist" and "eugenicist" today function essentially as epithets. It is understandable, perhaps predictable, that reform-minded historians would not seek to apply the terms to their intellectual progenitors.[35] But the same strand of Progressive Era historiography that has made "social Darwinism" into an epithet has also worked to mislead with respect to the influence of biological thought upon the newly professionalizing sciences of society. It has done so by also fashioning "social Darwinism" into a synecdoche for all things deemed nonprogressive in retrospect, which wrongly attributes to exemplars like Spencer and Sumner views they did not hold; which wrongly implies that progressives were somehow averse to Darwinian and other biological thought, when the opposite is true; and which also misleads with respect to the biological influences upon laissez-faire thought, which were, at least in part, Lamarckian rather than Darwinian.

These misunderstandings are compounded by the misleading claim that eugenics should be seen as a mere continuation of social Darwinism. Many eugenicists were reformers, thus opposed to laissez-faire, and

34. Of course, intellectual inconsistency did not stop some professed individualists from endorsing state control of human breeding. Sidney Webb (1910–11, 237), an enthusiastic eugenicist, understood this: "No consistent eugenicist can be a 'Laisser Faire' individualist unless he throws up the game in despair. He must interfere, interfere, interfere!"

35. The use of these terms as referents for all Progressive Era ideologies deemed nonprogressive in retrospect is of a piece with a Whiggishness that is sometimes found in Progressive Era historiography more generally. Progressive Era histories are often Whiggish in Herbert Butterfield's (1931) original sense of the term, that is, they depict their subject as a gradual march of progress, where good, forward-looking reformers continuously struggle with and ultimately overcome bad, backward-looking conservatives (Mayr 1990, 301).

many eugenicists were more Lamarckian than Darwinian with respect to inheritance. What is more, Progressive Era eugenics had a view of biological fitness wholly opposed to the Darwinian conception of fitness. And the eugenicist's case for state control of human breeding did not endorse natural selection; on the contrary, it ordinarily was predicated on a belief that natural selection did not or could not work. These important differences help explain why progressives were drawn to eugenics but not to social Darwinism.

The influence of biological thought should be no surprise, since Darwinian and other biological ideas influenced many aspects of the newly professionalizing social sciences. Social scientists of radically different outlooks could and did appeal to the biological thought of the day, this because Progressive Era biology (including Darwinism) was so protean, thus accommodating, with respect to the unit of selection, the effect of environment upon heredity, the effect of competition, and the nature of fitness. If one were to label as "social Darwinist" any social scientist who used a recognizably Darwinian idea, then nearly all Progressive Era social scientists—proponents and critics of reform alike—would be social Darwinists.

But because the term *social Darwinism* is associated with opposition to reform, it is important to recognize that, though modern Darwinism would no longer permit it, the eclecticism of Progressive Era biology readily accommodated a reform eugenics, which regarded the collective (race) as the unit of selection, which assumed that the environment could affect heredity—so that improving bad homes could also improve bad blood—and which saw biological fitness as racial, something prior to relative reproductive success.

In making Hofstadter a foil, I do not wish to be unfair, only to acknowledge his great influence. Hofstadter, after all, was not the first to critically join laissez-faire to Darwinism (and Darwinism to eugenics). The Hofstadter-inspired historiography, which presents Darwinian natural selection as the scientific instantiation (or expression or embodiment) of laissez-faire capitalism and which regards eugenics as so much social Darwinism, has deep intellectual roots in Left criticism of capitalism.[36] And, neither, of course, is Hofstadter alone. Other historians have

36. Engels read Darwinian natural selection as a mere projection of competitive Malthusian political economy upon nature and saw Galton's eugenics as the mere projection of Darwin back upon society. Historians and biologists on the Left have continued this venerable line of argument. One important problem with the claim that natural selection is just warmed-over

worked in this historiographical vein. But Hofstadter's telling—which reads eugenics as social Darwinism and social Darwinism as benighted opposition to reform—stands out because it has become canonical. It has influenced the process by which technical terms in intellectual history have devolved into epithets, a process that has, among the several consequences identified here, produced a kind of historical amnesia about the influence of biological ideas, notably eugenics, upon the reform thought and legislation that is the hallmark of the Progressive Era.

References

Adams, M., ed. 1990. *The Wellborn Science: Eugenics in Germany, France, Brazil, and Russia*. New York: Oxford University Press.

Bannister, R. 1973. William Graham Sumner's Social Darwinism: A Reconsideration. *HOPE* 4:89–109.

———. 1979. *Social Darwinism: Science and Myth in Anglo-American Social Thought*. Philadelphia: Temple University Press.

Barber, W. 1987. Should the American Economic Association Have Toasted Simon Newcomb at Its 100th Birthday Party? *Journal of Economic Perspectives* 1:179–83.

———. 1988. The Fortunes of Political Economy in an Environment of Academic Conservatism: Yale University. In *Breaking the Academic Mould: Economists and American Higher Learning in the Nineteenth Century*, edited by W. Barber. Middletown, Conn.: Wesleyan University Press.

Bary, H. V. 1972. *Helen Valeska Bary*. Regional Oral History Office, University of California, Berkeley, 1972–1973. Online Archive of California, http://ark.cdlib.org/ark:/13030/kt6z09n8m9.

Broberg, G., and N. Roll-Hansen, eds. 1996. *Eugenics and the Welfare State: Sterilization Policy in Denmark, Sweden, Norway, and Finland*. East Lansing: Michigan State University Press.

Broberg, G., and M. Tydén. 1996. Eugenics in Sweden: Efficient Care. In Broberg and Roll-Hansen 1996.

Bucur, M. 2002. *Eugenics and Modernization in Interwar Romania*. Pittsburgh: University of Pittsburgh Press.

Butterfield, H. 1931. *The Whig Interpretation of History*. London: G. Bell and Sons.

Chase, A. 1977. *The Legacy of Malthus*. New York: Knopf.

Childs, D. J. 2001. *Modernism and Eugenics: Woolf, Eliot, Yeats, and the Culture of Degeneration*. New York: Cambridge University Press.

---

liberal political economy is that, as William Coleman (2001, 39) has persuasively argued, the cofounder of natural selection, Alfred R. Wallace, was a socialist who wrote on political economy and who actively opposed competition, free trade, usury, and exports; who championed minimum wages, land nationalization, free bread for the indigent; and who argued that "capital" was "the enemy and tyrant of labour."

Coats, A. W. 1960. The First Two Decades of the American Economic Association. *American Economic Review* 50:555–74.

Coleman, W. 2001. The Strange "Laissez Faire" of Alfred Russel Wallace: The Connection between Natural Selection and Political Economy Reconsidered. In *Darwinism and Evolutionary Economics*, edited by J. Laurent and J. Nightingale. Cheltenham, U.K.: Elgar.

Coolidge, C. 1921. Whose Country Is This? *Good Housekeeping* 72:13, 14, 106, 109.

Croly, H. 1909. *The Promise of American Life*. New York: Macmillan.

Darwin, C. 1859. *On the Origin of Species by Means of Natural Selection, or The Preservation of Favoured Races in the Struggle for Life*. London: Murray.

———. [1871] 1913. *The Descent of Man, and Selection in Relation to Sex*. 2nd ed. New York: Appleton.

Degler, C. 1991. *In Search of Human Nature: The Decline and Revival of Darwinism in American Social Thought*. New York: Oxford University Press.

Dikötter, F. 1992. *The Discourse of Race in Modern China*. London: Hurst.

———. 1998. Race Culture: Recent Perspectives on the History of Eugenics. *American Historical Review* 103:467–78.

Dugdale, R. 1877. *The "Jukes": A Study in Crime, Pauperism, Disease, and Heredity*. New York: G. P. Putnam's Sons.

Ely, R. T. 1938. *Ground under Our Feet: An Autobiography*. New York: Macmillan.

Farnam, H. W. 1888. The State and the Poor. *Political Science Quarterly* 3:282–310.

Field, J. A. 1911. The Progress of Eugenics. *Quarterly Journal of Economics* 26:1–67.

Fine, S. 1956. *Laissez Faire and the General Welfare State: A Study of Conflict in American Thought, 1865–1901*. Ann Arbor: University of Michigan Press.

Fisher, I. 1907. Why Has the Doctrine of Laissez Faire Been Abandoned? *Science*, n.s., 25:18–27.

Fried, B. 1998. *The Progressive Assault on Laissez-Faire: Robert Hale and the First Law and Economics Movement*. Cambridge, Mass.: Harvard University Press.

Furner, M. 1975. *Advocacy and Objectivity: A Crisis in the Professionalization of American Social Science, 1865–1905*. Lexington: University Press of Kentucky.

Galton, F. 1869. *Hereditary Genius: An Inquiry into Its Laws and Consequences*. London: Macmillan.

Gilman, C. P. [Stetson]. 1900. *Concerning Children*. Boston: Small, Maynard & Co.

Gordon, L. 1992. Social Insurance and Public Assistance: The Influence of Gender in Welfare Thought in the United States, 1890–1935. *American Historical Review* 97:19–54.

Greg, W. R. 1868. On the Failure of "Natural Selection" in the Case of Man. *Fraser's Magazine* 78:353–62.

Hart, V. 1994. *Bound by Our Constitution*. Princeton, N.J.: Princeton University Press.

Hasian, M. 1996. *The Rhetoric of Eugenics in Anglo-American Thought*. Athens: University of Georgia Press.

Hofstadter, R. [1944] 1992. *Social Darwinism in American Thought*. Reprint, Boston: Beacon Press.

Jones, L. 1998. Social Darwinism Revisited. *History Today* 48:7–8.

Karp, L. 1982. Past Perfect: John Humphrey Noyes, Stirpiculture, and the Oneida Community. *American Journal of Medical Genetics* 12:127–30.

Kevles, D. 1995. *In the Name of Eugenics*. Cambridge, Mass.: Harvard University Press.

———. 1998. Eugenics in North America. In *Essays in the History of Eugenics*, edited by R. A. Peel. London: Galton Institute.

———. 1999. Eugenics and Human Rights. *British Medical Journal* 318:435–38.

Kropotkin, P. A. 1902. *Mutual Aid: A Factor of Evolution*. New York: McClure, Philips & Co.

Leonard, T. C. 2003a. More Merciful and Not Less Effective: Eugenics and Progressive-Era American Economics. *HOPE* 35:709–34.

———. 2003b. Review of *Darwinism and Evolutionary Economics*, edited by J. Laurent and J. Nightingale. *HOPE* 34:350–53.

———. 2003c. “A Certain Rude Honesty”: John Bates Clark as a Pioneering Neoclassical Economist. *HOPE* 35:521–58.

———. 2005. Protecting Family and Race: The Progressive Case for Regulating Women’s Work. *American Journal of Economics and Sociology* 64 (July): 757–91.

Ludmerer, K. M. 1972. *Genetics and American Society*. Baltimore, Md.: Johns Hopkins University Press.

Mayr, E. 1986. Evolutionary Theory: The Unfinished Synthesis. *Isis* 77:358–59.

McGerr, M. 2003. *A Fierce Discontent: The Rise and Fall of the Progressive Movement in America, 1870–1920*. New York: Free Press.

McLaren, A. 1990. *Our Own Master Race: Eugenics in Canada, 1885–1945*. Toronto: McClelland and Stewart.

Miller, K. 1917. Eugenics of the Negro Race. *Scientific Monthly* 5:57–59.

Morgan, M. 1993. Competing Notions of “Competition” in Late Nineteenth-Century American Economics. *HOPE* 25:563–604.

Orloff, A. S., and T. Skocpol. 1984. Why Not Equal Protection? Explaining the Politics of Public Social Spending in Britain, 1900–1911, and the United States, 1880–1920. *American Sociological Review* 49:726–50.

Paul, D. 1995. *Controlling Human Heredity, 1865 to the Present*. Atlantic Highlands, N.J.: Humanities Press.

Paul, D., and H. Spencer. 1995. The Hidden Science of Eugenics. *Nature* 374:302–5.

Pearson K. [1887] 1901. The Moral Basis of Socialism. In *The Ethic of Free Thought*. London: Black.

———. 1905. *National Life from the Standpoint of Science*. London: Black.

———. 1909. The Groundwork of Eugenics. *Eugenics Laboratory Lecture Series* 2. London: Dulau.

Peckham, M. 1959. Darwinism and Darwinisticism. *Victorian Studies* 3:19–40.

Raby, P. 2001. *Alfred Russel Wallace: A Life*. Princeton, N.J.: Princeton University Press.

Richards, E. H. [1910] 1977. *Euthenics, the Science of Controllable Environment*. New York: Arno Press.

Rodgers, D. T. 1998. *Atlantic Crossings: Social Politics in a Progressive Age*. Cambridge, Mass.: Belknap Press of Harvard University Press.

Roosevelt, T. 1907. A Letter from President Roosevelt on Race Suicide. *American Monthly Review of Reviews* 35:550–51.

Ross, E. A. 1901. *Social Control: A Survey of the Foundations of Order*. New York: Macmillan.

Schneider, W. H. 1990. *Quality and Quantity: The Quest for Biological Regeneration in Twentieth-Century France*. New York: Cambridge University Press.

Searle, G. R. 1976. *Eugenics and Politics in Britain, 1900–1914*. Leyden: Noordhoff.

———. 1998. The Early Years. In *Essays in the History of Eugenics*, edited by R. A. Peel. London: Galton Institute.

Soloway, R. 1990. *Demography and Degeneration: Eugenics and the Declining Birthrate in Twentieth-Century Britain*. Chapel Hill: University of North Carolina Press.

Stepan, N. L. 1986. Race and Gender: The Role of Analogy in Science. *Isis* 77:261–77.

———. 1991. *The Hour of Eugenics: Race, Gender, and Nation in Latin America*. Ithaca, N.Y.: Cornell University Press.

Suzuki, Z. 1975. Geneticists and the Eugenics Movement in Japan. *Japanese Studies in the History of Science* 14:157–64.

Wallace, A. R. 1890. Human Selection. *Fortnightly Review*, n.s., 48:325–37.

———. 1892. Human Progress: Past and Future. *Arena*, January, 145–59.

Ward, L. F. 1891. The Transmission of Culture. *Forum*.

———. 1915. *Glimpses of the Cosmos*. Vol. 3. New York: G. P. Putnam's Sons.

Webb, S. 1907. The Decline in the Birth-Rate. *Fabian Society Tract* 131. London: Fabian Society.

———. 1910–11. Eugenics and the Poor Law: The Minority Report. *Eugenics Review* 2:233–41.

Wilson, R. J. 1967. *Darwinism and the American Intellectual*. Homewood, Ill.: Dorsey Press.

Wylie, I. 1959. Social Darwinism and the Businessmen. *Proceedings of the American Philosophical Society* 103:629–35.

Walton H. Hamilton and the Public Control of Business

Malcolm Rutherford

American institutional economists have, from the beginning of the movement, been supporters of a greater degree of "social control" over the economy. It has even been claimed that the concept of social control, in the sense of "the consciously planned guidance of economic processes," is "the central organizing principle" or "guiding formula" of the institutionalist movement (Everett 1931), but the exact nature and techniques of social control suggested vary between different groups within the movement. Discussion of institutionalist views on the appropriate type of social control has focused on two main groups. The first is the Wisconsin group of John R. Commons and a number of his students who were proponents of the use of independent commissions to administer such things as public utility regulations, compensation for industrial accidents, unemployment insurance, and other labor legislation (Commons and Andrews 1936; Chasse 1986). The Wisconsin economists Edwin E. Witte, Arthur J. Altmeyer, and others were also involved with the development of the Social Security Act during the New Deal (Schlabach 1969). The second group consists of the advocates of some kind of "planning"; members of that group ranged from Wesley Mitchell, who supported indicative planning and countercyclical public works programs (Alchon 1985; Barber 1985), to Rexford G. Tugwell, Mordecai Ezekiel, and Gardiner Means, who were the central figures associated with the

My thanks to Fred Lee for information on the Cabinet Price Committee and to Mike Widener at the Tarlton Law Library. Research for this essay was made possible by a research grant from the Social Science and Humanities Research Council of Canada.

"structuralist" approach that had some influence during the first phase of the New Deal (Hawley 1966; Barber 1996). The New Deal planners pushed for a joint program of recovery and reform and favored some type of direct government planning and intervention in the economy in order to increase purchasing power, allocate investment, establish minimum standards, and correct for what they saw as various other failings of the market system.

This picture becomes more complex when we take into account the career of Walton H. Hamilton. Hamilton (1919) introduced the term *institutional approach* to the economics literature in 1918 and defined it in a way that placed special emphasis on its relevance to "the problem of control." Hamilton's interests spanned economics and law: he did his graduate work at the University of Michigan where he came under the influence of H. C. Adams and Charles Horton Cooley; he taught briefly at the University of Chicago and then at Amherst College from 1915 until 1923; he headed the experimental Robert Brookings Graduate School of Economics and Government between 1923 and 1928; and then he moved to Yale Law School where he remained until 1948. In all of his teaching and research he stressed a problem-centered approach and a creative search for programs of control (Rutherford 2003).

Hamilton was a member of the American Association for Labor Legislation (AALL), a supporter of workers' education, and a keen student of "the labor problem." During 1918 he worked with the War Labor Policies Board (headed by Felix Frankfurter) as an economic expert dealing mainly with reconstruction issues (Dorfman 1974). He maintained an interest in labor issues, particularly the problem of raising the standard of living for workers. In 1935 Hamilton served as U.S. representative to the meeting of the International Labour Organization (ILO) in Geneva (the first occasion the United States was officially represented). Outside labor issues, Hamilton had a special interest in the provision of medical services and in the problems of the bituminous coal industry. At Brookings and Yale Hamilton developed his interest in law and economics. Hamilton was a legal realist, opposed to legal formalisms, and became a well-known critic of the more "conservative" of the Supreme Court justices who sought to interpret the Constitution in ways limiting to social and economic legislation.

A number of Hamilton's students played prominent parts in the New Deal, particularly Mordecai Ezekiel (economic adviser to the secretary of agriculture), Isador Lubin (commissioner of labor statistics), Winfield Reifler (economic adviser to the executive council), Willard Thorp (director of the Bureau of Foreign and Domestic Commerce), Dexter Keezer (executive director of the Consumers' Advisory Board), and George Galloway (assistant deputy administrator at the National Recovery Administration). Hamilton himself joined the NRA in 1933 as a member of the Consumers' Advisory Board (CAB). With the successive changes to the organization of the NRA Hamilton became chairman of the Advisory Council of the NRA and then a member of the National Industrial Recovery Board. The debates over the NRA codes and price policy led, in 1934, to the formation of a Cabinet Committee on Price Policy, and Hamilton was appointed as director of studies. In July 1935 he was appointed as adviser on Consumers' Problems and director of the Consumers' Division of the NRA. In this capacity he was also a member of the National Emergency Council. Later in 1935 he was appointed by John G. Winant, the first chairman of the Social Security Board, as director of the Division of Economic Research of the Social Security Board.

As is well known, large parts of the New Deal legislation were found unconstitutional in Supreme Court rulings in 1935 and 1936, and those aspects of the New Deal relating to recovery from the Depression and the regulation of trade practices shifted from "planning" to a combination of fiscal policy and a more aggressive use of the antitrust acts (Hawley 1966). Hamilton also made this transition, and from 1938 to 1945 he was special assistant to the attorney general, working closely with his former Yale colleague Thurman Arnold on issues of antitrust and patents.[1] Hamilton's involvement with the New Deal thus spanned both its code making and later antitrust components. Afterward, he continued to write extensively on trade practice, antitrust, patents, judicial decision making, and the ongoing, and ever-changing, problem of the control of industry. In 1948 he retired from Yale and joined the Washington law firm of Arnold, Fortas, and Porter.

Hamilton's Institutionalism

In his original manifesto for an institutional economics, the most central of Hamilton's (1919, 312–13) arguments is that economics "should

1. Other Yale colleagues were also involved with the New Deal, notably Jerome Frank, William O. Douglas, and Thurman Arnold. Frank was one of the group of planners and was general counsel of the Agricultural Adjustment Act, while Douglas became head of the Securities and Exchange Commission. Frank (1933) spoke of the New Deal as involving "experimentalist lawyers" working with "experimentalist economists" in almost "interchangeable roles." See especially Gordon 2004.

be relevant to the modern problem of control." This "modern problem" had arisen out of new economic circumstances creating new social and economic problems and a growing demand for regulation. To have relevance to this problem of control, economics must "relate to changeable elements of life and the agencies through which they are to be directed": in other words, to institutional arrangements, in the sense of both the set of rules relating to economic behavior and the agencies through which the rules are established and altered. Such control "of the development of industrial society is contingent upon a knowledge of the bundle of conventions and arrangements which make it up," and the type of knowledge necessary is of a detailed nature. Moreover, institutional arrangements are constantly changing both from within and from outside developments (315).

Hamilton (1918) clearly rejects neoclassical "value theory" as a useful tool for the investigation of the nature and functioning of the "economic order." Such value theory ignores institutions. What is required instead is a "genetic" inquiry designed to analyze a problem in terms of how the current reality came to be, how it came out of the past, how it is changing, and how that change might be directed so as to better serve the end of human welfare. For Hamilton, institutional economics had as its basis an instrumental view of society and social institutions. It presented both "an invitation to detailed study" and an invitation to the formulation of programs of control (Hamilton n.d.b). In terms of "social welfare," or the ends to be pursued by these programs of control, Hamilton was not always clear, but a recurring ideal is that of raising a broadly defined "standard of living" for the bulk of the population—an ideal of "wise use, plentiful production and just distribution."[2] In Hamilton's view such a general criterion could only be made specific through particular inquiries aimed at establishing particular standards; standards subject to revision in the light of experience and further investigation.

Hamilton's view of the economic order borrowed heavily from Thorstein Veblen and Charles Horton Cooley. What Hamilton taught in his courses at Amherst and Brookings began with a discussion of the development of "modern industrialism" from the precapitalist manorial system. This process included the development of technology, culminating ultimately in the widespread adoption of large-scale machine methods

2. This quotation comes from chapter 5 of a draft book, *The Economic Order* (Hamilton n.d.e). Hamilton defines the standard of living to include physical, social, and intellectual needs and desires.

of production, and a complex of institutional developments relating to property and contract, the rise of markets, the adoption of pecuniary goals and incentives, the corporate form of organization, and the rise of what Hamilton called "the pecuniary order." This scheme of control developed out of elements "long in existence"; the instrumentalities it employs are "the corporation, the pecuniary calculus, and profit making." It grew partly out of tradition, partly as a result of conscious policy, but mostly as an unintended consequence of "judgments made with other ends in view." The system of pecuniary or business control is dominant, but Hamilton never forgets there are significant areas of economic life controlled by other institutions such as the family, professional organizations, and government. Government imposes limitations on "almost all forms of industrial activity, and controls some of them quite directly" (Hamilton n.d.d).

The key issue, of course, is the adequacy of this system of control to provide for the social welfare as Hamilton defined it. In the economics textbooks, competition is supposed to operate to reconcile the individual pursuit of pecuniary gain with the public interest, but Hamilton argues that competitive theory and the policies that it suggests apply only to an economy of "petty trade" and fail to provide an adequate analytical foundation for the understanding or control of large-scale industry and "big business." For Hamilton (1932b, 593) the fundamental issue is clear: "An economic order in which the productive processes belong to big business and the arrangements for its control to petty trade cannot abide." The task is to "devise a scheme adequate to the direction of great industry. In a world of change a society cannot live on a wisdom borrowed from our fathers."

Some Proposals for Control, 1923–32

Prior to his involvement with the New Deal, Hamilton developed proposals for the social control of various aspects of the economy (Dorfman 1974). Only some of these can be discussed here, but they all share an emphasis on the importance of increasing standards of living, the importance of the consumer interest, the need for detailed knowledge, and a view of institutional arrangements as instrumental and subject to creative innovation.

As the title suggests, Hamilton and Stacy May's *Control of Wages* (1923) is addressed to the problem of controlling wages in the sense of increasing the regularity of employment and of raising real wages to make "wages as nearly adequate as may be." It is presented as "the next step" in the "general campaign for the elevation of wages" (Hamilton and May [1923] 1968, 18–19; Hamilton 1922b). As might be expected, the argument stresses raising the productivity of labor, improving management, introducing new technology and equipment, improving organization, and eliminating various "wastes." There is, however, an equal emphasis on the improvement of the "economic arts," in particular policies to reduce business cycles and unemployment, including the introduction of a tax "assessed against irregularities in the volume of employment," with the receipts "disbursed as unemployment benefits" (Hamilton and May [1923] 1968, 66).[3] Additionally, Hamilton offers what he calls "a plan for the eventual 'liquidation of ownership' in natural elements, intangible assets, and other corporate property." The plan involves recalling all outstanding securities and replacing them with terminable annuities (of, say, fifty years) of equal value. This effectively "buys out all the returns due to ownership fifty or more years from now" (68–70), providing for future increases in wages.[4] Other institutional adjustments Hamilton and May discuss include collective marketing, collective research organizations, and the economies that might be generated through various schemes for the "unification of industry." This last possibility is approached in tentative terms, recognizing the problems of private monopoly power, the unsettled state of the debate over the nationalization of industries, and the preliminary nature of various other proposals for the unification of industry under the control of management representatives and workers, "of workers and consumers, or of workers alone." Hamilton calls the last type of scheme of control both "fascinating" and "promising," as it safeguards the interests of the public against private exploitation while also avoiding "the deadly sin of bureaucracy" (75–79).

3. Hamilton does not make it clear whether he is supporting pooled reserves or individual employer reserves, but the emphasis he places on penalizing employers for their particular contribution to unemployment and on the prevention of unemployment are more suggestive of what became the "Wisconsin plan" rather than the alternative "Ohio plan" formulated by William Leiserson, based on pooled reserves and insurance against risk principles. See Eisner 1967 and Schlabach 1969.

4. Hamilton mentions that this scheme is to be elaborated in a forthcoming article by himself and Willard L. Thorp titled "The Liquidation of Ownership" (Hamilton and May [1923] 1968, 80). A search of indexes failed to turn up any such publication.

The gains achieved in the ways outlined above need to be secured by the broad mass of labor and not just by some groups within the labor movement. Hamilton advocates collective bargaining by industrial unions and stresses the importance of spreading the gains achieved in the form of lower prices rather than as increased nominal wages. Unions need to give "constant attention to their interests as consumers" (90). A last important element in the real wage is the nonmonetary benefit provided by employers and the public goods provided by the state. Hamilton notes the extension of the role of the state in areas such as compensation for industrial accident, the provision of "an elaborate health service," educational institutions, and facilities for recreation. In the very near future the state may provide "some sort of guarantee of regular employment" (100).[5]

Some of the key themes in Hamilton's work on wages reappear in his later investigation of and recommendations for the coal industry. Coal was one area of research strongly emphasized in the Institute of Economics (later part of the Brookings Institution), founded in Washington, D.C., in 1922. In 1923 Hamilton was appointed as head of the companion Robert Brookings Graduate School of Economics and Government. Helen R. Wright also taught at the school, and she and Hamilton wrote two books on the bituminous coal industry (Hamilton and Wright 1925, 1928).

Hamilton and Wright's first book characterized the bituminous coal industry as beset by persistent excess capacity, irregular operation, low wages, unsafe working conditions, strikes and labor unrest, and supply interruptions. This state of affairs is contrasted with that suggested by the theory of competitive markets. The institutions of competitive free enterprise are supposed to ensure efficient operation, protection of the consumer, and conditions of work "as good as circumstances will permit" (Hamilton 1926). Instead, none of these conditions pertain. The problem, in Hamilton's view, is one of technological advance increasing capacity and creating a cost structure with high overheads and decreasing costs. Under these conditions competition leads to price cutting, low profits, and low wages. This is combined with uncoordinated

5. Hamilton and May are critical of marginal productivity theory, but primarily because it treats the interesting variables as givens. They admit that marginal productivity theory can be reconciled with most of their conclusions (Hamilton and May [1923] 1968, 176). Frank Taussig wrote to Hamilton concerning his 1922 article on wages that "your conclusions are pretty well in accord with those of the economists in general" (Hamilton 1922a).

investment decisions and bankruptcy laws that allow for reorganizations that retain the mining capacity in the industry.[6] The industry is characterized more by "chaos" than by an orderly state of normal profits and capacity matched to demand. The economic organization of the industry is "backward"; there is a "lag" between the technical development of the industry and its economic organization; the "scheme of arrangements" surrounding the production of coal fails to adequately serve the ends of workers or consumers. The result is unintentional; it is a system within which each individual tries to do good, but "evil comes of it" (Hamilton 1926, 225–26; Hamilton and Wright 1925, 256; Hamilton 1928b).[7] This argument goes well beyond more standard notions of market failure.

Hamilton and Wright's second book, *A Way of Order for Bituminous Coal* (1928), put forward a controversial proposal for reorganizing the industry. The book contains two dissenting opinions written by members of the Institute of Economics, something unique. The proposal is a modified version of one made by Henry Clay in 1919 for the British coal industry, and Clay's original memorandums are contained in an appendix to the book.[8] In the form given it by Hamilton and Wright, the proposal calls for the merger of all coal companies into a single enterprise of a corporate form but under the joint control of workers and consumers. The right to income from investment and the right to "a voice in control" are to be separated.

In the new company the existing ownership equities are to be exchanged by an issue of debentures upon "the basis of an equivalence of values," the interest payments on these debentures being a first charge on

6. There is a strong resemblance between Hamilton's analysis of the coal industry and Veblen's 1904 discussion of chronic excess capacity created by continuing technological change. See Veblen [1904] 1975, 217–55. Hamilton did not, however, apply the argument as generally as did Veblen.

7. Clarence Ayres wrote to Hamilton after reading his book describing the argument that "ours is a system in which each man can do good and evil come of it" as "more pregnant in meaning" than Veblen's maxims of business "baulking" industry—as it is more impersonal. It makes "confusion a misfortune of a confused transition rather than a conspiracy of malevolent freebooters." Ayres wonders if this is not "the point of departure for institutional economics" (Hamilton n.d.c).

8. Hamilton and Clay had come to know each other well and corresponded on this and other issues. Clay sent his proposal to the British Coal Commission as an alternative to nationalization of the coal industry under a government ministry, on the one hand, and unrestricted private enterprise, on the other. R. H. Tawney, a member of the commission, responded with the question "where does the State come in?" (Hamilton 1928a). Hamilton's proposal also has similarities to the scheme of control established for the German coal industry in 1919 (see Macgregor 1930). Neither Clay nor Hamilton reference the German case.

the new company. Control is to be given by a small number of shares of common stock, which entitle the various classes of holders to participate in various ways in the enterprise's direction. These shares pay no dividends, but represent the right to vote for a board member. Shares giving a right to vote for a voting board member are to be distributed equally to workers and consumers in a way that ensures the representation of different interests. Other shares giving the right to vote for a nonvoting board member are to be distributed to administrative and technical staff—their representatives on the board to provide advice, information, and criticism. The board is to consist of fourteen members (ten voting) plus a nonvoting chairman to be selected from without (Hamilton and Wright 1928, 166–73).

Hamilton was clearly pleased with this idea, and it is mentioned as an example of an inventive scheme of control in a number of his courses and published papers. His suggestions do not seem to have had the impact he hoped for, but Hamilton was closely involved in discussions about regulating the coal industry, both immediately before and during the New Deal, and it is quite likely that his involvement did result in the specific inclusion of representation of the consumer interest, which is a notable feature of the 1935 Bituminous Coal Conservation Act (Guffey Coal Act).[9]

Hamilton's innovative attitude is also apparent in his work on the provision of medical care. The American Association for Labor Legislation had begun studying compulsory health insurance (along the lines of European schemes) as early as 1912, and by 1915 it was actively promoting a model bill (Chasse 1994; Ross 2002). Despite initial support, the efforts of the AALL ultimately failed, but the pursuit of the issue was revived in the late 1920s because of increasing concern over the rising costs of medical care restricting access to medical services. Technical developments in medicine, advances in surgery, and higher physician's fees were all partly responsible. In 1926 a small group, including Hamilton, was formed to discuss a possible reorganization of medicine. Out of this came the Committee on the Costs of Medical Care (CCMC), which made a five-year study of the economics of health care. Hamilton was an important member of this committee.[10]

9. See Hamilton 1933b, 1933c. See also Hamilton 1933a, 1933d. This last refers to "Hamilton's Coal Bill" and the use of a rebate of tax to obtain the assent of the operators.

10. The committee eventually grew to forty-eight members. Wesley Mitchell was a member although less involved in the committee's work than Hamilton. The committee's research staff

The committee's final report was issued in 1932. It contained a set of majority recommendations, two sets of minority recommendations, and two individual statements of dissent, one written by Hamilton. The majority report favored group practice and the extension of basic public health services to the whole population, but while it recommended group payment schemes of various possible types, it stopped short of compulsory health insurance. The first minority report opposed group practice and any government involvement other than in the care of the indigent, and opposed voluntary insurance unless professionally controlled. This was the position adopted by the American Medical Association (AMA). Hamilton occupied the other extreme of the opinions expressed. For him, the majority report failed to go far enough and should have made a clear-cut recommendation for compulsory medical insurance and outlined a well-defined organizational alternative to private practice.[11] He argued that the majority report failed to keep the distinction between the technology of medicine and its organization clearly in mind, failed to place the problem in its proper social and historical setting, and failed to realize the essentially "instrumental character of the agencies which we employ toward health" (Hamilton 1932e, 190).

What Hamilton saw in the case of medicine was an older ideal of professional practice becoming converted into "a system of individual business competition" (193). But in medicine the market mechanism suffers from a number of deficiencies. The patient has insufficient knowledge to judge the quality of the service given; medical charges can vary substantially between doctors and are not usually known in advance; medical costs can be high, come unexpectedly, and be difficult or impossible to meet out of current income; and the incentives of money making may be inconsistent with professional standards and ethics. At the same time the technical advances in medicine were making medicine an increasingly complex "network of interlocking services" (193–94; Hamilton 1930b). Hamilton's solution was compulsory insurance, group practice, and the removal of "the aims and the arrangements for profit making" from the

included three of Hamilton's students from Brookings; one, Harry H. Moore, was the director of research. Hamilton planned to write a book on the economics of health, initially with Helen Wright as a coauthor. Some drafts were written, but no book was ever published (Hamilton n.d.f, g).

11. Eight signers of the majority report dissented on the issue of compulsory insurance alone. These included Wesley Mitchell. The authors of the first minority report were eight private practitioners and one representative of the Catholic hospitals (Chasse 1994, 1070; Ross 2002, 132).

practice of medicine (Hamilton 1932e, 195). This last was to be accomplished by making each group a corporation with a board of trustees made up of lay people, no one of whom should have any commercial interest in the venture. The professional staff should be paid by salary and promotion based on medical competence. The corporation could set aside reserves, establish pension funds, but it should not pay out dividends or engage in profit making. "In its larger outlines this scheme of organization is not a novelty; it is adapted to a profession engaged in public service; its value has been attested by its employment in education" (197). The model is that of the university. The involvement of the state "must be invoked to make membership compulsory," to ensure the collection of the premiums or taxes involved, and to make financial redistributions between centers if required, but it "is to be hoped that the concern of the state in the venture can be limited to a use of its power of compulsion in financial matters" (198).

The majority recommendations of the CCMC failed to withstand the organized opposition of the AMA, and Hamilton's proposals fared even worse. Hamilton did remain involved in health issues, and compulsory health insurance was discussed for inclusion in the Social Security Act. Continued opposition from the medical profession, however, resulted in Edwin Witte removing medical insurance from the bill, in order not to endanger the main provisions with respect to unemployment insurance and old age pensions (Schlabach 1969, 114; Hirshfeld 1970, 45–59).[12]

The Judicial Control of Industry

Hamilton's interests always spanned the disciplines of law and economics, but his concern developed in the 1920s and 1930s with the pronounced tendency of the Supreme Court to interpret the Constitution in ways limiting to the exercise of the state's regulatory power. The underlying question is "the kind of thing the Constitution is": is it "a fetish which must be served whatever be the resulting inability of the State to look after its own affairs," or is it "an instrument of government" and

12. The Social Security Act did provide federal grants to the states for public health programs, and in 1937 the movement for voluntary group prepayment of hospital costs resulted in the Blue Cross program. A leading figure in this was C. Rufus Rorem, who had been a member of the CCMC research staff (Chasse 1994; Ross 2002). For further information on the CCMC and the later campaign for compulsory medical insurance, see Perkins 1998 and Hirshfeld 1970.

an "instrument of public welfare" (Hamilton 1928c, 235; 1936a, 103)? Hamilton's special target for criticism was Justice Sutherland, who often spoke for the conservative majority of the Court,[13] while Hamilton's sympathies were more with the opinions of the "liberal" contingent of Justices Holmes, Stone, Brandeis, and Cardozo (after he replaced Holmes).[14] For Hamilton, as mentioned above, the coming of industrialism had created a host of new economic and social problems that demanded some response in the form of state regulation, including the regulation of prices, and in his view there was nothing in the Constitution that prevented the use of the state's police power in the cause of public welfare. Such prohibitions as Justice Sutherland discovered were not to be found plainly in the text of the Constitution but were the result of attaching new meanings and constructions to words, and to a reading into the Constitution of economic philosophies quite alien to the minds of those who had first constructed it (Hamilton 1936a; Hamilton and Adair [1937] 1972).

An example of the type of critical analysis of judicial decisions Hamilton provides is his article "The Regulation of Employment Agencies" (Hamilton 1928c). The majority of the Court had denied to the state of New Jersey the right to regulate the fees charged by private employment agencies. The key argument in the judgment written by Justice Sutherland is that employment agencies are "not affected with a public interest" so that the fixing of prices by the state is a "deprivation of property" without "due process of law." The reason given for employment agencies not being affected with a public interest is that employment agencies are "brokers," and previous judgments concerning theater ticket brokers had held that they were not affected by a public interest (231).

The questions Hamilton raises are many. Why is the statute not valid under the police power, as a regulation designed to correct a persistent and well-recognized evil? What exactly is the basis for "affectation with a public interest" if not a need for regulation evidenced by the importance of the business to the public and the failure of the competitive system to protect the public interest? Where does the category of "brokers" come from, all of whose business is not affected with a public interest?

13. The four most consistently conservative justices, Sutherland, Butler, McReynolds, and Van Devanter, were popularly known as "the four horsemen."

14. Hamilton was quite aware of the differences in approach of justices such as Holmes, Brandeis, and Cardozo. He was also not unaware of their failings. On Holmes and Brandeis, see Hamilton 1931d, 1941b; on Cardozo, see Hamilton 1938a.

Why does the basis of distinction lie in a mere stage of a marketing process with no connection to the issues of evils, regulation, or government control? Hamilton makes a contrast with the dissenting opinion written by Justice Stone (and supported by Holmes and Brandeis), which is "simple, clear cut, and direct." As the issue is the validity of an act of regulation, he "looks to see whether there was warrant for the specific exercise of power." He is interested in whether evils exist, whether they are grave and persistent and with adverse consequences for the public. He asks whether the regulation is suited to its purpose. He has no difficulty distinguishing ticket brokers from employment agencies in terms of their importance to the public. He sees the action of the legislature "as a proper regulation" designed to remedy a public evil. Hamilton sees the minority position as in accord with the longer legal tradition; it is Sutherland and the "conservative" majority who are providing the "radical innovations" and who "read into the Constitution of the United States the original ideas of ingenious attorneys for plaintiffs in error" (233–34).[15]

Analysis such as this led Hamilton to inquire more deeply into the beginnings and subsequent histories of interpretation of a number of legal concepts and doctrines. Most significant are his investigations of the key concepts of "affectation with a public interest" and "due process" (Hamilton 1930a, 1938c).[16] "Affectation with a public interest" is a term lifted from a decision of Lord Hale in England in 1676 on the regulation of charges at a public wharf. The term is not stressed, and it is not made a test for the right of the state to regulate prices. At that time the regulation of prices was a commonplace, and in England "even to this day Parliament decides for itself how far it may go in the control of industry" (Hamilton 1930a, 1094). The term came into American law in the case of *Mun v. Illinois* in 1877, over the regulation of charges by grain elevators. Here the representatives of the elevator operators argued the

15. Other decisions analyzed by Hamilton include a 1929 decision unfavorable to farmers' cooperatives written by Justice Sutherland (Hamilton 1929) and a 1931 decision favorable to the regulation of commissions paid by insurance companies to agents and written by Justice Brandeis (Hamilton 1931c). Hamilton also wrote on a number of the decisions concerning New Deal legislation that are dealt with below.

16. Hamilton also wrote pieces on the history of caveat emptor (1931a), of the concept of property (1932d), of the law surrounding compensation for workplace accident (1937), and of antitrust (1940a). Hamilton's former teacher and friend, Alvin Johnson, asked Hamilton to write the entries for the *Encyclopaedia of the Social Sciences* on accumulation, acquisition, affectation with public interest, caveat emptor, celibacy, collective bargaining, collectivism, competition, constitutionalism, Charles Horton Cooley, damages, freedom of contract, institution, judicial process, John Stuart Mill, and organization—economic, police power, and property.

principle to be a limitation of legislative action to only those businesses affected with a public interest. They lost the case, but the opinion of the Court accepted the principle. In successive decisions the principle went through some changes in definition, but by 1914 the principle had become "a general, if indefinite, invitation to the legislature to extend price control where the public concern demands it" (1099).[17] This began to change with the Supreme Court of 1921–23. The work of this Court was marked by the formal recognition of "affectation with a public interest" as a "definite test of constitutionality of price fixing regulation" (at least by the majority), but the same Court sought to narrow its range. Thus, throughout the 1920s "a phrase brought into constitutional law to sanction price fixing" was "consistently used to outlaw price fixing" (1100). The principle became a barrier to the ability of states to respond to public concerns via price regulation; the constitutional "test" of affectation being substituted for a recognition of police power and an appraisal of the need for and reasonableness of the regulation in question.

The injunction that "no person shall be deprived of life, liberty or property without due process of law" was contained in the Fifth Amendment, but until after the Civil War was regarded as a procedural concern only. After the Civil War the Fourteenth Amendment was passed to ensure the rights of the newly enfranchised blacks and contained similar language (Hamilton 1938c, 271). Hamilton traces the history of the attempts to read substantive rights into the due process clause. The first of these occurred with the well-known "Slaughterhouse cases" of the 1880s. Initially a corporation was given a monopoly on slaughtering, and the legal representative of independent slaughtermen attempted to argue that a property—the right to follow their trade—had been removed without due process.[18] The argument failed, but a few years later when the monopoly privilege was revoked, the corporation attempted the same line of argument. That too failed, but in a concurring opinion two justices effectively revisited the original case and argued that the original grant of the monopoly privilege was indeed unconstitutional and should never have been given. Thus, despite the losses to the older doctrine of police

17. A number of institutionalist writers of the 1920s looked to this principle of "affectation with a public interest" to provide a basis for legislatures to regulate prices quite broadly. See particularly Tugwell [1922] 1968. For a more sanguine view, see Clark 1926. Keezer and May (1930) also discuss the principle in detail. This book was their joint PhD thesis at Brookings.

18. John R. Commons also discusses this sequence of cases on the liberty, property, and due process clauses of the Fourteenth Amendment, but more with an eye to the shift in the property concept from tangible to intangible. See Commons [1924] 1968, 11–21.

power, the argument remained in use, acquiring "a momentum and an enhancing repute in the opinions in dissent." It was strengthened by an 1886 recognition that the term "person" included corporations and that extended to them the protection of due process (Hamilton 1938c, 284–86). In the 1890s, rulings on the ability of the Railroad Commission to set rates created, in the name of due process, a "judicial overlordship over what had up to that moment been set down as the province of the legislature." In later decisions the word "liberty" became defined to encompass "freedom of contract," and in 1905 and the case of *Lochner v. New York* due process "won in a clean-cut combat with the police power" (287–90).

The *Lochner* case concerned the regulation of the work hours of bakers, purportedly on grounds of public health. The majority opinion of the Court found freedom of contract an aspect of liberty and property that "a state may not abridge without due process of law." The opinion of the Court was "intended to be an apostolic letter to the many legislatures in the land appointing limits to their police power and laying a ban on social legislation" (291–92). The case, however, also occasioned Justice Holmes's famous dissent where he argued that the relation of the hours of bakers to public health was one of fact, that the liberty of the citizen "is interfered with by school laws, by the Post Office, by every state or municipal institution which takes his money for purposes thought desirable," and that "the Fourteenth Amendment does not enact Mr. Herbert Spencer's *Social Statics*" (*Lochner* 1905). Hamilton argues that while it "is common for latter-day liberals to set this down as the first blast of the trumpet in behalf of social oversight of human rights," the historian is more likely to see it "as a lance worthily broken in behalf of an ancient cause now in retreat" (Hamilton 1938c, 292).

In this manner—until the New Deal—economic regulation in the United States became increasingly circumscribed.[19] Even in the case of public utilities, problems had been created by the interpretation given to the due process clause and by court decisions on the valuation of the property of the public utilities.[20] Outside public utilities, primary

19. Regulation of hours of work were upheld where there were clear safety issues involving others, and in the case of women.

20. Utility companies complained that price regulation was depriving them of their property without due process. The courts reacted by attempting to find a basis for the valuation of public utilities based on reproduction cost. That the value of a property could not be established apart from its expected revenue flow was stressed repeatedly by Robert Hale. The discussion also involved John R. Commons and James Bonbright, as well as Hamilton. For Hamilton's contribution, see Hamilton 1938d.

reliance was placed on the antitrust laws to maintain competitive conditions. Hamilton, however, did not consider that the antitrust laws provided adequate protection of the public interest.[21] For Hamilton, the Sherman and Clayton Acts and the Federal Trade Commission were attempts by the state to enforce competition based on the textbook model of competitive markets. But that model is one that does not apply to a world of modern technology and big business. The antitrust laws, in their attempt to "stay the development of large scale enterprise and to make big business behave as if it were petty trade," embody and "express the common sense of another age" (Hamilton 1932b).

Hamilton (1932a, 1932b, 1932c) also points out the difficulties in translating economic concepts into legal categories such as that of "conspiracies in restraint of trade"; the clumsy and often inappropriate nature of cases at law in deciding issues of trade practice; the business tactics of delay and invention of new and alternative practices; the decisions made in one case sometimes becoming unfortunate and limiting precedents in others; and the highly uneven record of enforcement. But, for Hamilton, the most fundamental problems are that the antitrust laws may work against efficiency if that requires large-scale production, and that in certain industries—such as the coal industry—lack of competition is not the problem. Under certain conditions an enforced competition could lead to "waste and disorder." Isolated judgments by "the executives of rival businesses" do not necessarily "exorcise plant waste, eliminate surplus capacity, and articulate neat establishments into an orderly industry." The "tyranny" of overhead costs and excess capacity can lead to an "overdone competition" with unprofitable prices, low wages, and irregular production (Hamilton 1932c, 167). This line of argument had its origins in the 1890s criticism of the results of competition between railroads (Hadley 1896), and had been updated by J. M. Clark (1923) in his work on overhead costs.[22] Nevertheless, the antitrust laws did at least indicate an acceptance that business could not be left to its own devices and that business was indeed affected with a public interest. The danger of monopoly and other restrictive practices meant that the antitrust laws

21. Hamilton was an active participant in the debates over antitrust that developed in the late 1920s and early 1930s out of the 1926 proposals of the Committee on Revision of the Anti-Trust Laws of the American Bar Association, and the Swope plan of 1931 with its suggestion for industrial control and price-fixing by trade associations (Fetter 1932; Barber 1985, 121; Mayhew 1998, 193–95).

22. The 1890s literature on technological change, "surplus capital," and excess competition included work by Arthur T. Hadley, Charles A. Conant, and Jeremiah Jenks. This literature is discussed in Parrini and Sklar 1983.

could not simply be repealed but that they must be replaced by some other form of control.

Hamilton suggests that "order" might be achieved along three lines. First, competition could be retained but regulated to "escape the evils which attend it." The "plane of competition" could be established by law, and a body could be established to pass "in advance upon the practices of trade" and replace the judicial approach of the antitrust acts with an administrative procedure. Second, some industries could be recognized as monopolistic and regulated through commissions. However, Hamilton argues that the "dual control" inherent in commissions is a weakness, in that "private interests are able to do as they please, subject to the delayed approval or disapproval of the commission," and disagreements tend to end up in court. Third, there "is at least a possibility of contriving for certain industries a control from within," but it is essential here that control of the industry not be limited to those who make profits from it but also include labor and consumer interests (Hamilton 1932a, 11–12). He suggests no single solution for all industries. Industries vary in many ways, and schemes of control need to be tailored to the conditions of that industry. In all his writing on this subject Hamilton rejects "panaceas and creeds" in favor of "an intellectual and experimental attitude" (21).

The New Deal: Consumers, Codes, and Price Studies

The coming of the Depression, its persistence, and the obvious dislocation of the "economic order" only confirmed to Hamilton the pressing need for new forms of control. In a 1931 discussion of "ways out" he emphasized the paradox of a vast capacity to produce in excess of current production together with and an equally large capacity to use in excess of current consumption, and argued for some form of "centralized control of the conditions upon which the general welfare of the people in an industry rests." The solution lay not in individualism, or any other "ism," but in a system where decentralized decision making in business was combined with a social control that recognized the public interest in the performance of business and industry (Hamilton 1931e).

The National Industrial Recovery Act (NIRA) was passed in the summer of 1933. Title 1 of the NIRA declared a national emergency and stated the policy of Congress to promote the organization of industry for the purpose of cooperative action among trade groups, to "induce and maintain united action of labor and management," to "eliminate unfair competitive practices," to promote the full use of resources, to increase consumption by increasing purchasing power, to reduce and relieve unemployment, to improve standards of labor, and to rehabilitate industry and conserve natural resources (Lyon et al. 1935, 15–16). The act established the National Recovery Administration (NRA), which was to administer this policy through a set of industrial "codes," under which an industry agreeing to minimum wages and certain other labor conditions could establish trade practices to eliminate "unfair competition" and receive immunity from prosecution under the antitrust laws.

The original administrative structure of the NRA created three advisory boards, an Industrial Advisory Board, a Labor Advisory Board, and a Consumers' Advisory Board to advise the Recovery Administrator (General H. Johnson) on the codes. Even at the time it was recognized that the CAB worked under the handicap of having no organized pressure group behind it. Moreover, Johnson tended to identify "business prosperity" with the public interest, so that in the early days of the NRA there was "a general impatience with 'consumer interruption'" and a tendency to see the CAB as an "annoying and unnecessary fifth wheel calculated to slow up the recovery procession" (Lyon et al. 1935, 123–29; Campbell [1940] 1968, 31; Lynd 1934, 221). Nevertheless, it was also recognized that the explicit inclusion of consumer representation in the NRA (and even more so in the AAA) represented a significant development in the area of business regulation.[23] As stated by Robert Lynd (1934, 220): "The recovery machinery officially recognizes for the first time that the consumer is sitting in on the game."

The first executive director of the CAB was William Ogburn, but he resigned in August 1933 and was replaced by Dexter Keezer. Keezer recruited Hamilton to the CAB in October 1933. The CAB also appointed Corwin Edwards to head up a "Price Section" to undertake research on prices and price policies; Robert Brady to head up a "Standards Unit," which attempted to develop standard grades and other quality standards and have them established in the codes; and Paul Douglas to head a "Bureau of Economic Education," which was to work on establishing

23. Social scientists who were members of the CAB at various times included Hamilton, William Ogburn, Dexter Keezer, Robert Lynd, Gardiner Means, and George Stocking (Campbell [1940] 1968; Donohue 2003, 226–29). See also Lynd 1934, 1936; Keezer 1934; and Douglas 1934. For discussion of consumer representation in the AAA, see Campbell [1940] 1968. The AAA included an office of Consumers Counsel with a significant staff.

"consumers' councils" to provide a consumer organization.[24] The CAB's overall concern, however, was that the code-making machinery was being used to advance business interests by establishing minimum prices or some degree of price-fixing, effectively raising prices at the expense of consumers. As argued by Gardiner Means (1934b, 11), the codes were being used to raise prices to a point "where they yield a profit which could be justified only on a very much larger volume of business." The CAB's strategy in response was to undertake as much careful study of proposed codes as it could and to present well-documented arguments against provisions it felt were unreasonable. A model for these studies was provided by the submission made late in 1933 objecting to the price provisions in the petroleum code. This was produced by the Price Section together with board members George Stocking and Hamilton. Shortly after, Hamilton (1934) produced a published version.

The main argument about the petroleum code was that it proposed to establish prices much higher than those then existing, with serious adverse consequences for the consumer. Control of output was suggested as an alternative way to bring some "order" into the industry, provided that control was supervised by all the interests concerned and not just by producers. The brief also contained a more general argument in which Hamilton discussed the difficulties in transferring control of prices to an administrative board. In this part it becomes clear that Hamilton's reservations about the commission form of control had grown. He argues that commissions do not contain real consumer representation. The personnel with authority are government appointees, "and all of the indirection, exigency and pressure which we associate with the word 'politics' find expression in appointments and in judgment":

> The powers possessed by a commission to create or destroy property values and to divert income from one economic group to another make a commission a prize worthy of political capture. The system of regulation has put public utilities into politics; and a small compact group is usually, if not always, more powerful than a larger and unorganized host. (Hamilton 1934, 78)

24. Edwards's Price Section was absorbed into the Research and Planning Division of the NRA in April 1934. Douglas resigned in April 1934. Opposition to the original CAB plan to set up some 3,000 consumers' councils resulted in only about 150 being established. Brady left in the early summer of 1934 frustrated by lack of resources, but remained involved with issues of industrial standardization (Campbell [1940] 1968, 48–53; Donohue 2003, 240). Keezer left the CAB to take up the presidency of Reed College in July 1934.

Thus, any board or agency set up to control prices must have proper representation of consumers and not be dominated by the producer interest. It must also have available to it objectively determined (by independent technical staff) information on the "necessary social costs of production" that the prices charged would have to cover (96).

The early months of 1934 saw much criticism of the NRA codes from both inside and outside the NRA.[25] Two results of this debate are relevant here. In May 1934 an NRA Advisory Council was established to reconcile differences of opinion between the three advisory boards. Hamilton was the first chairman of this council and appears to have created a less-charged atmosphere within which proposals could be discussed and such evidence as was available assessed (Campbell [1940] 1968, 75). Given this, and the equal representation given to the three boards, the consumer point of view began to fare somewhat better. At the same time, and apparently in response to George Terborgh's (1934) critical analysis of the codes,[26] a Cabinet Committee on Price Policy was established. Isador Lubin, then commissioner of labor statistics, became the chair of this committee, and Hamilton was placed in charge of a study into prices and price policies.

The study as planned contained several "lines of investigation": first, a discussion of the price system in genetic, descriptive, and analytical terms with the goal of outlining the structure of the price system and "the adequacy with which it performs its function"; second, a quantitative study of the behavior of prices under the NRA; third, a series of case studies of price formation in particular industries; and, fourth, a series of studies on particular policy problems including a study of the NRA codes, the cost formula for price, the general problems of price control, and the operation of the antitrust laws. The case studies formed the core of the project and were presented as attempts "to discern the sources of order, and to diagnose the disorders, of various industries." The industries to be studied were chosen on the basis of data availability, public interest in the industry, and the contribution that the study

25. The NRA held a series of price hearings in January, there was a Senate debate on price and production policy under the NRA also in January, a conference for code authorities held in March, and in May the Darrow report on the NRA codes was released. Objections to the codes also came from the Department of Agriculture because of the effects on farm incomes, from the CAB, and from elsewhere within government. See Hawley 1966, 79–97.

26. George Terborgh had been a student of Hamilton's at the Brookings Graduate School. The reference to his book prompting the formation of the Cabinet Committee on Prices comes from a memo written by Leon Henderson to Miss F. M. Robinson (Henderson 1934b).

would make to "a general account of the price system." In some places Hamilton (1936b, 7) suggests that the industries were chosen as representing items important in determining "the standard of living." Included were automobiles, tires, gasoline, cottonseed, milk, whiskey, women's dresses, paper, wastepaper, razor blades, cigarettes, ice, and several others.[27] The goal was to complete a minimum of twenty case studies "to secure a picture of the broader aspects of the price system and to reveal those factors which any price policy on the part of the Federal Government must take into consideration" (Henderson 1934a; Means 1934a). This plan was never to be entirely carried out, as the Supreme Court decision declaring the code system unconstitutional came down in May 1935, resulting in the fairly rapid demise of the whole NRA organization. The price studies were first transferred to the Consumers' Division of the NRA (which also absorbed the Consumers' Advisory Board and the Consumers' Division of the National Emergency Council). Hamilton was named adviser on Consumers' Problems and director of the Consumers' Division,[28] but by the end of 1935 Hamilton had left for the Division of Economic Research of the Social Security Board, the Consumers' Division had been transferred to the Department of Labor, and in February of 1936 was reduced to the "Consumers' Project" within the Department of Labor and funded by the Works Progress Administration. Clarence Ayres took over the Consumers' Project and continued the price studies through to November 1936 when he resigned.[29]

27. Industries such as coal, movies, sugar are mentioned in some places. The first of the studies were completed in 1934, the last in 1936. They were confidential and not circulated. Hamilton even had a study of the market for art done by an artist, Robert Hallowell. Hamilton gave the piece to Mark Adams to revise. Adams eventually produced an essay "The Price of Art" in 1951 (Hamilton 1951). Irene Till wrote several of the studies. Her study of the milk industry also became her 1937 PhD thesis in political science from Columbia. She became Hamilton's second wife.

28. Campbell argues that in this capacity Hamilton did a poor job of promoting and ensuring some continued basis for the representation of the consumer interest. There is no doubt that Hamilton's major focus at this point was on the price studies. See Campbell [1940] 1968, 84, and Hamilton 1935a.

29. Ayres had been a close friend of Hamilton's since 1916 when they were both first at Amherst. Hamilton was Ayres's introduction to institutional economics (see Rutherford 2003). Ayres visited Washington to spend a month with Hamilton's group in the summer of 1935. This period and his time in charge of the Consumers' Project was his only employment with the federal government. According to Campbell, Ayres did not agree with Hamilton's ideas about the "functional representation of economic interests," in the form of industry, labor, and the consumer. Ayres thought this likely to lead to "fascism" (Campbell [1940] 1968, 86–87). He also had arguments with Robert Brady about standards for automobiles (Ayres n.d.).

A selection of the price studies (the case studies on automobiles, tires, gasoline, cottonseed, dresses, whiskey, and milk), together with an introductory and concluding chapter by Hamilton, was eventually published in 1938 (Hamilton and Associates 1938).[30] Given the highly concrete nature of these case studies, it is hard to summarize them or make generalizations—but this was a significant part of Hamilton's point. Here and elsewhere Hamilton argues that industries are not alike; they have their own particular sets of practices and conventions that have grown up within the trade; they differ in scale of enterprise and in the number of competitors; in the structure of costs and the existence of joint products; in the arrangements made with suppliers and distributors; in the impact of new technology or of new regulations; in advertising and sales strategy; and in the ability, and the exact methods used, to confine or limit competition. Each industry's particular pattern is also undergoing continuous change (Hamilton and Associates 1938; Hamilton 1940b). There is no sharp line of demarcation between competition and monopoly, nor even a line running from perfect competition through monopolistic competition, oligopoly, duopoly, to pure monopoly on which particular cases may be set down. To do so "is to make hypothetical economic phenomena" the subject of the exercise. The "tricks may be pulled off with neatness and intricacy; but the result is not a picture of the pragmatic reality called industry" (Hamilton and Associates 1938, 23).[31]

For Hamilton, to understand the variety of industrial practice, to get behind the abstractions of demand and supply, and to come to understand why a price is what it is could serve two important purposes. The first has to do with understanding what, if any, barriers stand in the way of improving the American standard of life; of bringing "the good things of life within the reach of the great mass of people" (Hamilton 1936b, 7). Here, the point of attack of the price studies "is what lies back of a price—to make it high or low—to restrict or enlarge supply—to bring it within the reach of the few or the many." They are thus part of a campaign against waste, disorder, and restriction, and for greater abundance and higher living standards (9). This is entirely of a piece with

30. The quantitative aspect of the study, "Recent Price Behavior," was completed by Willard Thorp (with a number of assistants) in 1934 but not included in the published selection. A copy is available in the Columbia Law Library.

31. Hamilton's price studies did not go down well with more orthodox economists. See the review by Mund (1938) and Hamilton's (1939a) reply titled "Industrial Inquiry and Sectarian Dogma."

Hamilton's earlier work on wages and the costs of medical care. The second function has to do with the design of business regulation and programs for control. Business interests and the mechanism of price do not necessarily lead to an industry functioning in a way compatible with the public interest, but any system of control has to be sensitive to particulars. Thus "the road towards industrial government runs by way of authority and the particular":

> The state in formulating public policy, must have a wide discretion, and statutes should be written in the broadest of terms. But a way of order and a program of control can be crowded into no set formula. The general standards of industrial code and legislative standard must be adapted to the shifting circumstances of particular industries. Since usage is forever on the make the exercise of authority must be grounded in a continuing exploration of industrial arrangements. (Hamilton and Associates 1938, 555)

Hamilton's involvement with the CAB, his chairmanship of the Advisory Board, and his membership on the National Industrial Recovery Board obviously brought him into close contact with the processes of code making under the NRA. Hamilton gave testimony to the Senate hearings in 1935 considering the continuation of the NRA. Apart from public utilities, Hamilton (1935b, 2047) divided industries into those where competition "works not perfectly but at least reasonably well," those where competition is "underdone" because of restrictive practices of some kind, and those where competition is "overdone," such as in coal and textiles. The last two cases represent areas for intervention, although the problems involved are quite distinct.

It is clear that Hamilton favored the retention of the NRA, although with some modifications. Hamilton wished to see a clear statement that all industry is affected by a public interest, to give the state the right "to break in whenever the State decides that the conduct of the industry is not serving the interests of all who have a stake in it" (2053); a clear positive affirmation that the codes must be constructed with a view to preventing monopoly, and not merely that they should not encourage monopoly; and that all interest groups, including consumers and workers, have input into the code making. In terms of the administration of codes, if the code controls prices or production, then the code authority must include more than the business interest (2046–50). If the code involves a public interest, then public officials should be involved in its administration;

no group "should be in the double position of an interested party and a judge of their actions at the same time" (2052). Further, the notion of "unfair competition" should be broadened to include unethical business practices that might lower the plane of competition, competition that is unfair to labor and competition that is unfair to the consumer. The provision of information to the code authorities should also be required.

In terms of the antitrust laws, Hamilton is clear that he has no quarrel with the ultimate purposes of the acts—to make business behavior conform to the public interest—but reiterates his view that the mechanism of legal proceeding and criminal prosecution is flawed. The issue is "whether we can devise better mechanisms than the Antitrust Act for accomplishing the same purpose" (2057). The antitrust laws and the Federal Trade Commission provide only "a measure of protection" of the public interest. Hamilton argues that "it is quite possible through the NRA to add to that another measure of protection and probably a more important measure of protection than has yet been achieved." The antitrust act is only a "tentative answer" to the problem of the control of industry: "It is an instrument, it is a mechanism, and not a final answer to the problem" (2058).

> I think the NRA can do a constructive job that the Federal Trade Commission and the Department of Justice cannot do, by devising administrative remedies against monopoly. I think they can also address themselves to the job of trying to find out why various industries are not turning out goods in greater abundance and why the American standard of living is as low as it is. That is a long time job; it is not a matter of panacea; it is a matter of detailed treatment. (2059)

It is no surprise to find Hamilton reacting negatively to the series of Supreme Court decisions that struck down the NRA code-making machinery in 1935, and then the Guffey Coal Act and parts of the Agricultural Adjustment Act in 1936. Hamilton outlines the development of Court decisions: in 1934 in the *Nebbia* case "it was willing to allow remedial legislation to take its course"; in the next year the Court first began to use "procedural devices" against federal legislation, but then moved to substantive issues to strike down the industrial codes of the NRA. By the winter the Court "was ready to pass the death sentence upon the Agricultural Adjustment Act (AAA); and in the spring of 1936 it laid on with abandon against all social legislation, state and national" (Hamilton 1938a, 17). Fear of the president's power and the "ghost of an imaginary fascism" deflected even Brandeis and Stone from their customary views.

In the NRA case the Court held that the NRA codes represented an unconstitutional delegation of legislative power to the president. Cardozo and Stone agreed, but made the point that Congress itself could not set up standards for regulation for all industries, given their variety and number.[32] In retrospect, Hamilton conceded that the NRA should have begun with key industries such as coal, oil, lumber, and textiles where "disorder was notorious," but argued that its deficiencies could have been repaired by new legislation (Hamilton and Associates 1938, 21).[33] The case concerning the AAA was decided by a majority of the Court who ruled the tax on processors to provide revenue to pay farmers to take land out of production to be coercive and unconstitutional. Stone, Brandeis, and Cardozo dissented on the grounds that the tax was levied in accord with legislation passed by Congress, and "Courts are not the only agency that must be assumed to have capacity to govern" (*United States v. Butler* 1936), a point with which Hamilton was in full agreement. The Bituminous Coal Conservation Act (Guffey Coal Act) was passed in 1935 to replace the NRA code and to regulate prices, minimum wages, maximum hours of work, and "fair practices." A tax was levied, but those who complied were given refunds. The act established a National Bituminous Coal Commission, a Coal Labor Board, and Consumers' Counsel. In 1936 the act was declared unconstitutional on the grounds that labor conditions were local, within state and not interstate evils, and did not fall under federal jurisdiction. Cardozo, Brandeis, and Stone dissented, expressing the view that coal production was an interstate business and that the conditions in the coal industry meant that "commerce had been choked and burdened; its normal flow had been diverted from one state to another; there had been bankruptcy and waste and ruin alike for capital

32. In an earlier case on the "hot oil" industry Cardozo had not objected to the delegation of powers, as the delegation was "narrow" and what could be done "is closely and clearly circumscribed both as to subject-matter and to occasion." Cardozo was in a minority of one in that opinion. See *Panama* 1935.

33. After the NRA decision a number of people, including Tugwell, Ezekiel, and Galloway, attempted to gather interest in an "Industrial Expansion Act." This act was modeled on the ideas contained in Mordecai Ezekiel's book *$2,500 a Year* (1936), which argued that a moderate standard of living could be attained by all via a planning agency similar in some respects to the AAA. It was also to use a processing tax, the receipts to go to those signing agreements on output, price, working conditions, etc. The effort picked up some support, and bills were introduced in 1937 (see Hawley 1966, 179–84). A copy of the bill and correspondence between Hamilton and Galloway about it can be found in Hamilton n.d.a. Ezekiel's later *Jobs for All* (1939) was a summary version of the industrial expansion plan (Ezekiel n.d.).

and for labor"; and that the liberty protected by the Fifth Amendment "does not include the right to persist in this anarchic riot" (*Carter* 1936). Hamilton poured scorn on the view that the meaning of interstate commerce was to be narrowly construed to apply only to the interstate movement of goods. Justice Sutherland claimed this interpretation was "used in the Constitution," but, as Hamilton argued at length, the Constitution was written by a group consisting in large part of those of a mercantilist mentality for whom "commerce" meant nothing less than the whole of production and trade (Hamilton and Adair [1937] 1972). The paradox is that "as industry has become more and more interstate in character, the power of Congress to regulate has been given narrower and narrower interpretation" (Hamilton and Adair [1937] 1972, 192).

In 1937, after Roosevelt's threat to pack the Court, but before any change in membership, the Court began a rapid process of reversing its opposition to social legislation. The Social Security and National Labor Relations Acts were upheld, and "a body of constitutional doctrine, lately overlooked or relegated to dissent, was rediscovered" (Hamilton 1938a, 19). A replacement Coal Act was passed in 1937 without the labor conditions, and was upheld.[34] New membership changed the attitude of the Court even further (Hamilton and Braden 1941), but the larger NRA experiment would not be revisited, and Hamilton moved on to consider other possible instruments for the control of business.

Antitrust and Patents

In 1938 Thurman Arnold was appointed head of the Antitrust Division of the Department of Justice. In the past Arnold (1937) had been a severe critic of the antitrust laws,[35] but he came into his new job determined that the antitrust should be revised so "that the government could

34. When this act was due to expire in 1941, it is interesting that Hamilton leapt to the defense of continuing with the "experiment" in control. Eugene Rostow, a Yale law school colleague of Hamilton's, wrote an article arguing that the 1937 act had been an experiment that failed to work. Conditions had changed, and expansion of the economy and the public interest would be better served by government spending and imaginative enforcement of the antitrust laws (Rostow 1941). Hamilton (1941a) replied with a defense of the 1937 act, that maintained that all the causes of past "disorder" were still present in the industry, and that both the coal act and deficit spending were "experiments" that would require adjustment as they proceeded.

35. In the Hamilton papers there is an undated piece called "Scattered Thoughts on Thorstein Veblen" written by Hamilton for Thurman Arnold. It ends: "This, I hope, supplies enough material for a bridge from Veblen to Arnold. Once the bridge is half way crossed, Arnold is on his own" (Hamilton n.d.h). For an interesting analysis of Arnold's thinking and his relationship to the legal realists, see Fenster 2003.

strike at market domination, regardless of how the power over prices had been acquired and regardless of motive or intent" (Hawley 1966, 411). Arnold had been a longtime colleague of Hamilton's at Yale, and between 1938 and 1945 Hamilton was a special assistant to the attorney general working on problems of patents, monopoly, and restraint of trade. For Hamilton, Arnold's approach to antitrust was not out of line with his own. Hamilton (1938e) wrote to Dexter Keezer that Arnold

> is definitely persuaded that if the Anti-Trust Acts are to serve a constructive purpose, they must come to grips with the web of usage in distinctive industries, so he wants to get a number of industrial studies underway. Each will appear as a memo and in form should be comparable to an opinion of the United States Supreme Court that grapples with the law as public policy and stakes its judgments upon a recitation of industrial fact.

On the same day Hamilton (1938f) wrote to the publisher of *Price and Price Policies* that Arnold is insisting that the Department of Justice "get down to concretions" and deal with the "web of industrial usage" and that Arnold's approach "is an application of the approach worked out in 'Price and Price Policies,' and I wish we had some way of advertising the fact."[36] The approach followed by Arnold and Hamilton was a case-by-case one, and one that also made greater use of devices such as the consent decree. Hamilton was never an advocate of smallness for its own sake; he was one of those who was "more pragmatic, more concerned with consumer welfare and the disciplining of price policies" than with the "preservation of small business or decentralization as a social good" (Hawley 1966, 297).

Hamilton's involvement included work on briefs on antitrust suits brought against the AMA for its actions against experiments in group health (Hamilton 1938b), the movie industry for its distribution practices, and many others (Hamilton 1940b). But the major products of Hamilton's time with the Antitrust Division were two reports for the Temporary National Economic Committee (TNEC): *Antitrust in Action* (Hamilton and Till 1940a) and *Patents and Free Enterprise* (Hamilton

36. The Arnold-Hamilton case-by-case approach did not find favor with all antitrusters. Frank Fetter clearly wanted a more general approach to antitrust policy. Paul Homan wrote to Jerome Frank and Hamilton expressing hope that the disagreements would not work to the detriment of the whole antitrust enterprise (see Hamilton 1939b). Homan was another Brookings PhD. Business also objected to the lack of guidance given by a case-by-case approach and its potentially arbitrary nature.

1941c). In the first of these studies, and in a related paper (Hamilton and Till 1940b), Hamilton repeats many of the concerns he had expressed before on the inappropriate nature of legal proceedings, particularly criminal proceedings, for dealing with matters of trade practice, and the problems of some industries having too much competition rather than a lack of it. In such industries where the problem is an "overplus" of competition, any concerted move against "disaster" may run afoul of the law (Hamilton and Till 1940a, 19). Hamilton also discusses the development of new forms of restraint, involving various forms of tacit collusion, price leadership, delivered price systems, quality standards, patents and license agreements, unequal bargaining power as between large manufacturers and their suppliers or distributors, and regulations originally enacted to protect a public interest from being turned into a "smoke screen for vested interest" (12–19).

Hamilton goes on to suggest two avenues of change, the first involving a "streamlining" of the antitrust acts and the second, a move to an administrative rather than a judicial base. Streamlining would involve providing adequate funding, a power of subpoena, a greater use of the equity decree in place of criminal actions, a shift from crime to tort, and a penalty equal to twice the total net income gained during the period of wrongdoing, as well as placing the burden of proof on the party that enjoys access to all the facts and providing the consumer with a cause for action (Hamilton and Till 1940a, 101–6). These reforms, however, Hamilton regards as insufficient, as they fail to penetrate to "the heart of the difficulty." What is required is a movement that develops the advisory opinion and consent decree of the Department of Justice into an administrative system that can provide for a flexible and timely case-by-case approach. This cannot "come into practice full blown" but must "begin as a cautiously experimental power" (108). An administrative system would allow for the approval in advance of "a code of industrial behavior," with the government and industry in cooperation spelling out "a line of business activity which is believed to accord with public policy, and in the furtherance of which immunity from prosecution is promised" (Hamilton and Till 1940b, 19). This process requires information about the industry to be gathered, analyzed, and kept up-to-date. Agreements cannot be permanent as conditions change, so that every measure is subject to correction. Agreements require oversight and policing, but with breaches treated as a civil offense and punishable by fines. A "Decree Section" should be established and be concerned with industrial analysis and remedies rather than litigation. Judicial review should be by a "specially constructed industrial court" with five or seven members well versed in the ways of industry.

As a "caveat" to his proposals Hamilton raises the problem of administrative processes being "captured" by the business interests they are supposed to regulate. Commissions have "closed public utilities to outsiders"; the various agricultural controls have been "sensitive to the plight of the farmers, negligent of farm labor, and indifferent to the general public who must pay the bill"; the NRA "staged a full dress performance of the hazards of the administrative process" in which wide powers were granted only to "become sanctions under which the strategic group could lord it over the industry" (Hamilton and Till 1940b, 25). This concern was to become increasingly insistent in Hamilton's work in the years after World War II.

The issue of patents and their use in certain industries to maintain privileged market positions had come to Hamilton's attention during the price studies. As he continued work on this issue, he came to see it as a preeminently important and particularly difficult policy problem. Knowledge is more important than real property, natural resources are largely what the current state of knowledge makes them, and modern industry is "nothing more than our accumulated technical knowledge" (Hamilton 1949b, 339). Abundant production and rising standards of living rest on the advance of knowledge and its dissemination.

Patents have as their purpose the promotion of technological advance, but Hamilton's investigations indicated to him that the existing patent system had numerous failings in achieving that end. Research and invention had become a matter of corporate research and development laboratories. In the hands of corporations the patent system could easily be used to create control of an industry. A flood of closely related products could be patented, blocking out other competitors; patents could be used to "fence" in an invention, "block" the work of rivals, or "trawl" for information; patent protection could be extended in time by patenting successive modifications; special terms and conditions could be written into patent licenses, dividing the market between producers by quota, or territory, or product, and setting prices for various users; patents could be pooled, resulting in a closed and collusive market; and international agreements involving patents could provide the basis for trade agreements between firms and international cartels (Hamilton 1941c; Hamilton and Till 1948).[37]

37. With the American involvement in World War II, Hamilton (1943b) also became concerned over Axis control of patents holding up the delivery of strategic materials.

Hamilton made a number of proposals to improve the patent system. Justice should push forward cases involving restrictive covenants in order to more clearly define what could and could not be included in a patent license. An easier and more expeditious method of validation of patents might prevent some pooling of patents, but where pooling was required for efficient production the pool should be accepted and placed under public authority. Patents not in use should be canceled or compelled to license. Higher standards for patentability should be established, or different types of invention given different types of patent. Here Hamilton wanted to differentiate between genuinely novel and important inventions and mere modifications or variations. Applications for reissue or renewal should be prohibited. He also suggested the establishment of a "Public Counsel on Patents" to exercise general oversight of patent grants, of assignments and leases, and of all patent litigation, and with a right to intervene in applications and institute suits to protect the public interest (Hamilton 1941c, 146–52).

These steps, however, "fall short" of an answer to the problem of accommodating the patent grant "to its corporate and industrial habitat" (156). If a "fresh slate" were at hand, a system of compulsory licensing might be best, but in the existing circumstances Hamilton suggested an expert commission of inquiry to consider a more fundamental redesign based on "further study and the formulation of a program" (163). A National Patent Planning Commission was established in 1942 but only produced a skimpy eleven-page report that "whitewashed" the patent system, ignored the major problems, made proposals that would, if anything, lower the standards of patentability, and suggested extending the time a patent grant could run (Hamilton 1943b).

The conclusion of his work on antitrust and patents was a growing concern on Hamilton's (1943a) part with the development of what he called "property rights in the market" or "market equities." These property rights could take the form of a wide variety of business practices; the requirements of a profession or trade; the control of a strategic ingredient or resource; the protection given to local industries or favored producers by state or national regulations; regulations originally adopted for public benefit turned into barriers to entry; and patents, patent licenses, and patent pools used as a basis for the control of markets.[38] Most significant,

38. Hamilton discusses professional associations such as the AMA, the spread of professional licensing to cover many trades and occupations, the control over news by the Associated Press, international cartels as operating in tin and rubber, Florida regulations on the citrus fruit industry, regulations on milk, and patents.

corporations had discovered that "regulation is a two edged thing," that controls can be captured and put to uses never intended (29).

In his work in the late 1940s and 1950s Hamilton elaborated on this theme and gave it more historical perspective. The failures of the market to properly control business in the public interest had resulted in a move toward regulation. But regulation broke down the older division between state and economy. The most-used form of regulatory device, the commission, was particularly susceptible to capture by the interests it was supposed to be regulating, and the campaign for regulation ultimately produced "its own counterrevolution" (Hamilton 1949a, 1957). The "interest to be regulated is compact, organized, mobile" and alert to opportunities. The public interest is general, sluggish, diffused, and "unable to effect a united front or move in time" (Hamilton 1949a, 85; 1953, 268). The business to be regulated has the initiative, the commission becomes bogged down in detail, staff who earn a reputation for understanding business can move into a career in industry, routines are established and maintained, and competition from new sources may be stifled to maintain older privileges (Hamilton 1949a, 83; 1957).[39] The NRA began as an exercise in price-fixing, but as these sanctions were toned down or defused "business gradually lost interest in the NRA." Despite the demise of the NRA it was "not without its effect on economic structure." Representatives of different companies had been brought together in Washington, and the NRA left many industries "much more tightly organized than they had been before" (Hamilton 1957, 97). This move toward a "private government of industry" making use of "the devices and procedures of politics" was much advanced by World War II. The War Production Board (WPB) brought business personnel to Washington to serve as public officials, and "a hierarchy of primary contracts" resulted in a consolidation of business empires. The NRA gave representation to labor and the consumer, but in the WPB "it was the business interest alone which was enthroned" (97–98).

All of these problems were compounded by the development of the corporation, its treatment as a natural individual by a series of legal "fictions," its internationalization, its ability to create subsidiaries and complex and intricate patterns of control, its ability to choose and change its domicile, and its ability to exist in perpetuity or dissolve itself and

39. Examples given by Hamilton include the Interstate Commerce Commission being given the regulation of canals and motor transport, to the advantage of the railroads, and the Civil Aeronautics Board discouraging low-cost carriers.

reappear under a new name. The techniques of public control encounter legal fictions that "have left fact far behind." The "elaborate web of 'as ifs' which the courts have woven,—have put corporate affairs pretty largely out of the reach of the regulations we decree" (Hamilton 1946a; 1946b, 4).

Conclusion

Hamilton's career of examination and experiment in control is revealing in many respects. It complicates the picture of the policy positions taken by institutionalists in the interwar period. The usual picture is to divide institutionalists into those who believed in commissions (mainly the Wisconsin group) and the "planners" such as Tugwell and Ezekiel. Bringing Hamilton into this indicates a much greater complexity and diversity of opinion within institutionalism. All the members of the institutionalist group used the rhetoric of "social control," but what was meant by that by different people varied significantly.

In Hamilton's case it is clear that he was not a proponent of big government, or of commissions as usually constituted, or of industrial government by trade association. His work on Supreme Court decisions leaves no doubt that he disagreed with the interpretation of the Constitution as severely limiting to the exercise of the state's police power, and it is quite clear that he thought that the state must have the power to govern and to regulate business in the public interest. At the same time, his suggestions for the coal industry have no direct role for government in the operation of the industry; he did not favor a British-style nationalization and was concerned about the inflexibility of bureaucracy. There is an obvious syndicalist element in his thinking about the management of the coal industry and in his notions of control by workers and consumers. His proposals for the provision of health services also avoid direct government involvement in the delivery of medical services; the model proposed being based on that of the university. Even in the case of the NRA where government agencies were more directly involved, he was trying to create a form of stakeholder control with input from industrialists, workers, and consumers, enabled and overseen by the state. This was Hamilton's version of industrial "self-government." His occasional use of that term led to accusations that he was suggesting a control by business interests alone, but that was never Hamilton's idea. Self-government of industry always meant, for Hamilton, the participation of all interests.

This notion of "representation of interests" does provide a commonality between Hamilton and Commons, but Commons's plans for commissions tended to include only business and labor interests, with the "public interest" represented by political appointees and not by consumers themselves. Hamilton was clearly not "producerist" in his orientation.

Hamilton's positions during the New Deal serve to break down some of the traditional equivalences drawn between those representing the consumer interest, those promoting antitrust in place of planning, and those of more neoclassical persuasion. It is noteworthy that Hamilton's concern with the representation of the consumer interest was shared by many planners, particularly those involved with the AAA such as Tugwell (1935), and had no connection with neoclassical theory. Hamilton's work also cuts across the more basic distinction usually made between the planners and the antitrusters. For Hamilton, antitrust, particularly if reformed, could play a vital role in combating restraint of trade, but this did not necessarily mean that there was no place for a reformed NRA. Indeed, Hamilton's various suggestions for an administrative approach to trade practice, a reformed NRA, or creating a "Decree Section" of the antitrust administration all have a strong resemblance. The common idea was to move away from a judicial approach to an administrative approach given to the task of working out acceptable trade practices in advance, and on the basis of detailed study. Perhaps the most controversial aspect of Hamilton's thinking was his notion of industries such as coal where competition is "overdone," and he obviously did not believe that more competition rather than less was the solution for every industry. It is here in particular that Hamilton departs from the more standard "market failure" view of regulation found among neoclassicals.

Hamilton's work also brings out the "experimentalist" and instrumentalist aspects of institutionalist policy thinking very well. Hamilton's approach was highly particularist and problem centered, but this approach was not accidental or ad hoc but well considered and closely linked to his rejection of orthodox "value theory" as well as his adoption of the pragmatic philosophy of John Dewey taught to him by Charles Horton Cooley. Hamilton's approach was not to define "failures" relative to a theoretical competitive norm but to investigate the actual workings of specific markets and to take an experimental attitude to policy. Hamilton was not wedded to particular instruments for policy, but his ends in view always remained the same: how to provide an institutional framework that would lead business to operate in a way consistent with the provision of a higher standard of living and a fuller measure of life to the average citizen.

Of course, one of the greatest themes in the literature on economics and government is the question of how to reconcile the individual's pursuit of economic gain with the broader public interest. There are those who believe that the market can perform this function and those who argue that other forms of control are required. For Hamilton, markets had proved insufficient to properly direct the operation of business to the public interest much beyond the stage of small-scale production and petty trade. The passage of the antitrust acts, while based on a faith in competition, were themselves a recognition that the market alone could not ensure the public good, and a judicial oversight of the activities of business was required. Antitrust had had limited success and did not always result in appropriate policy where technological efficiency demanded larger scale or some broader industrial coordination. The major alternative, regulation by administrative commission, had also been less than entirely successful. Commissions had been captured by the interests they were supposed to be regulating. Many supposed "controls" such as professional standards, licensing requirements, quality controls, and the like had been turned into sanctions. Patents, too, had been diverted from their proper function and become a vehicle for restriction rather than for technological advance and dissemination of knowledge. In general the "political arts" had not kept pace with the development of technology and of business and professional practice.

Hamilton's late position was that while there could be no return to laissez-faire, competition should be maintained where possible. This view was based, however, not on an acceptance of the idealized view of competitive markets but on the lack of adequate regulatory alternatives. Thus, "a great corpus of the law stands as proof of the incapacity of the industrial system to regulate itself," and there is a necessity for the direction of industry toward objectives that serve the general welfare. But "until the political arts reach a maturity they do not now possess the question of the maintenance of competition will remain insistent." Where competition needs to be superseded by another method of control the case needs to be made. Mergers should not be allowed where technology does not require it and where there are dangers in the concentration of economic power. The grant of patent should be limited to "its proper office." Government procurement should not encourage concentration or restrictive practices. The problem of the capture of commissions and administrative agencies will remain until "political invention contrives an adequate substitute." Businesses will continue to play a strategic game with the regulator and will continue to try to find new ways to effect their own control over markets. Any scheme of public control, no matter how ingenious, will require revision over time, as technology and business practice evolve. There is no panacea; the only way forward for economic control in the public interest is that of "eternal vigilance" (Hamilton 1957, 166–68).

References

Alchon, Guy. 1985. *The Invisible Hand of Planning: Capitalism, Social Science, and the State in the 1920s*. Princeton, N.J.: Princeton University Press.

Arnold, Thurman. 1937. *The Folklore of Capitalism*. New Haven, Conn.: Yale University Press.

Ayres, Clarence. n.d. Robert Brady Folder and Walton Hamilton Folder. Clarence Ayres Papers, Center for American History, University of Texas, Austin.

Barber, William J. 1985. *From New Era to New Deal: Herbert Hoover, the Economists, and American Economic Policy, 1921–1933*. Cambridge: Cambridge University Press.

———. 1996. *Designs within Disorder: Franklin D. Roosevelt, the Economists, and the Shaping of American Economic Policy, 1933–1945*. Cambridge: Cambridge University Press.

Campbell, Persia. [1940] 1968. *Consumer Representation in the New Deal*. New York: AMS Press.

Carter v. Carter Coal Company. 1936. 298 U.S. 238. http://newdeal.feri.org/court/298US238.htm.

Chasse, John Dennis. 1986. John R. Commons and the Democratic State. *Journal of Economic Issues* 20 (September): 759–84.

———. 1994. The American Association for Labor Legislation and the Institutionalist Tradition in National Health Insurance. *Journal of Economic Issues* 28 (December): 1063–90.

Clark, John M. 1923. *Studies in the Economics of Overhead Costs*. Chicago: University of Chicago Press.

———. 1926. *The Social Control of Business*. Chicago: University of Chicago Press.

Commons, John R. [1924] 1968. *The Legal Foundations of Capitalism*. Madison: University of Wisconsin Press.

Commons, John R., and John B. Andrews. 1936. *Principles of Labor Legislation*. 4th rev. ed. New York: Harper & Brothers.

Donohue, Kathleen G. 2003. *Freedom from Want: American Liberalism and the Idea of the Consumer*. Baltimore, Md.: Johns Hopkins University Press.

Dorfman, Joseph. 1974. Walton Hale Hamilton and Industrial Policy. In *Industrial Policy and Institutionalism: Selected Essays*, by Walton H. Hamilton. Clifton, N.J.: Kelley.

Douglas, Paul H. 1934. The Role of the Consumer in the New Deal. *Annals of the American Academy of Political and Social Science* 172 (March): 98–106.

Eisner, J. Michael. 1967. *William Morris Leiserson: A Biography*. Madison: University of Wisconsin Press.

Everett, Helen. 1931. Social Control. *Encyclopaedia of the Social Sciences*. Vol. 4. New York: Macmillan.

Ezekiel, Mordecai. n.d. Boxes 11, 12, 19. Mordecai Ezekiel Papers, Franklin D. Roosevelt Library, Hyde Park, N.Y.

———. 1936. *$2,500 a Year: From Scarcity to Abundance*. New York: Harcourt, Brace.

———. 1939. *Jobs for All through Industrial Expansion*. New York: Knopf.

Fenster, Mark. 2003. The Symbols of Governance: Thurman Arnold and Post-Realist Legal Theory. *Buffalo Law Review* 51 (fall): 1053–118.

Fetter, Frank A. 1932. The Economists' Committee on Anti-Trust Law Policy. *American Economic Review* 22 (September): 465–69.

Frank, Jerome N. 1933. Address to the Association of American Law Schools, Chicago, 30 December, Box J18, Folder 2. Walton Hamilton Papers, Tarlton Law Library, University of Texas, Austin.

Gordon, Robert W. 2004. Professors and Policymakers: Yale Law School Faculty in the New Deal and After. In *History of the Yale Law School*, edited by Anthony T. Kronman. New Haven, Conn.: Yale University Press.

Hadley, Arthur T. 1896. *Economics: An Account of the Relations between Private Property and Public Welfare*. New York: Putnam.

Hamilton, Walton H. n.d. Walton Hamilton Papers, Tarlton Law Library, University of Texas, Austin.

———. n.d.a. Box J45, Folder 1. In Hamilton n.d.

———. n.d.b. Box J5, Folder 6. In Hamilton n.d.

———. n.d.c. Clarence Ayres to Walton Hamilton, 3 May, no year, Box J45, Folder 1. In Hamilton n.d.

———. n.d.d. The Control of Industry, Box J3, Folder 3. In Hamilton n.d.

———. n.d.e. *The Economic Order*, Box J4, Folder 3. In Hamilton n.d.

———. n.d.f. Helen R. Wright to Hamilton, 18 November, no year, Box J4, Folder 5. In Hamilton n.d.

———. n.d.g. Medicine in the Making, draft, Box J12, Folder 1, and Box J41, Folder 4. In Hamilton n.d.

———. n.d.h. Scattered Thoughts on Thorstein Veblen, Box J29, Folder 3. In Hamilton n.d.

———. 1918. The Place of Value Theory in the Place of Economics I. *Journal of Political Economy* 26 (March): 217–45.

———. 1919. The Institutional Approach to Economic Theory. *American Economic Review, Papers and Proceedings* 9 (March): 309–18.

———. 1922a. Frank Taussig to Walton Hamilton, 11 October 1922, Box J5, Folder 5. In Hamilton n.d.

———. 1922b. A Theory of the Rate of Wages. *Quarterly Journal of Economics* 36 (August): 581–625.

———. 1926. The Problem of Bituminous Coal. *American Labor Legislation Review* 16:217–29.

———. 1928a. Henry Clay to Walton Hamilton, 24 January, Box J5, Folder 5. In Hamilton n.d.

———. 1928b. The Plight of Soft Coal. *Nation*, 4 April, 367–69.

———. 1928c. The Regulation of Employment Agencies. *Yale Law Journal* 38 (December): 225–35.

———. 1929. Judicial Tolerance of Farmers' Cooperatives. *Yale Law Journal* 38 (May): 936–54.

———. 1930a. Affectation with Public Interest. *Yale Law Journal* 39 (June): 1089–112.

———. 1930b. An Economist Audits His Costs. *Survey* 63 (January 1): 380–83.

———. 1931a. The Ancient Maxim Caveat Emptor. *Yale Law Journal* 40 (June): 1133–87.

———. 1931b. Competition. *Encyclopaedia of the Social Sciences*. Vol. 4. New York: Macmillan.

———. 1931c. The Jurist's Art. *Columbia Law Review* 31 (November): 1073–93.

———. 1931d. The Legal Philosophy of Justices Holmes and Brandeis. *Current History* 33 (February): 654–60.

———. 1931e. *The World-Wide Depression: Ways Out*. Pamphlet No. 71. New York: Foreign Policy Association.

———. 1932a. The Anti-Trust Laws and the Social Control of Business. In *The Federal Anti-Trust Laws: A Symposium*, edited by Milton Handler. Chicago: Commerce Clearing House.

———. 1932b. The Control of Big Business. *Nation*, 25 May, 591–93.

———. 1932c. The Problem of Anti-Trust Reform. *Columbia Law Review* 32 (February): 173–78.

———. 1932d. Property according to Locke. *Yale Law Journal* 41 (April): 864–80.

———. 1932e. Statement by Walton H. Hamilton. In *Medical Care for the American People*, by Committee on the Costs of Medical Care. Chicago: University of Chicago Press.

———. 1933a. Letter to Hamilton from an unknown correspondent (second page of the letter is missing) at Yale Law School, 19 May, Box J4, Folder 5. In Hamilton n.d.

———. 1933b. Nathan Margold to Hamilton, 27 April, Box J5, Folder 5. In Hamilton n.d.

———. 1933c. Norman Myers to Hamilton, 27 April, Box J5, Folder 5. In Hamilton n.d.

———. 1933d. Walton Hamilton to Norman Myers, 23 May, Box J46, Folder 3. In Hamilton n.d.

———. 1934. Consumers' Interest in Price Fixing. *Survey Graphic* 23 (February): 76–80, 95–96.
———. 1935a. The Consumers' Front. *Survey Graphic* 24 (November): 524–28, 565, 567.
———. 1935b. Testimony of Walton Hamilton. Hearings before the Committee on Finance, U.S. Senate, 74th Cong., 1st sess. Washington, D.C.: Government Printing Office.
———. 1936a. The Constitution as an Instrument of Public Welfare. *American Labor Legislation Review* 26:103–7.
———. 1936b. Why the Price Studies? *Consumer* 1 (January 15): 6–9.
———. 1937. The Living Law. *Survey Graphic* 26 (December): 632–35, 735.
———. 1938a. Cardozo the Craftsman. *University of Chicago Law Review* 6 (December): 1–22.
———. 1938b. The Doctors' "Union." *New Republic*, 7 September, 117–18.
———. 1938c. The Path of Due Process of Law. *Ethics* 48 (April): 269–96.
———. 1938d. Price—by Way of Litigation. *Columbia Law Review* 38 (June): 1008–36.
———. 1938e. Walton Hamilton to Dexter Keezer, 11 May, Box J9, Folder 8. In Hamilton n.d.
———. 1938f. Walton Hamilton to Hugh Kelly, 11 May, Box J22, Folder 2. In Hamilton n.d.
———. 1939a. Industrial Inquiry and Sectarian Dogma. *American Economic Review* 29 (March): 102–6.
———. 1939b. Paul Homan to Jerome Frank, 14 March, Box J31, Folder 3. In Hamilton n.d.
———. 1940a. Common Right, Due Process, and Antitrust. *Law and Contemporary Problems* 7 (winter): 24–41.
———. 1940b. *The Pattern of Competition*. New York: Columbia University Press.
———. 1941a. Coal and the Economy—a Demurrer. *Yale Law Journal* 50 (February): 595–621.
———. 1941b. On Dating Mr. Justice Holmes. *University of Chicago Law Review* 9 (December): 1–29.
———. 1941c. *Patents and Free Enterprise*. Temporary National Economic Committee, Monograph No. 31. Washington, D.C.: Government Printing Office.
———. 1943a. Property Rights in the Market. *Journal of Legal and Political Sociology* 2 (April): 10–33.
———. 1943b. Whitewashing the Patent System. *New Republic*, 30 August, 278–79.
———. 1946a. The Economic Man Affects a National Role. *American Economic Review* 36 (May): 735–44.
———. 1946b. *On the Composition of the Corporate Veil*. Publication No. 6. Philadelphia: Brandeis Lawyers' Society.
———. 1949a. The Genius of the Radical. In *Years of the Modern*, edited by John W. Chase. New York: Longmans, Green.

———. 1949b. A New Patent Policy. *Current History* 17 (December): 338–41.

———. 1951. Walton Hamilton to Mark Adams, 11 August, Box J26, Folder 1. In Hamilton n.d.

———. 1953. The Law, the Economy, and Moral Values. In *Goals of Economic Life*, edited by A. Dudley Ward. New York: Harper & Brothers.

———. 1957. *The Politics of Industry*. New York: Knopf.

Hamilton, Walton H., and Douglass Adair. [1937] 1972. *The Power to Govern*. New York: Da Capo Press.

Hamilton, Walton H., and Associates. 1938. *Price and Price Policies*. New York: McGraw Hill.

Hamilton, Walton H., and George D. Braden. 1941. The Special Competence of the Supreme Court. *Yale Law Journal* 50 (June): 1319–75.

Hamilton, Walton H., and Stacy May. [1923] 1968. *The Control of Wages*. New York: Kelley.

Hamilton, Walton H., and Irene Till. 1940a. *Antitrust in Action*. Temporary National Economic Committee, Monograph No. 16. Washington, D.C.: Government Printing Office.

———. 1940b. Antitrust—the Reach after New Weapons. *Washington University Law Quarterly* 26 (December): 1–26.

———. 1948. What Is a Patent? *Law and Contemporary Problems* 13 (spring): 245–59.

Hamilton, Walton H., and Helen R. Wright. 1925. *The Case of Bituminous Coal*. New York: Macmillan.

———. 1928. *A Way of Order for Bituminous Coal*. New York: Macmillan.

Hawley, Ellis W. 1966. *The New Deal and the Problem of Monopoly*. Princeton, N.J.: Princeton University Press.

Henderson, Leon. 1934a. Walton Hamilton to Isador Lubin, 8 October, Series: NRA Papers, Folder: Prices, Cabinet Committee. Leon Henderson Papers, Franklin D. Roosevelt Library, Hyde Park, N.Y.

———. 1934b. Leon Henderson to Miss F. M. Robinson, 11 May, Series: NRA Papers, Folder: Prices, Cabinet Committee. Leon Henderson Papers, Franklin D. Roosevelt Library, Hyde Park, N.Y.

Hirshfeld. Daniel S. 1970. *The Lost Reform: The Campaign for Compulsory Health Insurance in the United States from 1932 to 1943*. Cambridge, Mass.: Harvard University Press.

Keezer, Dexter M. 1934. The Consumer under the National Recovery Administration. *Annals of the American Academy of Political and Social Science* 172 (March): 88–97.

Keezer, Dexter M., and Stacy May. 1930. *The Public Control of Business*. New York: Harper.

Lochner v. People of the State of New York. 1905. 198 U.S. 45. http://laws.findlaw.com/us/198/45.html.

Lynd, Robert. 1934. A New Deal for the Consumer? *New Republic*, 3 January, 220–22.

———. 1936. Democracy's Third Estate: The Consumer. *Political Science Quarterly* 51 (December): 481–515.

Lyon, Leverett S., et al. 1935. *The National Recovery Administration: An Analysis and Appraisal*. Washington, D.C.: Brookings Institution.

Macgregor, D. H. 1930. The Coal Bill and the Cartel. *Economic Journal* 40 (March): 35–44.

Mayhew, Anne. 1998. How American Economists Came to Love the Sherman Antitrust Act. In *From Interwar Pluralism to Postwar Neoclassicism*, edited by Mary S. Morgan and Malcolm Rutherford. *HOPE* 30 (supplement): 179–201.

Means, Gardiner C. 1934a. Minutes of Meeting of Committee on Prices, 22 October, Series I, Folder: Price Fixing. Gardiner Means Papers, Franklin D. Roosevelt Library, Hyde Park, N.Y.

———. 1934b. The Consumer and the New Deal. *Annals of the American Academy of Political and Social Science* 173 (May): 7–17.

Mund, Vernon. 1938. Review of *Price and Price Policies*, by Hamilton and Associates. *American Economic Review* 28 (December): 818–20.

Panama Refining Co. v. Ryan. 1935. 293 U.S. 388. http://newdeal.feri.org/court/293US388.htm.

Parrini, C. P., and M. J. Sklar. 1983. New Thinking about the Market, 1896–1906: Some American Economists on Investment and the Theory of Surplus Capital. *Journal of Economic History* 43 (September): 559–79.

Perkins, B. B. 1998. Economic Organization of Medicine and the Committee on the Costs of Medical Care. *American Journal of Public Health* 88:1721–26.

Ross, Joseph S. 2002. The Committee on the Costs of Medical Care and the History of Health Insurance in the United States. *Einstein Quarterly Journal of Biology and Medicine* 19:129–34.

Rostow, Eugene V. 1941. Bituminous Coal and the Public Interest. *Yale Law Journal* 50 (February): 543–94.

Rutherford, Malcolm. 2003. On the Economic Frontier: Walton Hamilton, Institutional Economics, and Education. *HOPE* 35:611–53.

Schlabach, Theron F. 1969. *Edwin E. Witte: Cautious Reformer*. Madison: State Historical Society of Wisconsin.

Terborgh, George W. 1934. *Price Control Devices in NRA Codes*. Washington, D.C.: Brookings Institution.

Tugwell, Rexford G. 1935. Consumers and the New Deal. In *The Battle for Democracy*. New York: Columbia University Press.

———. [1922] 1968. *The Economic Basis of the Public Interest*. New York: Kelley.

United States v. Butler. 1936. 297 U.S. 1. http://newdeal.feri.org/court/297US1.htm.

Veblen, Thorstein. [1904] 1975. *The Theory of Business Enterprise*. Clifton, N.J.: Kelley.

Part 3

Doctrine Meets Policy

From Muddling Through to the Economics of Control: Views of Applied Policy from J. N. Keynes to Abba Lerner

David Colander

This essay tells a story of changing views about economists' conceptions of what economic theory has to say about the role of government in the economy.[1] It considers three views. One is the view of J. N. Keynes and Lionel Robbins, who argue that pure economic theory has little or nothing to say about policy, but that a separate branch of economics exists that should consider such policy issues. A second view is that of Alfred Marshall and A. C. Pigou, who argue that a "realistic" theory can be used to guide judgments on policy. The third view, which is most closely related to an "economics of control" view set out by Abba Lerner, connects pure theory, policy, and the role of government in the economy in a more direct way, drawing implications about policy and the role of the state from pure theory.

This essay discusses the evolution of these three views and argues that the first two are actually much more compatible than they at first seem. They both can be seen as a "muddling through" approach to policy, in which pure economic theory does not give much guidance for policy. The third view, in which pure theory gives direct guidance for policy, is incompatible with the other two. The essay concludes by arguing that the current textbook presentation of policy follows the third view and that,

I would like to thank D. P. O'Brien and participants of the 2004 *HOPE* conference, and especially Craufurd Goodwin, for their comments on an earlier version of this essay.

1. This essay is not a full consideration of the issues and does not discuss how outside events influenced economists' thinking. Instead it focuses on economists' changing methodological views about what the role of theory is and of how that theory should be used in thinking about policy.

while the first two are quite reasonable views, this third view is at best misleading and at worst simply wrong.

J. N. Keynes's Muddling Through

The standard methodological reference in the late 1800s is J. N. Keynes's *Scope and Method of Political Economy* ([1891] 1955). In it, Keynes, following earlier economists, divided economics into three branches—positive, normative, and art. He defined the branches as follows: "Positive science . . . a body of systematized knowledge concerning what is; normative or regulative science . . . a body of systematized knowledge discussing criteria of what ought to be . . . ; art . . . a system of rules for the attainment of a given end" (34–35). Keynes's book played an important role in clarifying many of the confusions that had existed in economics and became the standard methodological statement of the time. Keynes argued that maintaining a separate positive science quite distinct from applied policy, which was what he meant by the art of economics, was necessary to avoid confusions about the relation between theory and policy. For Keynes positive theory had no policy implications because of the complexity of those real-world policy problems. Applied policy was necessarily muddling through and should be seen as such.

Keynes was very definite about the highly limited role of theory in applied policy. He writes:

> Few practical problems admit of complete solution on economic grounds alone. . . . when we pass for instance, to problems of taxation, or to problems that concern the relations of the state with trade and industry, or to the general discussion of communistic and socialistic schemes—it is far from being the case that economic considerations hold the field exclusively. Account must also be taken of ethical, social, and political considerations that lie outside the sphere of political economy regarded as a science. (34)

> Thus, it would be generally agreed that, in dealing with practical questions, an abstract method of treatment avails less and carries us much less far than when we are dealing with theoretical questions. In other words, in dealing with the former class of questions, we are to a greater extent dependent upon history and inductive generalization. (63)

> We are, accordingly, led to the conclusion . . . that a definitive art of political economy, which attempts to lay down absolute rules for the regulation of human conduct, will have vaguely defined limits, and be largely non-economic in character. (83)

The methodology of applied policy for Keynes was quite different from the methodology he saw for positive economics. It was inductive, relying on history and educated common sense. Pure theory—positive economics—was used by Keynes as a backdrop for thinking about policy problems; it was useful to help organize one's thoughts but not to be applied to real-world problems. For Keynes, questions about the role of the state belonged in the art of economics; such questions could only be answered by addressing issues that went far beyond economic theory.

Answers about the role of the state were to be found in a broader philosophical tradition of liberalism. Such policy questions would be decided on economic, moral, practical, political, and social grounds. Economists in their role as individuals or as social philosophers might have something to say about such questions, but as economic theorists they had little to say because in that role they did not consider the noneconomic aspects of the questions. Economics was an input into policy; it did not come to policy conclusions.

In distinguishing between implications that could be drawn from positive theory and implications that could be drawn from the art branch of economics, Keynes distinguished theorems from precepts. A theorem was a conclusion that followed from positive economic theory; it concerned how the economy worked. It did not concern policy questions dealing with the role of the state. A precept was a rule of thumb that concerned policy; it followed from the art of economics and was not derived from economic theory but from introspection, induction, and an educated common sense. Pure theory (positive economics) played a role in developing that educated common sense because it revealed logical errors in initial commonsense reasoning, but otherwise theory was not involved in determining policy or the role of the state. There could be precepts about the role of the state, but there would be no theorems about the role of the state. For Keynes, and for classical economists more generally, the doctrine of laissez-faire was a precept, not a theorem.

The "precept/theorem" and "art/positive/normative" distinctions did not leave much of a role for pure economic theory in guiding economic policy. In terms of the then raging *Methodenstreit* between those favoring an analytic approach and those favoring a historical approach to economics, Keynes's solution gave applied policy to the historicists and gave the scientific branch of economics—positive theory—to the theorists. But his solution also left one with the feeling that the scientists had not won much, since, other than in some unspecified abstract way, positive economics was irrelevant for applied policy.

Keynes's view of theory has a long history in English classical economics and was most directly a continuation of the views of economists such as Nassau Senior ([1836] 1951). In this view theorems are simply logical proofs; they convey nothing other than the implications of assumptions one makes.[2] Theory was simply a system of logical deductions from a series of postulates derived from introspection, which are not themselves subject to empirical verification. Theory might be useful as a backdrop for pondering the role of the state, but theory would not answer the question of what that role was and would certainly not lend itself to specifying rules of actions that the state should follow.

The Marshallian Straddle

Methodological pronouncements are seldom followed, and although Keynes's work was generally accepted as the best statement of the state of methodology of the time, few economists carefully followed his methodological prescriptions.[3] An example is Alfred Marshall, who was a colleague of Keynes. Although clearly Marshall had read and discussed with Keynes the methodological issues that Keynes wrote about, Marshall proceeded to write his *Principles of Economics* with little direct reference to Keynes's work and did not distinguish between the art and science of economics. Instead, Marshall approached the distinction between theory and policy quite differently, specifically blurring the distinction between positive economics and applied policy, or the art of economics. In fact, in early editions of *Principles*, he argued against having a separate art of economics and focused on economics as a science.[4]

2. The philosopher Alexander Rosenberg (1992) has examined modern micro theory and has argued that it has these characteristics.

3. Economists then, as economists now, do what they do. Actual economics develops with only a weak tie to methodological prescriptions. More often than not, methodology serves as an *ex post* rationalization for what economists do rather than a guide to what they should do.

4. Marshall argued against the use of the phrase "the art of economics" in the early editions of *Principles*. However, as Marshall's editor points out, between the third (1895) and fourth (1898) editions, Marshall cut from his *Principles* a paragraph arguing against using the phrase "art of economics" ([1890] 1961, 2:154).

He could do this by changing what was meant by the concepts of science and positive economics. Marshall's concept of science was not the logical-deductive science that Keynes had in mind but instead a type of applied science, which was more a type of engineering than it was a pure science. For Marshall, science was about solving real-world problems, not understanding for the sake of understanding. Put another way, for Marshall "science" was a tool in the art of economics.[5]

The important point here is that for Marshall, the positive economics of Keynes was practically nonexistent; all economics was art. An economic theorist for Marshall was not a scientist but instead a policy economist who created useful tools that could explicate an actual real-world problem. Marshall simply dismissed the logical-deductive branch of economics as being useless and advocated a type of theory that was, in essence, a sub-branch of art. Marshall justified his position by arguing that economics does not avail itself to long deductive chains of reasoning and thus had to concern itself with shedding light on practical issues.[6]

Unfortunately, Marshall did not make clear precisely what he was doing, and he never discussed how his approach differed from Keynes's. He straddled the methodological issues, as he straddled many issues.[7] Even with his limited interpretation of theory, Marshall was extremely hesitant to draw policy conclusions. Policy was too complicated and involved too many noneconomic variables. For example, when he discussed the art of economics in the fourth edition of *Principles* he wrote:

5. Marshall's argument against art and his focus on economics as science must be understood in the context of the times; when he was writing, economics as a separate discipline did not yet exist. The majority of economists he dealt with talked about policy, not theory. Only a small minority did theory or followed a logical-deductive approach. As he was writing *Principles*, he was also petitioning Cambridge to set up separate tripos in economics and was very much concerned that the objectivity of economics be maintained (Marshall 1902). Given his institutional needs, it is not surprising that he combined the art of economics and positive economics, and called it economics rather than political economy. To have emphasized Keynes's distinction would have worked against his desire to set up a separate tripos in economics.

6. Consistent with that view in *Principles*, he placed all general equilibrium issues in a two-page footnote (Marshall [1890] 1961, mathematical note 21). Such theoretical issues could not be dealt with using the mathematical techniques available and thus were beyond theorizing.

7. For example, he eschewed mathematics but simultaneously structured his arguments in the *Principles* so that they could be deduced mathematically. (The mathematics were placed in an appendix if they were included at all.) He incorporated enormous institutional and historical insights into his *Principles*, but he simultaneously removed the term *political* from the name of economics discipline, naming his book *Principles of Economics* rather than *Principles of Political Economy*. This change in name further moved the profession away from Keynes's methodological perspective because the term *political economy* suggests that there is an applied branch of economics separate from the theoretical branch, and for Marshall that was not the case.

> Of course an economist retains the liberty, common to all the world, of expressing his opinion that a certain course of action is the right one under given circumstances; and if the difficulties of the problem are chiefly economic, he may speak with a certain authority. But on the whole, though the matter is one on which opinions differ, it seems best that he should do so rather in his private capacity, than as claiming to speak with the authority of economic science. (Marshall [1890] 1898, 2:154)

While such careful prescriptions about drawing policy implications from theory may seem to be similar to those of Keynes, there was a major difference between their views. For Marshall, positive theory was a tool of applied policy; it was a working abstraction, a tool, not a truth.[8] Since theory was only a tool, it was not a problem if one's theoretical apparatus incorporated some normative judgments and institutional realities as long as those value judgments were recognized and were useful in making the theory more applicable. As a tool, theory did not have to be pure; it simply had to be useful.

One can best see Marshall's approach to theory through the tools he devised. Consider the concept of consumer surplus, which Marshall developed as a theoretical tool useful in shedding light on some policy questions. It integrated the welfare of all individuals into an area under a curve and thereby included the implicit value judgment that an individual's welfare was comparable and interchangeable. As a tool of pure science, the models built on that assumption were useless, but as a tool of a practicing economist, the models could be useful in certain instances, as long as in applying the analysis one carefully considered the limiting assumptions on which the analysis was built.

Marshall generally limited the use of his tools to applications for which he thought they fit. For example, consider his view of utility and tastes. He specifically rejects William Stanley Jevons's and Carl Menger's view that economics should be seen as the science of meeting given wants and argues that our wants are not independent. He writes that "while wants are the rulers of life among the lower animals, it is to changes in the forms of efforts and activities that we must turn when in search for the keynotes of the history of mankind" (Marshall [1890]

8. J. M. Keynes (1922, v) summarized Marshall's approach to theory as follows: "The theory of economics is a method rather than a doctrine, an apparatus of the mind, a technique of thinking which helps its possessor to draw correct conclusions."

1961, 85). He further writes: "The higher study of consumption must come after, and not before, the main body of economic analysis; and, though it may have its beginning within the proper domain of economics, it cannot find its conclusion there, but must extend far beyond" (90–91).

For Marshall economic reasoning was an input into a broader policy analysis, and economic theory was an input into economic reasoning that is designed for the policy problem at hand. The difference between Keynes and Marshall is that for Keynes, theory is a deductive set of propositions involving long deductive chains of reasoning from initial assumptions. It is as pure as possible and avoids as many value judgments as possible. Modern general equilibrium theory would be an example of Keynes's pure theory. Theory, for Marshall, was makeshift; it specifically did not involve long deductive chains of arguments, but instead involved short chains of arguments, consistent with his "one thing at a time" approach. Its structure was determined by the policy problem one was addressing, and one would make generally accepted normative assumptions that fit the problem at hand in order to make the theory more useful. For Marshall it was acceptable to integrate value judgments into the theory as long as those value judgments were clearly expressed, and if one took them into account when drawing on theory to arrive at a policy conclusion.

Pigou's Realistic Economics

A. C. Pigou followed Marshall at Cambridge and set the tone for applied economics that was used in the 1920s and 1930s. While mindful of Keynes's distinction between art and science, Pigou followed Marshall in developing economic theory as a sub-branch of the art of economics rather than as a logical-deductive science. Pigou, however, is much clearer about his method, and he specifically states that he is not doing pure theory but is instead doing what he called "realistic theory." He writes: "Hence it must be the realistic, not the pure, type of science that constitutes the object of our search" (Pigou [1920] 2002, 6). To make this point even clearer, Pigou distinguishes between fruit-bearing theory and light-bearing theory (3). Fruit-bearing theory—realistic theory—is a branch of the art of economics; it is theory designed to solve particular policy problems. Light-bearing theory is pure theory, or theory belonging in Keynes's positive branch of economics.

As was the case with Marshall, Pigou has nothing to say about pure theory, which was what Keynes meant by positive economics; it simply was not part of Pigou's approach. Pigou's welfare economics must be seen in this light; it was not meant to be a final guide to policy. It was about precepts, not theorems. But, unlike Keynes, whose precepts were largely determined outside economic theory, Pigou's precepts were developed within his realistic theory that embodied generally accepted value judgments.

Since his realistic theory was a tool of the art of economics, the absence of any normative welfare judgments, and the consistency of the analysis among different applications, was far less important than it was for Keynes. As was the case with Marshall, Pigou normally accepted that normative judgments could be built into theory, as long as one was clear about what those judgments were and did not argue that those who disagreed with those value judgments were incorrect based on economic reasoning. Economic theory was a set of tools, not rules, for policymakers.

The approach Pigou took to utility theory was consistent with this policy approach. He specifically did not use the term *utility* but instead used the term *desiredness* (23). Desiredness was determinable by introspection and was comparable across averages of individuals.[9] For Pigou, desiredness was not a precise measure of a consumer's welfare but simply a rough measure for his or her material welfare to be used when thinking about policy issues and in explaining the results of economic analysis to others.

Since the tools were designed to come to a policy conclusion, the embodied value judgments had to be justified. Pigou spends much of his *Economics of Welfare* doing precisely that. For example, he writes: "It is fair to suppose that most commodities, especially those of wide consumption that are required, as articles of food and clothing are, for direct personal use, will be wanted as a means to satisfaction" (Pigou [1920] 2002, 24). For Pigou, an increase in consumption—meeting people's desires—did not mean that there was definitely an improvement in the welfare of society; he simply meant that it most likely would be an improvement. He devoted many pages of his *Economics of Welfare* to explaining why, as a general precept, one could use social dividend as a rough guide to welfare for many policy changes.

9. The term *utility* only shows up once in Pigou's *Economics of Welfare*, and then only to argue against its use.

His introspective use of utility led him to include two significant interrelated normative judgments in his analysis. First, he held that, in general, income going to rich people had less positive impact on society's welfare than income going to poor people. Based on this assumption, he could favor policies supporting redistribution from rich to poor if that transfer did not decrease the social dividend. He argued that such transfers "enable more intense wants to be satisfied at the expense of less intense wants" (89). Second, he argued that it was inappropriate to differentiate individuals' abilities to generate pleasure, thus specifically excluding the argument that the rich needed more money to fulfill their more refined tastes. Tastes, he argued, were changeable, and if the poor were given more income, they would develop more refined tastes.

Pigou did not deny that these aspects of his welfare economics involved very specific normative judgments, but, for him, they were reasonable judgments, shared with a large part of the population. They were also necessary judgments to make the tools relevant for applied policy. Since his was realistic theory, not pure theory, Pigou argued that such judgments were quite acceptable as long as one was clear that they were being made.

Lionel Robbins's Political Economy

Pigou's work on welfare economics provoked a reaction from Lionel Robbins, who, in his famous *Essay on the Nature and Significance of Economic Science* (1932), specifically criticized the Pigovian-Marshallian approach to theory and policy. His argument is similar to Keynes's argument in 1890 and thus is best seen as a call for the return to the methodology of Keynes's initial art-science distinction. Robbins essentially states that what Pigou and Marshall called theory was not theory at all but was instead something else. For Robbins theory is what Keynes meant by theory—logical abstract deductions—and is what Pigou had classified as "light-seeking theory" to contrast it with the "fruit-seeking theory" that Pigou was interested in.

In making his argument, Robbins resurrected the ordinalist approach to welfare analysis in which economic welfare was not material welfare, as it was for Marshall and Pigou, but, instead, a broader concept that implied satisfaction of desire. The difference between the two definitions had been remarked on by Vilfredo Pareto ([1909] 1971), who made a distinction between utility and ophelimity. Pareto's concept of utility was the equivalent of what Pigou called desiredness; it was determinable by introspection and was comparable across averages of individuals. Pareto's concept of ophelimity was the equivalent of Robbins's concept of utility. It referred to satisfaction of desire; it was not determinable or comparable among individuals; it was appropriate for pure science but was of little help in applied policy work. Marshall's and Pigou's economics took the Pareto utility approach; it was a rough-and-ready guide for policy that embodied generally accepted welfare judgments. Robbins's economics took the ophelimity approach; it concerned precise statements about the welfare of individuals that could be drawn from economic theory.

Robbins criticized the material welfare aspect of Marshall's and Pigou's analysis and chose his definition of economics, "the allocation of scarce resources among alternative ends," to specifically rule out the "study of the causes of material welfare" definition that he attributed to Marshall and Pigou. Robbins argued that any tools involving interpersonal welfare judgments had no scientific basis. Robbins's alternative definition both expanded and contracted the domain of economics. It expanded it because it now included all activities and goods, not just those that affected material welfare. But it simultaneously contracted the domain of economics by limiting the amount of interpersonal comparability that was allowed, since that comparability had no scientific basis.[10]

Given his definition of pure theory, Robbins was very careful to say that no policy conclusions followed from economic theory. In his 1981 Ely Lecture, which developed ideas in his book on classical economics (Robbins 1953), Robbins reflected on his argument and expanded on his distinction. There he argued that "the raison d'être of welfare economics" is to be "able to pronounce *as a matter of scientific demonstration* that such and such a policy was good or bad" (Robbins 1981, 4; emphasis in the original). He stated: "In the great work of Marshall and, still more, Pigou, we are assuming comparisons . . . (that are) . . . not warranted by anything which is legitimately assumed by scientific economics" (4–5). He cites Bentham as agreeing with him that interpersonal utility comparisons are "in vain" and that any economic analysis based on any assumption about such comparisons is unscientific and therefore outside the domain of economics.

10. For a discussion of the distinction between these two approaches, see Cooter and Rappoport 1984.

But as was the case with Keynes, Robbins did not stop there; he recognized that his definition of the science of economics was highly limiting and would mean that economics has little, if anything, to say about policy, since "all recommendations of policy involve judgments of value" (6). Thus, he specifically called for a separate branch of economics that he called political economy. He writes: "My suggestion here, as in the Introduction to my *Political Economy: Past and Present*, is that its use should be revived as now covering that part of our sphere of interest which essentially involves judgments of value. Political Economy, thus conceived, is quite unashamedly concerned with the assumptions of policy and the results flowing from them" (7, 8).

Robbins sees political economy as distinct from economics in the stricter sense of the word. It involves "all modes of analysis and explicit or implicit judgments of value." While he does not call it the art of economics, Robbins's political economy is an almost perfect parallel to Keynes's art branch of economics. Moreover, if one sees Pigou's realistic economics as a form of Robbins's political economy, not as pure theory, there is little difference between Robbins's and Pigou's view of how policy analysis needs to be conducted in reference to theory. Pigou was simply developing an approach that Keynes and Robbins said needed to be developed but did not develop and did not believe deserved to be called economic theory.

Abba Lerner's Economics of Control

The last writer I will consider in this paper is Abba Lerner, whose *Economics of Control: Principles of Welfare Economics* (1944) provided a template for the approach to policy that current textbooks take. Although Lerner was a student of Lionel Robbins (and Lerner specifically states that the ideas were likely absorbed from his teachers at the London School of Economics, including Robbins and Friedrich Hayek [Lerner 1944, viii]), Lerner's work does not fit nicely into Robbins's methodological position. Instead, it more closely follows Marshall's and Pigou's, since Lerner is drawing policy implications directly from theory. Unfortunately, he did not make clear the distinction between pure and realistic theory that Pigou made. Lerner thus left open the possibility that his policy conclusions followed from pure economic theory, not from a realistic theory that had already embodied numerous welfare judgments that needed to be discussed and accepted before one could apply the results of the analysis.

The likelihood that people would interpret his work as implying that policy conclusions followed from theory was increased because, unlike Marshall and Pigou who carefully discussed the limitations of theory to drawing policy conclusions, Lerner specifically applied his theories to policy and aggressively related theory to policy conclusions.[11] He made no distinction between precepts (derived from the art of economics embodying value judgments in the theory) and theorems (derived from pure theory and quite irrelevant for policy). Thus, he argued that while interpersonal comparisons of welfare were impossible, "probable comparisons" were not and that redistribution policy *should* be based on "probable total satisfaction" (Lerner 1944, 29). Consistent with this view, he drew out specific rules for how government could achieve the optimal distribution of income.

As opposed to developing tools for policy analysts, who would in turn develop policy precepts, as Marshall and Pigou did, Lerner developed specific rules of policy from pure theory, identifying precisely what government should do to maximize social welfare. These rules, because of their simplicity and clearness, became the template for the textbook presentation of both micro and macro policy discussions.[12] In microeconomics these rules became the rules of welfare economics involving the equating of marginal social costs with marginal social benefits. These rules, which are known as the Lange-Lerner rules, became the guiding rules of welfare economics.[13]

In macro, Lerner (1941, 4, 5) developed the rules of functional finance, which involved the government maintaining "a reasonable level of demand at all times" through appropriate fiscal policy and a monetary policy governed only by the need to maintain "the optimal amount

11. In doing so he followed the approach of David Ricardo ([1817] 1953), an approach characterized by Joseph Schumpeter (1954) as the Ricardian vice.

12. Lerner's early writing played an important role in the socialist calculation debate that was ongoing at the time, and Lerner was very much concerned with the arguments behind the state's role in the economy. In that debate Lerner advocated market socialism and argued that socialist planners could give directives to managers to price at marginal costs, thereby achieving maximum social welfare.

13. Specifically, government should adjust resources until the following series of equations are met: $Msb = p = mpr = mpc = vmf = msc$ (Lerner 1944, 96). His rules on income redistribution did not become part of the textbook template. Lerner agreed that we had no basis for making interpersonal welfare comparisons, but argued that because of the uncertainty principle, redistribution was more likely to improve social welfare than hurt it, and thus he supported redistribution and defined his welfare rules to include redistribution. Later economists switched to a welfare economic focus only on Pareto efficiency.

of investment" and by the functional needs of the economy, not by any precepts of "sound finance."[14]

These policy rules that Lerner developed were not presented as general guidelines to be used in combination with noneconomic considerations, as were the precepts of Marshall and Pigou. Instead, they were presented as firm rules based on economic theory. They were presented as forming the basis of policy—the blueprints that governments should follow—if government wanted to work in the social interest. For example, in the introduction to the *Economics of Control* Lerner (1944, 6) writes: "We shall concentrate on what would be the best thing that the government can do in the social interest—what institutions would most effectively induce the individual members of society, while seeking to accomplish their own ends, to act in the way which is most beneficial for society as a whole. . . . Here we shall merely attempt to show what is socially desirable."

In making his arguments, Lerner combined a much longer chain of reasoning into the purely economic analysis than either Marshall or Pigou had been willing to do.[15] Whereas Marshall's work was primarily partial equilibrium in nature and designed to solve specific policy issues, Lerner drew policy rules from general equilibrium theory, using long chains of reasoning, an approach that Marshall argued against.

Had Lerner followed J. N. Keynes's approach and presented his own work as pure theory, with little relevance for policy, Lerner's economics of control approach would have been consistent with that of previous writers. But Lerner did not take that view. He drew very specific rules about policy from theory, as one might do in a Pigovian-Marshallian framework. In doing so, he ignored the positive/art distinction of Keynes, the economics/political economy distinction of Robbins, and the fruit-seeking/light-seeking distinction of Pigou. In short, he moved away from a "muddling through" vision of applied policy, in which pure theory had no direct relevance for policy, a vision held by all previous writers, and

14. Unlike the other economists I have been discussing, Lerner also arrived at definite policy rules for macro policy. He did so because early in his career he became enamored of macroeconomics and became a leading expositor of Keynesian ideas. His exposition of these rules was precise, and they became the foundation for much of the textbook presentation of Keynesian economics.

15. Marshall was not alone in this; during the 1930s and 1940s when Lerner was writing, there was a larger movement occurring in economics from a Marshallian partial equilibrium method to a Walrasian general equilibrium method. Lerner's work was part of this broader movement.

replaced it with an "economics of control" vision of applied policy, in which specific policy rules followed from pure theory.

Conclusion

I am primarily a teacher of economics. The reason I am interested in the above history is that it sheds light on how we came to the particular structure of micro and macro that currently dominates the textbooks. That framework remains essentially the framework that Lerner developed, although in macro, with the demise of Keynesian economics, precisely what we are teaching students is unclear.[16] The microeconomic framework that we teach is a framework in which we teach students an applied policy approach where policy conclusions seem to be directly drawn from theory. What this history points out is that our current microeconomic textbook presentation would be unacceptable to Keynes, Marshall, Pigou, and Robbins.

Where they differed was not in their view of what policy conclusions could be drawn from theory but rather in where they saw economists fitting into the applied policy process. Keynes's and Robbins's pure theory leads to no applied policy rules; it leads to a framework that might be helpful in thinking about the art of economics, but it does not lead to any policy conclusions. For them, policy discussions belong not in economics but in a separate branch of economics, called either political economy or the art of economics. Marshall's and Pigou's realistic theory leads to applied policy rules, but it does so only because it starts with the premise that all applied policy necessarily involves value judgments, and Marshall and Pigou give explicit consideration to those value judgments and discuss numerous noneconomic issues. Even Lerner's framework, which combines the two approaches, retains an explicit consideration of distributional issues and is built on the assumption that governments have resolved these. Unfortunately, such considerations of the necessary element of value judgments in any discussion of policy are not presented in most economics texts, since they do not distinguish a separate "art of economics" branch for policy or make it clear that they are using tools that already embody normative judgments.

16. Even in macro, the models that many principles textbooks use to discuss monetary and fiscal policy retain significant elements of the ideas of functional finance, although authors are much more circumspect about the policy relevance of the models than were earlier textbook authors.

All of the economists I have considered, with the possible exception of Lerner, would have a problem with the current textbook microeconomics presentation, because it violates Hume's dictum—that you cannot derive a *should* from an *is*. They all accepted the need to go beyond pure economic theory *to have anything to say about policy or the role of the state*. For all of them, applied policy, and questions about the role of the state in the economy, is a muddle. For them the role of the economic theorist is not to give answers but to provide input into a broader policy decision process that goes far beyond economics. That insight has been lost in the texts, and that is sad.

References

Cooter, Robert, and Peter Rappoport. 1984. Were the Ordinalists Wrong about Welfare Economics? *Journal of Economic Literature* 22.2:507–30.

Keynes, J. M. 1922. Introduction to *Supply and Demand*, by H. D. Henderson. London: Nisbet.

Keynes, J. N. [1891] 1955. *The Scope and Method of Political Economy*. New York: Kelley and Mellman.

Lerner, Abba. 1941. The Economic Steering Wheel. *University Review*, June, 2–8.

———. 1944. *The Economics of Control: Principles of Welfare Economics*. New York: Macmillan.

Marshall, Alfred. [1890] 1898. *Principles of Economics*. 4th ed. London: Macmillan.

———. [1890] 1961. *Principles of Economics*. 9th ed. London: Macmillan.

———. [1902] 1961. A Plea for the Creation of a Curriculum in Economics and Associated Branches of Political Science. In Marshall [1890] 1961.

Pareto, Vilfredo. [1909] 1971. *Manual of Political Economy*. Edited by Ann S. Schwier and Alfred N. Page, translated by Ann S. Schwier. New York: Kelley.

Pigou, A. C. [1920] 2002. *The Economics of Welfare*. Reprint, New Brunswick, N.J.: Transactions Press.

Ricardo, David. [1817] 1953. *On the Principles of Political Economy and Taxation*. Edited by P. Sraffa and M. Dobb. Cambridge: Cambridge University Press.

Robbins, Lionel. 1932. *An Essay on the Nature and Significance of Economic Science*. London: Macmillan.

———. 1981. Economics and Political Economy. *American Economic Review* 71 (May): 1–10.

Rosenberg, Alexander. 1992. *Economics: Mathematical Politics or Science of Diminishing Returns?* Chicago: University of Chicago Press.

Schumpeter, Joseph. 1954. *History of Economic Analysis*. Edited from manuscript by Elizabeth Boody Schumpeter. Oxford: Oxford University Press.

Senior, Nassau William. [1836] 1951. *An Outline of the Science of Political Economy*. New York: Kelley.

Economists, Government, and Economic Policymaking in Israel: From "Crawling Peg" to "Cold Turkey"

Yakir Plessner and Warren Young

For decades, Israeli academic economists ventured for limited periods of time out of the ivory tower and became economic advisers to top policymakers. Some of those economists were Eitan Berglas, Michael Bruno, Ezra Sadan, Pinhas Zusman, and one of the authors of the present essay (Plessner). How academic economists perform as advisers to policymakers should be a legitimate public choice question, at least as long as one believes that people act largely in their own best interests (the possibility of some degree of altruism should always be admitted). More concretely, suppose that the economy is in State A and that the problem of getting it to State B arises. The question then is, asked how to get the economy from A to B, would an academic economist respond to the challenge identically whether she is asked by a student or by a politician who employs her? Put differently, should one expect economic advisers who hail from academia to come up with different economic-policy options than they would have come up with in the classroom?

While Bruno Frey (1983, 260–86) did address the topic of economic advising within the context of the democratic process, he did not explicitly consider the possibility of a split personality. Moreover, while the possibility of "cognitive dissonance" among economists has recently been examined (Darity and Young 2000), the issue of incentive structure facing economists as economic advisers has not been dealt with nor have

We are grateful to Jürgen Backhaus, David Colander, and Warren Samuels for helpful comments. All remaining shortcomings are, of course, our own. Although not cited in the text, the following works were important in the composition of this article: Halevi 1969, Lerner 1954, Patinkin 1956, and Zilberfarb 1991.

any examples been presented up to now. We do not suggest, of course, intellectual dishonesty. But there is no escaping the fact that the academic in a position of power faces different incentives from those faced in the academic environment. It may also be reasonable to expect that the sense of power, a huge novelty for academics, will cause them as advisers to consider possibilities that they would not consider in front of students. What we mean is that proximity to power could generate a different view of the world and of what can and cannot be done.

The incentive that is not present in academia is the desire, at least for a while, to stay on as adviser. Otherwise, the individual in question would not have assumed the post in the first place. This implies that when advice is provided, the adviser takes into account, to some extent, the impact of the advice on the prospects of staying on. It seems to us that where this might be particularly important is when the adviser has to confront the possibility that what the boss wants to achieve is unobtainable, or that trying to achieve the desired end could involve serious risks. It stands to reason that politicians do not hire an adviser to tell them what cannot be done. Telling the politician "I don't know ways to achieve this" likely diminishes the economist's stature in his or her own eyes.

We conclude that under this structure of incentives, different from the structure to which the adviser is used to in academia, he or she will likely respond differently in an advisory position than in the classroom. Israel's economic history is, we think, rich in examples of this nature. In what follows, we focus mainly on one such example, albeit one that had momentous consequences, in that it turned into a recipe for triple-digit, actually almost hyper, inflation.

Background

Historical

The history of erroneous advice imparted by academic economists to the Israeli government and central bank is long and touches on many aspects of the economy. The period on which this essay focuses is 1974–85, starting with OPEC 1, the tripling of oil prices by the newly formed cartel of major oil countries. The reason for this choice is that the inflationary process that developed following the Yom Kippur War, at the end of 1973, reaching hyperinflation levels in 1984–85, brought the Israeli economy to the brink of collapse. Hence the role that academic economists played must be deemed crucial.

Table 1 CPI Rate of Inflation (annual percentage)

Year	Rate of Inflation
1974	56.2
1975	38.0
1976	23.5
1977	42.5
1978	48.1
1979	111.4
1980	132.9
1981	101.5
1982	131.5
1983	190.7
1984	444.9
1985, first half	284.9

Source: Central Bureau of Statistics, Jerusalem

The main questions that economists faced were (1) what caused inflation, and (2) what policies should be chosen in order to stop or at least reduce it. Table 1 reveals the severity of the inflationary problem facing Israel at the time.

Three basic characteristics of the Israeli economy before the start of the period under consideration must be briefly described to put the evolving story in context. First, the exchange-rate regime was one of a fixed rate, as was the case worldwide under Bretton Woods. The last big discrete devaluation preceding the period on which we focus occurred in August 1971, when the Israeli lira was devalued by 20 percent, from 3.5 to 4.2 liras to the dollar.

Second, on the political front, the deep recession that Israel experienced in 1966–67, when unemployment reached an annual average rate of 10.4 percent of the labor force (and that came to an end in the aftermath of the Six-Day War), created a fear of unemployment that henceforth dominated economic policy priorities for a long time.

The third component concerns inflation. In the two years in which Israel came out of the recession, 1968 and 1969, inflation as measured by the CPI was 1.9 percent and 3.5 percent, respectively. But in 1970, inflation became a serious problem, when it hit 10.1 percent. To get a handle on the events that led up to the changes in economic policy that are the subject of this essay, one needs to recall the difference between cost-push and demand-pull inflations. Perhaps the best concise description of the initial phases of the inflationary period that followed the Yom Kippur War is by Martin Bronfenbrenner and Franklyn Holzman (1963, 613–14):

> Although cost-push theories of inflation are not in fact new, their revival in the 1950's has been called *The New Inflation*. . . . The title symbolizes reaction against the demand-pull orthodoxy of the prior decade but does not deny that cost-push may involve increases in money supply . . . particularly if decreases in output and employment are to be avoided. More important, the term "new inflation" embodies the opinion that the strength of economic pressure groups . . . , together with increased public concern with unemployment, had increased the likelihood (in many countries) of "disequilibrium" price and wage increases being validated by expansive monetary and fiscal policies.

Figure 1 illustrates the point. After inflation as measured by the CPI raced ahead of the wholesale price inflation in 1971 and 1972,[1] the two were almost identical over the first three quarters of 1973. But then came the surge in oil prices at the end of 1973, which meant that the average price Israel had to pay for imported oil in 1974 was 4.6 times the average for the first nine months of 1973 (Bank of Israel 1975, 59). Prices of other imported inputs increased as well: the price level of imports in the second half of 1973 was 26 percent higher than it had been in the first half of the year (Bank of Israel 1974, 63). These twin developments caused a huge surge in production costs: short-run aggregate supply moved violently up and to the left. The figure shows that in the last quarter of 1973 and throughout 1974, the wholesale price index surged ahead of the CPI. In the fifteen months from October 1973 to December 1974, the wholesale price index rose by 130.8 percent in annual terms, while the CPI rose by 121.3 percent. It is at this point that our story begins to unfold.

The Monetary System

To follow the argument below, it is also crucial to understand Israel's monetary scene immediately preceding the change. Monetary policy may be carried out by targeting one of three nominal magnitudes, regardless of the objectives of the policy. These are the nominal interest rate,

1. Wholesale price is defined as the price of industrial output destined for domestic uses.

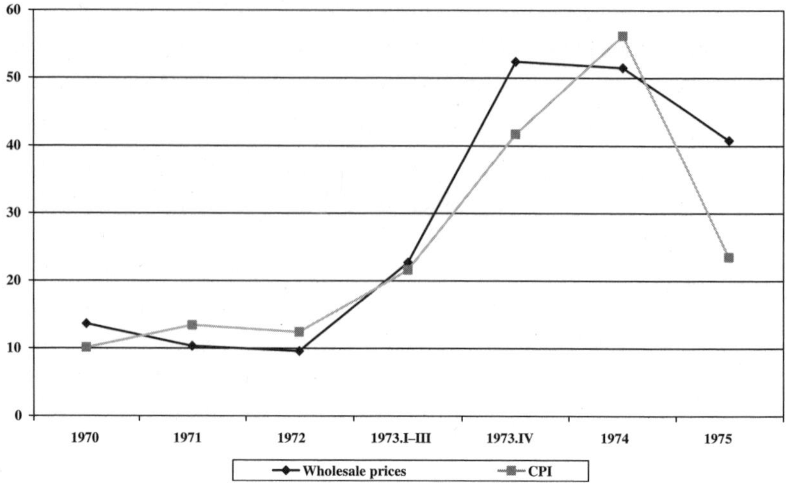

Figure 1 Rates of inflation, percent, annual terms

the nominal exchange rate, and some monetary aggregate, such as M_1. Our key observation is that Israel did not have a monetary policy, but at least the monetary system had been determined exogenously prior to the change.

Start with the fact that the Bank of Israel (henceforth BoI) had been completely under the thumb of the government.[2] This meant that it had no independent control over any of the nominal instruments of monetary policy. In terms of a monetary aggregate, the government could freely borrow from BoI, thus forcing it to print money at the government's pleasure. The amount of base money had essentially the status of an endogenous variable, whose value was largely determined by the budget deficit, on the one hand, and by foreign-exchange outflow, on the other.[3]

The natural response to this assertion is, why couldn't BoI intervene by using open market operations? The answer is to be found by reference to the saving regime extant that had been designed to channel the

2. Legally, nothing has changed between then and now; in practice, BoI has become one of the most independent central banks in the world.

3. Under a fixed exchange-rate regime, the central bank is obliged to sell foreign exchange at the official rate. Hence any purchase of foreign exchange by the public implies a reduction in base money.

public's savings into the government's hands. This, in turn, had been motivated by the desire to make the government the prime agent for allocation of capital in the economy. Briefly put, practically all of the public's savings were deposited in saving instruments backed by government-indexed, nonnegotiable, CPI-indexed bonds. For example, an individual would deposit a sum in a bank's saving scheme;[4] the bank would turn around and use the money to purchase government bonds; the government would then redeposit the money in the bank, with instructions as to whom this money may be lent. The important thing to remember is that the bonds backing the saving scheme could not be traded—they had to be held by the bank to maturity. Consequently, BoI never had a large enough stock of negotiable government paper to conduct effective open market operations, and thus could not target a monetary aggregate.

Consider next the interest rate. First, BoI could not change any interest rate without the government's approval. But perhaps more important, a sizable share of credit had been extended under myriad interest rates, fixed by the government for identifiable classes of borrowers. In 1975 there were thirteen "credit funds," managed by BoI, designed to finance activities such as "imports used for producing exports," "production of citrus and cotton," "revolving finance for industry," "revolving finance for agriculture." At that point almost 53 percent of the average bank credit had been extended under these "directed credit" arrangements (Bank of Israel 1977, 291). This means that interest rates could not be used as an effective monetary instrument, since more than half of the credit outstanding was shielded from interest-rate changes.

Finally, let us consider the exchange rate. The fact that it had been fixed did at least provide an anchor for the monetary system, thus preventing it from becoming endogenous. But the choice of exchange rates had not been motivated by any monetary considerations. Rather, the exchange rate was considered to be a tool for correcting balance of payments problems. Thus, even though the monetary system was under control in the sense that it was governed exogenously, the country did not have a monetary policy to speak of. This, in itself, can prove to be a very interesting case study, because the academic (and nonacademic) economists of the time never pointed out this key attribute of Israel's economy.

It is not generally possible to show what was not done, that is, to prove the nonexistence of facts (as opposed to theoretical constructs).

4. All such schemes required government approval.

We believe, however, that some important examples will serve to support our assertion in the case of Israel.

The first comprehensive description of the Israeli economy by an academic economist was *The Israel Economy*, by Don Patinkin (1960). While Patinkin (1960, 104) did point out the difficulties faced by the central bank in conducting effective monetary policy, he never pointed out that monetary policy of any kind had been impossible in principle under the arrangements extant. The impression that one derives from reading his analysis is that what hindered the central bank had been primarily the credit that it provided to the government. And again, in summarizing the causes of the inflationary process during the fifties, Patinkin (1960, 109) identified the inflationary finance of the government budget deficit as the main culprit, without pointing out that the central bank simply had no instruments available to offset the impact of such finance (e.g., high interest rates).

The next major academic description of the Israeli economy was *The Economic Development of Israel*, by Nadav Halevi and Ruth Klinov-Malul (1968; for a review, see Gass 1969). Both Halevi and Klinov-Malul were, as was Patinkin, members of the economics department of Hebrew University. Their discussion of monetary policy (1968, 6, 8, 10, 257–59) is quite similar to that of Patinkin, even though a decade separates the two studies. The impression one derives from their treatment is that the government-cum–central bank simply did not activate the sort of monetary policy required to curb inflation. They talk about "easing monetary policy" and "expansionary monetary policy" as though they were talking about a country that could make deliberate choices about which monetary policy it actually wanted to pursue.

The 1970s are dealt with in detail below and could be viewed as the continuation of the same failure to deal with the inability to conduct any monetary policy at all. So let us turn to the 1980s. The best example here is Stanley Fischer's article "Monetary Policy in Israel" (1982). Fischer enumerates no less than six classes of monetary policy instruments that BoI had at its disposal, albeit recognizing that it faced significant constraints on its ability to use them. Finally, in a memorandum by Avi Ben-Bassat (1982) of the research department of BoI, he came close to admitting that the implementation of any monetary policy at all was impossible. This can be surmised from the fact that, even though he appeared to say that BoI's monetary policy was aided by a number of interrelated instruments, its policy had concentrated on credit rationing—not through a price or reserve mechanism but through the imposition of quantitative limits on lending.

Wage Indexation

The supply shock clearly left Israel poorer than it had been, because export prices rose by much less than import prices. In the last quarter of 1973, export prices were only 31 percent higher than the 1972 average, while import prices rose over the same period by 51.9 percent (Bank of Israel 1974, 47). Thus, it now took a larger volume of exports than before to buy a given volume of imports.

But wage indexation in Israel never discriminated between the various sources of price increases. In particular, no mechanism had been set up to neutralize inflation caused by external supply shocks, from the basis for calculating wage indexation payments. As a consequence, workers got compensated for price rises that not only did not benefit employers but which actually hurt them. The upshot was that the external supply shock created a secondary supply shock caused by higher wages. That is, the system as it existed translated external supply shocks into a massive reallocation of value added. Labor's share increased at the expense of capital's share. The unavoidable consequence would have been a considerable rise in unemployment.

The evidence is unmistakable: the average real wage for the first nine months of 1974 was only 3.1 percent lower than for the comparable 1973 period.[5] Since, as noted, the government abhorred increased unemployment, it devalued the currency by a whopping 42 percent in November 1974. That sent real wages plunging: the average real wage for the last quarter of 1974 was 4.4 percent lower than the average for the first three quarters, and it was 7.4 percent lower than it had been in the first three quarters of 1973.[6] It went on to decline by another 1.5 percent over the following two quarters.

The medicine was effective, however, for only a short time. By the third quarter of 1975 the real wage already exceeded the 1974 average. Thus, the threat of increased unemployment was becoming a steady

5. For nominal wages, see Bank of Israel 1974, 254; for CPI, see table 6, "Consumer Price Index—Various Bases," produced by Israel's Central Bureau of Statistics (http://www.cbs.gov.il/price/t6_e.htm).

6. Comparing anything to the last quarter of 1973 is meaningless, because so much of the labor force was mobilized for the war.

feature of the economy. A way had to be found to stop the process of the initial supply shock from turning into a vicious race between wages and exchange rates, with the concomitant upward spiral of prices.

The New Policy

The method devised by professional economists to deal with the country's economic woes was aimed at averting a balance of payments crisis.[7] This was to be achieved by enhancing export profitability and reducing the demand for imported consumption goods. These, in turn, were to be attained by eroding the real purchasing power of wages. The erosion would render a decline in unit labor costs, thus enhancing international competitiveness while reducing the real incomes of wage earners, in turn causing a reduction in consumption demand, including, in particular, demand for imported consumption goods. The method of wage erosion may be described as a pincer movement, consisting of changes to the management of the exchange rate, on the one hand, and a redesign of the wage indexation system, on the other.

The Exchange-Rate Regime

The exchange-rate regime was transformed from a fixed rate, with periodic devaluations, to a crawling peg. The rationale was formulated as follows: large, discrete devaluations instigate expectations, resulting in runs on foreign-exchange reserves (Gafni, Zuckerman, and Sussman 1975). This is adverse in itself, but in addition it creates liquidity shortages in banks, as the public borrows in order to speculate on foreign exchange. BoI then feels obliged to allow banks to borrow at the discount window, thus injecting more liquidity into the economy. Once the devaluation takes place, the process goes into reverse: having realized the devaluation profits on foreign-exchange holdings, the public sells foreign exchange. Since the banks that buy turn around and sell to BoI, a lot of liquidity is injected into the system, which the central bank finds difficult to soak up (recall BoI's inability to engage in open market operations).

Devaluations also caused consumers to push forward purchases of big-ticket imported items, such as consumer durables and cars, for fear

7. Some of this material has been discussed in Plessner 1994. But the present is a much more comprehensive discussion.

that devaluation will render them dearer. There is also a political drawback to large discrete devaluations: the public considers these to signal economic-policy failures. Hence politicians hesitate to implement devaluations, even when they are called for on economic grounds.

A crawling peg has none of these disadvantages, a fact that had been recognized by other countries at the time. As we shall show, however, the institution of a crawling peg under the circumstances that prevailed at the time in Israel was a grave and potentially catastrophic mistake.

Two of the most prominent economists of the time, Michael Bruno and Zvi Sussman (1978), laid out in great detail the philosophy behind the transition to a crawling peg, in an article published in the wake of the complete floating of the lira in 1977. The arguments advanced by them in support of the change are the above mentioned. What is striking is what they had to say about the monetary system. The section that deals with the question is based entirely on the equilibrium equation $r_d = r_f + e^*$, where r_d and r_f are the domestic and world interest rates, respectively, and e^* is the expected rate of devaluation of the domestic currency. In other words, their entire attention was devoted to the impact on the monetary system of foreign-currency movements into or out of the economy.

Two years later, Fischer (1982), while being aware of the various classes of credit impervious to interest-rate targeting and of the government's ability to borrow directly from BoI, recommended that BoI target credit as its monetary instrument.

How unrealistic this recommendation was is evidenced by the chronic liquidity deficits that the commercial banking system exhibited. Table 2 reports the evolution of base money during the period under consideration. It is important to realize that in Israel's context, the actual equivalent of M_1 is the sum of broad-base money and liquidity deficits, something that drives home the assertion that BoI had no control over the monetary system. The only thing that prevented the monetary system from becoming endogenous was the fixed exchange rate.

Wage Indexation

The other part of the pincer movement concerned wage indexation. Indexation started before Israel gained independence. In earlier years, the system could in some respects be considered as a protection of workers against income redistribution at their expense. For example, price changes in fruit and vegetables were figured annually, so as to avoid

Table 2 Base Money (millions of lira)

Year	End of Period Base Money		Liquidity Deficit
	Narrow[1]	Broad[1]	
1972	5,004	5,482	47
1973	6,303	6,942	283
1974	6,889	8,064	67
1975	7,224	8,569	1,519
1976	10,549	11,958	287
1977	15,897	17,474	489
1978	20,358	22,618	2,841

Source: BoI, *Annual Report*, various years.
1. Narrow base money is M_1 as traditionally defined; broad base money is M_1 plus exemptions from liquidity requirements for the directed-credit funds.

instability because of seasonal variations. Since those result mainly from variations in supply, they cannot be viewed as favoring employers over employees. Similarly, housing prices were not included in the price index for purposes of indexation computations. The rationale here was that rents were controlled, and owner-occupiers should not be compensated for an appreciation of assets that they own.

But by the mid-1970s, all of this had atrophied. Indexation was at a rate of 100 percent of CPI, including everything. Even price rises that resulted from increased indirect taxes were included. It is still true, of course, that under a system where indexation was the only mode of wage increases, real wages could be eroded even under a steady-state rate of inflation—see figure 2. But indexation payments are never the only mode of nominal wage increases, especially in a heavily unionized environment, as was the case in Israel.

Enter the Sussman Commission, headed by Zvi Sussman, research director of the Bank of Israel. The commission comprised five members, three of whom had PhDs in economics. While its proposals contained many changes to the system of wage indexation that had existed in Israel, the one that concerns us here, and that the commission itself viewed as the most important proposal, dealt with the degree of inflationary compensation. Specifically, the commission proposed that wage indexation payments be made at a rate of 70 percent of the rate of inflation in the CPI. In the commission's own words,

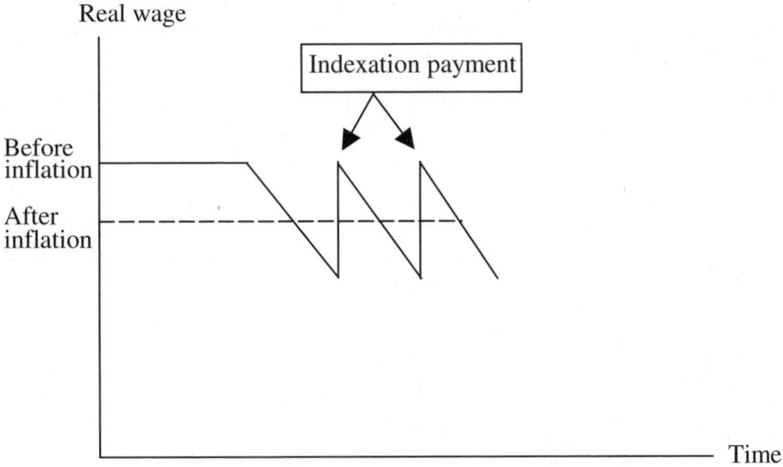

Figure 2 Erosion of real wage under steady-state inflation

> Such a rate will reduce the danger of over-compensation for price rises occasioned by the government's exchange-rate and taxation measures; fully compensating for price increases that result from such measures is bound to accelerate the inflationary process and under certain circumstances, even cause an increase in unemployment. (Sussman Commission 1975, 2)

The purpose is clear: Israel's balance of payments problem has been aggravated considerably in the wake of the oil crisis; and the commission, which submitted its recommendations in July 1975, had been aware of the change in the exchange-rate regime, designed to achieve real devaluation. In the absence of substantial economic growth, successful devaluation (i.e., a nominal devaluation that results in a real one), requires the diversion of resources from domestic to foreign uses. But to achieve such a diversion, the purchasing power of the domestic population must be reduced. If, then, the government can devalue without the workers being fully compensated for the price rises occasioned by devaluation, then their real wages will have been eroded, and so their purchasing power diminished. There is no doubt that erosion of real wages was the objective. Thus, the commission stated,

Table 3 Injections into the Monetary Base (millions of lira)

Year	Positive Injections			Foreign Exchange
	Government	BoI	Total	
1975	4,255	1,351	5,606	−5,271
1976	6,009	1,616	7,625	−4,301
1977	8,857	6,746	15,603	−10,256
1978	10,684	13,712	24,396	−19,984

Source: BoI, *Annual Report*, various years.

> from the standpoint of the government, indexation based on the CPI reduces the effectiveness of changes in the exchange rate and of indirect taxation. Price rises occasioned by devaluations are designed to boost exports and reduce the demand for imports. Indexation payments under these circumstances will not only push producers to further price increases, but will hurt the efficiency of exchange-rate policy as an instrument of solving the balance-of-payments problem. (Sussman Commission 1975, 5; see also Herschkowitz 1975)

The policy objective of the twin changes was thus clearly enunciated. Was this a good policy prescription?

The Failure

The Exchange-Rate Regime

What happened in fact is that the conversion to a crawling peg exchange-rate regime rendered the monetary system anchorless. This was particularly true because the amount of periodic devaluation was calibrated on the rate of inflation. And so, the exchange rate became a function of the monetary system, which itself was a function of the exchange rate. It is no wonder, then, that the nominal system roared out of control, as is evident from table 1. Another vantage point from which to view the loss of control is provided by table 3, which reports the sources of injection into the monetary base.

From the table it follows that there has been a dramatic change as of 1977: whereas in 1975 and 1976 BoI's share of injections to the monetary base was between one-fifth and one-fourth, in 1977 the share jumped to 43 percent, and by 1978 BoI became the main source for injections,

at 56 percent. What drove the process is clear from the last column—foreign-exchange hoarding. In effect, BoI was accommodating the public's hunger for foreign exchange.

The weapon of choice to combat the effects of inflation on the balance of payments was, at the time, the "crawling peg." After its inception in the mid-1960s (Meade 1964, 1966; Williamson 1965), the crawling peg was applied in many countries, albeit for the most part without much success. In theory, the crawling peg was more desirable than large discrete devaluations. But this is only if it were limited, according to James Meade, at least, to a maximum of 2 percent per annum (Meade 1964; McKenzie 1969). However, even though advocated by eminent theoreticians, such as Meade and John Williamson, early on it was shown that the crawling peg could be problematic in practice, especially as a result of speculation and constraints on interest-rate policy (Furth 1969; Willett, Katz, and Branson 1970).

For example, Mervyn King (2004) noted the importance of interest-rate policy to the failure of the recent Brazilian crawling peg exchange-rate regime. The Brazilian case was not the only time the crawling peg approach was utilized in Latin America. In the late 1970s, Argentina and Chile, among other countries, attempted to control inflation by applying the "tablita" (preannounced) crawling peg approach, that is, a decreasing rate of devaluation that was supposed to be less than the inflation rate. This was supposed to act as a mechanism for adjusting inflationary expectations. Had all gone according to what the economic advisers who advocated the approach thought would happen, the rate of inflation in these countries should have rapidly converged to the world rate plus the preannounced devaluation rate. In Argentina, the tablita was introduced at the end of 1978, and the inflation rate indeed went down, from about 335 percent in 1975 to about 88 percent in 1980. However, while inflation in Argentina, for example, decreased, its convergence to the preannounced devaluation rate was much slower than it should have been. A real appreciation of the Argentine peso occurred, deteriorating the current account balance. This, in turn, fueled expectations of devaluation and also brought about capital flight and a balance of payments crisis. In 1981 the tablita was abandoned (Ruge-Murcia 1997, 13). The pattern of what can be called asynchronous inflation and devaluation rate, with a subsequent deterioration in the current account and ensuing abandonment of the crawling peg, also occurred in Chile in 1982, after which Chile experienced a 15 percent drop in GDP (1982–83), accompanied by an increase in external debt and an inflationary upsurge (Morande 2001, 2).

In the transition economies of Eastern Europe, some success, in Hungary for example, was achieved in the short run by applying a crawling peg system, but this did not occur in the Czech Republic and Poland (Kutan and Brada 1999, 5–9). More recently, Turkey also abandoned the crawling peg after its failure (Akyuz and Boratov 2001). Thus, it is not surprising that after over a decade of increasing disappointment, the consensus among most economists has shifted from the crawling peg to advocating credible fixed and fully flexible exchange-rate systems (see, e.g., Mussa et al. 2000; Summers 2000; Edwards and Savartano 2000), or toward advocating exchange-rate bands (Williamson 1996; Frankel 1999).

But let us leave the last word to one of BoI's most senior economists. In a recent paper titled "Dollarization and Indexation in Israel's Inflation and Disinflation," Edward Offenbacher (2002, 5–6), acting director of BoI's Monetary Department, wrote, "In 1975, Israel introduced a preannounced crawling peg exchange rate regime (a type of tablita). This was one among a number of signals of willingness to accommodate inflation, rather than taking serious steps to fight it, another being indexation of tax brackets, also implemented in 1975."

It is important to point out in this context that in October 1977 the crawling peg was extended to its logical conclusion: Israel floated its exchange rate.

Wage Indexation

One of the more puzzling aspects of the wage indexation reform is that its architects had recognized the role of inflationary expectations in the formation of wage agreements. The Sussman Commission stated that

> another phenomenon, also with negative consequences for the economy, is the attempt to predict the rise in prices during the term of [the wage] contract, and base on the prediction the terms of the contract. If the predicted rise in prices turns out to be higher than the actual rise, cost-push inflationary pressures will intensify, and it is possible that this will even cause a contraction in output and in employment, and an increase in unemployment. . . . Wage indexation—being a mechanism for automatic linking of wage changes to price changes—is designed to obviate demands for wage increases during the term of

wage agreements, and prevent, during the negotiation for such agreements, wage demands that are designed to compensate for expected price changes. (Sussman Commission 1975, 4)

The commission members thus clearly understood the dangers associated with workers trying to insure themselves against anticipated inflation. It should also be remembered that the commission's deliberations took place after the revolution in macroeconomics because of the advent of rational expectations had already occurred. And yet the commission did not apply this understanding when it came to leaving part of the wage open to inflationary erosion. In other words, it appears as if in the minds of the commission members, the danger existed only in the total absence of indexation, not when indexation was only partial. The commission did, however, explain why it resorted to this tactic. It opined that the ideal method would be to construct a special consumer price index with a dual purpose. The normal CPI would still serve to measure overall price increases. But for purposes of wage indexation, the effects of changes in prices of imported goods, resulting from both world price changes and domestic changes in exchange rates, could be neutralized. Similarly, the effects of changes in indirect taxes could also be neutralized. The commission went on to assert, however, that the difficulties involved in calculating such an index were insurmountable. Hence the chosen alternative.

Figure 3 clearly indicates that the intent to erode the real wage failed. The figure portrays the evolution of the exchange rate[8]—the main tool for wage erosion—the price level, and real wage, where the deflator is the CPI. At first, after the big devaluation of November 1974, the wage rate did indeed decline somewhat. Then came a period of relatively steady devaluation, and the real wage caught up. But probably because of increased inflationary expectations, the real wage reached a local maximum in the second quarter of 1977. The pace of devaluation then accelerated from the third quarter of 1977, and real wages declined again—but never below their level at the beginning of the period covered. At the end of the period covered by the graphs, the average real wage was 19 percent higher than it had been at the beginning of the period. And if one continues to follow the evolution into 1979 and on,

8. The exchange rate here is relative to a basket of five currencies, representing the composition of Israel's foreign trade. These were, at the time, the dollar, the deutsche mark, the French franc, the sterling, and the florin.

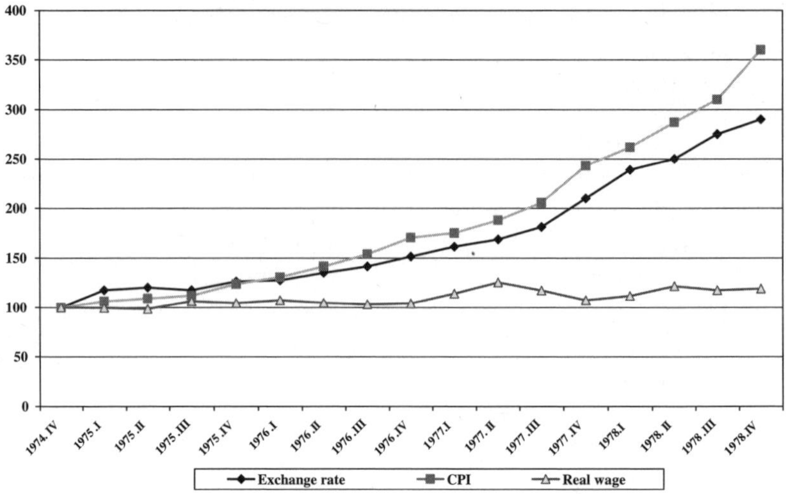

Figure 3 Index of exchange rates, consumer prices, and real wages

the picture becomes even more pronounced: the real wage reached the highest point for a decade in 1983.

One possible explanation for why the commission did not anticipate what would happen in the wake of the implementation of its own policy recommendations is its failure to take into account the moral hazard that the devaluation policy created for employers. To prevent unions from taking out insurance policies, as it were, against expected inflation, employers would have had to bargain hard, risking strikes. But the cost of doing so was not worth the gains, because there was a less costly alternative. Since the governments at the time were very concerned about the balance of payments situation, the employers could harp on that fear. So it was easy to grant pay demands and then turn around and besiege the government to devalue, lest exports be hurt because of loss of competitiveness. The upshot was a race between exchange rates and prices on one side, and nominal wages on the other. And in the end the unions won: the policy prescription was a total disaster.

The Failure to Learn the Lesson

No honest economist can criticize policy mistakes with hindsight. But economists are clearly entitled to a critical attitude when they detect a failure to change a policy prescription after it has become evident that the policy is a mistake. Unfortunately, in the case under consideration, the policy continued for at least six years after it had become clear to some economists that it did not work.

In BoI's 1978 report, published in May 1979, one finds the following passage:

> Wage increases in the private sector in 1978 are a consequence of demands for large wage increases, that were based on expectations of a continued fast pace of price increases, coupled with uncertainty regarding the rate of inflation; and the realization that the new indexation arrangements provided only partial compensation. In the circumstances the employers granted the workers' demands without serious resistance. The number of strikes [in 1978] was lower than it had been in 1977, and the private sector concluded an early wage agreement that was out of line with government policy. (Bank of Israel 1979, 183)

The paragraph quoted already includes all of the indications of the failure mentioned above. Particularly important is the allusion to the small number of strikes. The absence of strikes is usually a sign of conciliatory positions taken by employers. The argument is as follows: wage negotiations are conducted under uncertainty. Neither side has an exact knowledge of where the other side's "red line" is. As a consequence, if negotiations are tough, both sides risk crossing that line inadvertently. When employers do, a strike will ensue. Hence the absence of strikes indicates that employers did not engage in very tough bargaining.

In 1978 Israel the reason for the absence of tough bargaining is clear: employers could always appeal to the government to undo the excessive (from the point of view of productivity) wage agreements by accelerated devaluation, with its attendant inflation.

As noted, the failed policy persisted, causing ever-increasing inflation. Because the Israeli currency became so debased, the dollar was becoming more and more the preferred unit of account. Ultimately, even the prices in stores' windows were posted in dollars.

"Cold Turkey"

In July 1984 a general election took place, which resulted in a draw between the two main parties. As a consequence, a national unity government came into power in September. At that point it had become

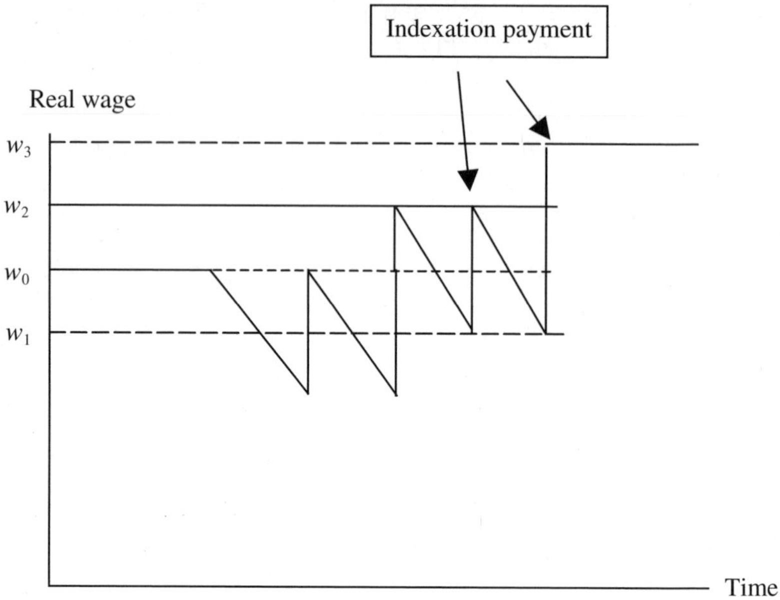

Figure 4 The impact of stopping inflation on the real wage

completely clear that inflation could actually cause the economy to collapse. But it still took until July 1985 to change the failed policies.

The key feature of the "cold turkey" medicine was a return to the exchange-rate regime that had been abandoned a decade earlier. This was accompanied by an agreement with the labor unions whose main component was a temporary suspension of indexation. The importance of this feature is demonstrated in figure 4, which is an extension of figure 2.

Suppose that unions, having realized that because of inflation their average real wage has declined from the preinflation w_0 to w_1, manage to secure wage hikes that restore the average to the preinflation rate. This implies that immediately preceding the indexation payment, the real wage is now w_1, and immediately after the payment it is w_2. Now suppose that inflation is suddenly stopped. Then the last indexation payment will bring the wage rate to w_3, higher than the preinflation rate. Note that this happens even under a steady-state rate of inflation and even when no inflationary expectations play any role.

The stabilization plan of 1985 is remarkable in that it exactly reversed the policy that had persisted for the preceding decade. While it managed to pull Israel from the brink of hyperinflation, it had design flaws of its own. In consequence, Israel suffered double-digit inflation for nine of the following eleven years.

This was followed by another policy prescription set out by the then governor of BoI, a well-known economist in his own right, Jacob Frenkel, that managed to eradicate the double-digit inflation. But its obvious flaws brought Israel to its current bout with deflation.

We may conclude by saying that in its fifty-six years of existence, Israel has, regrettably, never enjoyed good professional economic advising. Sometimes this was by commission, as in our story, and sometimes by omission, as academic economists failed to speak up against faulty policies adopted by politicians. While, of course, we cannot prove that the cause was incentives that distorted good judgment, the story is clearly consistent with this possibility.

References

Akyuz, Y., and K. Boratov. 2001. The Making of the Turkish Financial Crisis. Political Economy Research Center Paper (December). Amherst: University of Massachusetts.

Bank of Israel. 1974. *Annual Report 1973* (Hebrew). Jerusalem.

———. 1975. *Annual Report 1974* (Hebrew). Jerusalem.

———. 1977. *Annual Report 1976* (Hebrew). Jerusalem.

———. 1979. *Annual Report 1978* (Hebrew). Jerusalem.

Ben-Bassat, A. 1982. The Monetary Policy of the Bank of Israel. Memorandum, Bank of Israel, Jerusalem.

Bronfenbrenner, M., and F. D. Holzman. 1963. Survey of Inflation Theory. *American Economic Review* 53.4:593–661.

Bruno, M., and Z. Sussman. 1978. Flexibility of the Exchange-Rate System, Inflation, and Structural Changes (Hebrew). *Economic Quarterly* 99:270–94.

Darity, W., and W. Young. 2000. Reply to Ahiakpor. *HOPE* 32:915–18.

Edwards, S., and M. Savastano. 2000. Exchange Rates in Emerging Economies: What Do We Know? What Do We Need to Know? In *Economic Policy Reform: The Second Stage*, edited by A. Krueger. Chicago: University of Chicago Press.

Fischer, S. 1982. Monetary Policy in Israel. *Bank of Israel Economic Review* 53:5–30.

Frankel, J. 1999. No Single Currency Regime Is Right for All Countries or at All Times. NBER Working Paper no. 7338.

Frey, Bruno S. 1983. *Democratic Economic Policy*. Oxford: Martin Robertson.

Furth, J. 1969. International Monetary Reform and the "Crawling Peg"—Comment. *Federal Reserve Bank of St. Louis Review*, July, 21–25.

Gafni, A., B-A. Zuckerman, and Z. Sussman. 1975. Floating the Lira (Hebrew). Mimeo, Jerusalem.

Gass, O. 1969. Review of *The Economic Development of Israel*, by Nadav Halevi and Ruth Klinov-Malul. *Journal of Economic Literature* 7.4:1175–77.

Halevi, N. 1969. Economic Policy Discussion and Research in Israel. *American Economic Review* (supplement—surveys of National Economic Policy Issues and Policy Research) 59.4:74–118.

Halevi, N., and R. Klinov-Malul. 1968. *The Economic Development of Israel*. New York: Praeger.

Herschkowitz, M. 1975. The Significance of the New Indexation System. *Economic Quarterly* 87:270–76.

King, M. 2004. The Institutions of Monetary Policy. *American Economic Review*. 94.2:1–13.

Kutan, A., and J. Branda. 1999. The Evolution of Monetary Policy in Transition Economies. ZEI—Center for European Integration Studies Working Paper B 19. Bonn.

Lerner, A. 1954. Economic Stabilization and Economic Independence (Hebrew). *Economic Quarterly* 1.2:3–11.

McKenzie, G. 1969. International Monetary Reform and the "Crawling Peg." *Federal Reserve Bank of St. Louis Review* (February): 15–22.

Meade, J. 1964. The International Monetary Mechanism. *Three Banks Review*, September, 3–25.

———. 1966. Exchange Rate Flexibility. *Three Banks Review*, June, 3–27.

Morande, F. 2001. Exchange Rate Policy in Chile: Recent Experience. Paper presented at the "Exchange Rate Regimes: Hard Peg or Free Floating?" conference, IMF Institute, Washington, D.C., March.

Mussa, M., et al. 2000. Exchange Rate Regimes in an Increasingly Integrated Economy. *IMF Occasional Paper*, no. 193. Washington, D.C.

Offenbacher, E. 2002. Dollarization and Indexation in Israel's Inflation and Disinflation. Paper presented at the Eighth Dubrovnik Economic Conference, "Monetary Policy and Currency Substitution in the Emerging Markets," June.

Patinkin, D. 1956. The Middle East: Israel. *American Economic Review: Papers and Proceedings* 46.2:408–12.

———. 1960. *The Israel Economy: The First Decade*. Jerusalem: Falk Project for Economic Research in Israel.

Plessner, Y. 1994. *The Political Economy of Israel: From Ideology to Stagnation*. Albany: State University of New York Press.

Ruge-Murcia, F. 1997. Heterodox Inflation Stabilization in Argentina, Brazil, and Israel: A Historical Review and Some Stylized Facts. University of Montreal, CRDE Working Paper 0797, May.

Summers, L. 2000. International Financial Crises: Causes, Prevention, and Cures. *American Economic Review* 90.2:1–16.

Sussman Commission. 1975. *Report of the Commission for the Examination of Wage Indexation* (Hebrew). Jerusalem, July.

Willett, T., S. Katz, and W. Branson. 1970. Exchange Rate Systems, Interest Rates, and Capital Flows. Princeton Essays in International Finance, no. 78.

Williamson, J. 1965. The Crawling Peg. Princeton Essays in International Finance, no. 50.

———. 1996. *The Crawling Band as an Exchange Rate Regime: Lessons from Chile, Colombia, and Israel*. Washington, D.C.: Institute for International Economics.

Young, W. 2001. *The Impact of American Jewry on the Israeli Economy*. New York: American Jewish Committee/Ramat Gan: Argov Center, Bar Ilan University.

Zilberfarb, B. 1991. Foreign Exchange Market Liberalization: Anatomy of a Failure. In *Markets and Politicians: Politicized Economic Choice*, edited by A. Hillman. Boston: Kluwer.

From Continental Public Finance to Public Choice: Mapping Continuity

Jürgen G. Backhaus and Richard E. Wagner

To define public finance as the study of the economic activities of governments would command consensus among fiscal scholars, for all agree that government comprises the object that fiscal scholars study. That consensus dissolves, however, on closer inspection. What appears instead are two relatively distinct analytical orientations toward fiscal inquiry, reflecting different conceptualizations of the relationship between the polity and the economy. One orientation, which we label the Anglo-Saxon orientation, conceptualizes the polity as independent of or autonomous from the economy. The other orientation, which we label the Continental orientation, conceptualizes the relationship between polity and economy as mutual and reciprocal.

Within the Anglo-Saxon orientation, fiscal theorizing proceeds independently of political regimes and fiscal institutions. Taxes are treated as sacrifices regardless of the regime within which they are extracted. A fiscal scholar might well acknowledge that regimes differ in how much attention they give to the minimization of sacrifices, but the conditions for minimization are themselves independent of regime. Public finance is thus "the study of government intervention in the marketplace" (Jha 1998, xii). Within the Continental orientation, by contrast, public finance is the study of how people participate through political and fiscal institutions to generate fiscal patterns and outcomes (Buchanan 1967 is an exemplary treatment within this orientation). In this essay we first sketch

We should like to thank a number of conference participants for helpful comments and suggestions, and we should especially like to thank an anonymous referee for pointing out a number of ambiguities, the rectification of which has improved greatly the flow of the narrative.

the origins of the Continental orientation in the work of the cameralists, then describe the emergence of a distinct Continental orientation in the late nineteenth century, and close by noting how the development of public choice in the second half of the twentieth century is really a continuation of the Continental orientation toward public finance.

A Complaint and a Quarrel: Framing the Disjunction

In his 1896 treatise on public finance, Knut Wicksell ([1896] 1958, 82) complained that the theory of public finance "seems to have retained the assumptions of its infancy, in the seventeenth and eighteenth centuries, when absolute power ruled almost all Europe." Absolute power is the possession of an autonomous ruler or state. Such a state might be ruthlessly despotic or it might be relatively benevolent, but it will be autonomous in any case. Sacrifice theories of taxation can be construed in this setting as recipes for the practice of benevolence toward ruled subjects. Wicksell argued that under parliamentary democracies it made no sense to regard subjects as being ruled, for they participated in their own governance through parliamentary institutions. For Wicksell, the challenge to fiscal theorizing was to map the contours of such governance when government was not an agent of intervention into market-generated economic relationships but rather an arena in which people participated in their own governance. What resulted was political economy conceptualized as a seamless garment.

If Wicksell's complaint provides a glimpse into the disjunction between what were to become the Anglo-Saxon and Continental orientations toward public finance, the quarrel between Fredric Benham and Henry C. Simons over their sharply different evaluations of Antonio de Viti de Marco's treatise on public finance starkly exposed that disjunction. This quarrel occurred through Benham's and Simons's dueling book reviews that accompanied the publication in 1934 of de Viti's treatise, *Principii di economia finanziaria*, a book whose central arguments were first formulated in his 1888 book, *Il carattere teorico dell'economia finanziaria*. De Viti's treatise was a major statement of the Continental tradition of public finance, in that it sought to explain the observed phenomena of public finance in terms of economic principles as these play out in a parliamentary institutional setting. It was reviewed in the August 1934 issue of *Economica* by Benham, who asserted that de Viti's book "is probably the best treatise on the theory of public finance ever written" (364). Benham laments that the sorry state of public finance in England, which was dominated by the choice theoretic orientation that Wicksell decried (and which Benham associated with F. Y. Edgeworth and A. C. Pigou), could be improved greatly through a strong infusion of de Viti's orientation. Benham also noted the strong complementarity between the approaches taken by de Viti and Wicksell.

Simons reviewed the English translation of de Viti that appeared in 1936, in the October 1937 issue of the *Journal of Political Economy*. Simons (1937, 712) began by observing that "the Italian literature of public finance has long been held in high esteem; but its claims to distinction have rested mainly upon works which have been inaccessible to those of us who lacked facility with the language. The translations [both German and English translations were being reviewed by Simons[1]] of De Viti's famous treatise are thus doubly welcome, for they will make possible a more informed consensus, both as to the merits of Italian economics and as to competence of the interpretation and appraisal which it has received in other countries."

After describing this initial sense of eager anticipation, Simons offered his judgment: "Careful reading . . . has left the reviewer with no little resentment toward the critics who induced him to search in this treatise for the profound analysis and penetrating insights which it does not contain. The *Principii* is revealed to him, not as a great book, but as a . . . monument to . . . confusion" (713). Simons continued by asserting that "there is not a single section or chapter which the reviewer could conscientiously recommend to the competent student searching for genuine insights and understanding" (713).

Simons concludes by taking on Benham's review three years earlier: "If [de Viti's] book is 'the best treatise on the theory of public finance ever written,' one hopes that it may be the last. . . . To say that it is distinguished among treatises in its field is to . . . comment bitterly on the quality of economic thought in one of its important branches. To call it a great book, however, is a disservice to the cause of higher standards and better orientation in economic inquiry" (716–17).

This clash of appraisals, moreover, cannot be attributed to any kind of ideological clash over the role of government within society, for all three authors adhered to a generally classically liberal orientation in these

1. Actually, the 1932 German translation was of a 1928 edition of de Viti's treatise, whereas the English translation was of the 1934 edition, which is also the version that Benham reviewed.

matters. Simons worked within the Anglo-Saxon orientation of an autonomous state, with public finance serving as an instrument for appropriate intervention into the economic order. For Simons, improvements in public finance entailed improvements in the instruments of intervention. For de Viti, improvements in public finance would correspond to a deeper and more complete understanding of the actual course and pattern of fiscal activity. The intellectual enterprise that de Viti was engaged in was orthogonal to that in which Simons was engaged. There was nothing in de Viti that Simons could regard as providing a means for promoting better intervention, for instead de Viti sought to uncover the underlying economic logic to which governmental action conformed.

Cameralist Origins of Continental Public Finance

As a field of systematic academic inquiry, public finance arose with the cameralists in central Europe in the sixteenth century, as surveyed in Dittrich 1974 and Small 1909. Joseph Schumpeter (1954, 143–208) described the cameralists well when he referred to them as "Consultant Administrators." They were both consultants and administrators. They were consultants to the various kings, princes, and other royal personages who ruled throughout those lands. The term *cameralist* derives from *camera* or *kammer* and refers to the room or chamber where the councillors to the king or prince gathered to do their work. The cameralists were not, however, anything like contemporary academic consultants. They were real-world administrators engaged in such activities as managing mines or glassworks, as well as holding academic posts. Johann Heinrich Gottlob von Justi (1717–1771) is a good case in point. When he was appointed in Vienna, he was appointed in two capacities. First, he was to give lectures (in political rhetoric) at the Theresianum, a school the queen and empress had founded for training future civil servants. Second, he was made a superintendent of mines. Hence he prepared two inaugural lectures to be delivered in front of the empress. One lecture outlined what would become his entire rather complex system of cameralism and public administration, which is presented in Backhaus and Reinert forthcoming. The other lecture treated the organization of mines.

While cameralism has sometimes been described as a Germanic version of mercantilism, the differences between them are surely more notable than the similarities. Both originated within authoritarian political regimes and represented efforts to give good counsel to the heads of those regimes. Mercantilism arose among big players on the international stage: the English, the French, the Spanish, and the Dutch. The ability of these powers to influence events and terms of trade worldwide provided the background for mercantilist thought and practice. The stress on taxation and the prevalence of rent seeking and other forms of venality were products of the big-player standing of the mercantile empires.

In contrast, cameralism arose under conditions of high political fragmentation. The cameralist lands were necessarily price takers on the international scene. There was no concern within the cameralist lands about influencing terms of trade, about the use of colonies as instruments of policy, and about one's relative standing among the preponderant powers. The focal point of cameralist concern was on survival of the regime. Survival required a military capacity and economic development, which in turn required the acquisition of improved technologies, the improvement of human capital, the creation of new enterprises, and the growth of population.

This concern about development took place within regimes that were both absolutist and severely constrained. The prince was the ruler of his lands, and he could hope to pass his principality along to his eldest son. His ability to do this, however, varied directly with the extent of economic progress within his land. A prince whose land was supporting a growing population of energetic and enterprising subjects would both be wealthier and face better survival prospects than a prince of a land where the population was stagnant or declining, and whose subjects were dull and lethargic. Furthermore, population was mobile in fact, even if it was mostly tied formally to the land through feudal restrictions. Distances between lands were typically short. A peasant who traveled to a new land was not likely to be returned. In fact, it was the common law at the time that after a year plus a day, a peasant who had left the land and stayed in a city would be granted citizen's rights there. The rulers of the cameralist lands faced a competitive labor market. Indeed, the cameralist lands represented a kind of competitive industry among localized governments, much as Charles Tiebout (1956) tried to characterize some three hundred years later.

For cameralist public finance, state lands and enterprises were principal sources of revenue. If one were to construct a model of the cameralist vision of the state, it would look like a model of a business firm. Forests could be harvested,[2] game could be caught, and mines could be built

2. Actually, forestry as a science is just one aspect of cameralism. See Pfeiffer 1781.

and worked. The prince would also sponsor an assortment of commercial enterprises, including such things as the operation of a glassworks or a brewery. Taxes were a distinctly secondary source of revenue. Even in the late nineteenth century, enterprise revenues and not taxes were the primary source of state income in the formerly cameralist lands (Backhaus and Wagner 1987).

The cameralists' general predisposition against taxation as an instrument of public finance reflects an orientation that the state acts as a participant within the economic order. Individuals had their property and the state had its property. The state should be able to use its property to generate the revenues required to finance its activities. Or at least those enterprise revenues should support the major portion of state activity. Some of the cameralists argued that taxes should be earmarked for the support of the military, while all activities for internal development should be financed from the prince's net commercial revenues. In any case, a state contains many business enterprises within its boundaries, and with the state itself operating a subset of those enterprises. It was understood that the state would have significant expenses associated with its activities. These expenses, however, were not to become drains on the private means of subjects. They were to be met from the lands and enterprises that constituted the state's property. For instance, to achieve a particular objective in a sustainable way it was rather common to assign a revenue source such as a vineyard to a public hospital.

Revenues, of course, are only one side of the fiscal account. The cameralists also devoted much thought to the expenditure side. Much of that discussion had a kind of capital theoretic quality to it, where programs of expenditure today would generate increased revenue tomorrow. A great deal of the cameralist emphasis was placed on what is now called human capital, though it would not be appropriate to import too much of a conceptual framework into the cameralist writings. A good deal of this emphasis stemmed from the concern with population. A growing population was desirable, to be sure, but that population in turn had to possess useful skills and talents, good health, and an industrious attitude.

From Cameralism to Continental Public Finance

In both the cameralist and the mercantilist lands, the material of public finance was conceptualized in choice theoretic terms. While the rulers of the mercantilist empires faced different opportunities and constraints than did the rulers of the cameralist lands, the phenomena of public finance were the products of ruler's choices in both settings. Throughout the nineteenth century, however, parliamentary regimes were becoming increasingly common. It was in this context that Wicksell voiced his complaint about the outdated political presumptions of public finance theorizing. To be sure, Wicksell's complaint came perhaps a little late, at least with respect to Continental public finance, for the changes in political regimes were already being accompanied by changes in the orientation of fiscal scholars toward their inquiries, even as illustrated already by Christian Freiherr von Wolff (1740). The phenomena of public finance came increasingly to be treated not as simple choices by some ruler but as the emergent outcomes of complex processes of interaction within various forms of parliamentary governance, perhaps as would be conveyed by a notion of catallactical public finance.

In treating a catallactical orientation as the defining characteristic of Continental public finance as it emerged in the late nineteenth century, we are mapping the world of fiscal scholarship somewhat differently from that presented in Orhan Kayaalp's (2004) treatment of the history of fiscal theorizing. Kayaalp argues that fiscal thought can be organized coherently along five national lines. What we describe as the Anglo-Saxon orientation corresponds to Kayaalp's portrayal of British fiscal thought in terms of the sacrifice approach to taxation. The sacrifice approach is independent of regime and entails an autonomous state. Kayaalp further distinguishes among Italian, German, Austrian, and Swedish fiscal theorizing, all of which we treat under the rubric of Continental public finance because we think the similarities far exceed the differences. Kayaalp associates the benefit approach with Italian public finance, an emphasis on marginal utility with Austrian public finance, and a focus on institutional arrangements for collective choice with Swedish public finance. Yet all three of these elements were combined throughout the contributions to Continental public finance regardless of national origin. Although at the time scholarly citations were not common, it is obvious that Continental authors read each other's work carefully.

We should also note that Kayaalp treats German public finance as being animated by a vision of an organic state, which would place it outside the Continental orientation and would locate it instead within the domain of sacrifice theorizing and an autonomous state. This placement might have characterized a few cameralist writers from a didactic point of view, but it did not characterize German public finance as it took shape during the latter part of the nineteenth century, as we explain below. Indeed, great care must be taken not to misunderstand what was "organic" about the formulations of these authors. While "organic" notions are systematically used in Fichte 1800 and Schäffle 1878, and also to some extent in Wagner 1883, they are always used for illustrative purposes only and never as analytical arguments.

It is possible to use a language that speaks of states as responding to public needs without holding a vision of an autonomous or organic state. Object-oriented programming provides a good lesson in this respect. Mitchel Resnick (1994) gives a nice example in this respect. Consider a simple computer model of cars moving along a highway. When drivers enter the highway, they follow the rule of speeding up until they get within, say, five car lengths of the preceding car, after which they maintain that distance. This generates a model of an evenly spaced parade of cars crossing the computer screen. Into this stationary state inject some such action as a driver suddenly slowing down, perhaps because he or she is distracted by a wasp that has flown into the car. This single action creates a chain reaction among the following drivers. A traffic jam results, and this jam is an object in its own right along with the individual cars. The individual cars continue to move forward. The jam itself, however, moves backward. It would not make any sense to speak of the jam as if it were a gigantic car moving backward, for all of the individual cars within the jam are moving forward. The jam does reflect the actions of the drivers who comprise the jam, only the relationship among the drivers is interactive and not additive. To treat the jam as an object in its own right is not to treat it as organic or autonomous, for it emerges out of complex patterns of interaction. Modern computational techniques now allow us to probe the generation of such patterns in ways not possible a century ago.[3]

As parliaments came to first complement, then replace kings and princes, a transformation occurred in the pattern of property relationships and the associated patterns of governance. The sphere of private property expanded while the property holdings of states contracted. Taxes became more significant sources of revenue; state enterprises provided relatively less revenue. The state as a political entity was no longer

3. The entire picture of public finance practice can be described in terms of the driver who had to slow down, but it can also be described from the point of view of those drivers who have their destination in mind and move ahead anyway. To the extent this maneuvering was theory induced, it is part of what this essay tries to emphasize. See Seckendorff [1665] 1976.

independent of the individual citizens whose activities constituted the market economy, for those same citizens represented both the polity and the economy.[4] This transformation of political regime called for an effort to bring the phenomena of public finance within the same analytical framework as the phenomena of the market economy, taking due account of differences in institutional and organizational arrangements. Hence, scholars within the Continental orientation sought to explain fiscal patterns in terms of such concepts as subjective value, entrepreneurship, and political-economic equilibrium.

A Quick Excursion into Continental Public Finance

In this section we shall describe briefly a few examples from Continental public finance to illustrate our claim about a common orientation across national boundaries. That orientation centered on the desire to render sensible the fiscal activities of states within a framework of mutual determination of polity and economy. In this section, we shall treat briefly some selected figures who contributed to Continental public finance. Our purpose here is twofold. On the one hand, we seek to characterize the general, commonly held orientation toward public finance. On the other hand, we seek to illustrate some of the differences of analytical detail that found expression within this commonly shared orientation. Hence, we shall first consider some of the seminal Italian contributions, after which we move to the northern end of the Continent to examine Knut Wicksell, and then finish our excursion in the center of the Continent by examining some German and Austrian contributions.

Italian Fiscal Scholarship

The period roughly bounded by 1880 and 1940 was one of great flourishing for Italian scholarship on public finance.[5] The Italian scholars treated

4. Some rulers even in the twentieth century were proud not to levy taxes. Letters of tax forgiving are common as Christmas presents shortly before World War I, for example, in the two Mecklenburgs. The principality of Schaumburg-Lippe prides itself on never having levied taxes. The Kingdom of Prussia earned more than 50 percent of its revenues from public (competitive) enterprises, not including state monopolies. These revenues, in Wicksell's terms, are *consensual*, not imposed.

5. See, for instance, the 2003 special issue of *Il pensiero economico italiano*, which is titled "The Theory of Public Finance in Italy from the Origins to the 1940s."

public finance not just as one specialized field among several within economics, but as an independent object of study, partly in economics but also concerned with politics, law, and administration as well. Central to their analytical framework was the incorporation of the state into the economic process, along with the universal application of such economic categories as utility and profit across all organizational arrangements within society.

For instance, the ability of political enterprises to expand will depend on their ability to attract patronage. They might attract that patronage through their ability to exploit economies of scale or to provide services that people are willing to support, but which were somehow not being otherwise provided.[6] This would correspond to standard formulations of public goods theory. They might also attract patronage through subsidizing supporters at the expense of other, less influential members of society, as noted with particular clarity by Giovanni Montemartini (1900). The size and scope of political enterprises reflect the same economic principles as operate within the market economy, save only that those principles play out differently within different institutional regimes. The central analytical task in any case was to render sensible the complex and whole economic organization of society, as illustrated crisply in chapter 7 of Joseph Schumpeter's *Theorie der wirtschaftlichen Entwicklung* (1911; see Backhaus 2003).

The Italian tradition in public finance was soberly realistic. Whether people will support market or state provision of particular services will depend on which source of supply is less expensive to them. State provision may be cheaper for some people yet more expensive for others. If so, divisions of opinion will exist, with the outcome to be resolved through the exercise of political power as this is channeled and organized within some particular political framework. Whether the resulting outcomes are thought to be beautiful or ugly when appraised against some normative standard is beside the point.

Maffeo Pantaleoni (1883) sought to bring the budgetary actions of parliaments within the purview of the economic categories of utility, cost, and exchange. Particularly interesting in this regard was the emphasis he gave to the accretion of institutions and procedures over time as economizing devices that rendered manageable what would otherwise have been overwhelming complexity. In this, Pantaleoni recognized that

6. For instance, because of credit market restrictions, the state was the better debtor in these times.

budgeting was incremental and not zero-based. His treatment of parliament could perhaps be assimilated to that of a peculiar form of investment bank. Parliament was an intermediary that facilitated the organization of complex exchanges that brought together people who had programs for which they were seeking support with sources of support for those programs, recognizing, of course, that the offers of support typically were not volunteered.

Some years later, Pantaleoni (1911) treated the state as generating a system of political prices that existed parasitically on the system of prices generated through market relationships. For the most part, each buyer pays the same market price. For political pricing, however, each buyer may well pay a personally unique price. Political prices are in any event discriminatory prices, with the pattern of discrimination being dependent on the particular pattern of taxation being employed. In Pantaleoni's model, political prices could only exist parasitically, with market prices serving as the host. One interesting feature of Pantaleoni's formulation, noted in Wagner 1997b, is that there is a kind of natural limit to the extent of political pricing that inheres in the parasite-host relationship that political pricing entails.

The classic Italian orientation toward public finance is catallactical. The phenomena of public finance arise through interaction among fiscal participants. Those participants might comprise only a small subset of the society, as illustrated by models where ruling classes govern the masses. In other settings, those participants might include everyone in society, as illustrated by models of cooperative democracy. In any case, fiscal phenomena are objects to be subjected to scientific explanation just as surely as are market phenomena. The size of state budgets, the distribution of those budgets across programs, and the sources of revenue used are all objects for fiscal explanation within the Italian orientation.

Knut Wicksell and Catallactical Public Finance

Knut Wicksell's contribution to public finance, *Finanztheoretische Untersuchungen* (1896), contained three essays, the second of which made Wicksell a household word among public finance scholars after it was translated and published as "A New Principle of Just Taxation" in *Classics in the Theory of Public Finance* (1958), edited by Richard Musgrave and Alan Peacock. The first of Wicksell's three essays analyzed tax incidence while making use of Eugen von Böhm-Bawerk's framework of a structure of production. Wicksell's third essay, which occupied nearly half of the book, examined Swedish fiscal history, where Wicksell argued that the new principle he articulated in his second essay was congruent with various strands of Swedish historical tradition, as well as being capable of implementation in the Sweden of his time.

Wicksell's ([1896] 1958) second essay, on a new principle of just taxation, has been the main source of Wicksell's reputation in public finance. This essay asked what kind of institutional framework for parliamentary governance might make it possible for the state to act as a productive participant within the economic life of a society. Hardly anyone would dispute the statement that a government should expand its services so long as the value created exceeds the cost that people must bear through the value they must sacrifice to pay for those services. But how might this outcome be achieved? Wicksell sought to describe an institutional framework that would promote such an outcome, and in so doing showed how the Pareto principle could be made applicable to the state, which is something that Pareto did not think possible, as Pieter Hennipman (1962) notes.

The Wicksellian approach construes the state as a participant within the economic process. The state itself is a process or a framework of rules and procedures that governs human relationships. Fiscal phenomena do not result from the optimizing choices of some exogenous being but rather emerge through interactions among participants within various fiscal and political processes. Those interactions, in turn, are shaped and constrained by conventions, institutions, and organizational rules. Fiscal phenomena, like market phenomena, are catallactical and not choice theoretic phenomena.[7] The size and extent of governmental activity, within the Wicksellian orientation, is to be explained with references to the same principles used to explain other features of economic activity within a society. The same categories of utility, cost, demand, supply, production, and the like that are used to explain market phenomena are to be brought to bear on the explanation of fiscal phenomena.

Wicksell's particular institutional interest was his effort to describe a network of institutional relationships that would make it possible for

7. We should note that we are not using *catallactical* as a synonym for *voluntary*, but as an antonym for *choice*. Fiscal phenomena involve a mixture of exchange and duress, both of which we regard as catallactical, as distinct from choice theoretic phenomena. See, for instance, Wagner 1997a.

people in their capacities as taxpayers reasonably to say that their tax payments were directed as they wished. The ability for people to say this would locate government on the same plane as other economic participants. Wicksell assumed that through proportional representation it would be possible to select a parliament that would serve reasonably well as a miniature model of the Swedish population. If this parliament were then bound by a rule of unanimity, its decisions would conform closely to unanimity within the underlying population. The state would participate within the economic process on the same terms as other participants. Its size relative to that of other organizations in society would depend on the effectiveness of its officers in gaining acceptance for proposals in parliament, relative to the ability of other producers to gain favor from people.

Wicksell articulated a principle of unanimity, which he relaxed to a practical rule of approximate unanimity. Wicksell recognized that this shift to approximate unanimity involved the creation of a trade-off. True unanimity would ensure that people would not have to pay taxes for activities they were not willing to support. But it would also prove costly to any effort of trying truly to work out arrangements for collective support. Some modest movement away from unanimity might, Wicksell thought, be a reasonable compromise to expediency. James Buchanan and Gordon Tullock (1962) subsequently converted this compromise to expediency into a framework for constitutional analysis, which can be traced through to the contemporary scholarship on public choice and constitutional economics, as Richard Wagner (1988) explains.

Wicksell accepted Adolph Wagner's treatment of the state as a form of enterprise and sought to articulate a framework for governance that would more closely align principle and practice. In this, there is an often overlooked relationship between Wicksell's new principle of just taxation and the older tradition from Justi to Wagner that emphasized state entrepreneurship. When the crown offers a particular public service for adoption, it has to propose a scheme of taxation that closely fits the beneficiaries of this service. To the extent this fit is successful, near unanimity can be secured in parliament. This requires, however, that the landscape of political parties closely corresponds to different social groups that can be clearly distinguished in terms of their demands for particular services and for purposes of taxation. When that approach fails, and unanimity cannot be secured, the only recourse left is for the crown, acting in its capacity as the producer of goods and services for the public, to act entrepreneurially and finance the activity through the revenue generated by state enterprises.

Staatswissenschaften: The Germanic Science of State

Adolph Wagner (1883), perhaps the best-known figure in the *Staatswissenschaften* tradition, took account of the changes in political and property relationships over the preceding two centuries while carrying forward the cameralist orientation toward the state as a participant *within* society, as against being an intervening agent that acts *on* society. In particular, Wagner conceptualized the state as a type of enterprise located within the economy, though it was of a different sort from most commercial enterprises. In this respect, Wagner argued repeatedly that such state enterprises as railroads and mines can often pursue a leadership role in such areas as occupational safety, stimulating changes among private firms in the process (Backhaus 1997).

To contemporary readers, Wagner is best known for what is now described as Wagner's law of the increasing relative size of government. These days, Wagner's law is almost uniformly presented as meaning that the income elasticity of demand for state services exceeds unity. A large literature has emerged over roughly the past half century that brings increasingly sophisticated econometrical techniques to bear on probing the income elasticity of demand for state output, as a means of testing the applicability of Wagner's law. The first thing that should be said about this is that Wagner advanced no such formulation. He presented no quantitative statements whatsoever pertaining to income elasticity of demand. What he did was describe the changing patterns of property relationships over the preceding few centuries and explore what he thought were their implications for human governance. Over those centuries, state-held property had diminished in economic significance while the sphere of alienable private property had expanded.

This transformation in property relationships led to Wagner's effort to articulate a process of *qualitative* change in the types of activities undertaken by governments. Qualitative changes might, of course, correspond to quantitative increases in some measure of relative economic size, but they need not. For instance, people might initially draw their water from wells and deposit wastewater in septic fields. With increasing population density, conflicts among people over water would surely intensify, and this in turn would elicit state involvement. That involvement might entail governmental provision of water and sewerage facilities, thus increasing the G/GDP ratio. Alternatively, that involvement might entail governmental facilitation of the formation of new forms of cooperative enterprise that would have little or no impact on a G/GDP ratio. There would be a *qualitative* change in either case. The further and further extension of the state's tasks (*Aufgaben*) may very well involve an increase in state spending (*Ausgaben*), but this is not necessarily so. Wagner's emphasis is qualitative and oriented toward public entrepreneurship, which he sees simultaneously as a font of technological innovation and a source of revenue. Indeed, during the years when he wrote, half of the revenues of the Kingdom of Prussia stemmed from its railroad.

The changing character of property relationships and their implications for public finance were central to the legendary debate that took place between the two Austrians, Rudolf Goldscheid and Joseph Schumpeter, that is collected in Hickel 1976. It was during this debate that Goldscheid coined the term *fiscal sociology*, the contemporary relevance of which is sketched in Backhaus 2002. The particular topic of controversy was what to do with Austria's public debt at the conclusion of World War I and the breakup of the Hapsburg Empire. Behind this particular point of contention, however, lay two contrasting perspectives on property and public finance. For Schumpeter, the debt could be discharged through an extraordinary tax levy, with the bonds being incinerated and the matter put to rest. In contrast, Goldscheid argued for a recapitalization of the state, after which the state would once again, as in cameralist times, possess property whose revenues would provide the means to support state activities.

This debate about property and the state relates directly to Georgist-type arguments in support of site-value taxation. A state that provides services that make location there more desirable will experience rising land values because of the resulting increased demand for residency there. A tax on site values would not be a tax in the ordinary sense of the word, but would rather be a charge for those state-supplied services that elicited the increased demand for residency. As Fred Foldvary (1994) and Spencer MacCallum (1970) explain, it is the same for hotels, shopping centers, and other forms of privately organized community. For instance, a hotel offers a tied sale of a room and such public goods as security services, elevator transit, and parklike amenities. Those public goods increase the demand for residency within the hotel, which is expressed through a higher price that residents are willing to pay.

Public Choice and Continental Public Finance

During the great flourishing for Continental public finance from roughly 1880 to 1940, German and Italian were the primary languages through which the Continental orientation was expressed. The calamitous events surrounding Adolf Hitler and World War II had the side effect of dispersing many of those contributors elsewhere. This dispersal was accompanied by the rise of English as the lingua franca of economic scholarship. The Continental orientation continued to develop in the postwar period, only much of this development now occurred under the name of public choice and not public finance. Indeed, in most of the textbook literature today, public finance is presented as an admixture of Continental and Anglo-Saxon orientations, as illustrated nicely in such textbooks as Cullis and Jones 1998 and Blankart 2001. It is readily apparent from a perusal of contemporary texts in public finance that the two orientations have not been blended, for their respective analytical strands remain distinct and visible, although the texts differ in the relative emphasis they give to the two orientations.

In the postwar period the Continental orientation has been carried forward under the heading of public choice. Public choice is not truly a new formation on the intellectual landscape but rather a renamed extension of the Continental orientation, as Richard Wagner (2003) explains with reference to Italian fiscal theorizing in particular. For instance, Pantaleoni's (1883) effort to model budgetary outcomes with reference to the average intelligence within parliament, along with his emphasis on incremental accretion of conventions, resonates strongly with such recent public choice formulations as probabilistic voting (Hettich and Winer 1999; Coughlin and Nitzan 1981), democratic efficiency (Wittman 1995; Becker 1983), and incremental budgeting (Wildavsky 1984; Kraan 1996).

Amilcare Puviani's (1903) work on fiscal illusion has never been translated into English, though Buchanan (1967, 126–43) presents a précis. Puviani's work was, however, translated into German in 1960, and in his foreword to that translation Gunter Schmölders states that "over the last century Italian public finance has had an essentially political science character. The political character of fiscal activity stands always in the foreground. . . . This work [Puviani] is a typical product of Italian public finance, especially a typical product at the end of the 19th century. Above all, it is the science of public finance combined with fiscal politics, in many places giving a good fit with reality" (8). Where Schmölders speaks of political science and political character in connection with Italian public finance, he was referring to what subsequently came to be called public choice. The Continental orientation toward fiscal phenomena exhibits continuous development to the present, only it has undergone a change in name in the postwar period, from public finance to public choice.

References

Backhaus, Jürgen G. 1997. *Essays on Social Security and Taxation: Gustav von Schmoller and Adolph Wagner Reconsidered.* Marburg: Metropolis.

———. 2002. Fiscal Sociology: What For? *American Journal of Economics and Sociology* 61.1:55–77.

———. 2003. *Joseph Alois Schumpeter: Entrepreneurship, Style, and Vision.* Norwell, Mass.: Kluwer.

Backhaus, Jürgen, and Eric Reinert, eds. Forthcoming. *Johann Heinrich Gottlob von Justi.* Hildesheim: Olms.

Backhaus, Jürgen G., and Richard E. Wagner. 1987. The Cameralists: A Public Choice Perspective. *Public Choice* 53:3–20.

Becker, Gary. 1983. A Theory of Competition among Pressure Groups for Political Influence. *Quarterly Journal of Economics* 98:371–400.

Benham, Fredric. 1934. Review of *Principii di economia finanziaria*, by Antonio de Viti de Marco. *Economica*, n.s., 1:364–67.

Blankart, Charles B. 2001. *Öffentliche Finanzen in der Demokratie.* 4th ed. Munich: Vahlen.

Buchanan, James M. 1967. *Public Finance in Democratic Process.* Chapel Hill: University of North Carolina Press.

Buchanan, James M., and Gordon Tullock. 1962. *The Calculus of Consent.* Ann Arbor: University of Michigan Press.

Coughlin, Peter J., and S. Nitzan. 1981. Electoral Outcomes with Probabilistic Voting and Nash Social Welfare Maxima. *Journal of Public Economics* 15:113–22.

Cullis, John G., and Philip R. Jones. 1998. *Public Finance and Public Choice.* 2nd ed. Oxford: Oxford University Press.

De Viti de Marco, Antonio. 1888. *Il carattere teorico dell'economia.* Rome: Pasqualucci.

———. 1936. *First Principles of Public Finance.* London: Cape.

Dittrich, Erhard. 1974. *Die deutschen und österreichischen Kameralisten.* Darmstadt: Wissenschaftliche Buchgesellschaft.

Fichte, Johann Gottlieb. 1800. *Der geschlossene Handelsstaat.* Munich: Saur.

Foldvary, Fred. 1994. *Public Goods and Private Communities.* Hants: Elgar.

Hennipman, Pieter. 1982. Wicksell and Pareto: Their Relationship in the Theory of Public Finance. *HOPE* 14.1:37–64.

Hettich, Walter, and Stanley Winer. 1999. *Democratic Choice and Taxation*. Cambridge: Cambridge University Press.

Hickel, Rudolf, ed. 1976. *Finanzkrise des Steuerstaats: Beiträge zur politischen Ökonomischer Staatsfinanzen*. Frankfurt am Main: Suhrkamp.

Jha, Raghbendra. 1998. *Modern Public Economics*. London: Routledge.

Kayaalp, Orhan. 2004. *The National Element in the Development of Fiscal Theory*. New York: Palgrave Macmillan.

Kraan, Dirk-Jan. 1996. *Budgetary Decisions: A Public Choice Analysis*. Cambridge: Cambridge University Press.

MacCallum, Spencer H. 1970. *The Art of Community*. Menlo Park, Calif.: Institute for Humane Studies.

Montemartini, Giovanni. 1900. Le basi fondamentali della scienza finanziaria pura. *Giornale degli economisti* 21:555–76.

Musgrave, Richard A., and Alan T. Peacock, eds. 1958. *Classics in the Theory of Public Finance*. London: Macmillan.

Pantaleoni, Maffeo. 1883. Contributo alla teoria del riparto delle spese pubbliche. *Rassegna italiana* 15:25–70.

———. 1911. Considerazioni sulle proprieta di un sistema di prezzi politici. *Giornale degli economisti* 42:9–29, 114–33.

Pfeiffer, Johann Friedrich von. 1781. *Grundris der Forstwissenschaft zum Gebrauch dirigirender Forst- und Kameralbedienten, auch Privatgutsbesitzern*. Mannheim: Schwan.

Puviani, Amilcare. 1903. *Teoria della illusione finanziaria*. Palermo: Sandron.

Resnick, Mitchel. 1994. *Turtles, Termites, and Traffic Jams*. Cambridge, Mass.: MIT Press.

Schäffle, Albert. 1878. *Bau und Leben des socialen Körpers*. Tübingen: Laupp.

Schmölders, Gunter. 1960. Foreword to *Die Illusionen in der öffentlichen Finanzwirtschaft*, by Amilcare Puviani. Translated by Marianne Hartmann and Felix Rexhausen. Berlin: Duncker & Humblot.

Schumpeter, Joseph A. 1954. *History of Economic Analysis*. New York: Oxford University Press.

Seckendorff, Ludwig Veit von. [1665] 1976. *Teutscher Fürsten Stat*. Reprint, Glashütten: Auvermann.

Simons, Henry C. 1936. Review of *First Principles of Public Finance*, by Antonio de Viti de Marco. *Journal of Political Economy* 45:712–17.

Small, Albion. 1909. *The Cameralists: The Pioneers of German Social Polity*. New York: Franklin.

Tiebout, Charles M. 1956. A Pure Theory of Local Expenditures. *Journal of Political Economy* 64:416–24.

Wagner, Adolph. 1883. *Finanzwissenschaft*. 3rd ed. Leipzig: Winter.

Wagner, Richard E. 1988. The Calculus of Consent: A Wicksellian Retrospective. *Public Choice* 56:153–66.

———. 1997a. Choice, Exchange, and Public Finance. *American Economic Review*, Proceedings. 87:160–63.

———. 1997b. Parasitical Political Pricing, Economic Calculation, and the Size of Government: Variations on a Theme by Maffeo Pantaleoni. *Journal of Public Finance and Public Choice* 15:135–46.

———. 2003. Public Choice and the Diffusion of Classic Italian Public Finance. *Il pensiero economico* 11:271–82.

Wicksell, Knut. 1896. *Finanztheoretische Untersuchungen debst Darstellung und Kritik des Steuersystems Schwedens*. Jena: Fischer.

———. [1896] 1958. A New Principle of Just Taxation. In Musgrave and Peacock 1958.

Wildavsky, Aaron. 1984. *Politics of the Budgetary Process*. 4th ed. Boston: Little Brown.

Wittman, Donald. 1995. *The Myth of Democratic Failure*. Chicago: University of Chicago Press.

Wolff, Christian Freiherr von. 1740. Von einer Erwegung der Staatsgeschäfte. In *Gesammlete kleine philosophische Schriften*. Halle: Renger.

Corporatism and the Economic Role of Government

António Almodovar and José Luís Cardoso

In the interwar years several different conceptions of what a proper economic system should look like emerged, producing a rationale for a more significant economic role of government. Though inspired by different ideological and philosophical presuppositions, and pertaining to different national traditions of thought, such conceptions all strongly criticized the neoclassical belief in the self-healing properties of market equilibrium through the action of a purely spontaneous mechanism.[1] In this regard, since socialism was already known to be a possible alternative to the traditional liberal political and economic agenda (see Schumpeter [1942] 1976, 340), special attention should be given to the visions of partially alternative economic systems put forward by authors ready to finish with some of the political or economic tenets of the traditional liberal worldview but unwilling to embrace an unambiguous socialist doctrine.

Such was the case of the corporatists, who were ready to abandon extreme individualism while holding to individual property rights. And it was also the case of John Maynard Keynes, who was ready to accept the importance of a certain kind of political body (corporations) that could fill the existing gap between individuals and the state, and give an impulse to a necessary socialization of both consumption and investment.

We wish to thank Roger Backhouse, Brad Bateman, Steve Medema, Warren Samuels, and an anonymous referee for their helpful comments and suggestions. All translations from Portuguese and Italian into English are ours. The usual disclaimer applies.

1. As a matter of fact, this was more a liberal or Manchesterian notion than an original neoclassical one. Notwithstanding, the neoclassical economists, either as a school of thought or as an emerging mainstream school in economics, could be considered as the most likely inheritors of this nineteenth-century dogma (see Morgan and Rutherford 1998).

But even though the corporatists and Keynes did not believe in full-fledged laissez-faire, and thought that practical political reasons ought to prevail over the old established belief in the market's self-adjusting properties, they were unwilling to accept the pure and simple suppression either of capitalism or of the market system.

Contrary to the open debate about the likely survival of a socialist planned economy, which was generally perceived as a conflict between two entirely opposite systems, the discussion of reformers and third-way supporters was not, during the inter- and postwar periods, particularly active. All the same, it is possible to identify some major differences among those scholars and politicians who, although refusing to subscribe to a full socialist option, shared nevertheless a considerable lack of respect toward the conventional liberal (and neoclassical) views on how to balance social harmony and welfare with economic efficiency and steady progress.

The present essay deals with the debate over the proper political and economic rationale of economic organization and state intervention in the interwar years. During this period many economists questioned the classical liberal vision of the state and explored several alternatives for the economic role of government. These included socialism, which is well known, and corporatism, which has not received so far the attention it deserves. The corporatist movement was especially important in Italy and Portugal, though its historical significance and impact goes far beyond its original, fairly limited geographic frontiers. Corporatism is indeed closely related to the indicative planning movement in France, to aspects of the New Deal in the United States, and, generally speaking, to any economic and social policy issues about the building up of the welfare state. The corporatist alternative gave a much larger role to the state and was supported by philosophical and economic arguments. This essay explores the nature and history of corporatism, why it developed and why it eventually died out, or, more precisely, how it was partially integrated into the Keynes consensus that emerged from the post–World War II period.

Corporatism: A New Challenge to Liberal and Neoclassical Economic Principles

The development of economic ideas in the early twentieth century witnessed a variety of competing schools of thought that could roughly be divided into a proliberal approach and a prosocialist approach. This division took place in an atmosphere that favored the emergence of several different species of eclecticism, because of the more or less diffuse influence of the German historical school's criticisms of both classical political economy and its unsustainable version of liberalism.

This trend was particularly evident within current public opinion in some Continental countries, where the simultaneous acknowledgment of some version of the German historical school and the belated institutionalization of neoclassical economics may be partly explained by the public reluctance to accept the evolution of a theoretical and doctrinal discourse. Such a discourse seemed to be based not only on the idea that unplanned market equilibrium could always be reached through the free action of rational, calculating, optimizing economic agents but also on the claim that every other imaginary solution was necessarily worse. Regardless of the effects of an ever-possible lack of theoretical aptitude or analytical vocation, barriers to the acceptance of neoclassical economics among lay people and political agents were above all raised not against the new analytical constructs per se,[2] but mainly against the persistence of the dogma of a munificent self-regulating market mechanism and the incorporated belief in its overall social and political virtues.

The misgivings that we refer to here, once coupled with the long-established propensity of economists to disagree, would unsurprisingly lead to the clash of the neoclassical views with the pressing social and political awareness that prevailed during the interwar years. In an age of open long-lasting crisis, when people gradually start to lose their faith in the possibility of resuming their old livelihood, any conventional, dogmatic liberal stance was logically at pains to counteract the growing strength of the ideologies of alternative programs of economic organization. The followers of these alternative programs could reasonably argue that time and circumstances had finally come for people—and politicians—to try something different.

Those who were to advocate a corporatist solution had therefore at their disposal an atmosphere generically favorable to the proposal of new solutions for contemporary pressing problems—be it the labor question,

2. Although in different terms, the debate about the proper seat for political economy—either as a moral science, a branch of jurisprudence, or alternatively as a close ally of the natural sciences—was already considerably long when corporatist authors presented their own conceptions. If we look at Ugo Spirito's ([1933] 1934, 247–79) criticism of the misuse of mathematics by economists, it is fairly obvious that it is not as harsh as criticisms of the liberal dogmas.

the threatening development of socialism, or the seemingly rampant social and political instability. Furthermore, they were also in a position to take up and reorganize an immense cluster of previously developed arguments in order to build their own system. Departing from the objective contemporary evidence of social and political unrest, corporatist thinkers could rely on the ethical and social concerns previously expressed in 1891 by Leo XIII in the encyclical *Rerum Novarum*, or even on the social and economic disquisitions of several different types of nineteenth-century Catholic thinkers.[3] They could also use the nationalist and historicist revival fostered by the German historical school or the arguments for and against the emergence of trusts and monopolies to point out the existence of a new economic reality that could no longer be explained by traditional political economy. Last but not least, they could take on the political arguments put forward by all those who thought that democracy and mass political participation was one of the major causes of social unrest and political anarchy. On the whole, the corporatists were in a position where the major problems were those of selecting the suitable arguments and trying to systematize them into a single coherent and comprehensive proposal.

One possible path, along the ethical lines previously developed by Catholic thinkers, was to move from the ongoing discussion about the social or labor question to a more general assault on the liberal economic principle that the market could provide adequate means for sustainable human development, or even be able to properly assess and reward the individual contributions made by economic agents to both production and consumption processes. Going a little further, they could criticize the very notion of economic agents, namely, when individuals were relegated to the morally objectionable role of acting as a selfish, utility-driven *homo economicus*.

Such a concept, even if it was nothing but a concept, could serve as a fine example of what could be considered as the ongoing process of gradual destruction of human dignity and purpose in the hands of political economists. Moreover, they could even point out that the functioning of an extremely individualistic economic system, where persons were conceived and treated both as a kind of amoral automaton and as mere

3. Detailed information on the evolution of Christian and Catholic economic reasoning and action within France may be found in Battini 1995. Regarding Italy, De Rosa 2003 is quite useful. Abram L. Harris's (1958) essay on Heinrich Pesch also deserves to be mentioned here. For a general contemporary appraisal, see Turmann 1909 and Rist and Gide 1917.

commodities, was at the very origin of both socialism and communism. And, as a matter of fact, corporatist authors eventually deemed the liberal philosophy underlying capitalism and its political economy not only as responsible for the collapse of the social fabric but also for the emergence of socialism and communism, its inevitable and no less harmful counterparts.

Another possible path, now along the lines of nationalism and historicism, was to criticize the cosmopolitanism present both in classical political economy and in its socialist equivalent. Such cosmopolitanism could be considered as a serious threat to national cohesion and development, namely because as a rule this view was coupled with the utterly unacceptable liberal idea that the state could and should refrain from assuming a leading role in ensuring the proper economic and social development of a nation. This line of reasoning could either lead just to an argument against free trade and in favor of protectionism or otherwise be coupled with an array of additional arguments that would question the meaning of democracy and of existing systems of political and social representation. Unsurprisingly, this path would lead in due course to rethink the meaning of social classes and class interests and to a tentative reorganization of the established relationships between the individuals, the nation, and the state.

Corporatism envisaged as an inclusive economic system—either as a third way alternative or just as a different economic system—was therefore to be the result of a combination of different arguments and criticisms mainly directed not against capitalism per se but against its evils or excesses: excessive individualism, excessive democracy, excessive abstraction, excessive materialism, excessive liberalism, and excessive socialism included.

Since assembling this system took place across the interwar years—and was far from being fully standardized across both time and space when the allied victory of World War II put an end to the regimes that could be considered as tangible examples of corporatism[4]—there is no obvious single model that can be offered as a standard example of corporatism. Even so, it is possible both to highlight the essential theses advanced by some of its most renowned promoters and also to draw a fairly

4. There is a huge amount of literature relating to fascism and Nazism and to other authoritarian regimes that emerged during the interwar years. However, as we do not deal with those regimes in this essay but just with their eventual underlying corporatist views, most of that literature may be considered irrelevant for our present purposes.

accurate picture of the contemporarily perceived divergences within corporatist supporters.

Corporatism Defined

One of the main original interwar advocates of corporatism—now conceived not just as a mere expedient to ease the problems raised by the labor question but as a truly alternative system—was the Italian philosopher Ugo Spirito. According to him, corporatism not only represented a proposal for a new economic and social order but also implied the establishment of a new scientific device for explaining social and economic life. His main arguments (Spirito [1933] 1934) were directed against the shallow neoclassical notion of *homo economicus*, for he thought that its underlying principle—selfish individualism—ought to be replaced by a more socially responsible ethos to abridge the unacceptable value gap that existed between individual egotistic motivations and state comprehensive goals. This was a distinctive philosophical principle, noticeably quite different from the principles of logical positivism and utilitarian individualism that were embedded not only in neoclassical economics but also in several other schools of economic thought. Even so, Spirito thought that the fulfillment of self-interests could only be acceptable if in synchronization with national interest, which he defined as the common essence and motivation that was to be deciphered and properly safeguarded by the state.

As a consequence of this new philosophical foundation, the traditional notion of *homo economicus* was to be replaced by the notion of *homo corporativus*, so that a new and more accurate economic science could eventually emerge. The typical self-interest of the traditional economic agent was therefore to be replaced by an interested concern with the national, common values and objectives, and instrumental rationality would consequently apply within a broader institutional context—where individuals would be acting while citizens within the new framework of the corporations. Moreover, since individuals would start to operate within a less individualistic environment, their own personal abilities to choose and decide according to the rules of the utility calculus would become naturally tempered by the higher notion of social responsibilities and welfare. This construction is part of a broader approach to the process of socialization that explains how norms are internalized and so come to motivate individuals. In this sense, we may say that the corporatist movement plays an important role in changing the atomistic conception of individual behavior that characterizes neoclassical economics to a broader view of individuals as socially embedded (see Davis 2003). By doing so, it is the classical, old Millian tradition of the notion of *homo economicus* that is restored, highlighting the institutional and sociological nature of human behavior and establishing the context for human actions and motivations (see Persky 1995).

Spirito's influence was noticeable in the sorts of criticisms subsequently made by other corporatist writers about neoclassical economic theory.[5] However, the fact that he stood for a transformation of large firms into corporations—namely, by socializing its property among the workers, thus giving them both the possibility of co-ownership and codirection—was generally considered in Italy as an excessive, even somewhat socialist, proposal (see Micheletti 1998).

Still another key element of corporatist economic thought was the idea that class struggle between labor and capital was not an inherent condition to a capitalist economic and social organization—either if the struggle was about property rights and the ownership of the means of production or just about the problem of inequity in income distribution. Contrary to existing extreme solutions supported either by liberal or by socialist partisans, corporatist authors believed that it was possible to set up an economic and social system that could serve as a feasible alternative to both the capitalist lack of a minimum of social responsiveness and the socialist proposals in favor of the abolishment of private property. As they saw it, the long-lasting conflict between labor and capital—including the liberal resistance against all species of labor organization and the socialist support of trade unionism as a political weapon—was mainly because of capitalists' misconceptions about property rights, namely because they tended to forget the inherent social responsibilities that went along with those very rights.

By keeping themselves inflexibly attached to an extremely individualistic ethos, those who had the benefits of property favored the emergence of no less extreme socialist responses such as the equally absurd solution of entrusting the state as the sole owner of the fundamental means

5. These criticisms addressed the utilitarian foundations of neoclassical economics and its presuppositions of free competition, as well as the notion of spontaneous equilibrium and the consequent refusal to accept the need for some degree of state interventionism. Spirito's ideas and proposals have found considerable support in Italy from Gino Arias, Filippo Carli, and Massimo Fovel, among others (see Faucci 1990).

of production. Therefore corporatist authors such as Filippo Carli (1929) tried to build up a rationale that could lead property owners onto the right track. According to him, there was no doubt that private initiative was to be considered as the most effective and useful instrument for ensuring national development and national economic power; however, since private entrepreneurship was to fulfill a national function and not just merely an individual one, individual owners and entrepreneurs ought to understand that they were in fact responsible for ensuring that national interests and aims were actually achieved. Like in the above case of Spirito, Carli would also acknowledge that individuals could be left to pursue their interests and perform their economic action provided that they were also driven by a minimum of public spirit or social responsibility—or, to phrase it in the expressive words of the Spanish Jesuit philosopher Joaquín Azpiazu (1934, 192), provided that "a sense of duty" and "an hedonism more comprehensive than the purely individual one, which can be applicable to the family, the race, etc." was firmly established within individual consciences.

These contributions are important elements of an overall proposal for a middle-way path, equally apart from ongoing extreme and equally misguided alternatives, a sort of even-balanced system that would avoid either the obvious shortcomings of socialist economies (the overwhelming presence of the state and the consequent lack of individual freedom and of the essential stimulus provided by private property) or the social problems arising from the failure of competitive markets and liberal capitalism (absolute selfishness, extreme individual competition, a strictly utilitarian and materialistic ethos, appalling mass poverty, a significant waste of resources, the ruin of the social fabric, and the absence of national concerns). But, at least at this stage, this sort of solution may still be considered as a foreseeable result of the late-nineteenth-century mood toward eclecticism, that is, it may be considered as an unsurprising outcome of the widespread verdict on the meager likelihood of scientific and doctrinal truth to be the sole property of any particular school of economic thought. The attempt to take the best out of existing alternative approaches to social and economic problems in order to establish sounder foundations for a more effective system was therefore shared by many other schools of thought and authors who insisted on the intrinsic worth of a "third way."

Accordingly, these doctrines—if not even the initial corporatist experiments—were assessed in a generally sympathetic manner by all those who assumed collaboration and harmony between capital and labor both as a desirable goal and also as a potential driving force for further economic and moral development of modern societies.[6] Such an approach was successfully accepted and followed in France in the 1930s as revealed in the works of Eugène Mathon (1934), Roland Prè (1936), Maurice Bouvier-Ajam (1937), François Perroux (1938), and Gaëtan Pirou (1938). And the popularity of corporatist ideas in France explains the contradictory, twofold use they were subject to: on the one hand, the right one, they were the foundation for the implementation of social and economic policies during the Vichy regime; on the other hand, the left one, they were a source of inspiration for the indicative planning movement after World War II.

The strict defense of the superior value of the interests of the nation, as opposed to those of individuals, and the arguments in favor of a system of professional and occupational groups and bodies (corporations) that would provide a suitable environment for collaboration and encourage active efforts to reach social peace and lasting harmony between capital and labor, were therefore to be coupled with other ideas and proposals to complete the main features of a doctrinal system that sought to provide the appropriate response not only to the particular economic and social problems of the interwar period but also to the overall problems of proper national government and the attainment of common good.

According to Mihail Manoilesco (1936, 80–82), one of the most distinguished Romanian advocates of corporatism, the basic principle inherent in the concept of corporation was that "it is the function, and not the profession, that defines the corporative group in relation to the nation. As regards the profession it must not be considered socially as an egotistic means by which a certain category of men assures its existence, but as a means by which man renders himself useful to the community by accomplishing, just like the corporation, a certain socially necessary function."

In other words, within a corporatist economy the individuals were to become once more socially embedded as members—or working parts—of a natural organic whole, namely through the establishment of a series

6. Even so, the adoption of a more liberal tone by some third-way supporters would necessarily lead them to keep a certain critical distance from the loss of political freedom and individual rights typical of fascist or similar authoritarian regimes, while the adoption of a more socialist tone would lead other third-way partisans to stress the underlying class bias in favor of capitalist interests.

of links and socially meaningful relations according to individuals' natural vocations and ascribed occupation. These arrangements were obviously quite different from the liberal and socialist conception of labor unions, for they were mainly designed as professional or class organizations that could help offset to some extent the abuses of a threatening group of increasingly powerful capital holders. However important it might be, this difference was still not enough for the purpose of outlining an entirely alternative system.

Corporatism and Authoritarian Political Regimes

Alongside these principles and motivations, it should be emphasized that corporatism turned out to be embraced by—and to become a social and political instrument at the service of—some of the harsh dictatorial regimes that took shape in several southern European countries during the interwar period.[7] The corporatist movement in itself must therefore be perceived as part of a broader group of authoritarian experiments that did pervade and disturb the European and international political scene, especially after World War I.

These movements were triggered by the distress and general weariness experienced by several social groups in face of the vicissitudes of liberal regimes based on wavering democratic systems of political representation, regimes that more often than not were also afflicted with considerable financial and budgetary problems. The acceptance of an authoritarian alternative was often supported by a reaction against political corruption and a sense of parliamentary wastefulness and disorganization, but it was also supported by a growing belief in the intrinsic value of order, security, and stability—that is, social, political, and financial equilibrium. Finally, there was also an implicit acceptance that the recourse to the use of force could be a way to solve any eventual persisting social conflicts and to avoid the emergence of even bigger ones. Since the very possibility of both resuming the process of wealth creation and improving the pace of economic development seemed naturally linked

7. This point is particularly worth stressing, because it explains why the corporatist model has been constantly faced with a serious legitimation problem because of its etymological association with certain authoritarian and fascistlike interwar political experiences. The political discredit of corporatism after World War II is a consequence of that association, which very often precludes the development of a rigorous, historical analysis of its main features (see Kaplan and Minard 2004).

to political stability, the acceptance of a less democratic situation could prove to be the price to be paid for the preservation of these higher values.

As seen above, there were several philosophical and political arguments available for the corporatist authors to develop their own perspectives. Among them, Thomism may be said to occupy a privileged position insofar as it offered a comprehensive philosophical approach to the above-mentioned problems—that is, it did offer a thorough and accurate outline of the appropriate hierarchical relations to be established between the individual, the society, and the state. According to José Pires Cardoso (1950)—a leading Portuguese corporatist scholar—there was a contemporary renewal of interest for this philosophical tradition and particularly for its fundamental concept of common good as the key to understanding the proper hierarchical relationships to be established between the whole and its constituent parts. In face of the doubts and possible ambiguities over the ideal balance between individual freedom and national aims, the recuperation of Aquinas's views seemed to provide a balanced and satisfactory answer, for although stating the prevalence of the general over the particular he did not consider that humans ought to be entirely absorbed or annulled by society.

Pires Cardoso (1950, 42) takes a further step in order to stress that contrary to the extreme hierarchical perspectives upheld both by individualism and by sociologism, one ought to realize the fact that "the Common good is therefore acquired through a process of depuration and sublimation of an individual's particular good, and it crystallizes in a form that is different for each one of them. Different but not independent, since the Common good cannot have an existence as the top or the upper limit without the existence at the basis or departure of an individual's particular good."

This framework was complemented with the idea that corporatism could be considered as a natural hierarchical structure, since it managed to respect both the rights of the human person and the common good of the nation mainly through the successive processes of depuration and sublimation performed by a whole series of institutions, including the family, the corporations, and the state.

The establishment of the new corporatist organization was therefore deemed to be an important step for ensuring these fundamental objectives of order and social harmony, namely by formally entrusting the state with a fundamental and leading role in the initial part of the whole process, with the aim of achieving an effective control of the nation's social and economic life. The previous reflection on corporatism as a feasible solution for the labor question and on the ongoing conflicts between capital and labor was consequently transformed into a comprehensive "doctrine of the functional organisation of the nation" (Manoilesco 1936, 82), a doctrine that was finally based on the submission of the individual to the superior interests of the nation and to the preservation of its everlasting moral and spiritual integrity, a subordination to be ensured by force whenever needed.

Corporatism and State Intervention

A closer look at some corporatist experiments in the interwar period reveals that the guiding role played by the state in economic life was designed to achieve three essential objectives. The first was to consolidate the spirit of cooperation and mutual help between producers by establishing intercorporative agreements with the capacity to determine technical rules and standards, fix prices and wages, and reduce production costs. Second was to discipline and exercise an effective control over the production process by supervising the activities of corporations so as to prevent excessive fluctuations of supply in relation to demand and lessen the unexpected effects of free private enterprise. Third—and this was something that would give an overall coherence to the first two objectives—was to lessen the negative effects of the system of free competition and fix the limits and barriers to the entry of new firms in certain sectors of economic activity, which would thereby bring about the possibility of a certain distortion in one of the fundamental bases of the capitalist system, that is, the determination of the market equilibrium price.

Two of the main conceptual foundations of neoclassical economics—the market system based on the model of perfect competition and the price system—were criticized and downplayed by corporatist authors. Skepticism arising from the economic performances provided by the market, and consequently the compensatory function that was attributed to corporatist organizations and the state, had inevitable repercussions on how economic policy should be implemented. The basic premises of free competition, the spontaneous equilibrium of markets and nonintervention by the state, could never be welcomed by corporatist theorists, who were particularly receptive to a guiding economic principle based on the idea of protection and market regulation. As unconditional opponents of laissez-faire, these authors extolled the notion of a self-directed economy that nonetheless had nothing to do with the processes of spontaneous market equilibrium that were so much to the liking of neoclassical economists. The following excerpt, from another leading Portuguese author, clearly illustrates this distinction:

> Corporations therefore collaborate in the performance of a normative role. And this is why the activities of individuals and companies are now subjected to a form of discipline or, better still, are conditioned by certain initial positions that are implied by this discipline.
>
> We are far removed from automatic equilibrium: instead of this, we have a directed economy. But, in this case, such direction does not belong directly to the state, for it is the industries that, through their corporation, take the initiative of drawing up the rules and regulations. Afterward, it is the task of the government, as the representative of the national interest, to decide on these rules in the last instance, either approving them or rejecting them. Now, since the industries collaborate in their own discipline, it is said that we have instead a *self-directed economy*. (Ribeiro 1939, 61–62)

In a perfect corporatist economy, corporations should regulate economic activity through a complex system of bilateral monopoly markets. The self-directed economy thus presupposed that at the founding stage of the corporatist organization there would be massive state intervention, which thereafter would gradually decline in importance. While in place, however, state intervention should provide administrative and political direction to avoid the evil consequences of the market process, especially on the issues of unequal income distribution and wastage of resources.

The incentive for the creation of corporations embodied a logic of social and economic organization in which the realization of the general interest was previously measured by harmonizing the interests of the different individual agents and groups of agents operating in a market overseen by the state. Therefore the chance was not for planning for individual gains but rather for the achievement of the common good and net social advantage.

In this regard, corporatist doctrinaires were not alone in their preaching against the limitations of laissez-faire and "hands-off" policy (see Higgins 1951). The political environment of the interwar period was extremely favorable to the emergence and development of alternative responses to the prophets of the self-regulating market economy, as was the case with Keynes.

Corporatism and the Keynes Consensus

The impact of Keynesian doctrine on economic policy is usually discussed with a focus on the two decades following World War II,[8] by emphasizing the manipulation of aggregate demand via fiscal policy and public investment that was implemented in several European countries (see Hirschman 1989 and Tomlinson 1995). In this sense, the word *Keynesianism* does not refer to the economics of Keynes but rather to the broad consensus that developed on how to integrate the role of government into the liberal economic ideology.

However, one should not forget that Keynes's ideas were also put forward through his own involvement in British politics during the interwar period, namely through the advocacy of a program of public works that would afford a sound and sustainable remedy for unemployment (see Clarke 1988, 75–102). Besides the recognition of his merits in developing a new economic theory, he should also be acclaimed for the concern with practical reason and for the strong capacity to invent and develop proposals and plans to attack economic problems of daily life, at both the domestic and international levels (see O'Donnell 1989, 178–82).

Keynes was not alone in supporting interventionist expedients to solve the structural problems of the British economy. He could eventually be endorsed by some other experts belonging to the old neoclassical school (i.e., Marshallian-Pigouvian), though he was clearly putting forward a new political agenda, which implied the recognition of the limitations of the laissez-faire dogma of the old liberal tradition. According to Keynes, laissez-faire was neither a moral absolute nor a guiding principle for an ideal economic system, though he was ready to accept the instrumental nature of individualism and its role to achieve plenty and efficiency in the allocation of resources (see Fitzgibbons 1988, 163–80).

8. It is not our aim to discuss here in detail the immense range of literature produced on Keynes's conception of the economic role of government and the influence of his work in the implementation of economic policies. Since our main concern is a comparative one, the reader should bear in mind the outstanding contributions dealing with the different ways of approaching the subject, as presented in Hall 1989 and Thirlwall 1978. For a contemporary, engagé approach of economic policymaking in Keynesian lines, the reading of Harris 1947 and Lekachman 1964 always proves fruitful.

Keynes believed in a concept of government based on public interest and benevolent dictatorship. Economic policy measures fostered by governmental action were therefore an indisputable precondition to the general improvement of society. In one of his most persuasive essays, Keynes (1926, 294) sustained his strong criticism against laissez-faire dogmatic assumptions while stressing that it was not the very nature of the capitalist economic system that should be blamed:

> For my part I think that capitalism, wisely managed, can probably be made more efficient for attaining economic ends than any alternative system yet in sight, but that in itself it is in many ways extremely objectionable. Our problem is to work out a social organisation which shall be as efficient as possible without offending our notions of a satisfactory way of life.

The general argument in favor of governmental action notwithstanding, it should be stressed that for Keynes "the most important *Agenda* of the State relate not to those activities which private individuals are already fulfilling, but to those functions which fall outside the sphere of the individual, to those decisions which are made by *no one* if the State does not make them. The important thing for government is not to do things which individuals are doing already, and to do them a little better or a little worse; but to do those things which at present are not done at all" (291).

As for the ideal social organization Keynes might have in mind, it is worth noting that some of his opinions could be considered as fairly close to some of the arguments put forward by the advocates of corporatism. One situation where this convergence could occur may be exemplified by the following excerpt, when Keynes seemingly praises the medieval support of semiautonomous bodies within the state:

> I believe that in many cases the ideal size for the unit of control and organisation lies somewhere between the individual and the modern State. I suggest, therefore, that progress lies in the growth and the recognition of semi-autonomous bodies within the State—bodies whose criterion of action within their own field is solely the public good as they understand it, and from whose deliberations motives of private advantage are excluded, though some place it may still be necessary to leave, until the ambit of men's altruism grows wider, to the separate advantage of particular groups, classes, or faculties—bodies

> which in the ordinary course of affairs are mainly autonomous within their prescribed limitations, but are subject in the last resort to the sovereignty of the democracy expressed through Parliament.
>
> I propose a return, it may be said, towards medieval conceptions of separate autonomies. But, in England at any rate, corporations are a mode of government, which has never ceased to be important and is sympathetic to our institutions. It is easy to give examples, from what already exists, of separate autonomies which have attained or are approaching the mode I designate—the universities, the Bank of England, the Port of London Authority, even perhaps the railways companies. In Germany there are doubtless analogous instances. (288–89)

A potential agreement of positions at this level was of utmost importance, namely because the corporatist's endorsement of institutions such as guilds, corporations, and other intermediate bodies was constantly faced with a series of criticisms because of its genetic association with long-gone, medieval inefficient economic structures. The implicit support provided by Keynes to one of the ideal references of the corporatist model was therefore quite important, namely because Keynes could be considered as "the first major theorist to perceive certain emergent imperatives of capitalism and to link them explicitly with corporatism" (Schmitter [1974] 1979, 25).

Still another example of potential convergence may be found in the preface to the German edition of the *General Theory*, where Keynes (1936, xxvi) himself acknowledges that his theory is better adapted to the overall circumstances of an authoritarian regime: "Nevertheless the theory of output as a whole, which is what the following book purports to provide, is much more easily adapted to the conditions of a totalitarian state, than is the theory of the production and distribution of a given output produced under conditions of free competition and a large measure of laissez faire." The corporatist conception of the national economic role to be performed by the state in capitalist societies was therefore not incompatible with Keynes's analytical views, namely because a somewhat more active state—not necessarily an autocratic one—was in a better position to implement an economic policy designed to foster full employment, promote economic growth, regulate working conditions, cover individual economic and social risks, resolve labor conflicts, grant a growing participation of labor organizations in economic decision making, and promote the betterment of social conditions through income redistribution.

However, even if a certain convergence could be assumed as regards the denunciation of laissez-faire and the option for a further economic role of both the intermediate bodies and the state, the fact is that, on the other hand, Keynes's views could have serious implications for the maintenance of the social and economic equilibrium that was the hallmark of the existing corporatist states.

The *General Theory* also expressed a series of notions and assumptions whose acceptance would be almost impossible by corporatist standards. Keynes's acceptance of the unpredictability of economic agents and the unstable nature of economic life, his views on the inevitable precariousness of decision-making processes that were subject to assessments made by animal spirits, or even his acknowledgment of the contingency of the expectations and state of confidence of economic agents were quite at odds with the new pattern of individual and social behavior that was to underlie a full corporatist organization—one where the old individualistic and materialist *homo economicus* would give place to the new and socially responsive *homo corporativus*.

Besides, the prevailing financial and economic difficulties within several of the countries that favored a corporatist solution were also a considerable obstacle to the adoption of a strictly Keynesian economic policy (Hall 1989, 380–82). Accordingly, the guidelines of corporatist economic policy followed a different path and brought forward a series of dogmas that become extremely difficult to question: a quest for a balanced budget, the ideal of an orderly and nationally responsible behavior of consumers, an exaltation of the virtues of saving, an intransigent defense of the internal and external stability of the national currency (to avoid inflationary pressures) and the belief in a mythical system of full employment and an integrated labor market that was to be achieved through the workings of a corporation system. All this represented a substantially divergent prospect from the managed capitalism envisaged by Keynes.

Having said this, it is no less obvious that the array of changes advanced by Keynes on the issue of the state's role was obviously less demanding than those required by corporatist thinkers. There is no point in denying that Keynes himself was largely responsible for a certain ambiguity on these matters, for as Alvin Hansen (1953, 215) remarks about some chapters in the *General Theory*, "many would say that he threw caution to the winds and allowed his fancy to roam in an irresponsible manner." However, it is quite clear that Keynes did not get along with either the basic corporatist philosophical conceptions or corporatist proposals for a comprehensive ethical reorganization of economic and social life. The existence of these chief philosophical divergences, once coupled with the fact that Keynes was much more attached to economics than to any other specific field of social and political thought, was in fact more than enough to preclude any enduring and meaningful convergence with corporatism.

To disregard the philosophical differences between the underlying rationale for state economic intervention of corporatism and of Keynes would therefore be even more absurd than equating Keynes's concept of a "socialisation of investment" with "socialist planning," thus associating Keynes's name and work with the advocacy of a "planned economy."[9]

Likewise, it is easy to understand some of the major reasons for corporatist thinkers' discomfort over Keynes's views. To begin with, there was a fundamental incompatibility between the philosophical creed upheld by Keynes and the neo-Thomism that inspired many corporatist authors. In a full-fledged corporatist system, economics was to play an important but nevertheless secondary role in the face of both law and ethics. As a result, the establishment of a more efficient economic organization was not perceived as an end in itself but merely as a helpful and necessary means for ensuring a superior form of social organization. Keynes himself would not disagree with this view. But he did nevertheless consider it as nothing but an honorable long-term aspiration, for he was quite aware that the process of transmuting human nature should not be confused with the more accessible task of managing it. The eventual eradication of such drives as the familiar money-making passion that for so long had acted on humanity was therefore something that had to be dealt with circumspectly, and it was a process that was unquestionably still in its very early stages. Keynes's views were consequently less ambitious, for he would settle for the immediate establishment of practicable measures that could avoid the destruction of existing economic forms.

Conclusion

The interwar years were a period of open debate about the proper rationale for political and economic organization. This debate was not only

9. For a synthetic critical presentation of this erroneous identification, see Cairncross 1978 and Winch 1989.

quite lively among the supporters of both liberalism and socialism, but it also allowed for the emergence of new unconventional proposals by the corporatists and by Keynes. The former had on their behalf a seemingly rigorous philosophical approach to humanity and society, but they obviously faced the opposition of several renowned economists. We may therefore understand why Keynes's ideas were capable of simultaneously arousing both sympathy and animosity among the partisans of corporatism. He was not only an economist but a distinguished one, several of his economic insights could be useful for reinforcing the criticisms directed against "classical economics views," and his style proved to be effective in persuading people of the vital importance of committed state involvement for the survival of capitalism. Once selectively interpreted, Keynes's economics could supply still another powerful set of arguments not only against old economic concepts and techniques but also against the deep-seated economic liberal worldview. It is therefore perfectly reasonable to insist that Keynes and the corporatist thinkers were likely to converge, insofar as they shared a common enemy—old-fashioned liberal views—and also because they both tried to involve the state in finding relief for the economic inefficiency and associated social turmoil that came out of the workings of a traditional market system.

As for the economic role of the state, it is obvious that there was agreement that the state could no longer act purely as a guardian, for it had an unavoidable strategic role in managing and directing national economic life. Likewise, the auxiliary character of the role that was to be performed by the state was quite compatible with Keynes's views about those decisions, which were made by no one if the state did not assume the responsibility to make them.

When the war was finally over, socialism was entrenched in a significant portion of the world, and the vindication of a full-fledged corporatist organization was no longer viable. However, the same applied to a hypothetical return to the nineteenth-century liberal status quo. Little by little, Keynes's economic ideas ultimately conquered economists and governments on both sides of the Atlantic. But now, Keynesianism was no longer a third way, for it assumed simultaneously the character of an economic orthodoxy and the role of a shared doctrinal expression of trust in the overall potential of a new, dynamic, form of capitalism—one that finally had conceded a meaningful social and economic role to the state. Accordingly, it is not surprising to find that several of the less autocratic supporters of corporatism would willingly join the Keynesian ranks. In those countries where corporatism had a more significant impact, the espousal of a Keynesian stance was in fact a realistic alternative for keeping at least with some of the previous corporatist comprehensive ambitions—namely among those who still wanted the state to remain directly involved in a strategy of social and industrial development. Curiously enough, it was the question of economic planning that acted as the central axis of a new discourse, supposedly free of any preconceptions of an ideological nature, and now advocated along the lines of a more technocratic stance.

Seemingly, many of those obviously engaged in establishing a true third way had finally accepted Keynes's confidence about the fact that capitalism, provided that it was wisely managed, could be made more efficient for solving economic problems than any other alternative system yet in sight.

This idea also meets the modern notion of (neo-) corporatism, defined as "a specific socio-political process in which organisations representing monopolistic functional interests engage in political exchange with state agencies over public policy outputs which involves those organisations in a role that combines interest representation and policy implementation through delegated self-enforcement" (Cawson 1985, 8). According to this approach, the growing collaboration and exchanges between functional interests associations and the state, namely through the institutionalization of a regular, permanent collaboration between them, paves the way to the growth of state economic intervention beyond the usual Keynesian lines. It emphasizes the significance of political negotiation, interest intermediation, and informal coordination of conflicting objectives in present-day societies. And it ultimately shows that the historical experience of corporatism during the interwar period, as a particular form of state intervention, has a strong meaning and relevance for contemporary politics and economics.

References

Azpiazu, Joaquín. 1934. *El estado corporativo*. Madrid: Editorial "Razón y Fe."

Battini, Michele. 1995. *L'ordine della gerarchia: I contribute reazionarie e progressisti alle crise della democrazia in Francia, 1789–1914*. Torino: Bollati Boringhieri.

Bouvier-Ajam, Maurice. 1937. *La doctrine corporative*. Paris: Librairie du Recueil Sirey.

Cairncross, Alec. 1978. Keynes and the Planned Economy. In *Keynes and Laissez-Faire*, edited by A. P. Thirlwall. London: Macmillan.

Cardoso, José Pires. 1950. *Corporativismo*. Lisbon: Edição do Autor.

Carli, Filippo. 1929. *Premese di economia corporativa*. Pisa: Nistri-Lischi Editori.

Cawson, Alan, ed. 1985. *Organized Interests and the State: Studies in Meso-Corporatism*. London: Sage.

Clarke, Peter. 1988. *The Keynesian Revolution in the Making, 1924–1936*. Oxford: Clarendon.

Davis, John B. 2003. *The Theory of the Individual in Economics: Identity and Value*. London: Routledge.

De Rosa, Gabriele, ed. 2003. *I tempi della "Rerum Novarum."* Rome: Istituto Luigi Sturzo.

Faucci, Riccardo. 1990. Un'epoca di transizioni? Le coordinate teorico-istituzionali del periodo. *Quaderni di storia dell'economia politica* 8.2–3:3–22.

Fitzgibbons, Athol. 1988. *Keynes's Vision: A New Political Economy*. Oxford: Clarendon.

Hall, Peter A., ed. 1989. *The Political Power of Economic Ideas: Keynesianism across Nations*. Princeton, N.J.: Princeton University Press.

Hansen, Alvin. 1953. *A Guide to Keynes*. New York: McGraw-Hill.

Harris, Abram L. 1958. *Economics and Social Reform*. New York: Harper & Brothers.

Harris, Seymour E., ed. 1947. *The New Economics: Keynes' Influence on Theory and Public Policy*. London: Dennis Dobson Ltd.

Higgins, Benjamin. 1951. *What Do Economists Know? Six Lectures on Economics in the Crisis of Democracy*. Melbourne: Melbourne University Press.

Hirschman, Albert O. 1989. How the Keynesian Revolution Was Exported from the United States, and Other Comments. In Hall 1989.

Kaplan, Steven L., and Philippe Minard, eds. 2004. *La France, malade du corporatisme? XVIIIe–XXe siècles*. Paris: Éditions Belin.

Keynes, J. Maynard. 1926. The End of Laissez-Faire. In *Essays in Persuasion*, vol. 9 of *The Collected Works of John Maynard Keynes*. London: Macmillan.

———. 1936. *The General Theory of Employment, Interest, and Money*. London: Macmillan.

Lekachman, Robert, ed. 1964. *Keynes' General Theory: Reports of Three Decades*. London: Macmillan.

Manoilesco, Mihail. 1936. *Le siècle du corporatisme*. Paris: Félix Alcan.

Mathon, Eugène. 1934. *La corporation, base de l'organization économique*. Paris: Comité des États Généraux.

Micheletti, Andrea. 1998. Ugo Spirito. In *Il fascismo: Dizionario di storia, personaggi, culture, economia, fonti e dibattito storiografico*, edited by Alberto De Bernardi and Scipione Guarracino. Milan: Bruno Mondadori.

Morgan, Mary, and Malcolm Rutherford, eds. 1998. *From Interwar Pluralism to Postwar Neoclassicism. HOPE* 30 (supplement).

O'Donnell, R. M. 1989. *Keynes: Philosophy, Economics, and Politics: The Philosophical Foundations of Keynes's Thought and Their Influence on His Economics and Politics*. London: Macmillan.

Perroux, François. 1938. *Capitalisme et communauté de travail*. Paris: Librairie du Recueil Sirey.

Persky, Joseph. 1995. The Ethology of Homo Economicus. *Journal of Economic Perspectives* 9.2:221–31.

Pirou, Gaëtan. 1938. *Essais sur le corporatisme*. Paris: Librairie du Recueil Sirey.

Pré, Roland. 1936. *Le bilan du corporatisme: Italie, Autriche, Portugal, Allemagne*. Paris: Librairie Technique et Economique.

Ribeiro, J. J. Teixeira. 1939. *Princípio e fins do sistema corporativo português*. Coimbra: Coimbra Editora.

Rist, Charles, and Charles Gide. 1917. *A History of Economic Doctrines*. London: George G. Harrap & Company.

Schmitter, Philippe C. [1974] 1979. Still the Century of Corporatism? In vol. 1 of *Trends towards Corporatist Intermediation: Contemporary Political Sociology*, edited by Philippe C. Schmitter and Gerhard Lehmbruch. London: Sage.

Schumpeter, Joseph A. [1942] 1976. *Capitalism, Socialism, and Democracy*. London: George Allen & Unwin.

Spirito, Ugo. [1933] 1934. *Princípios fundamentais de economia corporativa*. Portuguese translation. Lisbon: Livraria Civilização.

Thirlwall, A. P., ed. 1978. *Keynes and Laissez-Faire*. London: Macmillan.

Tomlinson, Jim. 1995. An Unfortunate Alliance: Keynesianism and the Conservatives, 1945–1964. In *New Perspectives on Keynes*, edited by Allin F. Cottrell and Michael S. Lawlor. *HOPE* 27 (supplement): 61–85.

Turmann, Max. 1909. *Le développement du Catholicisme social depuis l'encyclique Rerum Novarum*. Paris: Félix Alcan.

Winch, Donald. 1989. Keynes, Keynesianism, and State Intervention. In Hall 1989.

The Rise of Free Market Economics: Economists and the Role of the State since 1970

Roger E. Backhouse

Between 1970 and 2000 there took place a remarkable and dramatic change in attitudes toward the role of the state in economic activity. An ideology favorable to management of the economy gave way to one in which state action was seen as raising more problems than it solved. The role of the market was extended, markets being created by government where they could not evolve spontaneously, and attempts were made to minimize the role of state-organized and state-funded economic activity. Thus nationalized industries were privatized; services provided by the state were outsourced to private contractors; industries were deregulated; taxes were cut; and attempts were made to reduce the level of government spending. This was much more than a simple change in attitudes toward economic policy: it was a radical shift of worldview, involving a transformation of attitudes across a wide range of the political spectrum as well as being associated with profound changes in economic theory.[1] Inequality in the distribution of income was allowed to rise to levels that would have been considered socially divisive a few decades before. This was based on the twin beliefs that high rewards were needed to provide the incentives required to generate high levels of productivity

An early draft of this essay was presented at a seminar at the University of Oporto in May 2004. I am grateful to participants there and at the *HOPE* conference in April 2004 for valuable comments. In particular, I wish to thank David Levy for drawing my attention to the importance of the Volker Fund and the Earhart Foundation, and to Steve Horwitz for directing me to literature that I had previously missed. An anonymous referee also made some very helpful comments.

1. Note that this does not imply anything about the success or otherwise of these changes, not even about whether competition was in fact increased or the level of government expenditure actually reduced.

and growth and that, even if the tails of the income distribution were getting bigger, there was enough mobility to stop people from getting stuck in those tails. This change in the climate of opinion was so profound that, unless it is addressed, it is impossible to understand what happened to economics in the second half of the twentieth century.

In this essay, no attempt is made even to outline the causes of this change in the climate of opinion, for to do that would involve venturing well outside economics to consider, for example, the rise to power of political figures such as Margaret Thatcher and Ronald Reagan, and the way they and their supporters managed to change not only economic but also political life.[2] That is beyond the scope of such a short essay. Instead, it tries to answer some questions about the role of economics in this transformation of attitudes.[3] Even this is complicated, for economic ideas were both influenced by this climate of opinion and at the same time contributed to it. Though there is an element of truth underlying both perspectives, it is an oversimplification to argue either that economists simply responded to this ideological change—as the "hired guns" of neoliberalism—or that the experience of the postwar era showed that older "socialist" ways of thinking were fundamentally flawed.

An important complication in this story is that the rise of free market economics, as the term is being used here, refers to two distinct changes. The first is the rise of groups and organizations that propagate free market ideas in various ways (these groups are very heterogeneous). The second is a shift in the consensus within the mainstream of economics toward free market ideas: many economists who (at least today) would not be considered (by themselves or by others) free market economists hold views that, in the 1950s, would have been associated with a commitment to free markets. These two developments are not the same thing at all. Indeed, there are considerable ideological and methodological differences between, for example, Austrians and mainstream economics. Though the former's reasons may be very different, some Austrians are as critical of organizations such as the International Monetary Fund (IMF) as are those who criticize it for propagating free market ideology. However, although these two developments are distinct, they are two sides of the change in attitudes toward the state that has taken place in the past three decades and need to be considered together.

2. Kelley (1997) discusses some of this.

3. Kelley (1997) looks at the origins of free market economics as it impinges on libertarian politics. While there is some overlap between his chapter 2 and the themes discussed here, because economics is secondary to his story, his focus is different.

To provide a focus, the essay starts, in section 1, with some accounts that relate economists' increased interest in markets to experiences during the postwar period. These are accounts of progress, in which economists are learning from the mistakes of their predecessors in designing overambitious and flawed schemes. Socialism and state intervention are fundamentally flawed, and economists have learned what can be done with markets. However, while such approaches may inspire practitioners, they beg many historiographical questions. Section 2 reviews the thesis, proposed by Sonja Amadae (2003), that the change in economics since 1970 should be seen as the rise of what she calls "rational choice liberalism," an approach to economics radically different from what was found in economics before the 1940s. Rational choice liberalism, which affected social science much more broadly than just economics, had its origins in the Cold War, but eventually served an ideology very different from that out of which it emerged. The essay then approaches the question through the social dimension. Free market ideas did not just develop: deliberate attempts were made to propagate them through a network of organizations. Some of these organizations, and the links between them, are outlined in sections 3 to 5: free market think tanks (private and outside academia) in section 3; universities and international organizations in section 4, and sources of funding that have sustained free market ideas in section 5. Section 6 then returns to the intellectual dimension, exploring how the techniques employed by economists, largely unnoticed, may have biased the conclusions in favor of market solutions and away from ones that involve state intervention. Finally, the connections between these ways of looking at the problem and Amadae's thesis are discussed and conclusions are drawn about how we should be thinking about the two-way relationship between economic ideas and the climate of opinion.

1. Learning from Past Mistakes

The reason most economists would, no doubt, give for the change in attitudes toward government is that they have learned that the foundations on which support for interventionist policies rested were inadequate. The postwar consensus that prevailed until the 1970s was biased in favor of government intervention because it took account of market failure (caused by public goods, externalities, imperfections of competition, limited information, myopia, and so on) but ignored government failure.[4] Governments were assumed to be concerned to maximize social welfare and to have the information they needed to achieve this. These attitudes were abandoned in all areas of economics in response to both developments in theory and experience of government intervention over the preceding decades.[5]

The transition was clearest in macroeconomics. Whereas it has previously been thought that governments could, at least in principle, have some choice over the level of activity at which they ran the economy, Milton Friedman (1968), in his presidential address to the American Economic Association in 1967, argued that any unemployment rate other than the natural rate would be accompanied by accelerating or decelerating inflation, which would eventually become unsustainable. The crucial element in his argument was that workers cared about their real wages, with the result that the level of unemployment should be related to the expected change in the real wage, not the nominal wage. The addition of a mechanism whereby expectations responded to experience of inflation resulted in the theory that inflation would accelerate if unemployment exceeded the natural rate. Governments, therefore, could not have a lasting effect on the unemployment rate and should not try to do so. This provided a theoretical justification for the monetary policy rule that Friedman had been advocating since the late 1940s: that governments should aim for a constant rate of growth of the money supply.

Friedman's style of argument was old-fashioned, out of tune with the trend toward more formal theorizing, but Edmund Phelps (1967) and colleagues (Phelps et al. 1970) showed how similar conclusions could be derived using models in which information was imperfect and agents made mistakes. This added respectability to the conclusions that Friedman had reached using less formal methods. His conclusions and those of Phelps appeared to be vindicated shortly afterward when, in response to the boom brought about by a decade of full-employment policy and high expenditure on the Vietnam War, commodity prices rose dramatically, culminating in the oil crisis of 1973–74. In the ensuing depression, inflation and unemployment rose simultaneously, exactly as Friedman had predicted would happen. Keynesian theory could provide no guidance, and politicians readjusted their priorities away from employment toward inflation. At the same time, econometric models, based on

4. Kelley (1997, chap. 1) considers the rise of this consensus from the perspective of developments, as seen from a free market perspective, after 1970.

5. References are relatively sparse in this section because the material is so well known.

Keynesian principles, focusing on detailed modeling of aggregate demand, broke down in the presence of major supply shocks. Robert Lucas (1976) offered an explanation that further restricted the scope for government intervention. The Lucas critique argued that not only would the private sector seek to anticipate inflation but it would also try to work out and respond to any predictable patterns in the policy regime. This meant that policymakers could no longer base their actions on observed regularities in private-sector behavior: they had to find out the structural parameters if they were to get models that would be invariant to the policy regime. Given that these structural parameters were assumed to be tastes and technology, and the properties these were assumed to exhibit, this implied a role for government intervention that was very restricted.

At the same time there was a movement away from supporting government intervention in microeconomics. Regulation was increasingly seen as creating perverse incentives and distorting resource allocation as much as curing such problems. Efficiency was seen as requiring private ownership of assets and the availability of markets that could establish competitive prices for goods and services. This led many governments to privatize industries owned by the state and to remove regulations over industries as varied as airlines and banking. Where regulation had previously been seen as the solution to problems such as externalities and natural monopoly, attempts were now made to create competitive markets. For example, the United States designed a system for trading permits to emit sulfur dioxide that proved more effective than regulation had been in limiting emissions by power stations. In Britain, competition was introduced into the marketing of electricity and gas, despite there being only a single distribution system for each of these commodities. In many countries, auctions have become the standard way to allocate licenses for rights that would previously have been allocated according to the government's judgment about which company would provide the best service. The most visible examples of this were perhaps the auction, in many countries, of parts of the radio spectrum available for third-generation mobile phones, and the creation of markets for a vast range of new financial products. This is the process described by John McMillan (2002) as "reinventing the bazaar."

One key element in the theory behind this was public choice theory, which dates back to the work of James Buchanan, Gordon Tullock, Mancur Olsen, and Anthony Downs around 1960. The conventional view of policy has been to see the government as optimizing some social welfare function. The political process determined the values on which government policy had to be based, and the role of economists was to understand the constraints and design interventions, such as regulations, taxes, or government activities, that would achieve those objectives. Public choice theory challenged this by approaching government decision makers, whether politicians, civil servants, or regulators, as motivated by their own ends. This meant that government policy came to be seen not as maximizing social welfare but as driven by the interests of those responsible for implementing it. Government failure was as pervasive as market failure. The very possibility of government regulation would lead to rent seeking—using lobbying and other activities designed to achieve better treatment—diverting resources away from productive activities.

This critique of government, which suggested that inefficiency was inherent in any government-run activities, fits well with the earlier critiques of socialism offered by Friedrich Hayek (1935) and others in the 1920s and 1930s. Hayek had argued that it was impossible (not just difficult) for any organization to have the information necessary to engage in efficient central planning. Hayek's critique of socialism and the public choice critique of government were both theoretical, but the experience of running state-owned enterprises and regulating the private sector was held to have provided numerous examples that showed it to be correct. The outstanding example was the communist world, where state control had been taken to extremes. By the 1980s the performance of these economies was being seen as greatly inferior to that of capitalist economies, and the collapse of the Soviet Union and its satellite regimes in the early 1990s was widely seen to have vindicated the claim that socialism was fundamentally flawed.

In macroeconomics, too, attempts were made to endogenize government behavior, making the assumption that bureaucrats and politicians were self-interested. There was some work on "political business cycles" in the 1970s. For example, William D. Nordhaus (1975) developed a model of the cycle in which politicians manipulate policy so as to maximize their chances of reelection by myopic voters who take account of performance during politicians' terms of office. After a period of inactivity, there was a resurgence of such work in the late 1980s when, in the context of rational expectations and forward-looking behavior, asymmetric information was used to explain how politicians might be able to manipulate the economy to their advantages. Alongside this was the literature on the time-consistency (or inconsistency) of optimal monetary policy. The interaction of private agents and government anticipating each others' actions might be a suboptimal inflation rate. To achieve a better outcome, government might have to "tie its hands," perhaps by publicly committing itself to a policy target or by delegating monetary policy to a conservative central bank. Political business cycle models were never fully accepted, considerable doubts having been expressed about the empirical support for such theories. It has been argued that, when account is taken on other constraints on central bank action, the issue of credibility is of little practical importance. However, between them, these theories have probably contributed to economists' skepticism about successfully using discretionary policy.

The change that has come about is well illustrated by the example of development economics. In the 1950s and 1960s, development economics offered various theories about why certain countries remained poor. These included climate and cultural factors as well as externalities and unequal bargaining power between rich and poor countries. Some economists (e.g., Ragnar Nurkse) argued that it was necessary to industrialize on a broad front so that each industry would benefit from the externalities created by expansion in other sectors. Others (e.g., Albert Hirschman and Gunnar Myrdal) argued for selective industrialization, to create strategic disequilibria, which would induce further development. Still others (e.g., Raul Prebisch) opted for protection and import substitution, to break out of the trap caused by deteriorating terms of trade. On the basis of these theories, development strategies were designed: some countries sought to industrialize behind protective trade barriers; others to develop agricultural exports; others to invest heavily in infrastructure. The results were very mixed. South Korea and other countries on the Pacific Rim succeeded; Brazil and other countries in Latin America failed to make the advances that had been expected. Much of sub-Saharan Africa stagnated. From the 1970s, in parallel to the changes taking place in other branches of economics, thinking about development changed. At the theoretical level, interest turned away from "grand theories" of development to the application of standard microeconomics, based on utility and profit maximization, to development problems, on the assumption that behavior was determined in just the same way as in developed countries. Thus peasant farmers' unwillingness to invest in fertilizer despite high expected returns was seen not as nonmaximizing behavior but as a rational response to the riskiness of such methods in comparison with traditional farming methods. At the same time there was a move, prompted both by the failure of many development strategies and by the financial problems faced by many developing countries when energy prices and interest rates both rose in the early 1980s, toward policies that emphasized fiscal discipline and market liberalization.

A decade later John Williamson (1990) could label a list of such ideas the "Washington Consensus." Implementing such reforms provided the "minimum conditions" for developing countries to make progress (Williamson 1990). This perspective reflected developments in public choice theory in the preceding two decades, according to which government officials were assumed to pursue their own ends rather than disinterestedly to implement policies that would promote social welfare. Thus policy was seen as achieving the "breakthrough, from a dirigiste, statist, 'mercantilist,' closed economy rendered unstable by populist macroeconomic policies, to an open, relatively stable economy using competitive markets to allocate resources" (Williamson 1994, 12). Stability and prosperity were associated with open economies and competitive markets and instability with closed economies and extensive government intervention. Williamson argued explicitly that experience, notably in East Asia, had shown that the traditional view that development required sets of policies different from the market-oriented policies that had characterized developed economies was wrong. What makes this view significant is that Williamson felt able to claim that the Washington Consensus embodied "the common core of wisdom embraced by all serious economists" (18). It was not, unlike in the 1950s, the view of a conservative minority. Furthermore, many economists would no doubt endorse the view that "the process of conversion from one [dirigiste] consensus to another [market oriented] in large areas of the world owed . . . [much] to the accumulating evidence of success of neoclassical policies, in particular in East Asia, contrasting with the dismal results of previous policies in so many other countries" (Polak 1997, 217).

A book that sums up this change is by William Easterly (2002), subtitled *Economists' Adventures and Misadventures in the Tropics*. He provides a catalog of "panaceas that failed": using foreign aid to raise investment in developing countries; raising the level of education; giving away contraceptives to reduce unwanted births; lending to poor countries that had not learned to control inflation. In all of these cases, policies were based on then fashionable ideas about what was necessary to promote development. In contrast, the successes of development are centered on the idea that "people respond to incentives."[6] He summarizes the basic principle of economics in two ways: "People do what they get paid to do; what they don't get paid to do, they don't do"; and, "People respond to incentives; all the rest is commentary" (2002, xii). This translates into development economics as, "If we do the hard work of ensuring that the trinity of First World aid donors, Third World governments, and ordinary Third World citizens have the right incentives, development will happen. If they don't, it won't." The failures of development economics, Easterly argues, arose from policies that violated these basic economic principles.

These examples illustrate the depth of the change that has taken place within economics. Part of the story has been a resurgence of conservative economics. Interest in Hayekian ideas is particularly strong in some of the transition economies of Eastern Europe. Within the mainstream of economics, clear examples are Friedman and Friedman 1980 or Barro 2002. However, alongside this renaissance of conservative economics has been a much broader shift in the climate of opinion, of which Williamson, Easterly, and McMillan provide good examples precisely because they do not fall into the conservative category. Williamson (1994, 18), for example, states explicitly that he defined the Washington Consensus sufficiently broadly to exclude many issues (such as the size of government, the extent of income redistribution, and the type of market economy to be sought) on which there was little agreement (and on many of which his views were the opposite of those held by neoconservatives). Similarly, Easterly (2002, 143) argues that for development to occur, government must provide health, education, and infrastructure services. He even admits that "the new incentive-based views of growth could turn out to be as badly misguided as the panaceas that failed" (143–44). Even more strongly, McMillan (2002, 226) concludes by pointing out that markets work only if they are well designed, that there are limits to what markets can achieve, and that "a modern economy simply cannot run on libertarian principles." All of these economists, from Friedman to McMillan, see economics as having learned from mistakes made in earlier periods. However, though economists might claim that no further explanation is needed—that new theories were adopted because they were better than the old ones—few historians would be happy to stop at such an explanation and alternative versions of the story need to be considered.

6. These phrases are the titles of parts 2 and 3 of the book.

2. The Ideology of Rational Choice

The most developed account of the transformation of economics during this period has been provided by Sonja Amadae (2003) as part of an account of the transformation of social science more generally. Her story starts with the sense of defeat among Western intellectuals in the 1930s and 1940s, and the perceived need to develop a philosophy of markets and democracy that would provide an alternative to Marxism. That philosophy was rational choice liberalism, the philosophy that became "the linchpin of the triumphant West's ideological victory over Soviet communism" (Amadae 2003, 4). It had three broad elements: the self-interested rational actor, set-theoretic and axiomatic treatment of human rationality, and a commitment to universal and objective scientific law (3). Rational choice theory extended beyond any one social science, or even the social sciences as a whole.

The key figure in Amadae's account is Kenneth Arrow, whose research "served to establish the disciplinary standard within economics" through his contributions to the fields of social choice, general equilibrium theory, decision theory, and the economics of information (Amadae 2003, 85), as well as informing U.S. government policy. The work that formed the basis for this influence, *Social Choice and Individual Values* (1951) arose directly from Arrow's role as a "defense intellectual whose career as a key contributor to the neoclassical synthesis in economics is inseparable from his Cold War policy role" (Amadae 2003, 85). In 1948, as an intern at RAND, he was given the task of determining a utility function for the Soviet Union that could be used in game theoretic analysis of nuclear strategy. This led to *Social Choice and Individual Values*, the first version of which appeared as a RAND report. Arrow's use of set theory rather than calculus severed the link between rational choice theory and utility theory, for rationality became defined in terms of transitivity, not in terms of preference fields (Amadae 2003, 108). It therefore became a tool that could be applied to social science in general, not simply to questions of consumer choice.

In the decades before Arrow's work, there had been intensive debate over the merits of socialism versus capitalism. Arrow's theorem provided a solution to that debate by showing that, if one held certain values, the notion of collective decisions that represented individual choices did not make sense. Given that socialism was about collective decision making, this provided a political philosophy that "triumphed over Marxism, Kantian moral philosophy, Rousseau's political theory, and classical utilitarianism . . . both providing a basis for American political and economic liberalism while simultaneously undermining the alternative social philosophies of communism, idealist democracy, and totalitarianism" (87). This book was based on four assumptions: "that science is objective; that it yields universal laws; that reason is not culturally relative; and that individuals' preferences are both inviolable and incomparable" (84). These four assumptions "provide both the structure for his [Arrow's] impossibility theorem and the basis of the mainstream Cold War consensus on social philosophy characterizing rational choice liberalism" (129).

Amadae argues that the effect of Arrow's book was to establish social choice theory as an alternative to welfare economics and that social welfare was completely undermined. Though social choice theorists worked on extending Arrow's result, trying to find ways round his impossibility theorem, she argues that this served to reinforce the underlying ideals on which it was based.[7] The other main effect was to underpin public choice theory as it emerged in the 1960s, most of which is based on the premise of individualism. Arrow himself claimed that his theorem indicted the market as much as democratic voting and that he had the same faith in the market as in social planning, but others have seen the case differently. Amadae (2003, 128) quotes Charles Rowley as an example: "Arrow's theorem provides incontrovertible support for market process and encouragement for those who seek to constrain the range of collective choice to the limited functions of the minimal state." As public choice theory spread through economics in the 1970s, this view of Arrow's theorem no doubt gained greater currency.

This view that rational choice theory marks a radical break with previous approaches to social science and that, though originating in the Cold War technocratic ideology, it later provided the foundation on which free market economics could be based is discussed further in the final section. Before that, however, other aspects of the story need to be considered.

3. Think Tanks

The shift toward market solutions did not occur spontaneously; it was actively promoted by groups of economists committed to opposing

7. See also Amadae 2003, chap. 8, "Consolidating Rational Choice Liberalism, 1970–2000."

socialism, making the case for free enterprise, and reviving the fortunes of liberalism. In the first stage, the most influential institution was, as the previous section has made clear, the RAND Corporation, which brought together the Cowles Commission, Princeton University, and many of the economists associated with the development of rational choice theory.[8] RAND was a think tank set up by the U.S. Air Force at Santa Monica, California, to prevent the scientific and technical expertise that it had brought together during the Second World War from being dispersed. It was established in 1946 as a division of the Douglas Aircraft Company to undertake research on air warfare. In 1948, by which time its staff had grown to 255, it separated from Douglas to avoid conflicts of interest and was established as a nonprofit organization, with H. Rowan Gaither Jr. as chairman of the board of trustees.

Gaither was involved with the Ford Foundation (from 1951 by far the largest American philanthropy) and was involved in writing the foundation's statement of aims. Faced with the choice between democracy and totalitarianism, it was essential to get objective impartial advice from a professional corps of experts: "To replace partisan controversy with objective fact" (Amadae 2003, 36). Philanthropies such as Ford "ha[d] no stockholders and no constituents . . . [and] represent[ed] no private, political or religious interests" and so were ideally placed to supply this. Once it had become a nonprofit organization, this description fitted RAND perfectly, and it began to receive considerable funding from the Ford Foundation as well as the Air Force. In 1953, Gaither became president of the Ford Foundation, despite the potential conflict of interest with his position at RAND. This marked a shift to the right at RAND, away from Eisenhower's more moderate Republicanism toward a more aggressive conservatism. According to Amadae (2003, 38):

> Hoffman [the previous Ford Foundation president] . . . was unequivocally opposed to using foundation resources in efforts to destabilize foreign political regimes. Gaither and his close associates . . . on the other hand, supported foundation efforts to further political and psychological warfare. Similarly, Gaither's support of the social and behavioral sciences as a tool for an expertly managed society contrasted with Hoffman's interdialogic, democratic cosmopolitanism. Under

8. This paragraph draws on Amadae 2003, 31–47. RAND stood for "Research and Development," though given its activities it was later suggested that a more appropriate translation would be "Research and No Development."

Gaither's tutelage, the Ford Foundation promoted research oriented toward national security.

Gaither served as a bridge between Ford and RAND. Under him, RAND, increasingly dominated by economists, produced "systems analysis," in which the principles of rational action provided the central organizing framework.

Though RAND played a crucial role in the development of the theory and arguably the ideology of the market economy, it was by no stretch of the imagination something that could be called a "free market" think tank. Though freedom was an important part of its ideology, its commitment to technocratic management and its location in relation to the U.S. Air Force placed it in opposition to much free market ideology. The rise of institutions aimed at promoting free markets and more systematically opposing government intervention came from institutions that lay outside government.

The best starting point for the rise of organizations aimed specifically at arguing the case for free markets is the Mont Pelerin Society (MPS), the first meeting of which took place in Switzerland, in April 1947.[9] Following on from an earlier meeting, "Le Colloque Walter Lippmann," held in France in 1938, Friedrich Hayek sought to bring together a group of intellectuals who could develop "a philosophy of freedom." The background was widespread pessimism about the future of capitalism and, with it, of free societies. John Maynard Keynes, Arnold Toynbee, Bertrand Russell, Oswald Spengler, T. S. Eliot, and Joseph Schumpeter had all argued that capitalism was doomed, with many of them predicting the inevitable coming of socialism. Hayek saw the task of the new organization not as trying to exert an immediate influence on policy but as having a long-term influence on the climate of opinion, comparing its task explicitly with that facing the earlier generation of socialist and new liberal intellectuals who had formed the Fabian Society.

Though Hayek wanted to include more historians and philosophers, the nature of his contacts meant that the thirty-nine people at the initial gathering (and hence the society that was formed in November 1947) contained a high proportion of economists: from Britain were Stanley Dennison, John Jewkes, Lionel Robbins, and Hayek himself; from the United States were Aaron Director, Milton Friedman, Harry Gideonse, Frank Graham, Frank Knight, Fritz Machlup, Ludwig von Mises, and

9. This account of the Mont Pelerin Society draws on Hartwell 1995 and Cockett 1994.

George Stigler, as well as four representatives from the Foundation for Economic Education (FEE) in New York City; from continental Europe, Maurice Allais, Walter Eucken, Carl Iversen, and Wilhelm Röpke.[10] However, of all these, Hayek was unquestionably the dominant figure, not just because he had been instrumental in forming the MPS but because of *The Road to Serfdom* (1944). As Keynes symbolized the philosophy against which they were fighting (see Cockett 1994, chap. 1), Hayek's book provided the manifesto of the new movement.[11] In Britain, *The Road to Serfdom*, in the words of one commentator, "succeeded in redefining the political debate . . . in a way that no single book or statement of belief has done since" (Cockett 1994, 97). In the United States, after Hayek had failed to find a publisher, Director and Knight had the book published by the University of Chicago Press.

The significance of the MPS is not that it played a major role in sponsoring either free market research or activities related to economic policy: it did neither of these. Instead, its importance lies in its being the center of a network. It linked several of the main institutions involved in the subsequent transformation of economics: the network of think tanks centered in the London Institute of Economic Affairs (IEA) and the Chicago school, and later the network centered on the public choice society. Other organizations, such as the Institute for Humane Studies (discussed below), performed a similar networking role, but the MPS was unique in the range of its contacts (including libertarians, Austrians, and mainstream economists) and in the period over which it operated.

While Hayek was preparing for the initial meeting of the MPS, he was approached by a businessman, Anthony Fisher, who had recently read *The Road to Serfdom* and wanted advice about influencing public policy for the better. Hayek's response was, "I would join with others in forming a scholarly research organisation to supply intellectuals in universities, schools, journalism and broadcasting with authoritative studies of the economic theory of markets and its application to practical affairs" (quoted in Cockett 1994, 124). This eventually materialized, in 1955, as the IEA. This had a different focus from the MPS in that it was concerned with what Hayek had called the "second-hand dealers" in ideas (123). The IEA was, as a registered charity, strictly nonpolitical, its

10. Hartwell 1995, 45–46, contains a complete list. The sixty-four founding members are listed on page 51.

11. The other book usually grouped with this is Popper 1952. Karl Popper, a colleague of Hayek's at the London School of Economics, also attended the initial meeting of the MPS.

aims referring not to free markets (which might have sounded political) but to "the study of markets and pricing systems as technical devices for registering preferences and apportioning resources" (132). However, it published a series of pamphlets and books, by academic economists as well as by journalists and political figures, exploring market solutions to economic problems, advancing many ideas (such as privatization, deregulation, and methods for creating markets) that eventually became government policy. Despite its nonpartisan position, it exerted a particularly strong influence on the Conservative Party under Margaret Thatcher. Beyond this, it arguably helped change the climate of opinion through advocating policies that had previously not been taken seriously (the "thinking the unthinkable" of Cockett's title) and through providing a stream of material that, in addition to being accessible to policymakers, was attractive to students as applications of microeconomic theory.

In setting up the IEA, Fisher was influenced by the Foundation for Economic Education in New York, which he visited in 1952. This was founded in 1946 by Leonard E. Read, supported by Mises and the journalist Henry Hazlitt (both at the initial MPS meeting), to "educate the world on the principles of free-market economics": "individual freedom," "private property," "limited government," and "free trade."[12] Like the IEA, it focused on retailing free market ideas, not on academic research. The same was true of the American Enterprise Institute (AEI), founded in 1943. Education in the principles of liberty was also the aim of the Liberty Fund, established in 1960 by Pierre F. Goodrich. Goodrich was closely involved with the MPS from 1951 till his death in 1973, when he left most of his estate to the Liberty Fund, which used it to finance an extensive program of conferences and publications (see Starbuck 2001).

The IEA, AEI, and FEE were not the first think tanks to be formed in Britain or the United States to analyze social policy.[13] In Britain, there was the Fabian Society (established in 1884), the National Institute of Economic and Social Research (1931), and Political and Economic Planning (1931). In the United States, there were the Russell Sage Foundation (1907), the Brookings Institution (1916), and the National Bureau

12. Taken from its Web site (www.fee.org, "About FEE"), which describes it as "America's oldest free-market organization."

13. For attempts to define and classify different types of think tank, see McGann and Weaver 2002 and Abelson 2002, on which this paragraph draws extensively. Discussion of Britain draws on Denham and Garnett 1998. These make the point that the think tank, despite claims to the contrary (e.g., Edwards 1997, 28) is not a uniquely American institution.

of Economic Research (1920). These, however, though rarely neutral in that their work had identifiable influence on policy (cf. Abelson 2002, 23), were based on the premise that disinterested social scientific inquiry could contribute to better policymaking and were engaged in academic research, the policy implications of which might emerge only in the long term. They have been described as "universities without students" (McGann and Weaver 2002, 7; Abelson 2002, 18–19). Even the Fabians, though politically committed, were convinced that the optimal strategy was a long-term one. These organizations differed from those established in what has been called the second wave of think tank creation, from 1946 to 1970, dominated by contract research. The major one (discussed in more detail in section 3) was RAND, founded in 1948 to undertake research that would aid U.S. defense policy. The Hudson Institute (established 1961) was modeled on RAND. Toward the end of this period the Urban Institute was established (in 1968) to focus on domestic problems.

In the 1970s there was a further change in the think tank landscape with the sudden proliferation of advocacy think tanks, closer to the IEA, AEI, and FEE in that they were committed to advocating certain causes and marketing their ideas in a way not true of previous generations of academic and contract-research think tanks. Many of these were committed to free markets: in that sense, unlike the earlier academic think tanks, they were not searching for new policies so much as applying policies they already accepted (cf. Denham and Garnett 1998). In Britain there emerged the Centre for Policy Studies (1974), the Adam Smith Institute (1977), and the Social Affairs Unit (1980), the last one set up with the active support of the IEA. In this period, Fisher was also instrumental in setting up the Canadian Fraser Institute (1975) and the International Center for Economic Policy Studies (1977), which later became the Manhattan Institute (see Frost 2002, chap. 8; Abelson 2002, 44–46).[14] Encouraged by these, Fisher embarked on a program to create institutes across the world through Atlas (founded in 1981): "A non-profit 501(c)(3) organization headquartered in Fairfax, Virginia, that brings freedom to the world by helping develop and strengthen a network of market-oriented think tanks that spans the globe," its mission being "to discover, develop and support intellectual entrepreneurs worldwide who have the potential to create independent public policy institutes and related programs, which advance our vision; and to provide ongoing

14. Frost discusses ways in which the Manhattan Institute differed from the IEA.

support as such institutes and programs mature."[15] At a dinner to celebrate the thirtieth anniversary of the IEA, Fisher referred to "a family of 40 institutes in 20 countries" (Frost 2002, 161).[16] By the end of the century, Atlas was working with or supporting 150 such bodies (Frost 2002, 157).[17]

The most important development in the United States was the Heritage Foundation, established in 1973. Despite the existence of the AEI, it was felt that there was a need for a more aggressive conservative body to influence policy to counter the efficiency with which liberal (Left) ideas were translated into policy via the Brookings Institution, seen as part of the Left's "finely-tuned policy making machine" (Edwards 1997, 2–3). This feeling became more acute after the failure of Barry Goldwater's 1964 presidential campaign, when many conservatives felt that even Republicans were pursuing centrist policies and were not doing enough to stand up to communism.[18] It was against this background that a group centered on Strom Thurmond and two other Republican senators, backed by Joseph Coors, set up the Analysis and Research Association (ARA) in 1971.[19] The aim was to provide members of Congress with more timely economic advice than the AEI was providing. For a variety of reasons this developed, in 1972, into the Schuchman Foundation, which also attracted funds from Richard M. Scaife and other businessmen. Because of differences on how it should operate, it was decided to form a new organization that would aim to feed directly into the policymaking process. This was given the name of the Heritage Foundation, founded in 1973. As late as 1977, when Edwin Feulner took over as its president, it was not clear that the foundation would survive (Edwards 1997, 24).

Over the following years, however, Feulner sought to use it to create "a new conservative coalition that would replace the New Deal coalition which had dominated American politics for half a century," focusing on educational choice, urban enterprise zones, supply-side economics, deregulation, and reductions in the size of government (32).[20] In 1979,

15. Quotations from www.atlasusa.org/aboutatlas/index.php?refer=aboutatlas.

16. For a directory of many such organizations, see the appendix to Frost 2002, 179–261.

17. For broader international surveys of think tanks, see Stone, Denham, and Garnett 1998 and McGann and Weaver 2002.

18. Feulner (2002, 67) claims that some, at this time, were predicting worldwide state socialism and the end of U.S. global power.

19. This account of the origins of the Heritage Foundation is based on Edwards 1997, chap. 1.

20. Edwards (1997, chap. 2) also provides an account of the Heritage Foundation's ideas on foreign policy. See Feulner 2002 for a shorter account.

when Jimmy Carter seemed likely to be defeated, the Heritage Foundation took on the task of designing a conservative program along these lines that an incoming Republican administration could take up—*Mandate for Leadership*, which sold fifteen thousand copies in the first year after publication. When Ronald Reagan was elected, this book, and with it the foundation, became securely established in the policymaking process (47–52). Feulner claims that its income grew at 300 percent annually from 1973 to 1980, at 14 percent annually from 1980 to 1990, and at 10 percent from 1990 to 1997. By 1997 its annual income was $35 million and its operating expenses $26.6 million, larger than even the much longer-established Brookings and Hoover Institutions.[21] A much larger proportion (61 percent) came from individuals than was the case with other large think tanks.

4. Universities and International Organizations

Within academia, the main center for research along free market lines was undertaken during the 1950s and 1960s at the University of Chicago. The core of the Chicago school was a group of Knight's students and protégés that formed in the mid-1930s: Milton and Rose Friedman, George Stigler, Allen Wallis, Aaron Director, and Henry Simons.[22] However, up to the 1940s, Chicago economics was very diverse, the turning point coming in 1945–46, when Oskar Lange and Jacob Viner left, and Friedman, Director, and Wallis joined the faculty (Stigler did not arrive till 1958). On his arrival, Friedman immediately assumed the intellectual leadership of the group, setting the tone of Chicago economics for the next quarter century. There was opposition to his ideas but this was greatly reduced with the departure of the Cowles Commission to Yale in 1953. Melvin W. Reder (1982, 32) sums up Friedman's influence as follows:

> This exposure to the force of Friedman's argument became a distinguishing characteristic of Chicago economists, faculty members and students. However much they might disagree with him on one or a number of issues, awareness of the strength of Friedman's case led Chicago economists to become interpreters of Friedman's views to uncomprehending outsiders. . . . [This] had the effect, in the 1950s and

21. Their operating expenses were $23.8 and $20.8 million, respectively. See Abelson and Lindquist 2002, 53. The figure for the AEI was $14 million.

22. See Reder 1982, 7–11.

early 1960s, of making all Chicago economists appear to be dominated by Friedman and, I suspect, had the further effect of bringing them much closer to his own views than they would otherwise have come.

The core of the Chicago school was its PhD program, within which Economics 301 (taught mostly by Friedman and Gary Becker) played a key role. This was a rigorous training program, with a high failure rate, that created economists with the Chicago style of thought (Reder 1982, 8–9). The primary commitment was to "good economics," where good economics meant the rigorous application of standard microeconomic theory. Over the years, this theory was applied to an increasing range of applied fields, enlarging the influence of the Chicago school. It was entirely possible to accept this way of doing economics even though one did not start from Friedman's or Stigler's ideological position. Faculty appointments were based, as in other universities, on "professional recognition." Thus in 1974, Friedman could note that eleven out of thirteen Clark Medal winners had either held or been offered a teaching position at Chicago. However, in applied fields, the emphasis was not on technical virtuosity but on "the interest and reliability of [an applicant's] empirical findings" (Reder 1982, 33): "In these (numerous) cases, adherence to TP becomes very important. Inconsistency of empirical findings with the implications of TP, especially if the investigator is not greatly concerned about the inconsistency, is considered to be poor performance." TP is short for tight prior equilibrium theory, defined by Reder (1982, 11) as "rooted in the hypothesis that decision makers so allocate the resources under their control that there is no alternative allocation such that any one decision maker could have his utility increased without a reduction occurring in the expected utility of at least one other decision maker." In other words, good empirical work supported the conclusion that the world was Pareto efficient. The implications of this for attitudes toward the state are clear.

A related interpretation argues that the distinguishing feature of Chicago economics was "a disciplinary self-critique" that "narrowed the boundaries of 'legitimate' economics in the attempt to entrench it in its area of scientific competence" (Emmett 1998, 135).[23] Starting in the 1940s, there was a shift away from examining what students had learned

23. There is a clear parallel here with Friedman's (1953) dramatic narrowing of the scope of economic theory to exclude the processes whereby business decisions were made.

about a field to whether they could apply price theory. This was institutionalized through the system of workshops, started by Gregg Lewis and formally integrated into the PhD program in 1952–53 (147). Though they covered a wide range of fields, the most prominent was Friedman's workshop on money and banking. These workshops helped define what was meant by "good economics" and to instill its methods into graduate students.

What came to be known as Chicago school was never synonymous with the economics department: there were members of the department who did not support Friedman's approach, and there were people outside it (e.g., Wallis, in the business school) who did. Though sympathetic with some of Friedman's views, Knight and Hayek did not agree with his way of doing economics and remained outside. Becker was appointed to the sociology department in 1983, alongside James Coleman, who was applying rational choice methods to sociology. Henry Simons, Aaron Director, and Ronald Coase had positions in the law school. As the list of Nobel laureates indicates,[24] by the 1980s Chicago economics had become a major influence on the profession and on other disciplines, notably sociology and law (Medema 1998). Outside the United States, Chicago economists saw themselves as exporting "good economics." Harry Johnson, a Chicago professor from 1959 to 1974, was simultaneously (1966–74) a professor at the London School of Economics (LSE). His main aim was to promote good economics, though critics such as Joan Robinson saw him as trying to turn LSE into a version of Chicago. The most substantial foreign link, however, came through an agreement, lasting from 1955 to 1964, with the Catholic University of Chile (Harberger 1997; Valdes 1995). On the basis of this experience, the program was extended to other countries in Latin America: Argentina and Colombia. Harberger (1997, 302) estimated that from 1955 to 1980, "more than half of the economists trained at leading foreign institutions studied at Chicago." Chicago-trained economists were responsible for many of the liberalization and reform programs pursued.

After Chicago, the second major network in the transformation of attitudes toward government was the one centered on Public Choice Society.[25] Modern public choice stems from a group of works published around 1960. Its institutional origins lie in the Thomas Jefferson Center

24. Friedman, in 1976; Schultz, 1979; Stigler, 1982; Miller, 1990; Coase, 1991; Becker, 1992; Fogel, 1993; Lucas, 1995; Heckman, 2000.

25. This draws heavily on Medema 1998. See also Mitchell 1988, 1999.

for Studies in Political Economy at the University of Virginia, by Buchanan and Warren Nutter, in 1957. This center brought together scholars "who wish to preserve a social order based on liberty" (quoted in Medema 2000, 303). They were trained as Chicago economists and, though convinced that liberty could best be sustained through free markets, they realized that there was a need to study how price theory could be applied to political economy—to problems of decision making that did not take place through markets—and the center began to focus on this through establishing, in 1963, a Committee for the Analysis of Nonmarket Decisionmaking. In 1967–68, the center collapsed, and Buchanan and Tullock established the Center for Study of Public Choice, at the Virginia Polytechnic Institute, in 1968. It remained there till it moved to George Mason University in 1983.

In 1963 the Thomas Jefferson Center held a conference on nonmarket decision making. By 1970 this had become an annual event, and sessions began to be held at the American Economic Association meetings. After the 1967 conference, the Public Choice Society was set up, and by 1971 it had five hundred members. Those attending the conferences and joining the society were a mixture of economists and political scientists, and they became a forum linking a wide range of people, most of whom shared with Buchanan and Tullock the rational choice approach. By the end of the 1990s, a sizable number of papers presented at meetings of the Public Choice Society were being published in mainstream journals such as the *American Economic Review*.

The group, or perhaps a collection of groups, most ardently in favor of free markets was the "Austrians."[26] These were economists, mostly in the United States, who sought to keep alive the traditions of Hayek and Ludwig von Mises. However, though Hayek's ideas on the market later proved an important influence on Austrian economics, in the 1950s it was Mises who kept a specifically Austrian tradition going at New York University, where he joined the faculty in 1946 and continued to teach until his death in 1973. His students there included Murray Rothbard and Israel Kirzner. When Austrian economics began to grow in the mid-1970s, these two were, along with Ludwig Lachman, from South Africa, the dominant figures. Starting with a conference in 1974, they began to organize as a distinct group centered on a small number of universities: New York, George Mason, and Auburn. New York University

26. This paragraph draws on Vaughn 1994.

established an Austrian Economics Program (with substantial support from the Sarah Scaife Foundation) and George Mason launched the Center for the Study of Market Processes (supported by several foundations, the largest supporter being the Koch Family Foundations).

The final type of institution that needs to be mentioned is international organizations, of which the most important are the IMF and the World Bank.[27] These were not connected with the rise of free market groups (indeed, most Austrians have been hostile to such large governmental organizations) but are an important part of the shift in opinion within mainstream economics. The IMF was dominated by economists, and its heart was considered to be its research department.[28] The IMF was important in the 1950s and 1960s in two ways. It contributed to the literature on international monetary economics, and it helped the international dissemination of economic ideas. It ran training courses for officials from member countries, undertook consultation visits, and entered into negotiations over standby credit arrangements. The result, according to Jacques Polak (1997, 217), was "in many cases to bring about a certain parallelism in economic thinking that greatly facilitated agreement on the conditions governing the extension of Fund credit when the need for a Fund arrangement presented itself." These channels of communication were among the factors that led to the emergence of the Washington Consensus in the late 1980s.

In the early decades of the IMF, lending was primarily to developed economies that were experiencing temporary balance of payments difficulties. The period was also one of comparative stability (the "Golden Age") with the result that payments deficits were generally on a limited scale. However, in the 1970s, when the world economy became more unstable, it was faced with much larger deficits and with much larger disparities between inflation rates than had been possible under the Bretton Woods system. The IMF therefore had to become involved in lending on a larger scale, recycling dollars accumulated by oil-exporting countries and helping oil importers fund much larger payments deficits than had been observed earlier. After the 1979 oil shock, to which many developed countries responded with more restrictive policies than had

27. This claim refers to the 1970s transformation. If the focus were on earlier periods, other organizations, such as the League of Nations (which commissioned influential studies in the 1930s) and the United Nations (important in postwar development economics) would have to be given more weight.

28. See Polak 1997.

been imposed after the 1973–74 shock, balance of payments and international debt problems arose on an even larger scale, this time encompassing many developing economies. The IMF responded to this need by greatly increasing countries' borrowing facilities. In 1983, quotas were twice as high in relation to trade as in 1972. The result was that the IMF began to impose stricter conditions on lending to ensure that the necessary adjustments took place. According to Polak (1984, 254), "There can . . . be no doubt that since 1981 the Fund's conditionality has been more demanding than it was in any earlier period." As the IMF became involved not simply in providing short-term funds itself but in negotiating credit packages—serving as an intermediary between countries that were in difficulties and commercial banks, aid donors, the World Bank, and other organizations—its role in imposing conditions on recipient countries grew. Furthermore, as it became more involved with developing countries, the conditions perceived as necessary to ensure financial viability became even more controversial than those imposed on developed countries and went beyond financial matters to include trade liberalization and other reforms.

In contrast to the IMF, economists played a minor role in the early years of the World Bank, there being only 20 on the staff as late as 1965.[29] Under Robert McNamara, the number of economists grew to 120 by 1969. One reason for this expansion was McNamara's belief that because loans would inevitably be small in relation to a country's total investment, it was important to disseminate ideas. The result was that greater importance was attached to research; over the next two decades, the number of economists employed at the World Bank rose to around 800. Many of them were undertaking academic research of a type that would not have been out of place in a university.

The World Bank's role changed in 1980 when it abandoned its previous practice of lending only to finance specific projects and introduced "structural-adjustment lending." The aim of this lending was to help countries overcome medium-term balance of payments policies without the adverse effect on growth that would be produced by traditional expenditure-reducing policies. Loans were made on condition that countries implemented reform programs, liberalizing their economies. Financial markets were to be opened up; the public sector was to be reduced; markets were to be deregulated; and controls on investment were to be

29. See Ferreira and Stern 1997 and De Vries 1997.

removed. Given the serious balance of payments problems faced by many developing countries during and after the 1980s debt crisis, such policies became a major political issue, as many criticized the World Bank and the IMF for being the main instruments of conservative policies to force governments to liberalize their economies at the expense of the poor.

5. Funding Free Markets

An important element in the story told in the previous three sections is funding. The institutions discussed in the preceding sections arose because there were people who wanted to pay for them. The picture of funding is complex and not enough is known to be able to describe it in any detail. However, it is important to make the point that funding may have played a role, if only for two reasons. The first is to make it clear that the preferences of potential funding sources can and do influence what is done: money does not flow automatically on the basis of some notion of quality independent of ideology or interests. The second is to point out the complexity of the picture.

When U.S. philanthropic foundations began, in the interwar period, to get involved in funding economic research by other organizations, one of their aims was to distance themselves from controversy that arose from employing researchers themselves (see Goodwin 1998, 74–78). The main foundations funding economics were Carnegie, Rockefeller, Sloan, and Russell Sage, along with many overseas organizations. From the 1950s these were joined by the Ford Foundation, which became able to fund research on a large scale once it had settled a dispute with the U.S. Treasury. In 1951 it was by far the largest foundation, with assets of $417 million, making it significantly larger than either Rockefeller's $122 million or Carnegie's $170 million. The aim of these bodies was to influence economists' behavior, through funding economists they thought were good and not funding those they thought were bad,[30] but overall their goals were generally to promote impartial, objective research, and bodies such as Brookings, the National Bureau of Economic Research, and the Social Science Research Council fitted the bill. Though not ideologically neutral, they had no overt political agenda. This was part of their ideology—that good social science research would promote the private

30. Craufurd Goodwin (1998, 76–77) provides some examples of such attempts to exert influence.

enterprise system and improve economic performance. It has been described as "scientific philanthropy" (cf. Parmar 2002, 15–16).

In the 1950s this policy continued, though it began to change. Ford put money into RAND, which, as explained above, took this ideology of scientific detachment even further. The association with the Cold War, the U.S. defense establishment, and anticommunism arguably involved a strengthening and focusing of an ideology already present. Ford's involvement with Chicago, like that of Carnegie and Rockefeller, was part of a much broader strategy of consolidating U.S. influence in Europe and the rest of the world by fostering pro-U.S. modernizing elites (Parmar 2002, 14). Henry Ford II caused the Ford Foundation's policy to swing to the right (Amadae 2003, 38). However, a technocratic vision of government, represented by the policies pursued by Robert McNamara (who came from the Ford Motor Company) in the 1960s as secretary of defense, could still involve what might be regarded as "big" government and "efficient" involvement of government in economic activities. The free world needed government as well as private enterprise.

Up to the 1960s, there were only two significant foundations committed to explicitly free market ideas: the Volker Fund and the Earhart Foundation. The Volker Fund supported the Foundation for Economic Education, the American participants in early meetings of the MPS, and many publications including the Volker Fund Series in Humane Studies and texts given away through the National Book Foundation. It helped bring Hayek to Chicago and supported Mises in New York, as well as other individuals such as Rothbard, who from 1952 to 1962 was paid for reviewing books for their suitability for distribution through the National Book Foundation. The Volker Fund's work was continued through the Institute of Humane Studies, set up in 1961 by F. A. Harper (who had been on the staff of FEE from 1946 to 1958) and which continued its educational programs.[31] The Fund was dissolved in 1962, a large part of its funds eventually going to the Hoover Institution.[32] The Earhart Foundation was, in its early years, important through its one-year fellowships. By 1957 these had gone to seventy-five graduate students in economics. Nine out of thirty-five Nobel Prize winners had previously received

31. A referee has suggested I should pay more attention to the many summer schools for undergraduate and postgraduate students that have taken place, which also helped create networks and encourage certain types of thinking. Assessing this is a major task, so here I can do no more than indicate that it may have been an important factor.

32. This draws on a number of sources including Kelley 1997, 62; George 1996.

an Earhart fellowship, including Becker, Buchanan, Coase, Friedman, Hayek, Lucas, Daniel McFadden, Vernon Smith, and George Stigler.

Many of the initiatives discussed above were the result of wealthy individuals deciding to commit money to promote the case of free enterprise. Hunold, who played a major role in the early years of the MPS, was a Swiss businessman. Fisher, who was behind the IEA, was the owner of Buxted Chickens, which was responsible for the successful introduction of broiler chickens into the U.K. (and was advised by an agriculture specialist he met through the MPS). Joseph Coors, of Coors brewery, was behind the Heritage Foundation. Also important was Richard Mellon Scaife, the chairman of the Scaife Foundations in 1973, pursuing a consistently conservative line, who became a trustee of the Heritage Foundation in 1985. Coors and Scaife initially put in \$250,000 and \$900,000, respectively.[33] Between 1985 and 2002 the Scaife Foundations contributed around \$20 million to Heritage.[34] Between the same years, the Lynde and Harry Bradley Foundation contributed over \$12 million, the John M. Olin Foundation over \$8 million, and the Castle Rock Foundation (founded with an endowment from the Adolph Coors Foundation) almost \$2 million, as total grants from foundations over this period came to \$45 million. However, from 1978 to 1997, such income accounted for around only a quarter of Heritage's income, between 40 and 50 percent of which came from individuals (Feulner 2002, 72). In the 1980s corporations provided almost as much as foundations.[35]

This financing is typical of the practice of a group of conservative foundations to focus resources on a select group of think tanks and other institutions. During the same period, the American Enterprise Institute received \$32 million from a similar list of foundations. A similar pattern can be found in foundation support for universities. Certain institutions have been targeted and receive consistent funding over a period of years, enabling them to develop. Given their importance to developments in economics during this period, good examples are the Center for the Study of Public Choice at George Mason University and Law and

33. This and the immediately following statistics come from www.mediatransparency.org. Note that data from some of the smaller foundations are incomplete, so this may slightly underestimate the total.

34. The Sarah Scaife Foundation, the Scaife Family Foundation, and the Carthage Foundation.

35. Data for the period since 1985 can be obtained from www.mediatransparency.org. Because of disclosure regulations, data on philanthropic foundations is more complete than for individuals or corporations.

Economics at Chicago.[36] For the former, the largest donor was the Scaife Foundations, followed by the Olin and Bradley foundations. Scaife and Olin illustrate the way funding has been provided consistently, much of it to cover general operating expenses rather than specific projects. Compared with the center's overall budget, the sums received have not been large, but they are significant and regular enough to have been very important. A similar pattern emerges for Chicago's Law and Economics, though the sums involved are larger, and it is the Olin Foundation that provided the bulk of the funding.

The point here is not that conservative foundations are large, because by the standards of the big foundations they are not. For example, Ford's assets in 2002 were $9,300 million, compared with Bradley's $485 million, and only three conservative foundations are in the top one hundred. Rather, it is that they have adopted a particular strategy, designed to influence ideas, in which they have been very successful. Funding to liberal causes has been as large, if not larger, but it has been less narrowly focused on achieving specific goals.[37]

6. Technique and Ideology

A final approach to the story is the spread of mathematical techniques within economics.[38] Here, the story concerns only the shift of opinion within mainstream economics, for many free market economists have rejected the methods that have come to dominate economics within the past fifty years. It is a story that is sketched only briefly, to illustrate a further possible dimension to the problem. It is a methodological argument that, to be persuasive, needs to be developed in considerably more detail than the confines of a single essay permit. Whatever view is held about the causes, there is little dispute that economics has become more technical in the period since the Second World War (see, e.g., Solow 1997). In the 1940s it was becoming hard for many of the older generation to keep up with recent developments, and, despite the increase in mathematical training required of economists, this has remained true. There were some

36. See also Covington 1997, 8–10.

37. A helpful discussion of this is provided in Schambra et al. 2004, which is a discussion of Krehely, House, and Kernan (2004) between a representative of the National Committee for Responsive Philanthropy and representatives of several conservative foundations (including Bradley). The figures are from page 6.

38. The argument in this section overlaps with Backhouse 2005 and is being developed in more detail in another paper.

fields where technical requirements had been high throughout the 1950s (for example, general equilibrium and social choice theory), but in the 1970s many fields that had previously been open to less technical work followed suit. Industrial economics, development economics, and even international trade and macroeconomics began to require understanding of mathematical techniques not required a decade earlier.

The conventional view is that the use of mathematics protects economists from ideology,[39] as well as from being accused of being driven by ideology.[40] However, there is another case that can be made. This is that the intellectual value judgments that underlie technical economics, *as it currently exists*, bias one toward conservative conclusions. Stigler (1959, 522) has argued that "the professional study of economics makes one politically conservative." He defined a conservative as someone who wishes most economic activity to be organized by private enterprise and believes that the forces of competition will generally hold private power in check and promote efficiency—an advocate of laissez-faire. In learning economics, one is drilled in the problems of all economic systems and how the price system solves these problems. Clearly, Stigler is not suggesting that any bias is involved here, but one might read it differently. For example, feminists have argued that male values underlie some of the basic value judgments underlying economic theory (see, e.g., Nelson 1993, 2001).[41]

The reason the use of mathematics can introduce bias is that economics, like any science, is based on a set of intellectual values, some of which are explicit but most of which are implicit. Without them it could not function. Some of these are very basic—not deliberately falsifying one's results, acknowledging one's sources, and so on. Above this are values of the type that Daniel Hausman (1992) has sought to identify, such as the desire for theories that are of broad scope and the desire for economics to stand "separate" from other sciences, such as psychology. However, the most important aspect of this is the desire for a particular form of rigor.[42] Economists prefer theories where all the assumptions necessary to derive the conclusions are specified.

39. See Hutchison 1964.

40. It has been argued that the reason why Samuelson's textbook could survive conservative criticism when Lorie Tarshis's book, which provided a similar exposition of Keynesian economics, could not, was that it was more technical.

41. The argument sketched below has much in common with some feminist arguments, such as Nelson's, but is taken in a different direction.

42. For a discussion of other types of rigor, see Weintraub 1998.

If economists were omniscient and their theories were able to take into account every possible type of interaction between people, the requirement that theories be rigorous in this sense might be irrelevant. Regrettably, this is not the case. Economists have at their disposal a limited range of theoretical and conceptual tools that can be used in their mathematical modeling. The result is that the desire to derive arguments rigorously means that they are confining themselves to saying what these theoretical tools allow them to say. Given the state of the techniques available to economists, pursuing this form of rigor has severely constrained what economists have been able to say—the models and theories they have been able to work with. Individual optimization and perfect competition have been, for the most part, adopted not because economists believe them to be correct but because they permit rigorous analysis. This is changing as economists create new techniques, but slowly. The result can be to introduce bias, in much the same way that Julie A. Nelson (1993) has argued that even the notion of "scientific detachment" has gendered content.

One innovation introduced with the new classical macroeconomics (NCM) in the 1970s was methodological. Edmund Phelps and others had shown that limited information could be used to explain unemployment in a way that was consistent with rational, profit-maximizing behavior. The NCM elevated this into a methodological principle: that tastes and technology were fundamental, and that behavior should be modeled as if agents took advantage of all the opportunities open to them. When combined with the assumption that private agents were infinitely farsighted (any other assumption would be arbitrary and arguably irrational) and could anticipate all systematic (and hence predictable) government policy measures, it became hard to avoid the conclusion that active macroeconomic intervention would be ineffective. When combined with public choice arguments about the public sector decision making, activist government policy was almost inevitably seen in an even worse light. The use of representative-agent models, for purely pragmatic reasons (simplifying models so that they could be handled rigorously) ensured that coordination failures could not occur, for the same preferences underlay all private-sector decisions in the economy.

The point here is not that the use of mathematics dictated these conclusions. It clearly did not, as the example of new Keynesian macroeconomics makes clear. The point is that, at least for a while, a set of intellectual value judgments that could be presented as if they were entirely independent of any ideology made it easy to derive certain types of result and difficult to derive others. Whether or not Robert Lucas and the other architects of the new classical macroeconomics had any ideological ax to grind (I am not making any claim on this), the seemingly value-free nature of the intellectual value judgments involved, and the claim that this was the rigorous way to do macroeconomics, probably persuaded many economists to adopt a more critical attitude toward government than they would otherwise have done.

Is this not simply scientific progress, or what in section 1 was called "learning from experience"? In deciding that the Keynesian models used in the 1960s had to be changed, economists were certainly learning from experience. Insofar as there was evidence for these assumptions, the case that NCM involved learning from experience can be made, as argued in section 1. However, it is possible to argue that there was much more to it than that: that, as well as being influenced by evidence and conscious reasoning, economists were swayed by intellectual value judgments that were made simply because economists thought, no doubt for various reasons, that this must be a better way to do economics. Just as Nelson (1993) argues that a commitment to scientific detachment can produce gendered ideas, this is an argument that the intellectual values that mainstream macro economists adopted in the 1970s biased them away from solutions involving government intervention in the economy.

7. Conclusion

The rise of free market economics is a story with many dimensions. The account given here does little more than scratch the surface and sketch an agenda for a larger project. The essay suggests that the change in economists' attitudes toward the role of the state is a very complicated problem: it involves the internal dynamics of the economics profession and outside pressures ranging from changes in the funding regime to changes in the political environment. My conjecture is that no simple story will ever be adequate to explain it. One reason is that it relates to something that is hard to define precisely—the climate of opinion within the economics profession. This is what distinguishes the concern of this essay from others: for example, John Kelley's (1997) concern with free market politics in the United States, or Richard Cockett's (1994) concern with the organizations through which free market ideas were channeled into U.K. government policy, or political scientists' concerns with the implications of think tanks for the democratic process (McGann and Weaver 2002). The rise of market economics is a broad phenomenon, encompassing both free market economics and a much broader movement among mainstream economists toward greater support for markets and away from confidence in direct government intervention and planning; spanning economic advice to governments and academic economics, microeconomics and macroeconomics, and much else. The overlaps are so great that much is lost when different parts of the phenomenon are analyzed separately.

One way to interpret these developments is to outline the variety of histories that can be written.[43]

1. *Learning from mistakes*. This is the internalist account, or "Whig" history. It is the one that the majority of practicing economists, almost by definition, must subscribe to, for their own views are the latest available, and they would not hold them if they did not consider them superior to what had gone before.[44] On its own terms, such histories can provide convincing accounts of why economics changed in the 1970s toward a more free market economics. The point about the accounts given in section 1 is not that they stand up to detailed scrutiny but that they illustrate the types of account that most practicing economists would offer.
2. *Changes in the demand for economic ideas*. This involves looking more broadly than has been possible here at the patrons of economics (cf. Goodwin 1998). As the "effective demand" for economic ideas (demand backed up with cash) has changed, so has supply responded. In this story wealthy individuals, corporations, and those in control of foundations hold the key to what has happened. It has even been suggested that the key lies in the distribution of income—as the top 1 percent of the population has become

43. This list is not exhaustive. One theme that could be taken up is the political links of economists and the relationship between their political involvement and their economics. For example, little has been said here about libertarianism or anarchism as a political movement in which some of the economists discussed here were involved (see, e.g., Tucille 1971; Gerson 1997). Another line of inquiry would be to explore the generational shifts more systematically by analyzing the periods when economists entered and left the profession—for example, when those with memories of the Depression retired—and the effects of this on the age profile of the discipline.

44. Frequently outsiders see ideology where insiders see good economics. Thus Jacob Viner, when he returned to a conference in Chicago in 1951, having left the faculty five years before, commented on how it was ideologically loaded (Reder 1982, 7 n. 19). To insiders, it was no doubt "good" economics.

vastly richer compared with middle- and low-income earners, politics have become more polarized and funding for organizations that pursue policies favored by the rich increases (cf. Krugman 2003, 220–21).

3. *Academic entrepreneurship*. This story focuses on those who created the new institutions (of which those discussed here are the tip of the iceberg). The environment within universities and the financial context in which economists operate have changed dramatically in the past twenty years.[45] The creation of research centers has become almost a condition for doing research, and the ones discussed here illustrate centers that have been successful. Bodies such as the IMF, the World Bank, and central banks can be written into such a history as a new institutional forum where academic research and policymaking go together. Free market think tanks represent a similar form of entrepreneurship outside universities. Though they have generally aimed not at conducting basic research but at influencing policymakers, they have two other effects. They help change the climate of opinion and hence the range of ideas considered acceptable to entertain. In addition, they have provided new channels through which economic ideas can flow (or be directed); the existence of such channels may well influence supply.[46]
4. *Ideology*. This covers at least three different histories. One is Amadae's story of the Cold War ideology that operated through RAND and associated organizations in the 1950s, whose effects may persist up to the present day. Though it was not about free market economics, as the term has come to be understood, rational choice theory can be seen as having laid the foundations for the subsequent ideological shift. A second is to focus from the start on the attempt to revive free market economics, in opposition to the technocratic approach of RAND and the economic mainstream of the 1950s and 1960s. This history starts with the Mont Pelerin Society, or perhaps with early Austrian economics. A third is a history in which ideology is not something that comes into economics from

45. See the introduction to Mirowski and Sent 2002.

46. This is not to imply any disingenuousness on the part of suppliers. It may be that if new publication opportunities arise, and if such publications influence promotion decisions, those whose work fits with what is demanded will be more likely to obtain promotion than those who do not. Economists whose work fits will be selected over those whose work does not.

outside, in whatever guise, but is something that arises from within economics—from the basic intellectual value judgments on which the subject rests.

5. *Important individuals*. In Amadae's history, Arrow plays the key role in establishing rational choice liberalism, and by implication the case for free markets, as much through helping establish a set of intellectual values as for establishing a specific approach to economics. Against this, one might wish to argue that it was Friedman who set the tone of so many of the changes that took place in the 1970s, after which Chicago came to seem the center of economics rather than one of its peripheries. However, the institutional story emphasizes the importance of Hayek, a figure who is completely neglected in economists' internalist histories, as someone who effectively dropped out of serious economics in the 1940s. Hayek, though not a part of the Chicago school of economics, was connected to it; he was the inspiration for much Austrian economics; and he was behind the creation of many of the free market think tanks that began to transform the policy arena from the 1970s onward.
6. *The internal dynamics of the economics profession*. It is arguably not an accident that dissenters began to feel the constraints of orthodoxy in the 1970s. For much of the twentieth century there had been discussions about the role of the economics profession in society, and this had come to fruition (whether for good or ill) in the 1960s.[47] Accompanying this was the attempt to forge a consensus in which economists were technicians with access to a specialized body of knowledge that could be applied. This served to render life more difficult for dissenters, quite apart from the political turmoil of the Vietnam era and quite apart from the ideological implications discussed above. The timing may owe something to the cycle of generations: the 1970s was when the generation that came into the profession in the 1940s had reached the top.

The aim here is not to argue for one rather than another of these histories. They can all be made coherent and are legitimate ways of viewing how economists' attitudes toward government have changed. Taken individually, however, none is adequate. For example, economists were

47. See Kelley 1997 and Coats 2001. For a longer perspective, see also Bernstein 2001 and, on Britain, Middleton 1998, especially chapter 7.

clearly reacting to what they had learned, and they had to respond to what happened in the 1970s and after. However, evidence needs to be interpreted, and different interpretations, and hence paths for the subject, are conceivable. This account clearly begs the question of whether other paths might have been taken, and of the criteria that caused economists to consider modern theory an improvement on what went before, and whether external factors might not be important in explaining some of the choices made. Similarly, the Cold War may offer a plausible account of the origin of rational choice liberalism. But welfare economics did not die with the advent of social choice theory; there was great continuity between economics before and after the 1950s. Though it could be argued that the foundations of the subject had been severely damaged, the Arrow-Debreu theorems and the emergence of "Pareto efficiency" as a standard item in the economic theorist's tool kit gave welfare economics a new lease on life. It was altered profoundly by Arrow's theorem, but welfare economics was much more broadly based than just rational choice theory, even though the rhetoric of rational choice may have been used as a useful label for a very broad range of theorizing. When we turn to histories that focus on funding and entrepreneurship, there are questions about why the ventures discussed here, which (as some conservatives are quick to point out) are on a small scale compared with government funding of research through higher education and other institutions, could have done more than facilitate changes that were somehow implicit in the situation economists were facing (which turns attention back to the first history). There are also very severe problems of cause and effect. As for the intellectual bias caused by value judgments, this is clearly only a part of the story: explicit political biases seem likely to be important as well.

One response to the inability of any of these stories to encompass the whole history is to argue that they are layered: that some lie beneath others. The lessons from experience may, for example, provide the opportunities that are taken up by academic entrepreneurs who, through their identification of opportunities, are able to attract funding. What this amounts to is saying that there are causal links running from one story to another: in this case from the lessons of successes and failures of economics to the institutions and funding. However, to suggest that some of these stories lie beneath others is to suggest that causal links lie in but one direction. There are good reasons to believe that this is not so. Take the previous example: the lessons that economists choose to draw from their experiences will depend on the presuppositions of those with the most voice, and this may depend on funding, support within academia, and other factors. Causal links are likely to run in many directions, perhaps not surprisingly as these histories are themselves constructions placed on events.

The change in economists' attitudes toward the state discussed here yields several paradoxes. Friedman was central to the rise of the Chicago economics department and the development of a more critical attitude toward government within the mainstream; yet his methodology is unorthodox, having more in common with that of Wesley Clair Mitchell than with the mathematical economics and econometrics that has become dominant. It is paradoxical that Hayek's star has risen at precisely the time when a style of economics that, even more than Friedman, he rejected has come to the fore. The propagation of rational choice theory, which has lain behind much of the move toward free markets, by organizations and individuals committed to strong and efficient government is another. These reinforce the conclusion that we need a history sufficiently thick to encompass most, if not all, the stories that have been told here.

References

Abelson, D. E. 2002. *Do Think Tanks Matter?* Montreal: McGill-Queens University.

Abelson, D. E., and E. A. Lindquist. 2002. Think Tanks in North America. In *Think Tanks and Civil Societies: Catalysts for Action*, edited by J. G. McGann and R. K. Weaver. New Brunswick, N.J.: Transaction Press.

Amadae, S. M. 2003. *Rationalizing Capitalist Democracy*. Chicago: University of Chicago Press.

Arrow, K. J. 1951. *Social Choice and Individual Values*. New York: Wiley.

Backhouse, R. E. 2005. Economists, Values, and Ideology: A Neglected Agenda. Forthcoming, *Revue de philosophie économique*.

Barro, R. J. 2002. *Nothing Is Sacred: Economic Ideas for the New Millennium*. Cambridge, Mass.: MIT Press.

Bernstein, M. 2001. *A Perilous Progress: Economists and the Public Purpose in Twentieth-Century America*. Princeton: Princeton University Press.

Coats, A. W. 2001. The AEA and the Radical Challenge to American Social Science. In *Economics Broadly Considered: Essays in Honor of Warren J. Samuels*, edited by J. E. Biddle, J. B. Davis, and S. G. Medema, 144–58. London: Routledge.

Cockett, R. 1994. *Thinking the Unthinkable: Think Tanks and the Economic Counter-revolution, 1931–1983*. London: Harper Collins.

Covington, S. 1997. *Moving a Public Policy Agenda: The Strategic Philanthropy of Conservative Foundations*. Washington, D.C.: National Committee for Responsive Philanthropy.

Denham, A., and M. Garnett. 1998. Think Tanks, British Politics, and the Climate of Opinion. In Stone, Denham, and Garnett 1998.

De Vries, B. A. 1997. The World Bank as an International Player in Economic Analysis. In *The Post-1945 Internationalization of Economics*, edited by A. W. Coats. *HOPE* 28 (supplement): 225–44.

Easterly, W. 2002. *The Elusive Quest for Growth: Economists' Adventures and Misadventures in the Tropics*. Cambridge, Mass.: MIT Press.

Edwards, L. 1997. *The Power of Ideas: The Heritage Foundation at Twenty-five Years*. Ottawa, Ill.: Jameson Books.

Emmett, R. 1998. Entrenching Disciplinary Competence: The Role of General Education and Graduate Study in Chicago Economics. In *From Interwar Pluralism to Postwar Neoclassicism*, edited by M. S. Morgan and M. Rutherford. *HOPE* 30 (supplement): 134–50.

Ferreira, F., and N. Stern. 1997. The World Bank as an "Intellectual Actor." In *The World Bank: Its First Half Century*, edited by D. Kapur, J. Lewis, and R. Webb. Washington, D.C.: Brookings Institution.

Feulner, E. 2002. The Heritage Foundation. In McGann and Weaver 2002.

Friedman, M. 1953. The Methodology of Positive Economics. In *Essays in Positive Economics*, edited by M. Friedman. Chicago: University of Chicago Press.

———. 1968. The Role of Monetary Policy. *American Economic Review* 58:1–19.

Friedman, M., and R. Friedman. 1980. *Free to Choose: A Personal Statement*. Harmondsworth, U.K.: Penguin.

Frost, G. 2002. *Anthony Fisher: Champion of Liberty*. London: Profile Books.

George, S. 1996. Comment la pensee devint unique. *Le monde diplomatique* (August): 16–17.

Gerson, M. 1997. *The Neoconservative Vision: From the Cold War to the Culture Wars*. London: Madison Books.

Goodwin, C. D. 1998. The Patrons of Economics in a Time of Transformation. In *From Interwar Pluralism to Postwar Neoclassicism*, edited by M. S. Morgan and M. Rutherford. *HOPE* 30 (supplement): 53–81.

Harberger, A. 1997. Good Economics Comes to Latin America. In *The Post-1945 Internationalization of Economics*, edited by A. W. Coats. *HOPE* 28 (supplement): 301–11.

Hartwell, R. M. 1995. *A History of the Mont Pelerin Society*. Indianapolis, Ind.: Liberty Fund.

Hausman, D. M. 1992. *The Inexact and Separate Science of Economics*. Cambridge: Cambridge University Press.

Hayek, F. A., ed. 1935. *Collectivist Economic Planning*. London: Routledge.

———. 1944. *The Road to Serfdom*. London: Routledge.

Hutchison, T. W. 1964. *Positive Economics and Policy Objectives*. London: Allen and Unwin.

Kelley, J. L. 1997. *Bringing the Market Back In: The Political Revival of Market Liberalism*. New York: New York University Press.

Krehely, J., M. House, and E. Kernan. 2004. *Axis of Ideology: Conservative Foundations and Public Policy*. Washington, D.C.: National Committee for Responsible Philanthropy.

Krugman, P. 2003. *The Great Unravelling: From Boom to Bust in Three Scandalous Years*. London: Allen Lane.

Lucas, R. E. 1976. Econometric Policy Evaluation: A Critique. In *The Phillips Curve and Labor Markets*, edited by K. Brunner and A. H. Meltzer. Carnegie-Rochester Conference Series on Public Policy. Amsterdam: North Holland.

McGann, J. G., and R. K. Weaver, eds. 2002. *Think Tanks and Civil Societies: Catalysts for Ideas and Action*. New Brunswick, N.J.: Transaction Press.

McMillan, J. 2002. *Reinventing the Bazaar: A Natural History of Markets*. New York: Norton.

Medema, S. G. 1998. Wandering the Road from Pluralism to Posner: The Transformation of Law and Economics in the Twentieth Century. In *From Interwar Pluralism to Postwar Neoclassicism*, edited by M. S. Morgan and M. Rutherford. *HOPE* 30 (supplement): 202–24.

———. 2000. "Related Disciplines": The Professionalization of Public Choice Analysis. In *Toward a History of Applied Economics*, edited by R. E. Backhouse and J. Biddle. *HOPE* 32 (supplement): 289–323.

Middleton, R. 1998. *Charlatans or Saviours: Economists and the British Economy from Marshall to Meade*. Cheltenham, U.K.: Edward Elgar.

Mirowski, P., and E.-M. Sent, eds. 2002. *Science Bought and Sold: Essays in the Economics of Science*. Chicago: University of Chicago Press.

Mitchell, W. C. 1988. Virginia, Rochester, and Bloomington: Twenty-five Years of Public Choice and Political Science. *Public Choice* 56:101–19.

———. 1999. Political Science and Public Choice, 1950–1970. *Public Choice* 98:237–49.

Nelson, J. A. 1993. Value Free or Value-less? Notes on the Pursuit of Detachment in Economics. *HOPE* 25.1:121–45.

———. 2001. Economic Methodology and Feminist Critiques. *Journal of Economic Methodology* 8.1:93–97.

Nordhaus, W. D. 1975. The Political Business Cycle. *Review of Economic Studies* 42:169–90.

Parmar, I. 2002. American Foundations and the Development of International Knowledge Networks. *Global Networks* 2.1:13–30.

Phelps, E. S. 1967. Phillips Curves, Expectations of Inflation, and Optimal Unemployment over Time. *Economica*, n.s., 34.3:254–81.

Phelps, E. S., et al. 1970. *Microeconomic Foundations of Employment and Inflation Theory*. London: Macmillan.

Polak, J. J. 1984. The Role of the Fund. In *The International Monetary System: Forty Years after Bretton Woods*. Boston: Federal Reserve Bank of Boston.

———. 1997. The Contribution of the International Monetary Fund. In *The Post-1945 Internationalization of Economics*, edited by A. W. Coats. Durham, N.C.: Duke University Press.

Popper, K. R. 1952. *The Open Society and Its Enemies*. London: Routledge.

Reder, M. W. 1982. Chicago Economics: Permanence and Change. *Journal of Economic Literature* 20:1–38.

Schambra, W., et al. 2004. "Axis of Ideology" or Excess of Mythology: A Look at the National Committee for Responsive Philanthropy's Latest Report on Conservative Foundations and Public Policy. www.ncrp.org/PDF/HudsonTranscript.pdf.

Solow, R. M. 1997. How Did Economics Get That Way, and What Way Did It Get? *Daedalus* 126:39–58.

Starbuck, D. 2001. *The Goodriches: An American Family*. Indianapolis, Ind.: Liberty Fund.

Stigler, G. J. 1959. The Politics of Political Economists. *Quarterly Journal of Economics* 73.4:522–32.

Stone, D., A. Denham, and M. Garnett, eds. 1998. *Think Tanks across Nations*. Manchester: Manchester University Press.

Tucille, J. 1971. *It Usually Begins with Ayn Rand*. New York: Stein and Day.

Valdes, J. G. 1995. *Pinochet's Economists: The Chicago School in Chile*. Cambridge: Cambridge University Press.

Vaughn, K. I. 1994. *Austrian Economics in America: The Migration of a Tradition*. Cambridge: Cambridge University Press.

Weintraub, E. R. 1998. Controversy: Axiomatisches Missverständnis. *Economic Journal* 108:1837–47.

Williamson, J. 1990. *Latin American Adjustment: How Much Has Happened?* Washington, D.C.: Institute for International Economics.

———, ed. 1994. *The Political Economy of Policy Reform*. Washington, D.C.: Institute for International Economics.

The Role of Government in the History of Political Economy: The 2004 *HOPE* Conference Interpreted and Critiqued by the General Discussant

Warren J. Samuels

Ideas on the economic role of government have been a major source and a major part of the history of economic thought. The topic is rivaled only by ideas on the distributions of income and wealth, and on the historiographic, ontological, and epistemological themes with which it is often blended. One cannot expect one conference to cover every aspect or to deal thoroughly with any one aspect. This conference, organized by Peter Boettke and Steven Medema, included various kinds of papers and raised a number of issues on the subject of the economic role of government in the history of political economy. This commentary has two sections. Section 1 examines the linguistic and historiographic issues raised or illustrated by the conference papers and their discussion. Section 2 proposes a solution to one problem, the interpretive base on which to approach the topic of the conference.

The principal lesson of this report is the importance of three questions and of the answers given them: First, what is the interpretive baseline for the positive and normative *analysis* of the economic role of government? Second, what is the interpretive baseline for *efforts to control and legitimize* the use of government for economic purposes either narrowly or broadly defined? Third, what is the interpretive baseline for differentiating between papers on the role of government in the history of economic thought that are essentially positive and not overtly

This essay is dedicated to Steven G. Medema. His donation of part of his liver to his Uncle Gordon is evidence of Steve's remarkable moral nobility. I am indebted to Jeff Biddle, Leonides Montes, and Malcolm Rutherford for comments on an earlier version of this essay.

ideologically directed, and those that seek to enlist and promote an ideological agenda?

Only about one-half of past annual supplements to *HOPE* have had chapters approximating commentary on their respective conference themes, papers, and discussions, and these have varied greatly in format. For example, volume 28, *The Post-1945 Internationalization of Economics* (1996), has two short comments coupled with a lengthy report on discussions and an interpretive conclusion, the latter two by A. W. Coats. Volume 29, *New Economics and Its History* (1997), has a concluding part titled "Dynamics of the Development of Ideas," with chapters on economists' responses to anomalies and to arbitrariness coupled with John Davis's concluding chapter offering a historiographical view à la Andrew Pickering of the problem of doing recent economic thought. In volume 30, *From Interwar Pluralism to Postwar Neoclassicism* (1998), Mary Morgan and Malcolm Rutherford's introductory chapter presents an integrative summary of the contributions (as do such chapters in numerous other volumes) in identifying the principal historiographical and interpretive issues. In volume 32, *Toward a History of Applied Economics* (2000), Roger Backhouse and Jeff Biddle identify interpretive problems pertaining to the concept of applied economics; the sociology of economics; the treatment of applied economics in the history of economic thought; the interplay of facts, theories, and techniques; and the competition among conceptions of applied economics and the applicability of certain economic theories. Volume 33, *The Age of Economic Measurement* (2001), contains a chapter on perspective by Theodore M. Porter that raises historiographical and sociological themes pertinent to the topic. Volume 34, *The Future of the History of Economics* (2002), includes an afterword in which Philip Mirowski ruminates on the status of the history of economics in the discipline of economics and on the motivations of historians of economic thought and of those who hire them. The discussion in section 1 is more or less consistent with the central tendencies of past efforts. Alas, it is not possible here either to examine the individual papers in extensive detail or to recount or attribute to individuals the particular positions and views expressed in discussions. Section 2 does, however, depart from past practice in offering a solution to an important problem. My reason for doing so is due to two factors: my (and others') frustration with the ambiguities deployed in many discussions and my lifetime of studying the *problem* of studying the economic role of government both as such and as a part of the history of economic thought. Inasmuch as my proposal involves a model, or group of models, all the cautions about the limits of primitive terms and models apply, reflexively, to it.

1. Linguistic and Historiographical Problems Raised or Illustrated by the Conference Papers and Their Discussion

The Psychology of Collegiality

Most participants in the conference already knew, or knew of, one another. Two characteristics of the conference thus seem inevitable. One characteristic was the friendly collegiality that participants displayed toward one another. Hard questioning of authors was undertaken in a manner intended to avoid giving offense. A second characteristic, expressed in private and not publicly at the sessions, was a twin displeasure on the part of an unknown number of participants. One displeasure was that the George Mason attendees did not refrain from projecting their beliefs. The other displeasure was that no one, not even those displeased, challenged them for doing so. (The situation likely would have been no different had a group of Marxist Post Keynesian historians of economic thought been substituted for those from George Mason.)

The following points seem apposite. (1) Meetings of the History of Economics Society are lauded for their collegial tone. This conference was no different. (2) One cannot expect any group to leave its belief system outside the door of the conference room. Even if members of a group wanted to do so, it would be difficult to accomplish. (3) A conference in which verbal swords were overtly crossed could easily become, like much of U.S. politics, obnoxious and unattractive. (4) The problems pertaining to interpretive base were exhibited by most if not all participants; the term *laissez-faire*, for example, was frequently used as a primitive term. Such is a principal motivation for section 2. (5) Both projection of belief and response of quietude introduce strain. Which is more culpable is partly an empirical question and partly one of selective perception unaided by some unequivocal metric. The skewed beliefs of others are more readily perceived than are one's own. (6) Presumably the supply of projected belief and the demand for quietude in response have some degrees of elasticity; what constitutes the relevant prices may be equivocal. (7) The existence of opportunity cost is ubiquitous. The cost of collegiality was that underlying issues were not seriously raised and discussed. The cost of such a discussion may or may not have been the loss of collegiality. (8) Projection of one's belief system or adoption of quietude is unlikely to occur at every opportunity. Some but not all will tend to wave their flag at every opportunity, whereas others will dissent only on occasions they consider important (the Louis Brandeis principle). (9) Different people likely had varying reactions to the projection of strong beliefs, and many, perhaps most people likely were reasonably content with the quietude. (10) That several papers projected a particular belief system and criticism was muted suggests that they were already sufficiently discounted. (11) No reasonably well-known participant surprised anyone with ideas deviating from his or her usual positions. The George Mason folks, in particular, are avid promoters of their point of view, especially the ideas of James M. Buchanan, and tend to use every opportunity to do so. (12) It is not unreasonable for different perspectives to be held on this issue. (13) Dissent need not be raucous. (14) If people know in advance that self-promoting ideological papers are discouraged, they should be able to exercise self-control. (15) Given the perceivable excesses on each side, too much self-promoting ideology is preferable to censorship. People do not have to listen or heed what others say, but the others should be able to say it. (16) The problem is derivative of the larger problem of multiple interpretations; however, multiplicity does not alone yield aggressive marketing.

Problems of Language and Historiography

Frank H. Knight told a class in 1933–34, "There is no established economic usage for anything in economics" (Ostrander 2005). Seventy years later the same observation still applies—to the whole of economics, to the field of law and economics, and to the field of law. Definitions of words encompass and give effect to theories. No one theory can answer all our questions, and no one definition can accommodate all theories. Legal-economic "reality" is so complex and kaleidoscopic, and the standpoints from which it can be approached are so numerous, that multiple definitions of reality, not one, are expectable. Similarly, static and dynamic evolutionary complexity, multiple analytical and normative standpoints, and competing judgments as to both whose interests should count and the consequences thereof, are to be expected (see Samuels 2001).

Words, models, 2 × 2 and larger matrices, and dichotomies of various kinds are used to define reality. All include certain variables or factors and structure them in particular ways, while excluding other variables or factors. Some terms involve primitive, undefined words, words with widely honorific appeal but whose putative substance is selectively identified by different auditors or readers. Some terms reify in the absence of substance.

The fourteen papers and their related discussions at the conference were laden with such usages and problems of language and of historiography. The present author's subjective examination yields the following linguistic and historiographical problems or issues:

- Defining reality or framing discussion by use of primitive terms: *laissez-faire*, *public interest*, *human nature*.
- Defining reality or framing discussion by use of selected models, including dichotomies: models of pure conceptual a-institutional abstract economy versus institutionalized actual economies; models of relation of pure theory to policy; human nature; ordinary life versus perspective of philosopher = laissez-faire versus intervention = unintended beneficial order versus utilitarian intervention; justice versus utility versus equity; police; tripartite model of society (domains of market, moral rules, law and rights); epiphenomena versus underlying causes.
- Internalism versus externalism re: source of ideas.
- Practice versus ideas as driving force.
- Giving effect to selective emphasis using materials/processes essentially or arguably recursive in nature: epiphenomena versus underlying causes, cause versus consequence, economic versus political variables, laissez-faire.
- Rational reconstruction.
- Giving effect to selective emphasis in case of multiple paradigms: criteria of policy evaluation, interpreting Smith.
- Problem of interpretive base: the meaning of laissez-faire, normative evaluation of policies, religion, criteria of policy evaluation, corporatism, legal foundations of economy.
- Multiple definitions, hence disagreements.
- Belief versus definition of reality: laissez-faire, corporatism, free market economics, eugenics, Darwinism.
- Motivation of economists.

The author's subjective examination yields the following characterizations of how history of economic thought (HET) is done in the fourteen papers (some papers were classified in more than one category):

- Objective attempts to make sense of HET: Young, Bateman, Leonard, Rutherford, Colander, Backhouse, Meardon
- Objective attempt to use past ideas to make sense of present ideas: Farrant and Paganelli, Marciano
- HET interpretation as vehicle of ideology-driven approach: Boettke and Horwitz, Backhaus and Wagner, Almodovar and Cardoso, Peart and Levy
- HET interpretation on the basis of a theory of economic role of government: Boettke and Horwitz, Peart and Levy
- HET as history of policy and of policy advice, as vehicle for criticism of policy and of advice: Plessner and Young, Boettke and Horwitz

Accordingly, multiple definitions were used, multiple stories were told, and selective perception and emphasis were evident. That such was the case at times became *the* story.

Primitive Terms, Dichotomies, and Models: Two Examples

This report cannot possibly present a comprehensive account and critique of all of the conference papers. Two of them, however, provide ample opportunity to illustrate certain important points, especially the use of primitive terms that lack substantive content until selectively subconsciously provided by reader or auditor, and the use of dichotomies or models that exclude all variables other than those selectively included therein.

Peter Boettke and Steven Horwitz discuss the role of the state in the history of political economy using development economics as a case study of how economists think of the role of economic theory. They utilize several reality-defining dichotomies. They stress that tensions exist in each case that must be negotiated and worked out, and that each dichotomy involves not matters of Truth but an incentive system.

Nonetheless, they strongly tend to treat each definition (insofar as they provide definitions), each pair in a dichotomy, and each model as if it were self-subsistent. Among the dichotomies they deploy in defining reality are (1) voluntary *or* coercive authority; (2) the state as activist and corrective player *or* referee; and (3) the self-perception of economists as saviors *or* as scholars. Combining (2) and (3) Boettke and Horwitz form a 2 × 2 matrix with government as player and as referee on the vertical axis and economist as student and as savior on the horizontal axis.

Several problems arise with these terms and the dichotomies etc. they are used to form. (1) The categories are undefined though in actuality they are multifaceted, often recursive, and permit variable specification. What is voluntary and what is coercive is a case in point (Samuels 1997). Who is a scholar and who a savior is another case in point. How does one classify Friedrich Hayek: Is he a savior or a scholar? (2) The construction of the state as activist player versus referee neglects and even obfuscates the fact that even referees make choices. Government, with all its branches, is a process in which choices are made at all stages; no hard-and-fast categories of legislation, enforcement, and interpretation/review exist—they are worked out. (3) The linguistic formulation "getting institutions right" (or "getting prices right") seems to presume that there is a right institution or a right price, whereas rightness is one of the categories whose substantive content must be worked out. Culture matters, just as institutions matter; but whose culture, whose habits and mores, and which institutions? (4) A further dichotomy is that between constructivist rule-making rationality and allocative rationality. But this too is open-ended: allocative rationality includes the allocation of resources to change the rules; and rule-making rationality may include conceptions of how allocation is best undertaken, the price mechanism being only one mode. (5) The historic dichotomy to which some or much of the foregoing gives effect is that between knowledge for the purpose of knowing and for control. It has the same problems of language and other infirmities as do the other dichotomies.

Jeffrey Young's paper on Adam Smith's theory of the role of the state posits one dichotomy, between unintended order and intervention, and then presents a fuller account of Smith's complex system using parallel dichotomies. Young commences with the perceived tension between Smith's "natural liberty" and the extensive list of government interventions found in the *Wealth of Nations* (*WN*) compiled by Jacob Viner. One conference participant noted that Young's was a Hayekian reading of Smith; true enough, though, in my view, Young's reading can serve as a proxy for many other readings.

Young's basic dichotomy, between unintended order and intervention, defines reality with primitive terms. It parallels Hayek's distinction between nondeliberative and deliberative decision-making processes, the former associated by him with spontaneous order and the latter with coercive intervention. One fundamental problem is that all decision-making processes are combinations of Hayek's deliberative and nondeliberative decision making, or of Young's unintended order and intervention (Samuels 1995, 1999). This enables selective identification of institutions and processes as one or the other and selective ideological emphasis on one or the other.

Young's further dichotomies are between those with (in Griswold's [1999] terminology) the perspective of ordinary life and those with the perspective of the philosopher, between those who conventionally use local knowledge and those who formulate and use knowledge of the system, and between those who take life as it comes and those who perceive dysfunctional individual choices and market failures. While Young identifies other important elements in understanding Smith, his central vision is that of the tension between the perspective of ordinary life and the perspective of the philosopher, and a related and "similar tension between laissez-faire and intervention." In Young's complex view, the former yields the model of unintended beneficial order while the latter provides a model of utilitarian intervention. Again, these are not self-subsistent categories. Tension exists between the perception of order and the perception of a problem(s) requiring intervention. This tension exists in the minds of both ordinary people and philosophers. Ordinary people perceive problems and seek their redress through government—change of law by law. So do philosophers. Young's formulations recognize both that the philosopher's analyses are rooted in ordinary life and that anyone from ordinary life could become a philosopher. One suspects that the foregoing parallels similar elements in the working out of the impartial spectator process. One suspects, too, that Young's (and Hayek's) dichotomies refer less to conflicting domains and more to how each role or attitude is maintained by individuals.

A further tension within Smith is between, on the one hand, the trade of the philosopher, which "is, not to do anything, but to observe everything" (*WN*, I.i.9), and, on the other hand, as Young puts it, "the philosopher's job to offer the statesman advice to correct the problem" consequent to order being perceived to be not always either beneficial or equitable, and, in a different context, to critique both the content of the moral sentiments and rules promoted by the impartial spectator and the process by which they are formed. These critiques can include, for example, tension between standards of virtue and conduct and between activity coming under the headings of benevolence and justice, respectively—again reminding us that the content of what the impartial spectator stands for is in a continual process of being worked out. The work of seeking change is rooted in ordinary life. The problem of conflicting claims, customs, institutions, and conceptions of morality must be worked out; and the working out is guided by the philosopher as teacher.

Young's model posits as different decision-making processes what is, in actuality, a set of roles. These roles are not always easily distinguished, and, more important, they are performed by the same individuals. A common and perhaps obvious implication is the tension between those who are content with existing order, those who perhaps see in it the natural order of things, and those who are not content, who perceive problems of one sort or another. But these are not different people; they are the same people with mixed perceptions and policy preferences.

The model with the twin modes of order, unintended order, and order through intervention is only the first part of Young's impressive comprehensive interpretation of Smith. Young's account of Smith's position on the role of the state also includes tensions between three policy norms: between justice and utility and between commutative and distributive justice, or equity; four types of intervention; the three duties of the sovereign in the *Wealth of Nations*; and the maxims of taxation. These all involve selective perception, primitive terms, and tensions.

Young maintains that Smith's overall philosophical position is complex but that it is possible to give, in part, a coherent account of Smith's position on the role of the state in terms of the tensions between justice and utility and between commutative and distributive justice, or equity. It is in this context that the tensions between the contented and the discontented and between laissez-faire and intervention take place. The obvious implication for me, and I think for Young, is that while one can give a coherent account of Smith's overall system, one cannot necessarily derive from it particular unequivocal solutions to problems. The situation is akin to the pattern-model solutions of Hayek and Charles Wilber.

An even fuller account of the complexity of Smith's system would include, first, Smith's tripartite model of society: the formation of moral rules (*The Theory of Moral Sentiments* [*TMS*]), the operation of the market (*WN*), and the operation of government and the formation of legal rules and rights (*Lectures on Jurisprudence*) and, second, Smith's diverse philosophical—epistemological, epistemic, and ontological—position: comprising elements of several different and competing paradigms, namely, supernaturalism, naturalism, empiricism, historicism, secularism, individualism, rationalism, and so on. The fact of three domains permits, even engenders, analysis in one domain that disregards the operation of and interaction with the other domains—for example, the freedom of the "free market" vis-à-vis social control through moral and legal rules. The fact of these multiple paradigms explains how it is possible not only to give *a* coherent account of Smith's theory taken as a whole but *several* such accounts, each grounded on some combination and interpretation of the foregoing. Definitions and models (including dichotomies) frame discussion by omitting some variables and including others, the latter structured in particular ways. Even the varied use of particular terms can have varied framing effects: One can have a narrow versus a broad conception of the role of police—meaning policy—in Smith's system. One can but need not extend opposition to mercantilism to an affirmation of general laissez-faire.

Young's formulations, even if adopted by others, can be questioned along linguistic and historiographical lines. (1) To refer to public utility as "the final cause" seemingly attributes to public utility a causal role, indeed an independent and transcendent causal role, whereas public utility is an attribution whose substantive content must be worked out by people. (2) To say that "Smith derives these rules from the supposed interactions of ordinary people in society" should not be taken too strongly. Smith, like any person, can find putative illustrations of rules or the rules that seem to cover particular illustrations. I do not envision Smith claiming a great power here. Even functioning as a philosopher, anyone can do so. Both types of examples are performed by each person in the process in which moral rules are formed and the impartial spectator process operates.

Young illustrates but perhaps does not stress explicitly enough several tensions within Smith's system. (1) Young quotes Smith apropos of causation, "we observe the means adjusted with the nicest artifice to the ends which they are intended to produce" (*TMS*, II.ii.3.4). He also quotes Smith apropos of justice, to the effect that the existence of society does not require perfect justice (*WN*, IV.ix.28). (2) Moral rules and other principles are said to be due to God, but also to human reason. (3) Smith the methodological and normative individualist is accompanied by Smith the methodological and normative collectivist. (4) The problem of continuity versus change is represented by Smith quoted in affirmation of the ruler seeking to accommodate, "as well as he can, his public arrangements to the confirmed habits and prejudices of the people" (*TMS*, VI.ii.2.16) and also in affirmation of the need to change practices and laws, embedded in customs and traditions, that live on beyond their original justification. Also, (5) though approval of moral rules and government interventions must receive the approval of the impartial spectator, we know precious little about Smith's views on the process through which the moral and legal rules enforced by the impartial spectator are formed. I would speculate that parallel to, even constitutive of, the efforts to manipulate public opinion are similar efforts with regard to the impartial spectator process. People with concentrated interests in the rules will have an interest in influencing that process. (6) Young correctly points out that actions once coming under the category of benevolence may later come under the category of justice. An implication of this is the growth of the category of justice and therefore of government activities related thereto—what some will perceive as "bigger government." (7) Young concludes by calling attention to the "dialectical . . . tension between laissez-faire and intervention." He thereby indicates that whether or not the content of moral and legal rules is to be changed must be worked out—and will be worked out by people whose conflicting perceptions of things tends to reduce to such a dialectical tension.

Young's is a linguistic model with several distinct characteristics: the categories are designated by primitive terms and are substantively empty, numerous different amplifications can be made of them, numerous different stories can be told, and, in practice, both the identification of the problems to which his model of Smith are to be applied and their solutions must be worked out. The model is neither self-applying nor self-subsistent.

The foregoing is true of *all* models of Smith. Even though some or many historians of economic thought (and others) want to know what Smith *really* meant and others want to know the specific rules and policies to which Smith's analysis necessarily leads, his models lack the power to generate unique determinate results. Such desires simply underline the quest for absolutist formulation and for results that have determinacy and closure. But real-world phenomena fit his categories only on the basis of normative premises made operative through the process of working things out.

Definitions and models are useful for what they can do; their limits include what they exclude, how they handle what is included, and therefore the stories they tell and the stories they cannot tell. Above all, the stories they are used to tell depend on the addition of some normative premise that enables that story rather than some other and through which some belief rather than another is projected.

Multiple Definitions and Stories. All terms in economics can be defined in different ways, no theory can answer all our questions, and different models portray their respective domains of relevance differently. The powerful implication of the foregoing is that different definitions and different models as well as different theories in economics tell different stories. Inasmuch as correspondence with reality as a test of theory is inconclusive, other criteria for the adoption and rejection of theories etc. are used, such as ideology.

Selective Emphasis in a Recursive World. Economists, including historians of economic thought, confront the problem of modeling a world of recursive relationships. This situation facilitates selective emphasis through the exercise of conscious or unconscious choice. Whether one focuses on the world defined in terms of those who pursue ordinary lives or those who pursue the life of a philosopher (Boettke and Horwitz's savior), or deliberative and nondeliberative processes, or Smith's system of social science with the three spheres of moral rules, market, and law, and so on, neither component of a dichotomy or trichotomy is self-subsistent and independent of the other. They not only interact; they help change each other. The same is true of the multiple paradigms that entered into Smith's approach to his work. In all cases of Smith interpretation, the interpreter willy-nilly selectively emphasizes one or another element in whatever is taken to be Smith's model and does so by adding a normative premise. No wonder that such different interpretations and stories can be told about Smith.

Belief System versus Definition of Reality. Raised by but not brought up at the conference is the problem of whether economic theory and doctrine on the economic role of government is a system of belief or a definition of reality. Also not arising was Smith's distinction in the *History of Astronomy* between seeking and acquiring truth, which is eminently desirable, on the one hand, and seeking the answer that allays the tumult of the imagination, as well as provides social recognition and moral approbation (Samuels and Henderson 2004, chap. 1), which was the more probable successful and practicable goal.

That a belief is not necessarily indicative of reality is a matter treated by numerous thinkers. Freud found that people believe or act as if they believe in the omnipotence of thoughts, or of words. They act as if they believed that words alone can have an effect on the world.[1] Pareto identified certain beliefs as rationalizations[2] or myths that are essentially metaphysical and aprioristic assertions, allegations, and speculations that have no foundation (even no possible foundation) in fact; they are imaginary principles (Samuels 1974, 34 and elsewhere). Louis Menand (2001, 212) writes of the "fetishization of words" and that "concepts . . . [are] the means, and not the ends, of inquiry." Menand himself writes of the "idolatry of ideas," the "idolatry of concepts," and "the danger of principle" (374, 425). A two-centuries-long "tradition" from Adam Smith and Kant through Wittgenstein and G. L. S. Shackle can be identified in which the description of science and other endeavors involves belief more likely than truth. Smith anticipates (in both his theory and his practice) the ideas of the later Wittgenstein (1958), in which Wittgenstein rejects as conclusive the correspondence-with-reality theory of language—that science and language are the mirror of nature—and affirms language being more likely tools of expression and inquiry—as means of projection, not necessarily of correspondence. Smith anticipates Karl Popper insofar as Smith treats first principles and conjectural anthropology, psychology, and history as conjectures in Popper's sense—albeit without Popper's correlative process of refutation—that is, as a thought experiment, an investigative tool, a tool isolating a number of manageable variables. Smith anticipates Kenneth Boulding's theory in which he affirms that what counts is not some imposing reality but our image of putative reality (Boulding 1956). Smith approximates Charles S. Peirce's concept of abduction, combining abstract formulations that lead him to concrete examples and generating (or illustrating) examples that enable him to formulate abstract accounts. But throughout he composes stories hopefully amenable to the psyche. Smith anticipates Thomas Kuhn's (1962) approach to science, namely, social constructivism, nonmaterial criteria of evaluation, and so on—implicitly challenging the descriptive accuracy of traditional ontology and epistemology. Finally, Smith

1. Robert Paul (1991, 273) writes, "The basis of this attitude is the narcissistic overvaluation of one's own psyche and one's power to determine events. In at least part of the mind, the reality principle is rejected as too great a narcissistic blow."

2. Pareto used the term "derivation"; the comparable term "rationalization" comes from Robinson 1921.

anticipates Pierre Bourdieu's concept of *habitus*, a body of principles that generates and organizes practices and representations, deeply internalized and persistent mental schemes that frame and organize thought, schemes that conceptualize and help reproduce social arrangements (paraphrased from Smith 2002) but otherwise have no necessary relation to any ultimate reality.

2. The Problem of Interpretive Base. Laissez-Faire: Belief System and Sentiment versus Definition of Reality

Laissez-Faire and the Historian of Economic Thought

After centuries of intellectual study of the economic role of government, much of what is said about government reflects sentiment, primitive terms, and substantively empty models, and has very little nonideological and analytically meaningful to say about both the economic role of government and the process through which that role is worked out and given substance in actual economies. Most theories of the economic role of government are not efforts to describe or explain the economic role of government in an objective, arm's-length manner. They are normative theories laden with ideological or substantive agendas for government. Even theories that ostensibly reject agendas for activist government have their own agendas. The theories themselves are part of the process of working out the economic role of government. This is, ironically, notably true of the doctrine of laissez-faire. Laissez-faire is not a doctrine of the economic role of government in one sense but is necessarily so in another. It is not a doctrine that describes or explains. It is a doctrine that people use in working out the economic role of government. I hope to show these points below.

I am cognizant, indeed emphasize, first, that it is impossible to eliminate the ideological element; second, that all models have limits, even one's favorite(s); and third, that my critique of others' use of laissez-faire is self-referential. I recognize and insist on the limits of my proposed baseline. Fourth, I also recognize the necessity of the ideological, that is, valuational, element used in working out the economic role of government. But the application of the doctrine of laissez-faire does not drive itself. In practice it is driven by antecedent normative premises as to whose interest counts added to the doctrine. Laissez-faire sentiments, moreover, are systemic to Western civilization and, perhaps, to all people. The doctrine is driven by a cultural value system and a desire to be left alone, individualism, antagonism to decision making by others in which we do not personally participate, and, inter alia, pragmatic considerations of self-interest. Some uses are indiscriminate, some self-consciously selective. All uses, however, must involve some premise as to which individuals' self-interests are to count.

The chief cause of my dismay at the scarcity of objective, nonideological (relative to the ideological) analyses of the economic role of government is the combination of studied ignorance and high-priestly pretense associated with the sentiments that are both cause and consequence of the idea of laissez-faire. This is not because I have opposite sentiments; quite the contrary. It is because I prefer knowledge to ignorance and candor to pretense. (These are the values behind my approach.) Affirmation of laissez-faire is no theory of what the economic role of government is all about in the actual world.

Economists, including historians of economic thought, have largely not—repeat, largely not—taken an objective analytical view of government. Instead they have partaken of their cultural background and the dominant belief system, taken a belief system for reality, assumed the role of high priest of the market economy, and been as pragmatic as their fellow citizens.

My laments along this line were largely quietly kept to myself during the conference. Parallel to what is said above about the psychology of collegiality, even though I was an active participant in conference discussions, I did not want my personal sentiment to take over the conference, though perhaps I lacked courage. As this is my assigned commentary, I have no reluctance in giving it prominence here.

Assume that I was running for public office and my platform states that I will promote the public interest and the common good, that I will promote meaningful positions and a worthy mode of life for everyone, that in doing so I will comport with the will of the Deity and with the designed natural order of things. You would be entitled to declare that these terms are primitive, undefined terms that lack substantive content. My point is that much writing in the history of economic thought is in the same position. Mere invocation of "public interest," for example, is not enough. The "public interest" does not have an independent existence. Governments seek to define for the people and to legitimize the meaning of "public interest" it will pursue, as do the private people who seek to have government define "public interest" in ways promoting their interests. Governance is the process of working out what "public interest" is to mean. The same is true of the "will of the Deity" and the "natural order of things." Each term elicits affirmative evocations but is presumptuous, self-serving, and otherwise substantively empty. Whose conception of the program of Providence are we to accept, that of the physiocrats or that of the Social Gospel?

When historians of economic thought repeat the language of laissez-faire as used by the subjects they study, they must treat laissez-faire as a primitive, undefined term that lacks substantive content unless they have evidence to the contrary. They cannot meaningfully say anything about the subjects' concepts of laissez-faire unless the subjects address specifically what laissez-faire means and what governmental activism is taken for granted. Some governmental activism will be taken for granted, willy-nilly. Two different authors may invoke the concept of laissez-faire but mean different things by it—just as two different theorists may invoke ceteris paribus and mean different things in it. When historians of economic thought discuss their subjects' ideas on the economic role of government, these ideas must in part be treated as matters of psychology and sentiment that may or may not bear any objective, material relation to what is actually going on. The subjects may only be giving vent to their sentiments and not relate to any particular policies, or relate only to a particular issue of policy. However laden with selective perception and expressed in terms that are primitive in nature and whose substantive content is provided by auditors and readers, their ideas are contributions to the process of working legal-economic things out.

If one cannot state what activities of government are ruled out by a subject's use of laissez-faire, and why, then one should say so. If it is clear that the subject intends to rule out mercantilist protection, then, once "mercantilist protection" is defined in accordance with the subject's use, one should avoid the presumptuous extension of the concept of laissez-faire to other things. Perhaps one should indicate, to the extent possible, how the subject's use comports or conflicts with the baseline herein proposed (or some other).

Historians of economic thought should follow such a prescription if they are to elicit the meaning of what their subjects are saying and not merely rehearse primitive terms that are otherwise empty of content but whose use reiterates certain sentiments. Historians of economic thought should be cautious and not think that we have said more than we, or the original authors, have actually said. Without further specification of intent, the use of the term is inconclusive and meaningless.

A counterargument to the foregoing is that using the proposed interpretive base will open the door to change, and minimization of legal change is preferred. Even apart from the irony that the counterposition comprises an activist agenda of legal change of its own, a chief defect of the objection is that the legal-economic system not only already but fundamentally encompasses legal change. The sentimental burden of legal change may be onerous, but it is inexorable. No one can be, no one is, in favor of the entire status quo being made permanent. Inter alia, changing definitions of the status quo by its advocates requires choice between alternative definitions of the status quo and correlative legal change (Samuels 2004b). The argument amounts to a high-priestly obfuscation of the fact of legal change and constitutes the manipulation of political psychology rather than an objective analysis of what is actually going on—which includes such high-priestly activities.

If we did a better job of knowing what the economic role of government was all about, independent of particular issues and particular positions on those issues, we might project fewer, and be less exposed to, misleading and wrong propositions from both Left and Right and perhaps, just perhaps, do a better job of going about governing ourselves. At the very least, selective antecedent normative premises might be made clear; and certain linguistic constructions, or code words—such as "nonintervention" and "free market" on the Right and "the people" and "human rights" on the Left—might no longer misconstrue and mislead. Any of the foregoing would be a major contribution to economic discourse.

A Personal Digression

I write as an institutionalist historian of economic thought: a Wisconsin institutionalist student of the economic role of government and a historian of economic thought who happens to be an institutionalist. Institutionalism has had two types of scholars of the economic role of government. The overwhelmingly preponderant group pursues the same general course as, for example, Walton Hamilton and Edwin Witte: seeking change of the interests to which government gives its support. They *knew* that government was already deeply, ubiquitously, and importantly involved in the status quo as social control. They wanted to change the interests government promoted in and through that involvement. To the extent that they and others used the language of increasing social control they were following common linguistic practice. They knew better. Witte rarely used that language; he typically dealt with the change in interests directly. This group, especially the Wisconsin contingent, actively seeks to change whose interest is protected. But, like John R. Commons, they knew that no increase in social control was involved, although they appreciated why it might appear that way. They knew that government was not intervening into situations in which it hitherto had been absent. This first group is activist, has a deep understanding of the extant economic role of government, and at worst suffers to some extent from the ambiguities, misleading implications, and obfuscations of ordinary language—aside from whether one agrees with their agendas for legal change.

The second group, in which I reside, is not, or not as, activist (though its members have their own personal social preferences). It has, nonetheless, relative to the first group, the same view of the economic role of government in any status quo and is typically more sensitive to the fragilities of language. Unlike Hamilton and Witte, and unlike Buchanan and Hayek, I have not presumed that my work as a scholar should concentrate on remaking the legal-economic world.[3] My work as a scholar emphasizes, in part, the depth, ubiquity, and importance of the economic role of government. It may appear congruent with other beliefs, but it is not so intended. By other beliefs I mean the "statism" formerly attributed to me by Buchanan and the "socialism" attributed to me by the businessman-father of at least one of my students. The same applies to colleagues who find it difficult to accept as the functional or analytical equivalent of property rights the protection, say, of worker, consumer, and environmental interests—itself a manifestation of the power of the concept "property." If I analyze what the economic role of government is all about, in terms of theories of social control and social change; if I examine protective labor legislation, for example, not as an intrusion on property rights but as the development of property-right equivalents; or if I examine regulation as a mode of changing property rights, and deregulation as the analytical, functional equivalent of regulation in changing rights, and so on; or if I interpret institutional economics, in part, as

3. I grant that I have tried to influence, that is, to change the substantive, methodological, historiographical, and linguistic view of historians of economic thought—always in a self-referential way—and the legal-economic model of economics, always in an objective and suitably well-defined way.

an approach to problem identification and problem solving—I am only trying to define reality, not change or putatively improve it. What Hamilton and others may consider a demand for regulation, and others a demand to deregulate, I perceive as a demand for changing the law. The activist sees social control in legal change; the observer-analyst sees social control throughout the status quo. My proposed baseline derives from my positive study of the economic role of government.

An Interpretive Base

Both my position and my model can be understood better if one has to answer the question, what is the result of positing that government is both ubiquitous and important? One could respond that such is the point at issue—it should be neither. But, I reply, just assume, like it or not, that government is, in fact, inexorably both ubiquitous and important. This is a positive, not a normative, matter. What difference would that make in our conversations about the economic role of government? Instead of the sentiment of laissez-faire, so readily the object of selective political psychological manipulation, what if we employed empirical and logical reason?[4] The term *laissez-faire* is a hallmark of the American belief system. The term has both a conceptual and historical dimension. Conceptually, *laissez-faire* has been the set of ideas deployed by social control institutions and much of the general population to describe, explain, and rationalize various actions and inactions by government. The precepts of laissez-faire include such beliefs as the sanctity of private property, the harmony of interests, the importance of saving and capital to economic growth, and minimalist or nonactivist government, that the government had little or no constructive role to play in the economy—reinforced by such other beliefs as the Protestant ethic and self-determination. These precepts have been part of Americans' self-perceptions, albeit in varying strengths.

The historical dimension of laissez-faire is more difficult to specify, but, depending on its definition, it is more myth than reality. This is, in part, because the conceptual dimension is misleading. It is not an accurate representation of the history of the economic role of government in the United States—or anywhere else, for that matter. The fact is that whether one likes it or not and wishes to admit it or not, the importance

4. The conflict between sentiment and reason is well known in numerous early writings, notably those of Adam Smith and David Hume.

of government has been enormous. The rhetoric has not been reality, though the idea of laissez-faire has been selectively useful in the mobilization and manipulation of political psychology. Contrary to the sentiment of laissez-faire, government has been ubiquitous and important. The most descriptive name for what transpired is not laissez-faire but *pragmatism*. People, especially those in business, turned to government for help in solving problems. Social theorists may model such activity in terms of the use of government as an institution of social control, social change, and social construction in erecting the legal foundations of their economic system. In practice both elite groups and common people treated law as an economic alternative and government as a means to economic and other ends, all of which had to be worked out.

The state has been an important factor in the American economy from the beginning. The state does not have to be brought back in; it never left. Government was a mode of transforming a rural and agricultural economy to an urban and industrial one. The means was the transformation of the law and of government itself.

I now outline why and how this has been the case.

Economic theory usually posits a given, transcendent economic system largely devoid of attention to institutional details. Economic theorists prefer to deal with a pure abstract a-institutional conceptual economy. Government in this model is an exogenous institutional detail. Yet tension exists within the domain of the policy implications of economic theory: Government is also treated as endogenous and an object of social construction, each economist endeavoring to reconstruct it in some favored image. The role of government in the history of political economy is the same for economists as it is for ordinary economic actors, namely, an object of control. The sentiment of laissez-faire is juxtaposed to inexorable policy activism. Economists engaged in the policy arena are economic actors; and, like those who live more ordinary lives (pace Young), approach the use of government pragmatically.

The general proposition characterizing the economic role of government is that government is an object of capture and use by whoever can get into a position to do so.

"Political capitalism," the term but not the definition borrowed from Max Weber, is a system or situation in which gain or advantage accrues to those with political power or prerogative. All systems are systems of political capitalism: the former Soviet Union, the United States, Guatemala, South Korea under Rhee and today, feudal Scotland, Taiwan,

Cuba under Batista and under Castro, Germany under Hitler, and so on. The difference between them is not that in some no one has more influence or benefits more from legal arrangements than in others—they all are so characterized—but *who* has captured and used the state to advance their purposes and deploy the belief system among the population to legitimize their position. Marx's theory of the withering away of the state is misleading and obfuscating, in fact, quite wrong. Power over people remains, only the identity of the people with power over other people has changed.

Private property is both what it is because of government and a check on the power of government—given suitable legislators and judges. During the period of transformation from the old to the modern state and economy, new forms and new meanings of property arose and old ones fell. Property was not protected because it is property; it was property because it was protected. But such did not prevent claims invoking the sacred character of property and the need to protect property against the claims of those who wanted government to protect their interests just as it had protected others, as property.

The foundations of the economy are legal in character, but are not given once and for all time. Changing the legal foundations is not intervention by government into a situation in which it hitherto has been absent, but change of the interests to which government gives its protection. Law is important.

For all practical purposes in a market economy, the baseline includes market allocation of resources within a legal framework that—in choosing and changing the elements of the legal framework—inevitably channels that allocation. It also includes the pragmatic use of government as an instrument of change.

Laissez-faire posits noninterventionism, meaning that government should not intervene in the economy, or should get off of the backs of the people. But so-called intervention typically is a change of the interests to which government gives its support. It typically does not mean the intrusion of government into an area in which it hitherto has been absent. It means change of law by law. Government "interferes" to control the "interference" by others. Freedom—freedom to manufacture and to trade—is a function of the total system of freedom and control. Legal rules both limit and enhance the individual's range of operative discretion, typically differently for different people. A historic example is the contest between labor and capital over the legal status of unions.

Law is ubiquitous. Some body of law applies to every sphere of life. The possibility, even the meaningfulness, of "minimal" government is asymptotic to zero. Consider the development of new technology, for example, enabling surrogate motherhood or enabling the copying of music over the Internet. The prevalent assumption is that the new activity must be brought under some law, some law must be adopted that establishes the rights of all interested parties. Some people want to promote it; others want to prohibit, limit, or otherwise control it. The controversy is about who the parties are and what their rights will be, and not whether there should be a law. Once again, such looks like governmental activism, unless the new law resembles our concept of the natural order of things.

The belief that some laws or programs provide a greater or more significant economic role for government is a matter of selective perception and is wrong or misleading. Like it or not, government is important in every system, and the principle of selective perception helps explain the situation using two lines of reasoning. Consider Alpha-Beta situations in which two parties are in the same field of action such that government policy promoting Alpha's interests is tantamount if not analytically equivalent to either negating Beta's interests or rendering them exposed to Alpha's choices. Much of what government does is choosing between Alphas and Betas; legal change—replacing L^1 with L^2—involves changing the interest to which government gives its support.

Thus, for example, regulating Alpha protects Beta and deregulating Alpha no longer protects Beta but leaves it exposed to Alpha's choices. Both regulation and deregulation, in this model, are means of creating, destroying, and re-creating rights, only for different people. If one takes Alpha interests and government protection of them as the natural state of affairs, or posits regulation as antagonistic to freedom, then government regulation of Alpha in favor of Beta will seem like an increase in the power and role of government and a decrease in freedom, whereas government is not intruding into a situation in which it hitherto has been absent, it is only changing the interest to which it gives its support.

Another example is central planning. Central planning seems to overwhelm conventional notions of individual rights, markets, and so on. But if one defines those directly and indirectly in charge of planning as Alpha and all others as Beta, government is involved in both, assigning rights to Alpha and not to Beta. Transition from plan to market assigns rights to Beta and not Alpha. By failing to see the Alpha power at work in the planning system and by being preoccupied with the collectivist ideology of central planning, one also fails to appreciate the Alpha-Beta nature of the situation.

Still another example involves the adoption of social welfare programs "for the first time." Such a situation or system (the welfare state) seems like the opposite of a regime of private property and individual responsibility as well as a more significant role for government. But if one thinks of social welfare programs as the protection of interests, and if one thinks of private property as the protection of interests, then neither regime—private property and welfare state—involves a more significant role for government than the other. Any differentiation between the two is a matter of selective perception: both constitute protection of interests but private property has been given a privileged position in law, ideology, and consciousness. And if one thinks of welfare-state programs as matters of sordid politics, one should study the history, for example, of changes in property law and in corporation law.[5]

Further Comments

The concept of laissez-faire is fundamentally ambiguous. Sentimentally, laissez-faire stands for an economic system based on institutions of private property, private enterprise, competition, markets, meaningful private choice, and a presumption against government activism; markets govern resource allocation. It is an idealization of the Western economic system, a projection of certain individualist sentiments. Laissez-faire is used therefore in three contexts: as minimization of legal change given the status quo; as a particular vision of an economy inclusive of the foregoing; and, somewhat ironically, as a program of legal change to bring about the realization of that particular vision. While discussion here focuses on the first, all three involve much government, as seen in the foregoing. Laissez-faire seems an attractive solution to social problems and escape from the burden of choice in part because movement toward an idealized image is perceived as neither government nor change, in part because it seems to abstract from the details of property rights, competition, and so on.

5. Agricultural economist James D. Shaffer told the present author the following: Speaking before a Farm Bureau group—a group supportive of subsidies to farmers while critical of welfare programs—Professor Shaffer once began his talk by saying, "Good morning, welfare kings and queens." The audience was not receptive to the implicit equation of subsidies and welfare.

Laissez-faire is fiction, an exercise in wishful thinking and the language of those who opposed certain proposed changes, but not their own preferred changes. The concept has mixed sentimental and existential or substantive meaning, suffused with selectivity in application and ambiguity of meaning. Certain sentiments are effectively expressed, yet are fundamentally inconclusive with respect to the issues to which they are addressed, generally represented by the question, what should government do? The question is more complicated than the phrase and its underlying sentiment lead most people to expect. Laissez-faire is a simplistic and disengaging view of complex real-world problems, the dynamics of change, and the need for collective decision making. Accordingly, no country could or has practiced laissez-faire, though much has been done in its name and though its ostensible domestic program has been combined with imperialism—Great Britain in the nineteenth century and by others.

People who believe they have problems in pragmatic, democratic regimes seek government help, if they have the power to do so. Working all this out is messy. Politicians seeking reelection must attend to citizen attitudes and perceptions of problems, problems likely to be very real. For this and numerous other reasons, changing the legal rules governing property rights and other institutions happens frequently—to the dismay of believers in strict laissez-faire.

Apropos of the uses of laissez-faire: First, government is projected as an evil, to be removed from the backs of the citizens. Second, already existing important governmental activities are taken for granted, treated as natural. In these, officials' principal functions are to enforce the law, and neither expand their scope nor introduce change. Third, typically inexplicit in ordinary discourse, government is the object of reform, making government do the correct things for the right people. The first use minimizes government; the second minimizes change of law and the interests protected by government; and the third minimizes control of the agenda by the wrong people.

This orientation faces fundamental problems. First, conflicts exist between the three uses considered as agendas for government. Second, all three are applied selectively, therefore inconsistently, with resulting ambiguity and inconclusiveness. Third, economic policy is a function of contests among elites and between elites and nonelites to determine who are the right people to control and benefit from government. Fourth, tension exists between economic and social conservatives. The former want to enhance and the latter to constrain the range of private discretion allowed by law, generally but not necessarily in different spheres of life. Fifth, government is already ubiquitous.

Two related ironies persist. First, some strains of activism are equated with laissez-faire and thus are acceptable. Second, although laissez-faire is associated with opposition to social control, in the United States the doctrine of laissez-faire is frequently—and, of course, selectively—deployed by the institutions of social control, notably politicians within government.

Young's essay may understate the role of police—meaning policy—in Smith's system. Police is one of the main branches of jurisprudence, although, as Young notes, not identified as one of the duties of the sovereign in the *Wealth of Nations*. The *Lectures on Jurisprudence* reflect the ubiquity of law, of police, of policy. Young's view that instances of police "would be few" is simply wrong. Smith took for granted in the *Wealth of Nations* the police function he intended to spell out in his written version of what we have as the *Lectures*. This is a common problem, because of Smith developing a tripartite model of society and in each case largely treating it as self-contained.

One related center of interpretive gravity is the degree to which one associates mercantilism with monarchism and its manipulation of the economy in pursuit of the monarch's interests. Smith *seems*, at least in part, to extend his opposition to mercantilism to an affirmation of a general laissez-faire or limited-state model. But this extension may be erroneous, whether undertaken by him or by his interpreters. It depends on what one means, what one takes for granted, by *laissez-faire*. Young correctly indicates that the dismantling of the "entire system" of mercantilism "is actually a far-reaching policy of intervention into the existing economy." But he also says, "Another way of looking at it is to say that the laws of justice must replace the laws of police." But the laws of police is a broader category than mercantilism; the laws of justice includes laws of police.

When compared with mercantilism and Soviet-type planning, laissez-faire seems to have substantive meaning, similarly with laissez-faire as a putative solution to problems arising within a market economy. But in no case does it accurately portray the legal foundations of the economy and the modes of their change and reconstruction.

Special caution should be given to definitions of the economy as independent of government and to definitions of government as independent of the economic aspirations and perceived problems of economic agents as well as to definitions of the baseline of laissez-faire—the roles of government that are unstated, unexamined, and unseen because finessed by the usual "protect property and contract"—like definitions.

The Market-Plus-Framework Approach

Consider the consequence of assuming/recognizing the ubiquity of government or of social control in general. Analysis can go two routes. One route recognizes that all areas of life are covered by a body of law, as above.

The second route is the market-plus-framework approach to the economic role of government. In this model, the market is a function of firm decision making and of the institutions constituting the framework, say, law and morals. Markets operate within frameworks of moral and legal rules that structure and operate through the markets they help form. The model gives effect to both (1) private choice and (2) social control. Changing the law seems to some people like substituting law for the market, whereas it is only a change in the interests whose protection comprises, in part, the framework function of government. The market, in whatever form it exists, exists in part because of government; changing the interests to which government lends its support is neither the replacement of the market nor the intrusion of government into an area in which government hitherto has been absent. Problems inevitably arise over the substance of the rules, the mode of determining rules, relative reliance on and relation between moral and legal rules, and changing the rules. The model postulates joint processes: optimizing market resource allocation and reforming the framework within which optimization takes place.

In the commonsensical market-plus-framework model, two matters are clear: law is a fundamental part of the system, ubiquitous and important; and legal change is also, as technology, values, power structure, and other variables change.

The market-plus-framework approach to the economic role of government does not, indeed cannot, answer all the questions we might have. It does establish the point, contrary to those who dislike the exercise of governmental choice, that government already is in the status quo, that so-called intervention is not the intrusion of government into a situation in which it hitherto has been absent but a change of the interests to which government is giving its support, and that government itself is an object of capture and use by economic interests located in markets. Thus it helps establish the further point that "the market" is not independent of government; rather, markets are a function of government and of firms—whose power is a function of government, which is in turn a function of the use made of government by firms—such that limiting legal change amounts to deferring to the status quo of firms, a status quo that might itself otherwise lead to legal change. Recursive systems are complex and difficult to fathom; the idea of a static status quo is almost meaningless.

The reader should inquire whether the market-plus-framework model is subject to the same critique given in section 1 and if not, why not; or if so, what is the difference. The answer is, yes. The model is composed of primitive terms: market, law, morals. Their content is formally empty. The model has its limits. The difference is subtle. Several of the papers given in the conference presented a model, some in the form of a dichotomy, that framed the author's efforts to reach policy conclusions and, it seems, served in their own minds to generate policy conclusions. (If the latter is not the case, the authors felt no need to say so.) The market-plus-framework model represents an effort to identify and relate certain variables to each other. The relationships portrayed between them are not limited to one-directional causality. The relationships are recursive; the variables influence each other. While the model can help frame policy discussions, the model cannot frame efforts to reach policy conclusions; they cannot yield policy conclusions. For example, the model posits markets as a function of law and morals. The model cannot yield answers to such questions as which law, which morals, what relationship between law and morals, and what relative reliance on law and morals. Nor can the model yield answers to the question whether a particular law constitutes framework-filling activity or a particular intervention. The distinction may seem obvious, but unless people can agree on such basic issues as whether a change in property law or the antitrust laws are one or the other, the model cannot help.

The same is true of using the model to tell stories about causation using only one explanatory variable to the exclusion of others. For example, markets are a function of the actions of government, religion, and firms; government and religion are mutually influential or determining; so too with government and firms; and markets are especially a function of firms and government (Samuels 2004a, 2004b). One can tell a Coasean story about how firms, in making ordinary decisions about in-versus outsourcing, determine markets, to the exclusion of firm predatory behavior and government action. By adding a normative premise any of these stories may be given normative status. But the normative status is driven by the normative premise, not by the model. It is the normative premise that enables that story rather than some other and through which some belief rather than another is projected.

I am more interested in having discussions of the economic role of government be coherent and meaningful, rather than empty and ambiguous, than in establishing my approach as the baseline for laissez-faire, even though I consider it empirically accurate.

Governance

The concept of laissez-faire runs afoul of *governance*, defined as decision making importantly affecting other people. Official government is one institution of governance; others include other governments, international organizations, domestic and foreign corporations, nonprofit organizations, organized religion, education, and custom. Government has formal responsibility for the division of power within the nominally private sector and between the private and public sectors. But government is an object of a ubiquitous contest over its control. Limiting government does not limit governance. The use of laissez-faire has been, in fact, a means of promoting nongovernmental governance, not the elimination of control/governance, as one might think.

Some of those who appreciate that the sentiments expressed by "laissez-faire" are sentiments of freedom also understand that "freedom" is no single-valued concept. Freedom for whom, from whom, to do what, in what system with what structure, are only a few of the questions one must pose. Freedom for the one may be coercion for another (Samuels 1995, 1997).

Conclusion

My caution about belief being not necessarily indicative of reality when it comes to the economic role of government is self-reflexive; it applies to my own understanding. And surely I do not desire to exclude any other well-thought-out baseline. I pose, however, the following questions: (1) If my arguments are assumed to be correct, how does that affect the usual arguments about the economic role of government? (2) Various authors write of different schools of economic thought. On what basis does one choose between them as to their positive analysis of the economic role of government? (3) If my arguments are shown to be erroneous, what positive model better describes the economic role of government, and with what effect?

This is no easy task. Adam Smith provided, in his *Lectures on Jurisprudence*, considerable evidence of fundamental governmental activism, considerably amplifying his three agenda items in the *Wealth of Nations*. Yet numerous conflicting interpretations of what he said abound in the literature. Most other authors in the history of thought on the economic role of government do not go as far as Smith. Without specification of a base, the use of the term *laissez-faire* is meaningless except as a sentiment, a means of manipulating political psychology, and a pointer to a capitalist market economy. Somewhere I read of *laissez-faire* being used to refer to the unlimited authority of a ruler.

At best the term indicates a relative phenomenon, yet it is typically used in an absolutist manner. It offers little insight into the conditions leading to legal change (change of law) or into the precise meaning of laissez-faire as an economic system, or into the details of the sentiment itself. It is often used in the sense of "authority in fundamentals and freedom in all else," but without a sense of the fact of and need for legal change. Laissez-faire as description is usually misleading, because it omits or obfuscates the ubiquity and importance of government. The physiocrats apparently did not use the term, but François Quesnay et al. did express the sentiment. When Quesnay writes about the "entire freedom of commerce" and reliance on the natural order, neither orientation prevented strong roles for government in his system. The "natural order" is his/their version, not that of another devotee of naturalism. The "entire freedom of commerce" is only within the law—the law required, according to the physiocrats, by the natural order. It will be obvious to anyone not besotted by the sentiment of freedom or by the naturalism that, except for the opposition (which is not total) to mercantilism, their system is loaded with government/law. Their "fundamentals" and therefore authority are deep and wide ranging.

At worst, laissez-faire is a tool of obfuscation, aimed (for example) at diverting the masses from using government to promote their interests while allowing business to do so. The term is a linguistic device to manipulate political psychology. On one level it is misleading because those who deploy it themselves pragmatically take recourse to government and legal change whenever they have a grievance or other problem. On a deeper level the term is misleading because it neglects and obfuscates the existence and importance of government/law in the status quo. Government/law is fundamental to the legal-economic nexus, or to the market-plus-framework model, and legal change/change of law is fundamental to the process of working things out.

After more than two centuries it is time for historians of economic thought to take a more objective, a more analytical, and a more profound approach to a foundation concept widely associated with our discipline.

References

Boulding, Kenneth E. 1956. *The Image: Knowledge in Life and Society*. Ann Arbor: University of Michigan Press.

Griswold, C. L. 1999. *Adam Smith and the Virtues of Enlightenment*. New York: Cambridge University Press.

Kuhn, Thomas S. 1962. *The Structure of Scientific Revolutions*. Chicago: University of Chicago Press.

Menand, Louis. 2001. *The Metaphysical Club*. New York: Farrar, Straus and Giroux.

Ostrander, F. Taylor. 2005. Notes on Frank H. Knight's Course, Economic Theory, Economics 301, University of Chicago, 1933–1934. *Research in the History of Economic Thought and Methodology* 23B:22–74.

Paul, Robert. 1991. Freud's Anthropology: A Reading of the "Cultural Books." In *The Cambridge Companion to Freud*, edited by Jerome Neu. New York: Cambridge University Press.

Robinson, James Harvey. 1921. *The Mind in the Making*. New York: Harper.

Samuels, Warren J. 1974. *Pareto on Policy*. New York: Elsevier.

———. 1993. The Growth of Government. *Critical Review* 7:445–60.

———. 1995. Society Is a Process of Mutual Coercion and Governance Selectively Perceived. *Critical Review* 9:437–43.

———. 1997. The Concept of "Coercion" in Economics. In *The Economy as a Process of Valuation*, by Warren J. Samuels, Steven G. Medema, and A. Allan Schmid. Lyme, N.H.: Edward Elgar.

———. 1999. Hayek from the Perspective of an Institutionalist Historian of Economic Thought: An Interpretive Essay. *Journal des Economistes et des Etudes Humaines* 9.2–3:279–90.

———. 2001. Some Problems in the Use of Language in Economics. *Review of Political Economy* 13.1:91–100.

———. 2002. The Rule of Law and the Capture and Use of Government in a World of Inequality. In *Economics, Governance, and Law: Essays on Theory and Policy*. Cheltenham, U.K.: Edward Elgar.

———. 2004a. The Buchanan Colloquium on the Status of the Status Quo: Reports on a Conference. *Research in the History of Economic Thought and Methodology* 22A:219–56.

———. 2004b. Markets and Their Social Construction. *Social Research*, forthcoming.

Samuels, Warren J., and Willie Henderson. 2004. The Etiology of Adam Smith's Division of Labor: Alternative Accounts and Smith's Methodology Applied to Them. In *Essays on the History of Economics*, by Warren J. Samuels, Willie Henderson, Kirk D. Johnson, and Marianne Johnson. London: Routledge.

Shackle, G. L. S. 1967. *The Years of High Theory*. New York: Cambridge University Press.

Smith, Christian. 2000. Force of Habit: Hostility and Condescension toward Religion in the University. *Christianity Today*, vol. 8, no. 5 (September–October). www.christianitytoday.com/bc/2002/005/13.20.html.

Wittgenstein, Ludwig. 1958. *Philosophical Investigations*. Oxford: Blackwell.

Contributors

António Almodovar is a professor of the history of economic thought at the University of Porto, Portugal. He has published and edited several books on the history of Portuguese economic thought. His research interests also include the classical economists and the economic ideas of the interwar period. He is a member of the editorial board of the *European Journal of the History of Economic Thought.*

Jürgen G. Backhaus holds the Krupp Chair in Public Finance and Fiscal Sociology at Erfurt University. Between 1986 and 2000, he was chair of the public economics department at Maastricht University. In September 2004 he was awarded an honorary doctorate by the University of Thessaly (Greece). He has published 59 books and monographs, about 200 articles in refereed journals and book chapters, 28 scholarly notes, and 63 reviews. His research interests span economics, but also neighboring disciplines such as law, fiscal sociology, and environmental sciences. In 1994 he founded (with Frank H. Stephen) the *European Journal of Law and Economics*, of which he is the managing editor.

Roger E. Backhouse is Professor of the History and Philosophy of Economics at the University of Birmingham (U.K.). He is author of *The Penguin History of Economics/The Ordinary Business of Life* (2002).

Bradley W. Bateman is the Gertrude B. Austin Professor of Economics at Grinnell College where he teaches the history of economic thought and writing. He is the author of *Keynes's Uncertain Revolution* (1996) and the editor, with Roger Backhouse, of the *Cambridge Companion to Keynes* (2006). His current research involves the influence of religion on the American economics profession.

Peter Boettke is a professor of economics at George Mason University and the editor of the *Review of Austrian Economics*. He is a Senior Research Fellow at the Mercatus Center at George Mason.

José Luís Cardoso is professor of economics and history of economics at ISEG, the Institute of Economics and Business Administration of the Technical University of Lisbon, Portugal. He has published several articles and books on the history of Portuguese economic thought in a comparative perspective. His research interests also include economic history and the methodology of economics. He is the general editor of the series Classics of Portuguese Economic Thought and coeditor of the *European Journal of the History of Economic Thought.*

David Colander is the Christian A. Johnson Distinguished Professor of Economics at Middlebury College. A former president of the History of Economics Society, he is currently working on a book with Buz Brock titled *The Economics of Muddling Through.*

Andrew Farrant is on the faculty of the Department of Economics at Dickinson College. His research interests are political economy and the history of economic thought.

Steven Horwitz is the Associate Dean of the First Year and a professor of economics at St. Lawrence University. He is the author of two books, *Microfoundations and Macroeconomics: An Austrian Perspective* (2000) and *Monetary Evolution, Free Banking, and Economic Order* (1992), and he has written extensively on Austrian economics, Hayekian political economy, monetary theory and history, and macroeconomics. His work has been published in professional journals such as *HOPE*, the *Southern Economic Journal*, and the *Review of Austrian Economics*. He has also conducted public policy research on banking regulation for the Heartland Institute, Citizens for a Sound Economy, and the Cato Institute.

Thomas (Tim) C. Leonard is lecturer in economics at Princeton University. His current research concerns the influence of biological, especially eugenic, thought upon Progressive Era political economy. He has also recently published on the economics of science, the history of distribution theory in twentieth-century economics, and the ethics of trade in inalienable goods.

David M. Levy is director of the Center for Public Choice and a professor of economics at George Mason University. The Sandra Peart–David Levy volume, *The "Vanity of the Philosopher": From Equality to Hierarchy in Post-Classical Economics*, published in 2005 by the University of Michigan Press, represents many years of research motivated by the possibility that the issues debated in the past are with us still. The Summer Institute for the Preservation of the Study of the History of Economics, founded by Levy and now directed by Peart, is an effort to create a venue where historians of economics and other specialists in economics can discuss these live issues. Levy has recently been elected to the executive board of the History of Economics Society.

Alain Marciano is an associate professor at the University of Reims Champagne Ardenne. He is the author of two books on economics and philosophy and a coeditor of the *Elgar Companion to Economics and Philosophy*. He has published various papers on law and economics and on public choice theory. His research interests include the nature of rules and institutions, their evolution, and the links between human nature and the nature of rules.

Stephen Meardon is a visiting assistant professor at Williams College. His interests lie in past and present studies of international trade, economic geography, and the economies of Latin America. His recent works on the history and historiography of geographical economics appear in *HOPE*, the *American Journal of Economics and Sociology*, and edited volumes. He is currently studying the connections of the nineteenth-century American tariff controversy to other political debates, including slavery, international copyright, and imperialism.

Steven G. Medema is a professor of economics at the University of Colorado at Denver. He also serves as editor of the *Journal of the History of Economic Thought*. His research interests include law and economics, public economics, and the economic role of government in the history of economic thought. His most recent books include *Economics and the Law: From Posner to Post Modernism and Beyond* (with Nicholas Mercuro) and the forthcoming *The Hesitant Hand: Market and State in the History of Modern Economic Thought*.

Maria Pia Paganelli is an assistant professor of economics at Yeshiva University. She works on eighteenth-century monetary economics, David Hume, and Adam Smith.

Sandra J. Peart is a professor of economics at Baldwin-Wallace College. In 2005–6, she will be a Fellow for the American Council on Education. Her book (coauthored with David M. Levy), *The "Vanity of the Philosopher": From Equality to Hierarchy in Post-Classical Economics*, was published by the University of Michigan Press in 2005. She is also editing the Hayek-on-Mill volume of *The Collected Works of F. A. Hayek*. With David Levy, she is editing *The Street Porter and the Philosopher: Conversations on Analytical Egalitarianism*, a collection of papers presented at the Summer Institute for the Preservation of the Study of the History of Economics.

Yakir Plessner is an associate professor emeritus at the Hebrew University of Jerusalem and a former adviser to the minister of finance of Israel and deputy governor of the Bank of Israel. He has written a book on the economy of Israel and published papers in agricultural, environmental, macro, and monetary economics.

Malcolm Rutherford is professor of economics at the University of Victoria, British Columbia. His interests cover institutional economics, the history of economics, and the history of American economics. He is the author of *Institutions in Economics: The Old and the New Institutionalism* (1994). Recently his work has focused on the history of the American institutionalist movement in economics between the wars. He has published a series of papers on this topic in *HOPE* and the *Journal of the History of Economic Thought*.

Warren J. Samuels is a professor emeritus of economics at Michigan State University. His principal current project is on the use of the concept of the invisible hand. His most recent book is *Essays on the History of Economics* (2004).

Richard E. Wagner is Holbert L. Harris Professor of Economics at George Mason University. His primary scholarly activities involve teaching and writing about public finance, economic sociology, and macroeconomics, all approached from within a generally emergent and evolutionary orientation.

Jeffrey T. Young is the A. Barton Hepburn Professor of Economics at St. Lawrence University, where he has taught since 1980. He has also taught at the University of Colorado in Denver and at Marshall University, and he has been a research visitor at the University of Newcastle in Australia and an honorary research fellow at Glasgow University. His research interests are the economics and moral philosophy of Adam Smith and David Hume as well as the key figures of British classical economics. His publications include two books and journal articles that have appeared in respected international journals.

Warren Young is an associate professor of economics at Bar Ilan University. His books include *Interpreting Mr. Keynes* (1987); *Harrod and His Trade Cycle Group* (1989); *Oxford Economics and Oxford Economists* (with Fred Lee, 1993); *Atomic Energy Costing* (1998); *IS-LM and Modern Macroeconomics* (edited with B. Zilberfarb, 2000); *The Open Economy Macromodel: Past, Present, and Future* (edited with A. Arnon, 2002); *Economics, Economists, and Expectations* (with W. Darity and R. Leeson, 2004); and *Open Economy Macromodels: Origins, Development, and Debates* (with R. Boyer, forthcoming). He has published papers in *HOPE* and other journals. His current research focuses on the history of open economy and real business cycle models and the economics of energy and regulation. He is also symposia and book review editor, *European Journal of Political Economy*.

Index